State of White Supremacy

State of White Supremacy

RACISM, GOVERNANCE, AND THE UNITED STATES

Edited by Moon-Kie Jung, João H. Costa Vargas,

and Eduardo Bonilla-Silva

Stanford University Press
Stanford, California

Stanford University Press
Stanford, California

Printed in the United States of America on acid-free, archival-quality paper

Library of Congress Cataloging-in-Publication Data

State of white supremacy : racism, governance, and the United States / edited by
Moon-Kie Jung, João H. Costa Vargas, and Eduardo Bonilla-Silva.
    p. cm.
Includes bibliographical references and index.
ISBN 978-0-8047-7218-1 (cloth : alk. paper)--ISBN 978-0-8047-7219-8 (pbk. : alk.
paper)
1. Racism--United States--History. 2. Minorities--United States--Social
conditions. 3. United States--Race relations. 4. United States--Politics and
government. I. Jung, Moon-Kie. II. Vargas, João H. Costa (João Helion Costa).
III. Bonilla-Silva, Eduardo.
E184.A1 S76 2011
305.800973--dc22   2010043506

Typeset by Bruce Lundquist in 10/14 Minion

To the memories of Kiwane Carrington and countless others
who have lost their lives to racial state violence

and

to the memories of Michael Zinzun and countless others
who have risked their lives in resistance

CONTENTS

ACKNOWLEDGMENTS

The history of this book has been somewhat fitful, marked by periods of un-expected ease and difficulty. It began with our earlier volume, a special issue of *Critical Sociology* on racism and antiracism. David Fasenfest, the journal's editor, encouraged us to publish the issue in book form through a series he edits. We were taken with the idea of working on a book but wanted to take it in a different direction, one focused on the intersection of racism and the state. With this narrower aim in mind, we drew up a wish list of possible contributors whose work we admired. To our pleasant surprise and lasting thanks, they all agreed to participate and, as you can see, trusted us with their critical and brilliant scholarship. For reasons David was aware of and sym-pathized with, we were ultimately forced to move the project out of his book series. We thank him for his steadfast support throughout.

Sharing our high regard for the contributors and their contributions to this book, Stanford University Press expeditiously and expertly guided it to publication. A number of anonymous reviewers for, and before, Stanford were generous and helpful. Executive editor Kate Wahl, assistant editor Joa Suorez, production editor Mariana Raykov, and copy editor Jeffrey Wyneken were, in a word, excellent.

That books are collective efforts may be a truism, but it is one worth re-peating. We benefited greatly from ongoing conversations with colleagues and students in Austin, Durham, Urbaign, and beyond. In particular, we would like to extend our fondest appreciation to our graduate students, past and present, who have continually pushed us to explain, clarify, and improve our ideas. The book was conceived while its first editor enjoyed sunshine and the stimulating company of exceptional faculty, staff, and fellow fellows at Stanford University's Center for Comparative Studies in Race and Ethnicity.

We owe a big debt of gratitude to our friends and families, who to our amazement continue to suffer and support us. Eduardo gives special thanks to his "usual suspects": "I know a lot of people in sociology and a lot of people claim they know me, but Tyrone A. Forman, Amanda E. Lewis, and David G. Embrick are among the very few people I can truly call friends in Amerika. Last but not least, to the person with whom I share all my ideas, work, and sociological passion before they see the light of day, my wife and fellow traveler in sociology, Dr. Mary Hovsepian."

To the list of loved ones acknowledged in his previous book, Moon-Kie would like to add his partner Caroline H. Yang and niece Seri Lamson Jung. Three-year-old Seri, following in the giant footsteps of her sister and god-cousin, bravely stepped up this time to take responsibility for any errors that remain. Well, she nodded.

State of White Supremacy

Introduction

CONSTITUTING THE U.S. EMPIRE-STATE AND WHITE SUPREMACY

The Early Years

Moon-Kie Jung

The U.S. wars in Iraq and Afghanistan have stirred, once again, much talk of an "American empire." Despite sharp disagreements, the general consensus has been that the United States is a relatively new and decidedly informal, or noncolonial, empire, particularly compared to the European powers of the past. Even for many of the dissenters the only true foray into formal empire-building by the United States was at the turn of the last century, consequent to the Spanish-American War. Otherwise, the United States has been distinctly a nation-state, even if an informally imperialist one. Against this prevalent assumption I make three arguments: the United States has never been a nation-state; the United States has always been an empire-state; the United States has always been a racial state, a state of white supremacy.

My strategy in this chapter is simple and straightforward: I discuss several concepts and apply them in, by turns, broad and fine strokes to the case of the United States. I examine the origins and early development of the U.S. empire-state during the long nineteenth century, drawing on evidence from constitutional law.[1] None of the concepts or applications are, or should be, controversial in and of themselves. Taken together, they may cohere into something more original and useful, particularly in my own discipline of sociology.[2]

My intention is not to specify a new theory but to outline the basic elements of a framework upon which theorizing can take place. The emergent empire-state approach aims to bring together studies of race, the state, and empire. It also allows us to make unified sense of, and see connections between, the divers histories of peoples who have been racially subjected to and have struggled against the U.S. empire-state, without overlooking significant differences and particularities. I begin with a few words on a few concepts and introduce the argument that the United States has always been an empire-state, not a nation-state. I flesh out this idea in the subsequent sections, analytically separating the two defining dimensions of colonialism: the hierarchical differentiation of spaces and of peoples. Focusing on the acquisition and disposal of "territories" and on American Indian sovereignty, I show how U.S. state formation has always entailed the racial construction of colonial spaces. Given the racial subjection of various peoples of the U.S. empire-state, which has been overwhelmingly, but mostly group-specifically, documented, I ask whether and on what basis we should study the imperial subjection of colonized and noncolonized peoples within the same framework, which I answer through an analysis of a counterintuitive Supreme Court case, *Dred Scott v. Sandford*. I conclude with some thoughts on the chapters that follow.

RECONCEPTUALIZING THE U.S. STATE

More than two decades after its first publication, Michael Omi and Howard Winant's (1986) widely and justly celebrated *Racial Formation in the United States* is still one of the rare exceptions to the ongoing mutual nonrecognition and disengagement between theories of racial formation and of state formation (Goldberg 2002: 3–4). They argue that the U.S. state is "inherently racial" and "from its very inception has been concerned with the politics of race." Further, they predict that "race will always be at the center of the American experience" (Omi and Winant 1994: 5, 81–82).

I agree that the U.S. state is inherently racial and, in all likelihood, will always be racial. As "inherently" and "always" signal, Omi and Winant are not proffering purely empirical statements about the U.S. state but theoretical claims about its intrinsic character. But on what basis can we make such assertions, and how has the U.S. state been racial? I suggest that the questions remain considerably unanswered, and unanswerable, because the U.S. state is almost universally assumed to be, and to have been, a nation-state.

A *nation* is, as Benedict Anderson memorably put it, "an imagined political community—and imagined as both inherently limited and sovereign." A categorical identity, it entails direct membership and is "always conceived as a deep, *horizontal* comradeship" (1991: 6, 7; emphasis added). *States* are "coercion-wielding organizations that are distinct from households and kinship groups and exercise clear priority in some respects over all other organizations within substantial territories" (Tilly 1992: 1). Both of these definitions are as accepted and acceptable as any and could be substituted with others without much consequence.

My contention is that for the United States, the political community to which the state has been coupled has never been the nation. I do not mean in the trivial sense that the *nation-state* is an ideal type that no actual nation-state fits precisely but that the United States has not been a nation-state in a fundamental, square-peg-in-a-round-hole sense. By virtue of the assumed internal horizontality of nations, nation-states imply politically uniform populations of *citizens*, or state members. As a corollary, territories over which nation-states claim sovereignty are politically uniform spaces, symbolized in atlases by evenly colored, neatly bounded blocks. The United States has never come close to achieving these political "ideals" and, in all probability, is constitutionally, both literally and figuratively, incapable of doing so.

The polity to which the U.S. state has always laid claim in fact, if not in rhetoric, is an empire. Unlike nation-states, *empire-states* (Cooper 2005) are not horizontally uniform but hierarchically differentiated. Empire-states entail the usurpation of political sovereignty of foreign territories and their corresponding populations. In terms of geography, an empire-state encompasses spaces of "different degrees of sovereignty" (Stoler 2006: 128), territories of unequal political status. In terms of belonging or membership, the peoples of an empire-state effectively, through de jure and de facto practices, have differential access to rights and privileges. These conditions are what George Steinmetz (2008: 591) refers to as the "sovereignty" and, following Partha Chatterjee (1993), "rule of difference" criteria of *colonialism*, the formal supplantation and exercise of sovereignty over territories and peoples. Here, I would add a caveat to the rule-of-difference criterion. Steinmetz writes, "Where conquered subject populations are offered the same citizenship rights as conquerors in exchange for their assimilation into the ruling culture, we are better off speaking of modern state making rather than colonialism" (2005: 348; see also Cooper 2005: 27). But if we were to view the rule of difference from the vantage point of subject populations, like the indigenous peoples of North America and Hawai'i, we would find that the *imposition* of "equal" citizenship can be, and by many is, seen as a practice of colonial rule (Bruyneel 2004). In other words, without the consent of the colonized, unilaterally ridding the rule of difference through assimilation, rather than decolonization, may not eliminate but instead reproduce and even deepen colonial domination. After all, extermination and assimilation were both constitutive of the U.S. state's genocidal colonial policies toward American Indians in the nineteenth century and beyond, summed up respectively by the infamous quotes "The only good Indian is a dead Indian" and "Kill the Indian in him and save the man" (Wolfe 2006: 397).[3]

RACIALIZED SPACES OF THE U.S. EMPIRE-STATE

The continual misrecognition of the United States as a nation-state, not least by the state itself, has been integral to U.S. nationalism, and its attendant sense of exceptionalism, and thereby to the formation, fortification, and imperception of the United States as an empire-state. "Generat[ing] the mirage of its own disappearance [through] its informal, universalistic, and euphemistic form," Steinmetz (2006: 137) notes, "American power . . . does not typically annex and permanently occupy foreign lands—with the important exceptions of the westward expansion of the continental state, Hawai'i, and the colonies created from the spoils of the Spanish-American War."[4] Although the informal facet of the U.S. empire has been immense, the "important exceptions" have been important but hardly exceptional, which is readily apparent when we take in their spatial expanse: the overland and overseas annexations of the long nineteenth century stretched from the original thirteen states westward to the Eastern Hemisphere, northward to above the Arctic Circle, and southward to below the equator and, with certain exceptions like the Philippines, are still under the formal jurisdiction of the United States.

Many may object that the great majority of the lands under U.S. sovereignty, past and present, have been states and incorporated territories. In the early twentieth century, in a series of what are referred to as the *Insular Cases*, the Supreme Court invented a legal distinction between *incorporated* and *unincorporated* territories, distinguishing those slated to become states from those that could be kept and governed indefinitely as territories (Burnett and Marshall 2001b). Uncritically adopting this official distinction, which was crafted to deal with the newly acquired territories in the Caribbean and the Pacific, most analysts have considered unincorporated territories (such as Guam and Puerto Rico) as the only bona fide U.S. colonies. As a consequence, the temporal depth and spatial breadth of the U.S. empire-state have been routinely and often grossly underestimated, and its history oversimplified.

The deviant case of Hawai'i was revealing. Like the island colonies obtained through the Spanish-American War, Hawai'i was seized in 1898, located overseas, and inhabited predominantly by nonwhites—Native Hawaiians and migrant laborers from China, Japan, and elsewhere. However, unlike these other colonies, Hawai'i was slotted into the newly invented "incorporated" category, the same one to which all past and then present U.S. territories on the North American continent retroactively belonged. The decisive difference was that Hawaii's economy and politics had long been dominated by white settlers from the United States, foremost descendants of missionaries from the Northeast. It was precisely because U.S. white supremacy was already and sufficiently guaranteed that Hawai'i was incorporated while other overseas territories were not. Still, principally because of its concerns about the nonwhite-majority population, Congress would not grant Hawai'i admission into the Union as a state until 1959 (R. J. Bell 1984; Jung 2006; Merry 2000; Osorio 2002).[6] On the flip side, we can infer that the relatively short and smooth transition of most territories to statehood was also underwritten by white supremacy, that the taken-for-granted certainty of white dominance was a necessary condition of possibility.[7] And in the antebellum period, the transition always took into account the delicate sectional balance of power in the U.S. Senate between the North and the South, evening out the numbers of "free" and "slave" states admitted. Needless to say, the equilibration helped to preserve and prolong the white supremacist institution of slavery (Sparrow 2006).

In addition to acquiring and ruling territories, incorporated and unincorporated, U.S. empire-state formation has always entailed the construction of colonial spaces in relation to the indigenous peoples. But the Constitution was evasive. "Indian" appeared twice in the original Constitution, in the Three-Fifths and Commerce Clauses, but neither mention dealt directly with Indian lands.[8] Nonetheless, given the intrinsic coloniality of the U.S. state, built as it was on soil that was once exclusively the domain of Native Americans, constitutional questions about their political status were unavoidable. The initial answers were proffered in the early nineteenth century in three related Supreme Court cases, whose prevailing opinions were penned by Chief Justice John Marshall. In *Johnson v. M'Intosh* of 1823, the Court formally invoked the extraconstitutional, and profoundly white supremacist, doctrine of discovery as the basis of U.S. sovereignty over Indian territories, adopting and adapting the centuries-old colonial logic and rationale of European rule over non-Europe: "This principle was, that discovery gave title to the [European] government by whose subjects, or by whose authority, it was made, against all other European governments, which title might be consummated by possession." In other words, each European power acquired title to non-European lands that it "discovered," to the exclusion, and customarily with the tacit agreement, of other European powers. The Court reasoned that "original inhabitants" retained their "right of occupancy" and use of land, but their rights and "sovereignty, as independent nations," were "necessarily, to a considerable extent, impaired" and "diminished," as the "ultimate dominion" lay with the European "discoverer."[9] Corollarily, the latter held the right of preemption, the "exclusive right to extinguish the Indian title of occupancy, either by purchase or by conquest."[10] According to the decision, the United States, upon gaining its independence, inherited this unmistakably colonial relationship from Britain.

The remaining two rulings further specified the relationship. The 1831 case of *Cherokee Nation v. Georgia* determined whether the Cherokee, and by extension other Native American nations, constituted a state and, if so, what kind of state. On the first question, the Court decided in the affirmative: "They have been uniformly treated as a state from the settlement of our country. The numerous treaties made with them by the United States recognize them. . . . The acts of our government plainly recognize the Cherokee nation as a state, and the courts are bound by those acts." At the same time, indigenous peoples were not "*foreign* States." Rather, they were deemed to be "domestic dependent nations" in a "state of pupilage" with a relationship to the United States "resembl[ing] that of a ward to his guardian," striking a rhetorical echo for the unincorporated territories to come.[11] A year after *Cherokee Nation v. Georgia*, the inferior but definite sovereignty of Indian nations was affirmed in another case involving the Cherokee and the state of Georgia, *Worcester v. Georgia*. "Indian nations" were recognized as "always [having] been considered as distinct, independent political communities, retaining their original natural rights, as the undisputed possessors of the soil, from time immemorial," but, per the discovery doctrine, "with the single exception of that imposed by irresistible power."[12] And the authority of that imposition by the United States lay entirely with the federal government.[13]

The scope of federal authority grew and turned out to be without limit. A half century of white settler encroachment and violence, genocidal warfare, cession treaties, and removals onto reservations later, the Supreme Court weighed in on *United States v. Kagama* in 1886 to uphold a new federal law that intruded on the internal affairs of Indian reservations for the first time.[14] Extending the logic of the Marshall opinions, again on extraconstitutional grounds, the Court further undermined Native sovereignty and conferred on Congress plenary, or complete, power over Indians (Wilkins 1997). Having already passed a law in 1871 to no longer deal with Indians bilaterally through treaties, Congress was now constitutionally empowered to, and did, legislate unilaterally to reorder and seize Indian lands and otherwise regulate Indian lives.[15] In 1903, the Supreme Court outdid itself again. Asserting that the "plenary authority over the tribal relations of the Indians has been exercised by Congress from the beginning" and that, citing *Kagama*, "Indian tribes are the wards of the nation. . . . communities dependent on the United States," the Court, in *Lone Wolf v. Hitchcock*, declared that Congress, but not Indians, could disregard existing treaties at its discretion: "When, therefore, treaties were entered into between the United States and a tribe of Indians it was never doubted that the power to abrogate existed in Congress."[16] Attesting to the ruling's manifest racism, a U.S. senator responded at the time: "It is the *Dred Scott* decision No. 2, except that in this case the victim is red instead of black. It practically inculcates the doctrine that the red man has no rights which the white man is bound to respect, and, that no treaty or contract made with him is binding" (Matthew Quey as quoted in Wilkins 1997: 116).[17] Lest we dismiss such cases as relics of the past, the ruling in *Lone Wolf,* like those in the *Insular Cases*, still obtains, as does, it should be clear, the U.S. empire-state (Aleinikoff 2002; Biolsi 2005; Sparrow 2006).

RACIALIZED PEOPLES OF THE U.S. EMPIRE-STATE

The hierarchical differentiation of space and the hierarchical differentiation of people, both immanent and foundational to empire-state formation, are plainly related. Since the hierarchical differentiation of space is not about space in itself but about the *politics* of ordering space, it is inextricably, always already about the politics of ordering people. And, as argued above, the construction of U.S. colonial spaces—whether they be Indian lands, incorporated and unincorporated territories, the "several states," or the United States as a whole—centrally turned on the racialization of their inhabitants, on the production and reproduction of white supremacy. With little controversy, at least on the left and even among liberals, we could probably agree that certain populations were colonized by the U.S. state: the indigenous peoples of North America and Hawai'i, Mexicans of northern Mexico/southwestern United

States, and peoples of the so-called unincorporated territories. (With a little controversy, we could also acknowledge that most, if not all, of them continue to be colonized.[18])

What about other peoples of color, others subjected to racial domination? In much of the literature on colonialism, the binary oppositions of colonizer/colonized, European/native, and citizen/subject are unproblematically assumed to refer to the same relationship. How then should we conceive of *noncolonized, nonnative subjects*?

The racial domination of Blacks in the United States, for example, has not been one of colonial domination: the formation of the U.S. empire-state did not entail the expropriation of lands over which Blacks had prior claims. So, while it may be of undoubted relevance with respect to colonized peoples, like Native Americans or Puerto Ricans, how does the imperial, rather than national, character of the U.S. state significantly impinge on how we understand the racial domination of Blacks and other noncolonized peoples of color, who have been systematically treated as less than white citizens?

In an empire-state, racial domination of colonized peoples does not happen in isolation from that of noncolonized peoples, and vice versa. Though qualitatively different, they are intimately and intricately linked. Rather than a series of self-contained, dyadic relations between whites and various racial others, white supremacy comprises a web of crisscrossing discursive and practical ties. It is a unified, though differentiated, field that calls for a unified, though differentiated, theoretical framework. For instance, in the afterglow of the Louisiana Purchase of 1803, President Thomas Jefferson envisaged in the newly acquired territory an expanded "empire of liberty" in which his vaunted citizenry of white yeomen could grow and flourish. He also saw potential solutions to vexing racial problems supposedly posed by those beyond the pale pale of citizenship: "the means of tempting all our Indians on the East side of the Mississippi to remove to the West" (as quoted in Meinig 1993: 78) and of "diffusing" and thereby defusing Blacks, slavery, and the dreaded threat of insurrection, made all too real by the Haitian Revolution (Freehling 2005: 70). Such articulations of empire, white supremacy, racialized citizenship, and colonial and noncolonial subjection were not rare or limited to the early nineteenth century and the ruling elite. To take an example from the turn of the twentieth century, the state and the public, military and civilian officials, legislators and judges, academic and popular commentators, officers and soldiers, business and labor leaders, editorialists and cartoonists, and many others apparently could not imagine, talk about, write on, wage war against, or govern the newly colonized peoples of the former Spanish colonies and Hawai'i without references to Blacks, Native Americans, and the Chinese. They compared, differentiated, analogized, contrasted, transposed, extended, ranked, and homogenized. As much as the imperialists, anti-imperialists— whether white former abolitionists, Black antilynching activists, or white trade unionists in the anti-Chinese and anti-Japanese movements—made the associations, though with obviously divergent intentions and effects (Jacobson 1998; Kramer 2006; Murphy 2009).

The U.S. state, itself a unified but differentiated field, is a principal agent, or set of agents, in the field of white supremacy. Like other agents, it too confronts and helps to reproduce the field that is a unified but differentiated whole: it makes certain distinctions between colonial and noncolonial imperial subjects as well as within those categories, but it also generates identities, parallels, and overlaps. Explicitly and implicitly, intentionally and unintentionally, the state thus divides *and* unites as it rules. (It thereby sets barriers against and, dialectically, possibilities for coalitions of resistance.) The Supreme Court, compared to many nonstate agents and even among state institutions, has relatively fewer degrees of freedom, constrained as it is, at least nominally, by stare decisis and the Constitution itself.[19] Nonetheless, it too continually affirms the interconnectedness of practices of racial rule, the overall "unity" of a "'complex structure' . . . in which things are related, as much through their differences as through their similarities" (Hall 1980: 325). To illustrate, I turn to a case that is identified hardly ever with empire and almost exclusively with African Americans: *Dred Scott v. Sandford* (1857).

Marking one of the most significant moments in the history of African Americans, the *Dred Scott* decision denied U.S. citizenship to Blacks, both "free" and enslaved, in no uncertain terms, drawing an unambiguous distinction between "the citizen and the subject—the free and the subjugated races." According to the odious opinion of the Court, authored by Chief Justice Roger Brooke Taney, the Constitution was unequivocal in distinguishing between the "citizen race, who formed and held the Government, and the African race, which they held in subjection and slavery and governed at their own pleasure."[20]

Evincing the complex unity of white supremacy, this case, quintessentially about Blacks, could also be seen, in a nontrivial sense, as a part of Native American, Asian/Asian American, Pacific Islander, and Latina/o histories. Toward the start of his opinion, right after summarizing the question before the Court, Taney takes a seemingly gratuitous detour for a long paragraph. It is entirely devoted to contrasting the "situation . . . of the Indian race" to that of "descendants of Africans": since the "colonial" era, "although [Indians] were uncivilized, they were yet a free and independent people, associated together in nations or tribes and governed by their own laws. . . . These Indian governments were regarded and treated as foreign Governments as much so as if an ocean had separated the red man from the white, and their freedom has constantly been acknowledged." Therefore, although they were "brought . . . under subjection to the white race . . . in a state of pupilage," Indians could "without doubt, like the subjects of any other foreign Government, be naturalized by the authority of Congress . . . and if an individual should leave his nation or tribe and take up his abode among the white population, he would be entitled to all the rights and privileges which would belong to an emigrant from any other foreign people."[21]

A decade before, however, the Supreme Court, in another opinion written by Taney, had arrived at a contrary conclusion. In *United States v. Rogers* (1846), lands held by Indians were judged to be "a part of the territory of the United States" that had been merely "assigned to them." Further, ever since European "discovery," "native tribes . . . have never been acknowledged or treated as independent nations."[22] How do we account for the inconsistency? In *Dred Scott*, Taney contradicted his earlier opinion regarding Indians to forestall a presumably more dire contradiction regarding Blacks. In 1790, Congress had passed a law restricting the right of naturalization to "aliens being free white persons."[23] Evidently not satisfied with this statutory proscription, Taney sought to *constitutionally* block even the future possibility of naturalized citizenship for Blacks. One of the two dissenters in the case, Benjamin Robbins Curtis conceded, needlessly, that Congress's constitutional power of naturalization was confined to "aliens."[24] But he went on to note that being "colored" did not itself pose a constitutional barrier and that, in fact, American Indians and Mexicans had already been made U.S. citizens through treaties.[25] The other dissenter, John McLean, likewise remarked: "Under the late treaty with Mexico, we have made citizens of all grades, combinations, and colors. The same was done in the admission of Louisiana and Florida."[26]

Presumably because they had uncontroversially been seen as "aliens" before U.S. annexation, Taney did not bother to address Mexicans of the Southwest or nonwhites of the Louisiana and Florida territories in his opinion. He

also granted that "color" was not a constitutional hindrance to naturalization.[27] But, though not explicitly pushed by Curtis, the issue concerning Native Americans could not be so easily dispensed with: some Indians who had
been born under U.S. sovereignty according to previous rulings, including his
own, had been accorded U.S. citizenship. If they could be naturalized, why
could Blacks not be? Taney resolved the apparent dilemma by insisting that
the Constitution "gave to Congress the power to confer [citizenship] upon
those *only* who were born *outside* of the dominions of the United States" and
asserting that Indians, abruptly redefined as "aliens and foreigners," fit this
description.[28] Thus lacking the capacity to "raise to the rank of a citizen anyone born *in* the United States who . . . belongs to an inferior and subordinate
class," Congress could not naturalize Blacks even if it were so inclined.[29]

In *Dred Scott*, ruling on Blacks led to a reexamination into the rule of Indians (and Mexicans and others). The racial subjection of one was related to the
racial subjection of the other, evidencing a common field of white supremacy.
The articulation in this instance was one of difference. To refuse U.S. citizenship to all Blacks, the Supreme Court was provoked to state explicitly how
Native Americans were dissimilar, modifying its previous view on Indian sovereignty. In this way, the Court instituted and justified the differential treatment of the two "subject" populations, one rooted in slavery and the other
in colonization. At the same time, the decision also alluded to the inevitable
imbrications of imperial subjection. In support of the Court's opinion, Taney
cited a number of state laws that ostensibly formed a consensus against the
idea of Black citizenship. Though not commented on by the Court, three of
the statutes—two forbidding intermarriage with whites and one prohibiting
travel without a written pass—applied not only to "any negro" or "mulatto"
but also "Indian."[30]

The decision in *Dred Scott* with regard to Black citizenship was overruled,
at least formally, by the passage and ratification of the Thirteenth, Fourteenth,
and Fifteenth Amendments to the Constitution during Reconstruction. But
some of its reasoning survived to be debated anew decades later. One of the
arguments put forth by the plaintiff Dred Scott was that his residence from
1836 to 1838 at Fort Snelling, where he had been taken by his owner, had made
him free. With the Missouri Compromise of 1820, which had simultaneously
admitted Missouri as a slave state and Maine as a "free" state to maintain sectional balance, Congress had prohibited slavery in the remaining territories of
the Louisiana Purchase lying north of 36 degrees and 30 minutes latitude; this

area included the part of Wisconsin Territory in which the aforementioned army post stood.

The Supreme Court rejected Scott's claim, concluding that Congress had overreached: the Missouri Compromise, already voided by the Kansas-Nebraska Act of 1854 by the time *Dred Scott* made its way to the Court, was unconstitutional.[31] According to Taney, Congress's constitutional "Power to dispose of and make all needful Rules and Regulations respecting the Territory . . . belonging to the United States" (Article IV, section 3) was immaterial: the Territorial Clause pertained only to the territory claimed by the United States at the time of the Constitution's original adoption and could "have no influence upon a territory afterwards acquired from a foreign Government."[32] The lone means to acquire and, implicitly, govern additional territories was instead through the Admissions Clause: "New States may be admitted by the Congress" (Article IV, section 3). From acquisition to admission, temporary territorial governments organized by Congress were permissible, but it had no plenary power to "establish or maintain colonies . . . to be ruled and governed at its own pleasure." Just as in the several states, Congress had "powers over the citizen strictly defined, and limited by the Constitution," but "no power of any kind beyond it."[33] Thus, legislating as it did for the Louisiana Purchase territories in the Missouri Compromise, Congress had overstepped its definite powers and infringed on U.S. citizens' right of property, the "right of property in a slave."[34]

Having pronounced that Congress had "no power . . . to acquire a Territory to be held and governed permanently in that character," *Dred Scott* was bound to reemerge when various state and nonstate actors were clamoring for just that in the overseas territories annexed at the turn of the century, and others were mobilizing in opposition. It appeared extensively in *Downes v. Bidwell* (1901), "generally considered the most important of the *Insular Cases*"; Justice Edward Douglass White's opinion in the case, immediately about tariffs on Puerto Rican goods, introduced and detailed what would eventually become the controlling doctrine of territorial incorporation (Burnett and Marshall 2001a: 7).

Somewhat dissonant with the amply deserved infamy of *Dred Scott*, Taney's opinion on territories perversely took on a kind of "premature anti-imperialist" quality (Levinson 2001: 130). For the four dissenting judges in *Downes*, the Constitution included all territories when referring to the "United States" and was fully in effect there. As John Marshall Harlan averred in his dissent, "The Constitution is supreme over every foot of territory, wherever situated, under the jurisdiction of the United States, and its full operation cannot be stayed by any branch of the government."[35] In the opinion signed onto by all of the dissenters, Chief Justice Melville Weston Fuller drew on *Dred Scott*, noting that "the Court [had been] unanimous in holding that the power to legislate respecting a territory was limited by the restrictions of the Constitution."[36]

In the lead opinion in *Downes*, Henry Billings Brown took a diametrically opposing position. For him, the "United States" referred strictly to the constituent states. The Constitution applied to any given territory only if, and only to the degree, Congress explicitly extended it. Brown discussed *Dred Scott* at great length and concluded that Taney's thoughts on territories were irrelevant as legal precedent (Sparrow 2006: 88): the question in *Downes* was "readily distinguishable from the one" on slavery, and that *Dred Scott* had taken up the territory question at all had been unnecessary and "unfortunate."[37]

White's concurring opinion, joined by two others, split the difference between the maximalist and minimalist definitions of the "United States." Like Brown, he affirmed Congress's plenary power over territories, which had been disputed by *Dred Scott* but had been sustained, both before and after it, in other cases. But he disagreed with Brown's criticism of *Dred Scott* and partly sided with Fuller: "the principle which that decision announced, that the applicable provisions of the Constitution were operative" in U.S. territories was still valid. The issue was not, per Brown, "whether the Constitution is operative, for that is self-evident, but whether the provision relied on is applicable" to a given territory, a question that hung on "its relations to the United States."[38] Some territories, like the continental ones and Hawai'i, were "incorporated" into the United States. Others, like Puerto Rico and by extension the other former Spanish colonies, "had not been incorporated into the United States, but [were] merely appurtenant thereto as . . . possession[s]." In other words, the "United States" included some territories but not others, although all were "subject to [U.S.] sovereignty."[39] The precise meaning and consequences of "incorporation" remained fuzzy, but this and subsequent cases seemed to suggest that the Constitution "fully" applied in the incorporated territories.[40] For the unincorporated territories, White's opinion, though theoretically different, had identical practical implications as Brown's: "only certain fundamental constitutional prohibitions"—underspecified but certainly fewer than in incorporated territories—"constrained governmental action there" (Burnett and Marshall 2001a: 9–10). In 1904, White's doctrine of territorial incorporation was adopted by a majority of the Court for the first time, in *Dorr v. United States*. Among other things, the opinion of the Court quoted the same passage from Curtis's opinion in *Dred Scott* that White had cited in *Downes*.[41]

As in *Dred Scott*, and later *Insular Cases*, race and citizenship were pivotal in *Downes*. A major impetus and impact of legally inventing the category of unincorporated territories were the prevention of incorporating their inhabitants on an equal footing with white Anglo-Saxon citizens and the empowerment of Congress to calibrate how unequal the footing should be. In his lead opinion in *Downes*, Brown gave voice to the animating fear: what would happen if Congress did not have the discretionary power to determine the citizenship "status" of a territory's "inhabitants"?[42] After all, if territories "are inhabited by alien races . . . the administration of government and justice according to Anglo-Saxon principles may for a time be impossible."[43] But those "alien races" had no cause for worry, for "there are certain principles of natural justice inherent in the Anglo-Saxon character which need no expression in constitutions or statutes to give them effect or to secure dependencies against legislation manifestly hostile to their real interests." To give credence to this paternalistic argument, Brown cited a number of cases involving noncitizens who *already* lacked constitutional protection—one dealing with American Indians, *Johnson v. M'Intosh*, and several dealing with Chinese "aliens [who were] not possessed of the political rights of the citizens of the United States." Thanks to Anglo-Saxon self-restraint, the inhabitants of the new territories, or any territory, would likewise not be "subject to an unrestrained power on the part of Congress to deal with them upon the theory that they have no rights which it is bound to respect"—the last phrase an obvious, if not obviously negative, allusion to *Dred Scott*.[44]

White's concurring opinion sounded the same alarm about citizenship. He illustrated his point with a hypothetical example, appealing to the discovery doctrine espoused in *Johnson v. M'Intosh*, among other cases, and tacking on a bit of feigned concern about the potential tax burden on the colonized to his paramount apprehension about racial fitness for citizenship:

Citizens of the United States discover an unknown island, peopled with an uncivilized race, yet rich in soil, and valuable to the United States for commercial and strategic reasons. Clearly, by the law of nations, the right to ratify such acquisition and thus to acquire the territory would pertain to the government

of the United States. *Johnson v. M'Intosh*, 8 Wheat. 543, 595, 5 L. ed. 681, 694.…
Can it be denied that such right could not be practically exercised if the result
would be to endow the inhabitants with citizenship of the United States and
to subject them, not only to local, but also to an equal proportion of national,
taxes, even although the consequence would be to entail ruin on the discovered
territory, and to inflict grave detriment on the United States, to arise both from
the dislocation of its fiscal system and the immediate bestowal of citizenship on
those absolutely unfit to receive it?[45]

Worse yet, as pointed out by Brown, even if immediate bestowal of citizenship could be avoided, "children thereafter born, whether savages or civilized,
[would be] … entitled to all the rights, privileges and immunities of citizens.
If such be their status, the consequences will be extremely serious."[46] He closed
his opinion with a warning: "A false step at this time might be fatal to the development of what Chief Justice Marshall called the American empire."[47]

Brown's reference to "children thereafter born" stated aloud what must
have implicitly informed the other judges' discourse on citizenship. He was
alluding to *United States v. Wong Kim Ark* (1898), a case decided by the same
court just three years earlier. If we go a little further back, nine years before
Wong Kim Ark, the Supreme Court, in *Chae Chan Ping v. United States*, had
unanimously upheld the racially based Chinese exclusion laws of the 1880s,
specifically the Chinese Exclusion Act of 1888.[48] The broader effect of the decision was to establish Congress's plenary power over "aliens," which like the
plenary powers over American Indian sovereignty and over territories still
obtains to this day (Aleinikoff 2002). (A corollary effect was that the constitutional sanction afforded to Congress to legislatively contravene international
treaties, with China in this particular case, provided precedential support
for the 1903 ruling in *Lone Wolf* that gave similar sanction to abrogate treaties with Native Americans—yet another example of the interconnectedness
of racial rule, the imbrications of colonial and noncolonial imperial subjection.[49]) However, even the patent anti-Chinese racism of the Court had its
legal limits. Both Congress and the courts had consistently denied the right of
naturalization to Chinese migrants and would continue to do so until 1943.
But given the Fourteenth Amendment—"All persons born or naturalized in
the United States, and subject to the jurisdiction thereof, are citizens of the
United States" (section 1)—the Supreme Court could not but acknowledge in
Wong Kim Ark the birthright citizenship of "all children here born of resident

aliens," including the Chinese.[50] Consequently, as argued by Brook Thomas, "*Wong Kim Ark* forced any Justice[s] intent on denying citizenship to residents of the insular territories to restrict the definition of what comes within the territorial limits of the United States" (2001: 96; see also Levinson 2001: 132). And restrict they did.

On racial grounds, the Court chose to define the "United States in a domestic sense" as being composed of states and incorporated territories, and relegated the inhabitants of the unincorporated territories in Asia, the Pacific, and the Caribbean indefinitely to something always less than full citizenship—that is, colonial subjection. Initially denied U.S. citizenship, residents of today's unincorporated territories, except American Samoa, have been accorded it over the years, with or without their consent. Yet, in the context of the colonial relationship between the U.S. state and these territories, characterized by congressional plenary power, U.S. citizenship has never meant equality, not just informally but formally, and territorial inhabitants have been systematically withheld certain privileges and immunities.[51] (The same goes for American Indians, on whom U.S. citizenship was imposed, if not earlier through treaties or legislation, through the Indian Citizenship Act of 1924.)

With the exception of one justice, the same Supreme Court that heard *Wong Kim Ark* and *Downes* had also been on the bench for *Plessy v. Ferguson* (1896).[52] One of four dissenters in *Downes*, Harlan had been famously lone in that role in *Plessy*. Insisting that "there is no caste" and that the "Constitution is color-blind," he predicted, "In my opinion, the judgment this day rendered will, in time, prove to be quite as pernicious as the decision made by this tribunal in the *Dred Scott Case*" and "stimulate aggressions, more or less brutal and irritating, upon the admitted rights of colored citizens." Referring to Taney's opinion, he argued that the postbellum amendments to the Constitution were supposed to have "eradicated these principles" of excluding Blacks from the "rights and privileges which [the Constitution] provided for and secured to citizens of the United States."[53] Here, Harlan used *Dred Scott* to analogize the state-endorsed racial subjection of antebellum Blacks to what would follow from *Plessy*.

A former slave owner from a slave-owning family, Harlan has been hailed for his judicial antiracism (Chin 1996; Przybyszewky 1999; Sparrow 2006; Yang 2009). A product of its time, however, it had definite limits. Harlan's "antiracism" was one within the boundaries of white supremacy, one for *legal* equality that he was certain would not upset but safeguard white dominance:

"The white race deems itself to be the dominant race in this country. And so it is in prestige, in achievements, in education, in wealth and in power. So, I doubt not, it will continue to be for all time if it remains true to its great heritage and holds fast to the principles of constitutional liberty."[54]

Harlan's opinion was firmly anchored to the notion of equal *citizenship*, and his temporal comparison of the plight of Blacks led to a second comparison. His discussion of Blacks' *Dred Scott* past and *Plessy* future segued to a timeless contempt for the Chinese:

> There is a race so different from our own that we do not permit those belonging to it to become citizens of the United States. Persons belonging to it are, with few exceptions, absolutely excluded from our country. I allude to the Chinese race. But, by the statute in question, a Chinaman can ride in the same passenger coach with white citizens of the United States, while citizens of the black race in Louisiana, many of whom, perhaps, risked their lives for the preservation of the Union, who are entitled, by law, to participate in the political control of the State and nation, who are not excluded, by law or by reason of their race, from public stations of any kind, and who have all the legal rights that belong to white citizens, are yet declared to be criminals, liable to imprisonment, if they ride in a public coach occupied by citizens of the white race.[55]

The Louisiana law that the decision upheld, mandating racial segregation of railway trains, did not mention the Chinese, nor did it indicate to which of "the white, and colored races" they belonged, nor did it confine its purview to citizens (*Revised Laws of Louisiana* 1897: 762–63). Yet, in discussing the subjection of Blacks, Harlan evidently felt compelled to do all three.[56]

Toward the beginning of his dissent, Harlan wrote: "While there may be in Louisiana persons of different races who are not citizens of the United States, the words in the act 'white and colored races' necessarily include all citizens of the United States of both races residing in that State. So that we have before us a state enactment that compels, under penalties, the separation of the two races."[57] The initial clause of the first sentence—and the wording of the statute itself, with its ambiguous conjunctions and punctuation— was unclear on how many "races" there were, but by the end of the sentence Harlan definitively settled on two and equated "colored" with Black. He also narrowed the scope of the case to "citizens" and then further narrowed the scope to "citizens of . . . both races": constitutional protections were for U.S. state members only, and U.S. state membership included two and only two "races," Black and white. The tragedy, from his vantage point, was that the U.S. state would permit and abet the maintenance of racial distinction and inequality between these two categories of citizens. But he saw no contradiction between this "color-blind" jurisprudence and his acceptance and advocacy of other racial distinctions and inequalities, namely those concerning the Chinese (Yang 2009). That persons "belonging to [the Chinese race] are, with few exceptions, absolutely excluded from our country" was how it should be; likewise for their inability to "become citizens." What rankled Harlan was that the "few" Chinese who were in the country would be able to "ride in the same passenger coach with white citizens," while Black citizens could not. For him, the Chinese quintessentially constituted the *citizen*'s racial other—two mutually exclusive categories. In this light, Harlan's remarks on the Chinese in *Plessy* were hardly a throwaway digression at odds with his otherwise commendable antiracism but spoke to a vital component of a coherent racism that prefigured his (and only one other justice's) unwillingness to recognize even the birthright citizenship of U.S.-born Chinese two years later in *Wong Kim Ark* (Levinson 2001; Yang 2009). The difference between Harlan and the other justices was not that he was antiracist and they were racist, but that he and they drew, at the dawn of the twentieth century, the "color line,—the relation of the darker to the lighter races of men [and women] in Asia and Africa, in America and the islands of the sea"—differently in relation to U.S. citizenry and empire (Du Bois 1965 [1903]: 221; Chin 1996; B. Thomas 2001).

OVERVIEW OF THE BOOK

The empire-state approach to the United States advocated here does not and—as this chapter was not drafted before the others—could not explicitly inform the chapters that follow. But it is compatible with and, further, serves to highlight a couple of key themes running through them. First, the chapters continually reveal the false promise of liberalism for people of color—variably false over time and across groups, but false no less. The deeply entrenched patterns of racial domination and inequality, as all of the chapters attest to and document, simply do not square with the liberal notion of a nation-state of equal citizens. The United States does and always did encompass under its sovereignty many people formally denied the rights and privileges of full citizenship and still more people, though legally entitled, informally denied them. Second, chapter after chapter, we are reminded that states are unmistakably "coercion-wielding organizations" (Tilly 1992: 1). For people of color, state violence is hardly just a background presence—the unobtrusive back-stop of coercion securing everyday conditions of consent and freedom—that can be taken for granted and implicitly and explicitly relied upon for the protection of interests and indeed bodies. Rather, it is routinely oppressive, deadly, and in your face. All states, of course, are coercion-wielding, but the vast racial inequalities in the application of state violence in the United States make far more sense when we recognize that they are not anomalies and that equal citizenship to this purported liberal nation-state has not and does not come close to capturing the lived lives of millions of people.

Racialized and gendered from the beginning, modern "liberal" states like the United States, Charles Mills incisively argues, do not represent a radical break with hierarchically structured premodern societies, as commonly believed: "For people of color, the modern polity is the white settler state expropriating them, the colonial state enslaving them, the imperial state colonizing them." Attending to both the durability of "white supremacy's social substructure" and the historical specificity of its articulations, Dylan Rodríguez relates the seemingly unrelated historical moments of Reconstruction and the colonization of the Philippines, "tracing white supremacy's animus through two apparently disparate archival settings." Deftly taking us from contemporary Washington, D.C., and North Carolina to Enlightenment Europe back across to nineteenth-century and contemporary United States, Eduardo Bonilla-Silva and Sarah Mayorga conceive of citizenship, rooted in "bourgeois liberal individualism" and bound to the racial "nation-state," as a tactical resource at best and doubt its liberatory potential for people of color.

The next two chapters consider public education, the state institution that has been so crucial to the reproduction of racial inequalities. Offering a comprehensive overview of the current state of educational inequalities, Amanda Lewis and Michelle Manno report on the various means by which racial inequalities are generated. No longer as explicitly racist as before the civil rights movement, these mechanisms include differential school funding, teacher quality, teacher expectations, tracking, placement in special education, and school discipline. The gains of the civil rights movement prove to be even more circumscribed in George Lipsitz's chapter on the Supreme Court's recent gutting of school desegregation efforts. Shamelessly hypocritical and ardently protective of white privilege, the Court's ruling in *Parents Involved in Community Schools v. Seattle School District No. 1 et al.* (2007) makes a mockery of the already enfeebled *Brown v. Board of Education* and conjures up ghosts of *Dred Scott*, with "Black people still hav[ing] no rights that whites are obligated to respect."

Through a meticulous analysis of Florida's welfare-to-work program, Sanford Schram, Richard Fording, and Joe Soss discuss what they refer to as neoliberal paternalism in poverty governance. Simultaneous turns toward actively fostered market principles and a punitive brand of paternalism are leaving the Latina/o and especially Black poor more vulnerable, "underscor[ing] how the enduring factors of race, place, and their interaction are critical to the logic of the emerging forms of new poverty governance." Joy James explores the racial and sexual politics of the case of Ben LaGuer, a Black Puerto Rican man dubiously convicted and imprisoned for raping a white woman, and its articulations with the electoral politics around Deval Patrick's successful run to be Massachusetts's first Black governor and the long history of sexual-racial violence in the United States.

Given the extraordinary rise, size, and racial character of the carceral state, I would argue that prisons and prisoners (and former prisoners) should be seen for what they are: imperial spaces and subjects. What about "aliens," who like territorial inhabitants and American Indians are still subject to congressional plenary power? Are they citizens-in-waiting of this supposed nation of immigrants, or are many, especially the undocumented, subjects indefinitely without rights that the state and its citizens are bound to respect? How distinct is the line between citizen and subject, and how is it drawn? In her study of a five-day "immigration sweep" in 1997 by federal immigration and local police agents in Chandler, Arizona, Mary Romero suggests that the state draws this line solidly, and racially, *around* the Mexican-origin community and porously within, giving little regard to such legal niceties as formal citizenship or residency status. Along similar lines, Junaid Rana recounts two recent events, one of "panic" and another of "peril," involving the racialized figure of the "Muslim." He demonstrates that "racial constructions of potential terrorists are instrumental to anti-immigrant narratives that rely on ideas of illegality and criminality."

Over the course of the history of the United States, people of color and women have been the most frequent targets of terror, much of which has been perpetrated, endorsed, or ignored by the state. Against this backdrop, Andrea Smith critiques the prevailing politics of organizing against "hate crimes." "When organizing against racial and/or gender terror adopts the strategy of making this terror a crime," she argues, "it actually serves to reproduce patriarchy and white supremacy by masking the sexism and the racism of capital-ism and the nation-state." Looking to the activism of "indigenous women and feminists of color," she advocates "the construction of alternative governance systems that do not rely on the colonial nation-state." João Costa Vargas pro-poses to "decenter the United States . . . by recentering it in the Black Dias-pora." Guided by the overarching concept of genocide, he details the varied *and* connected practices of domination, in the United States and Brazil, that result in the "ongoing endangered and prematurely terminated lives of Black people"—the material bases of the Black Diaspora. But genocide is continu-ally survived and resisted, dialectically marking the Black Diaspora as "not only a geography of death but also, necessarily, a set of shared ontological and political knowledge that is immanently insurgent."

GENEALOGIES OF RACIAL RULE

Part 1

1 LIBERALISM AND THE RACIAL STATE

Charles Mills

Liberalism is hegemonic. The antifeudal political philosophy of individual rights and freedoms that emerges in the modern period in opposition to absolutism and natural social hierarchy has unquestionably become, whether in right-wing or left-wing versions, the dominant political outlook of the day. Poststructuralism, communitarianism, multiculturalism, and other bodies of political thought may flourish in the radical academy. But in terms of influencing public policy and mobilizing political players in the real world, liberalism is certainly the main (if not the only) game in town. The seeming collapse of socialist ideological-political alternatives has made a liberal framework the central normative reference point for claims about the justice or injustice of the social order, whether by appeal to free-market or social-democratic ideals.

What then does liberalism have to say about racial oppression? Racial oppression is, after all, the distinctive injustice of the modern world. This follows from the simple fact that—at least according to the consensus of scholars—it is only with modernity that race even comes into existence as a category of identity and as a social reality.[1] Class oppression may date from the period when technological advance creates a social surplus that makes slavery possible; gender oppression may go back even further, to the sexual division of labor in hunter-gatherer societies. But the advent of race and social orders structured around race is a very recent development in human evolution. Moreover, by modern standards race is distinctively horrific insofar as it facilitates enslavement and genocide at the very time when human equality is supposed to have been established as a dominant norm. Whether as a self-owning Lockean appropriator or a self-directing Kantian being, the liberal individual is supposed to be protected by the liberal state, and any infringe-ment of his or her rights corrected for. And what more flagrant violation of the liberal ideal of the rights and freedoms of the individual could there be than people's reduction to chattel status or mass killing merely because of their "race"? One would expect, therefore, that liberal moral theory and liberal po-litical theory would historically have made the analysis and condemnation of racial injustice and the correction of racial oppression a priority, since liberal-ism and racism developed in the same historical period.

But these expectations would be disappointed. Far from being in prin-cipled opposition to racism, as a blatant infringement of individual rights and freedoms, liberalism has too often been complicit with it. The origins of both in modernity have tended to be manifested more in symbiosis than contra-diction, with the liberal individual being so conceptualized that whiteness is a prerequisite for individuality. And the liberal state, correspondingly, has historically functioned as a racial state, the Lockean sovereign denying self-ownership rights to people of color and the Kantian state treating nonwhites as subpersons incapable of self-rule. In effect, liberalism, far from being color-less, has been a racialized white liberalism, in which both descriptive assump-tions and prescriptive norms have been shaped by race. If liberalism is to be reconstructed to become the vehicle of an effective program of racial justice, a prerequisite must be an acknowledgment of this history and a self-conscious rethinking and self-purging in light of it.

RECONCEIVING LIBERALISM

Let me begin with a brief sketch of the standard narrative of the origins of liberalism. In the orthodox account, liberalism develops in opposition to the political absolutism and social hierarchy of the medieval world. By contrast with the central categories of this sociopolitical system, liberalism makes the morally equal individual its theoretical focus rather than the social estates of feudalism and, before that, antiquity. Both descriptively, in terms of how we think of the genesis of the polity, and normatively, in terms of moral ends, the individual is supposed to be the central reference point. So conceived, liberal-ism obviously represents a sharp break with the political assumptions of the thousands of years that preceded it. As Paul Kelly (2005: 17) writes, "Equality . . . is a peculiarly modern value," one that "[p]re-modern world views such as those of Plato, Cicero or St Augustine have little place for," linked with "the idea of the modern individual emerg[ing] as a distinct bearer of ethical significance." Rather than hierarchically ordered social groups, we have morally equal individuals whose rights must be respected by a state that owes its legitimacy to their consent. We get a periodization that looks like this:

Liberalism and Modernity: The Standard Narrative

ANCIENT SLAVERY
social estates (citizens/slaves), social hierarchy, moral inegalitarianism, nonliberal ideology, nonliberal state

MEDIEVAL FEUDALISM
social estates (lords/serfs), social hierarchy, moral inegalitarianism, nonliberal ideology, nonliberal state

MODERN MARKET SOCIETY
individuals, social equality, moral egalitarianism, liberal ideology, liberal state

The shift from the premodern (ancient, medieval) to the modern thus involves a major change in the conceptualization and justification of the sociopolitical order, the understanding of the polity, and the view of the human beings who inhabit it. In political theory, the main conceptual vehicle of this change is social contract theory. Social contract theory urges us to think of society and the political order as if they had been voluntarily created by presocial, prepolitical human beings (Gough 1978; Lessnoff 1986; Boucher and Kelly 1994). We know, of course, that such creatures never existed. Human beings are always in societies and are always regulated by some kind of political system. The societies may be small, technologically undeveloped, and politically egalitarian, but they are still societies and not the "state of nature." Anthropology 101 gives the lie to social contract theory. But while false as a historical account, contractarianism nonetheless captures, metaphorically, two important truths, one being factual, the other, normative.

The first important truth is that society and the political order are in fact human creations (though not creations ex nihilo). They are not divinely ordained systems or natural organic growths but are "artificial." As such, the metaphor historically played a valuable role in (partially) demystifying the conservative, naturalistic, and frequently inevitabilist views of the sociopolitical order inherited from antiquity and the medieval world. Humans created society and the polity; humans can recreate society and the polity. The second important truth is that the human creators of society and the polity are morally equal, so this moral status should be reflected in the social structures and political institutions they bring into existence.[2] These structures and institutions should not embed social hierarchy and political oppression. In the words of Murray Forsyth (1994: 37), "The emergence of the notion of the social contract is hence linked intimately with the emergence of the idea of the equality of human beings." So the metaphor also historically played a valuable role in (partially) discrediting the ideologies of natural hierarchy inherited, again, from antiquity and the medieval world. Contra Plato, Aristotle, and feudal ascriptive hierarchy, egalitarianism was the appropriate norm for the contractors' political relations with one another.

The significance of the contract metaphor as expressing two key claims of modernity central to liberalism should therefore be obvious. Yet in both cases, as I have emphasized, its revisionist scope was only partial. The Whiggish picture in the standard narrative above is fundamentally misleading in that the "contractors" were conceived of not as raceless but as white (more precisely, as white men). The potentially radical and far-reaching implications of a liberalism and an accompanying contract theory that included everybody were thus severely truncated. White men were deemed fully capable of creating the sociopolitical order, but white women and nonwhite "savages" and "barbarians" were not. White men were represented as morally equal to one another, but white women and nonwhites were depicted as morally unequal. Thus the hierarchy actually targeted by the contract was not at all general but limited to only one dimension of the overall system of domination. What was really seen as illicit was that some white men, on the grounds of their superior birth, should rule despotically over other white men (the absolutist political ideology of Sir Robert Filmer, Locke's [1988] main adversary in the *Two Treatises of Government*). It was hierarchical white male social estates that were denied validity. As feminist theorists such as Carole Pateman (1988) have shown, gender "estates" were not even seen as sociopolitical but natural, taken for granted. The natural inferiority of women, far from being challenged, was in fact inscribed in the contract through a rewriting of gender relations. And the social categories of white and nonwhite, racial "estates" that had not even existed in the premodern period, were now, with modernity, established. White male natural hierarchy was discredited at the same time that white-nonwhite natural hierarchy was introduced. White-male-over-white-male despotic rule was repudiated at the same time that the despotic rule of white males over everybody else was legitimized. The famous free and equal individuals of social contract theory were not sexless and colorless but universally male and usually white.

From the beginning, then, liberalism developed as a political philosophy that was both gendered and (largely) racialized. The qualification is necessary because liberalism's record on race is less uniformly exclusionary than its record on gender, a manifestation of the relative historic recency of white supremacy as a system of domination in comparison to thousands of years of patriarchy. Both Sankar Muthu (2003) and Jennifer Pitts (2005), among others, have argued that there is a white liberal tradition of anti-imperialism and antiracism. But other scholars (see, for example, Trouillot 1995; Bernasconi 2001; Sala-Molins 2006) have been more skeptical about some of the theorists Muthu cites as supposed exemplars (Diderot, Kant), and the point of Pitts's book is to trace how, by the midnineteenth century, "imperial liberalism" does become the norm. At the very least, then, one could say that if there has ever been a consistently anti-imperialist and antiracist strain within white liberal *theory*, it has generally been subordinate. And certainly on the level of *practice*, in the policies of the actual liberal states of the period, it was not effective. I conclude that the conventional chronological and normative mapping of the transition from the premodern to the modern depicted above needs to be replaced with a more realistic picture, which takes both gender and race into account, thereby covering the entire human population and not just the white male minority:

Liberalism and Modernity: The Actual Story

ANCIENT SLAVERY
social estates (citizens/slaves, men/women), social hierarchy, moral inegalitarianism, nonliberal ideology, nonliberal state

MEDIEVAL FEUDALISM
social estates (lords/serfs, men/women), social hierarchy, moral inegalitarianism, nonliberal ideology, nonliberal state

MODERN MARKET SOCIETY
(white male) individuals, social estates (whites/nonwhites, men/women), social hierarchy, moral inegalitarianism, liberal (racial-gendered) ideology, nonliberal (or racial-gendered liberal) state

Note how dramatically this conceptual shift alters our perception of both liberalism and modernity. Instead of seeing liberalism as breaking sharply with the hierarchical political philosophies of the ancient and medieval worlds, we now see it as significantly continuous with them. Instead of ignoring the racial exclusions of modernity, or treating them as aberrational, as is standardly done, we now identify them as constitutive of the new variety of racial social estates that joins the (enduring) social estate of gender. Instead of assuming moral egalitarianism as the actual norm, we acknowledge the reality that the sociopolitical order remains a hierarchical one, though the ideological rationale for hierarchy and for demarcating particular sets of human beings as superior and inferior has somewhat changed. Above all, instead of theorizing as if all humans come to count as "individuals" in modernity, we recognize that there are racial and gender prerequisites for attaining this status that exclude the majority of the population.

Liberalism, then, is really nonliberalism, at least if measured by the (unrealized and unintended, though proclaimed) ideal of actually being predicated on the personhood of all humans. Alternatively phrased, liberalism is the exclusionary hierarchical ideology of the racial-gendered system established by modernity: racial patriarchy (Pateman and Mills 2007: chap. 6). And the role of the state—as in the sociopolitical orders of premodernity—is to privilege a minority of the population (white males) at the expense of the majority.

RACIAL OPACITY: OBFUSCATING
THE RACIAL NATURE OF RACIAL LIBERALISM

The obvious question then becomes, If this is indeed the actual nature of liberalism, how has it been successfully concealed all these years? What conceptual sleights of hand, revisions and rewritings, strategic silences and darknesses have made such obfuscation possible? In what follows, I will focus on race, the theme of this book, although the gender exclusions that make actual liberalism a gendered as well as a racialized ideology are of course equally important.

The starting point is what could be termed the principle of "racial opacity." If the modern epoch is continuous with the ancient and medieval periods in being founded on social hierarchy, it is discontinuous both in the pretense that this is not the case and in the emergence of the concept of the individual. The two developments are in fact interconnected. Transparency in government becomes one of the central values of the liberal contractarian tradition since the government now has to be justified to equal individuals. Thus in the most famous twentieth-century text of that tradition, *A Theory of Justice* (1971: 16), John Rawls emphasizes that the "principles of justice" regulating an ideal society must meet "the condition of publicity": "It is characteristic of contract theories to stress the public nature of political principles." By contrast with premodern states explicitly and unapologetically founded on natural hierarchy, the liberal contract polity is supposed to arise from the freely given consent of human beings having equal natural rights. So the contractors would have no motivation to agree to principles that did not safeguard those rights. They choose rules that protect everybody, and everybody knows what the rules are. The ideal of transparency seeks to ensure that "Society is not partitioned with respect to the mutual recognition of its first principles" (582). If an occasional gap between theory and practice opens, this shortcoming is contingent rather than structural, a result of unhappy circumstances rather than a systemic dynamic. The normative basis of the polity is the recognition of the Lockean-Kantian personhood of its members, and this commitment to the just treatment of all should pervade the transactions of everyday life. We are supposed to see others as our moral equals, expect to be seen by them the same way, and should conduct our interactions in the light of the norm of reciprocal respect (133). The Lockean-Kantian *Rechtsstaat* is an "ethical commonwealth" regulated by norms able to withstand the light of day: "No right in a state can be tacitly and treacherously included by a secret reservation" (Immanuel Kant, cited in Rawls 1971: 133 n. 8).

But what if the actual contract that founds the polity is a racial one, which demarcates full persons from subpersons, moral equals from unequals, and uses color-coded rules that differentially regulate the two populations? (Mills 1997). What if the Lockean-Kantian *Rechtsstaat* is actually a *Rassensstaat*, a "racial commonwealth" in which the founding principles of justice prescribe different schedules of rights for whites and people of color? What if disrespect for nonwhites is not contingent but structurally built in to the political system? It would mean that transparency cannot be the regulating ideal for government, because it would reveal too much. Instead, the actual norm, whether admitted or not, must be an opacity that is not the result of happenstance but epistemically and morally linked to the reproduction of the polity. The whitewashing, the whiting-out, of crucial aspects of the origins and routine workings of government becomes an organic part of the smooth functioning of the white racial state, and required by racial liberalism.

What I am calling racial opacity can thus be seen as a principled anti-transparency on matters related to race, the occultation and blocking from "sunshine laws" of the racial "partitioning" and "secret reservations" of the "first principles" on which the polity has actually been founded. Even during the phase of overt white domination, this principled opacity was in operation to a certain extent, as manifest for example in the pretense that under

Jim Crow "separate" could really have ever been "equal." But it becomes absolutely central in the current phase of putative "post-raciality." Racial opacity will be manifest, I suggest, not merely at the empirical level (such as the actual workings of government agencies, the details of public policy) but also at the conceptual level (the very theoretical tools employed to grasp the nature of the polity).

History and Political Science:
Histories and Concepts of the Racial Polity

The most obvious manifestations of racial opacity are the sanitized histories of the United States (and their equivalents in the other white settler states), which were prevalent in the academy up to only a few decades ago, and which continue today to be influential in high school education. These texts whitewash the history of aboriginal conquest and genocide, African slavery, Mexican annexation, anti-Asian exclusion, and Jim Crow. Michel-Rolph Trouillot (1995: 27) suggests that "any historical narrative is a particular bundle of silences," and the goal here has long been a strategic silence on the centrality of racial subordination to the making of the polity. Thus simply on the empirical level, in terms of the crucial facts, people with such a (mis)education will be disadvantaged in understanding the true nature of their society, since abstract concept-formation at least in part involves generalization from particulars, and these racial particulars will be missing from or marginalized in the official narrative. In his important two-part article on the "politics of memory of slavery," Thomas McCarthy (2002, 2004) argues that just as progressive postwar German historians demanded that the Holocaust and its relation to German anti-Semitism be confronted rather than evaded, so there needs to be a *Vergangenheitsbewältigung*[3] on slavery in the United States (2002: 631–32). As he points out,

> [T]he professional and public history of slavery, the Civil War, and Reconstruction were dominated by pro-Southern, antiblack perspectives until after World War II. . . . [A]betted by the pervasive racism of the period—in the North and West as well as in the South and across the boundaries of social class and political party—professional historians did in fact manage to achieve a high degree of historiographic agreement along racist and nationalist lines. This included a romanticized version of antebellum plantation life with softened images of slavery, a depiction of abolitionists and Radical Republicans as extremist agitators, and an account of the outrage of Reconstruction, replete

As a countermeasure, I propose that we shift the analytical angle from the state to the ruled. From the vantage point of the Native peoples of North America, the birth of the United States as a state was at once the birth of the United States as an empire-state. If we accept that England had established colonies in North America, usurping the political sovereignty of Native American peoples and territories, what changed after the colonies broke away and founded a state, or a federation of states, of their own? For the indigenous, the United States immediately became one more empire-state with which they had to contend. After all, as Christopher Tomlins (2001: 365) reminds us, the colonists declared independence, "in large part, in order to free themselves from imperial constraints that restrained their own colonizing (or to use the preferred anodyne phrase, their own 'westward movement')."

Taken as a whole, the abiding colonial logic was to wrest land away from indigenous sovereignty and control. The vulgar and deadly immodesty of the U.S. state's and its white citizens' colonial ambition has rendered metropole and colony largely overlapping and, at times like the present, nearly coterminous, a condition of possibility for assertions that the United States has been a nation-state, not an empire-state. Native survival and resistance, above all, have been what put the lie to such claims. Indigenous territories under colonial rule today consist minimally of the Indian reservation lands, maximally of the entire United States, and quite reasonably of all the lands that were never ceded.

Colonial rule over Indian-held lands was one of the fundamental issues for the United States from the beginning. Under the British, a royal proclamation in 1763 had drawn a line along the Appalachian Mountains to keep Indians and white settlers apart, prohibiting, if futilely, the latter from the western portion, which extended to the Mississippi River and was designated Indian territory. The postindependence status of the territory was a crucial issue since some former colonies, as a carryover from the British era, had claims to it, while others did not. To resolve the matter, all of them ceded their claims to the federal government, creating the first U.S. "territories." In this way, the very formation of the U.S. state hinged on lands occupied by Indians but over which it asserted ultimate sovereignty. The issues originally raised by the trans-Appalachian territories would continue to shape, bedevil, and haunt the geography of U.S. empire-state formation, namely the acquisition and disposal of territories, and American Indian sovereignty.

The blueprint for the nascent state, the U.S. Constitution expressly acknowledged the reality of spaces under U.S. sovereignty that did not enjoy equal standing with the "several states"—in short, colonial spaces. In Article IV, section 3, it vested Congress with the "Power to dispose of and make all needful Rules and Regulations respecting the Territory or other Property belonging to the United States." The "United States" was therefore not literal: it comprised not only the states but also other political spaces, which were to be ruled ultimately as Congress saw fit and would not have voting representation in the federal government. The constitutionality of further acquisition of territories was initially and periodically uncertain. Nonetheless, by 1853, with the Gadsden Purchase from Mexico, the United States had assumed sovereignty over the entire area of today's forty-eight contiguous states, with that of sixteen future states still composed of territories.

The Constitution did not address how territories could be transformed into states, merely stating, "New States may be admitted by the Congress into this Union" (Article IV, section 3). The widely held assumption during the nineteenth century was that the process followed the principle set out in the Northwest Ordinance of 1787 for the disposal of the northwestern portion of the trans-Appalachian territories (Sparrow 2006): temporary governments organized by Congress, followed by "establishment of States, and permanent government therein . . . on an equal footing with the original States, at as early periods as may be consistent with the general interest" (section 13).

The acquisition of overseas territories in the late 1890s, particularly the former Spanish colonies of Guam, the Philippines, and Puerto Rico, profoundly upset the tacit assumption. Above all, racism toward their nonwhite, non-Anglo-Saxon inhabitants incited the uproar and debate, both among imperialists and anti-imperialists, and centrally informed the construction of "unincorporated"—and, simultaneously, "incorporated"—territories. But this categorical bifurcation of territories did not suddenly inject racism into a hitherto nonracial practice of empire-state formation. Rather it laid bare the white supremacist underpinnings.

Acquiring territories, even under the assumption that they would be turned into states, has always been a racist process. The politics around conquering and taking possession of Texas and what would become the U.S. Southwest from Mexico, for example, had been patently structured by anti-Mexican racism, as numerous studies have shown.[5] The new overseas territories of 1898, however, provoked a more radical doubt of whether white supremacy could be maintained through the usual colonial practices of the U.S. state, a doubt resolved through the *Insular Cases*' doctrine of territorial incorporation.

with Southern white "scalawags," grasping Northern "carpetbaggers," and impudent black freedmen.

Not until the end of the 1960s was this "ruling consensus" overturned. But "public historical consciousness" still lags far behind the new antiracist historiography, in that many white Americans still "think of legally institutionalized racial oppression as ending with emancipation . . . and most are quite ignorant of institutionalized racism in the rest of the country" (634). Unsurprisingly, then, whites justify their current resistance to any measures of remedial racial justice by referring to a slavery long abolished, not realizing the enduring pervasiveness of racial discrimination across the country at large that would continue into the postbellum period.

But apart from these mystified histories (and one could tell similar tales with respect to the experiences of Native Americans, Mexicans, and Asians), racial opacity is manifest at the conceptual level also, in framing assumptions and overarching terms that reinforce this misleading historical picture. There is an interplay, a back-and-forth, between cognitive levels. The whitewashed history seems to confirm the validity of the deraced concepts; the deraced concepts orient us away from looking for disconfirming racial evidence.

In political theory, this pattern of obfuscation is most clearly represented by what has come to be called the "anomaly" view of American racism. As Rogers Smith's (1997) illuminating *Civic Ideals* demonstrates, the dominant tradition in American political science depicts American racism as a deviation from national norms. Through a detailed study of the work of three leading theorists of American political culture, Alexis de Tocqueville, Gunnar Myrdal, and Louis Hartz, Smith shows that even when (as with Tocqueville and Myrdal in particular) they recognize racism—the central theme of Myrdal's book, after all—they still frame it in such a way that it is "anomalous" to American political culture. The United States is conceptualized as *essentially* an egalitarian liberal democracy, and the long actual history of racial domination and subordination is conceptually firewalled by the categories of "anomaly," "dilemma," "deviation," and so forth. Even though Tocqueville, for example, "correctly saw racism as prevalent throughout the nation," he still wrote in "unqualified terms about America's supposedly egalitarian conditions" and relegated "blacks and Native Americans to the status of tangents in a final chapter" (22). Myrdal's (2003 [1944]) famous book, *An American Dilemma*, was of course focused precisely on racism, and he conceded that "far from being an exceptional or marginal phenomenon, moreover, the nation's racial ordering . . . affected virtually all aspects of American life" (Smith 1997: 23). But again, when it came to the question of how we should conceive of this racial ordering, it was in terms of a violation of the liberal egalitarian ideals that white citizens were, nonetheless, still thought of as endorsing, thereby giving rise to the tragic "dilemma" of the title. In sum, writers in the Tocquevillian mode read "egalitarian principles as America's true principles, while treating the massive inequalities in American life as products of prejudice, not rival principles" (27). Thus the United States has not historically been a white supremacist state; it has been a liberal egalitarian state with a few unfortunate deviations.

Finally, as the last quote indicates, there is a fallback option when the centrality of racism to the history of the United States, and the West more generally, is too blatant to be denied. This is the *psychologizing* of racism. In her history of the Black American anticolonial movement from the 1930s to the 1950s, Penny Von Eschen (1997) points out that as late as the 1940s, race and racism were discussed in Black political circles in an intellectual framework that took for granted that they had to be contextualized in a political economy not merely local but global, and related to the long history of European conquest and the racial regimes thereby established. Organizations now as mainstream as the NAACP had no difficulty seeing the links and common genealogy between white supremacy and white colonial rule, between Jim Crow at home and Nazism in Europe. But the advent of the Cold War and McCarthyism made the drawing of such theoretical connections dangerous. Thus by the 1950s a new paradigm emerged that rewrote "racism as an anachronistic prejudice and a personal and psychological problem, rather than as a systemic problem rooted in specific social practices and pervading relations of political economy and culture" (157). This conceptualization, which would become hegemonic, removes race from the category of the political altogether, and blocks any attempt to understand racism in terms of a social structure and a polity that are organized around racial subordination. Instead, the whole set of issues is displaced into a different discourse: a transdisciplinary shift is achieved that renders the attempt to raise such questions theoretically incoherent, conceptually confused. In effect, we are, decades later, still trying to fight free of the hegemony of this new postwar paradigm; either racism's centrality to the polity is denied or, if reluctantly conceded, psychologized, so that in neither case does it have implications for orthodox political categories and taxonomies.

Political Philosophy:
The Social Contract Metaphor and Its Moral Economy

Let us now turn to the distinctive contribution of political philosophy. The revival of Western political philosophy stimulated by John Rawls's 1971 *A Theory of Justice* also resurrected social contract theory, which had been widely judged to be dead. What I want to suggest is that the resurrection of the social contract metaphor in postwar liberal political philosophy has played a key cognitive role in preserving opacity about the true nature of the racial polity and its actual moral economy.

Above I pointed out the truths captured by the contract metaphor: factually, the role of human causality in sociopolitical creation; and normatively, the ideal of moral egalitarianism. In contrast, the truths it conceals are the dominant role of one subset of humans (white males) in the shaping of the modern world; and the accompanying denial of equal moral status to the majority of the population in the resulting modern sociopolitical order. The current version of the contract is of course explicitly hypothetical in character, having no pretensions to describe what has actually happened. Yet insofar as it draws on and links itself with the writings of the classic seventeenth- and eighteenth-century political theorists, it reproduces a set of assumptions about the polity that are profoundly misleading. To reply that the contract is "only a metaphor" is to misunderstand the extent to which our cognition is shaped, consciously and unconsciously, by the figures we employ (Lakoff and Johnson 1980). I would contend that we are so oriented in conceptual space by this metaphor that certain questions, particularly about race, never even arise.

What image does the metaphor conjure up? It is a picture of people of recognized equal moral status consensually bringing into existence a social order and a political system that protects their rights and interests. Within the pre-Colombian Americas, within precolonial, preinvasion Africa, Asia, and Australasia, such an image could have some legitimacy. But as we have seen, in the modern epoch, which is supposed to be the paradigmatic period for the applicability of contractarianism, it has none whatsoever. The experience of people of color in modernity—the experience that makes them "people of color" in the first place—is one of expropriation, genocide, enslavement, and colonization. On the factual level, then, the metaphor does not at all correspond to nonwhite history. Rather, the idea of a consensual contract is a framing that represents the white (male) experience of modernity, whether in Europe itself or in the "new Europes" created by white settler populations in the non-European world. Thus even in the seemingly abstract and hypothetical realm of philosophy, supposedly stratospherically removed from vulgar empirical reality, we see the ideological influence of distinctive group experiences and distinctive group perspectives. Even when purged of the original racist restrictions that would have limited personhood to whites, the underlying assumptions (consensuality, recognized equal moral status), the overarching narrative (the common state of nature, the joint agreement to establish a just polis), the negative poles to be avoided (the feudal-absolutist state), and the normative priorities (ideal justice) continue to reflect the distinctive features of the European experience.

For people of color, the modern polity is the white settler state expropriating them, the colonial state enslaving them, the imperial state colonizing them. The state is imposed rather than consensually constructed; equal moral status is denied on the basis of their putatively closer connection (as "savages" or "barbarians") to the state of nature; coercion rather than agreement is the norm; the negative pole is not feudal absolutism but white "absolutism," which is established rather than overthrown; and the normative priority, correspondingly, is the immediate ending of the injustice of the white-dominated polity. Insofar as contemporary liberalism continues to work within the traditional framework, it remains a racial liberalism, not in the sense that it explicitly privileges whites but in the sense that its architectonic continues to reveal the conceptual orientation and normative assumptions arising from the interests and the positioning in the world of the group that originally created it. In what it takes for granted, what it ignores, what it highlights, what it obfuscates, what it chooses to recall, and what it chooses to forget, contemporary liberalism reveals its whiteness.

We can see this clearly in the moral economy presupposed. As earlier emphasized, the key claim of the liberal narrative is that the transition to the modern epoch is marked by the replacement of a moral economy of group hierarchy and correspondingly differentiated ethical-juridical status by a moral economy of individuals in egalitarian relationships with one another. Assuming moral objectivism to be valid (that moral truths are not dependent on people's opinion), then it has always been the case that people are morally equal, throughout all the historical epochs demarcated. But what is supposed to distinguish modernity is that this moral equality becomes generally recognized; any exclusions are exceptions. This is the standard narrative one finds in introductions to political philosophy. Thus Will Kymlicka (1990: 5) writes,

"[T]he idea that each person matters equally is at the heart of all plausible [modern] political theories." Very similarly, Philip Pettit (2007: 22–23) glosses Ronald Dworkin in saying that "all plausible, modern political theories have in mind the same ultimate value, equality. . . . [E]very theory claims to treat all individuals as equals." And Paul Kelly's (2005: 13) introduction to liberalism states that one of the two basic philosophical claims of "egalitarian political liberalism" is that "All individuals are of equal and ultimate moral value."

But this claim—represented as virtually axiomatic—is in fact quite false once race is taken into account. It can only be maintained as true by defining "person" or "individual" as white, which would of course concede what must be hidden, that actual liberalism is racial liberalism. The assertion either downplays the history and importance of racism (racism was marginal) or denies its moral significance (racism had no implications for moral status). Both theses are completely false. Racism was central to the Western tradition; and racism is inter alia a normative theory of moral statuses. Thus it was not at all the case that all "persons" (if taken to refer to human beings generally) mattered equally and were treated equally in liberal theory. Rather, there was a partitioning in the ranks of humanity that was color-coded, and people of color, even when conceded to be human (by no means always the case), were denied the status of full personhood. The reduction of racism to individual "prejudice" by today's liberalism evades the actuality that what is involved is a theoretical ethical-political norm—on a par with the comparably developed ideologies of antiquity and feudalism (see the revised narrative, above)—about who is deserving of equal rights on the basis of racial prerequisites, and who is not.

This ontological division has always been recognized by theorists and activists in the antiracist tradition, including some white progressives, but especially, of course, people of color. In his famous preface to Frantz Fanon's (1968 [1961]) classic *Wretched of the Earth*, Jean-Paul Sartre (1968: 26) states, "There is nothing more consistent than a racist humanism. . . . On the other side of the ocean there was a race of less-than-humans." Fanon (1967: 8) himself, in *Black Skin, White Masks*, would write, "At the risk of arousing the resentment of my colored brothers, I will say that the black is not a man." Frederick Douglass (1950–75: 126) says, "My *crime* is that I have assumed to be a man." W.E.B. Du Bois (1965 [1903]: 271) describes Black Americans as this curious "*tertium quid*," this third thing "between men and cattle." In short, there was a category in Western political thought for people of color as entities of an inferior moral status, with a diminished schedule of rights. Modern racial liberalism (which is actual liberalism) is, like the ideologies of the premodern period, hierarchically structured. Just as they had different rules for citizens and slaves, and for lords and serfs, racial liberalism has a different set of rules for whites and people of color. But this cannot be admitted within the existing conceptual framework. If Locke, Hume, Kant, Mill, Hegel, and others are the key political theorists of modernity, and they are all committed to the equality of persons, then how could writings on race have any place in the canonical Western narrative? It follows then that political theorists from the antiracist, anti-imperialist, anti-white-supremacist tradition of people of color (such as Douglass, Du Bois, and Fanon) can be excluded from the textbooks that construct the canon of Western political theory. Their work could not be significant because they are addressing an exceptional state, anomalous racial exclusions, when the dominant norm from modernity onwards has been inclusion.

Correspondingly, racial liberalism has to excise the struggle against this form of ascriptive hierarchy from the historical and political narrative, producing the triumphant periodization of the first account ("The Standard Narrative," above) rather than the continuing inegalitarianism of the second, revised account ("The Actual Story," above). In the orthodox story, Locke and Kant are depicted as the champions of the new ideals of freedom and equality. Ascriptive hierarchy is limited to white male class inequality, so that its defeat becomes the defeat of social hierarchy and moral inegalitarianism simpliciter. Equal moral personhood is thus taken to be established by modernity, the equal rights and freedoms of all individuals (retroactively rewritten as all humans) being a product of the European antifeudal battle (and the American Revolution being coded as the New World's triumph over the Old World's absolutist domination). The new system of racial "estates" established by modernity is denied, empirically, through a mystified history and, conceptually, through the nonrecognition of white supremacy as itself a political system, whose justificatory ideology is racism. Meanwhile, the role of Locke's and Kant's own racial views in contributing to the construction of this system is either obscured altogether or theoretically marginalized. Locke's justification of aboriginal expropriation and investments in African slavery are not brought together in the same intellectual framework as his advocacy of liberal parliamentarianism and limited government, so that he can be simply represented as the Whig defender of antifeudal antiabsolutism (Bernasconi and Mann 2005). Kant is characterized as the advocate of an unqualified moral egalitarianism—"Kant's is an ethics of the people, of moral egalitarianism. . . . Respect is an attitude due equally to *every* person, *simply* because each is a person, a rational being capable of moral self-determination" (Sullivan 1989: 197)—and not as one of the key founders of modern scientific racism (Bernasconi 2001; Mills 2005). With a few unimportant exceptions, according to this narrative, equal personhood and equal respect become the established norms of modernity.

But this moral economy is of course completely fictitious, an artifact of white historical revisionism now (in a different phase of white supremacy) embarrassed by the exclusions of the past. In his study of race in international affairs, Frank Füredi (1998) points out that up to World War II, the superiority of the white race, and its entitlement to run the world, was taken for granted by all shades of white political opinion. It was only with the war, the discrediting of (overt) racism by Nazism (the outrageous genocide of Europeans on European soil, as against the acceptable genocide of non-Europeans on non-European soil), and the radical heightening of anticolonial struggles by the participation of peoples of color in the armies of their "mother countries" that racial equality as a global principle began to be seriously considered as an ideal to which it would be prudent to at least give lip service. Previously, the ideologies and practices of the European and Euro-settler states over several centuries had made it clear that people of color were *not* equal. The single event that epitomizes this commitment most clearly could be said to be the vetoing by the "Anglo-Saxon nations" (Britain, the United States, Canada, Australia, New Zealand, South Africa) at the 1919 Versailles Peace Conference of the Japanese delegation's proposal to insert a "racial equality" clause in the League of Nations Covenant (Lake and Reynolds 2008: chap. 12). What should—if the conventional narrative of modernity was correct—have been a routine and reflexive inscription of standard liberal boilerplate (all humans are equal) was instead seen as a radical and unacceptable principle, making it explicit that only whites were equal. Racial liberalism's norms are different from nonracial liberalism. Modernity's actual moral economy lifts white persons above nonwhite subpersons.

This history—less than a century past, and with massive documentation available if one wants to look for it—should be undeniable. Yet, astonishingly, it has been denied, at least in terms of its racial significance and implications for ethical-political theory. A revisionist history was created after World War II, a racial opacity, which continues to shape moral, political, and philosophical discourse today, over sixty years later, blocking recognition of the fact that a planetwide normative division existed between those deemed equal and those deemed unequal.

The reality then is that there has been an ongoing struggle (still incomplete) against racial ascriptive hierarchy that has been global in scope, and that dwarfs the limited white male struggle against class ascriptive hierarchy among whites. The abolitionist movement, the anticolonial struggle, the fight against the color bar and the color line, can all be illuminatingly seen as a battle extending over hundreds of years to overthrow racial liberalism and establish racial equality as the actual planetary norm. Thus historian Thomas Borstelmann (2001) speaks of "the era of global white supremacy," and suggests that by World War I "a global struggle for racial equality" had begun, "what might be called the international civil rights movement of anticolonialism." It is a struggle whose cost has been immense, involving millions of lives, and far more comprehensive in its scope than the limited intra-European squabble. Yet we do not see it as such because we are still operating with the obfuscatory categories of a whitewashed racial liberalism that now pretends to be inclusive but retains the conceptual architectonic and misleading narrative of the European and Euro-settler experience. If modernity establishes equal rights for everybody, if class hierarchy is the only form of ascriptive hierarchy, if "individual" is race-neutral, then how could there be any need for such an "international civil rights movement" when this victory has long since been won?

Normative Consequences: The Mis-orientation of "Justice"

Finally, what are the normative implications of liberalism's racialization? Liberalism is not just a political theory but a normative theory about the good polity. And in the revival of political philosophy stimulated by Rawls's (1971) work, the question of social justice has been moved to center stage. Whereas classical social contract theory had focused on issues of political obligation, Rawls's version made the adjudication of the justice of what he called society's "basic structure" the main goal of the contract. So it might have seemed that whatever the shortcomings of the liberalism of the past, this new, presumptively nonracial liberalism would make it a priority to deal with racial injustice. After all, who could deny the centrality of racial injustice to the history of the United States? Not only was it established through expropriation of Native land, but it was the only modern Western nation with large-scale plantation slavery on its own soil, so that its "basic structure" was foundationally shaped by white supremacy (Fredrickson 1981).

But as with classical liberalism, these expectations would be disappointed. Classical racial liberalism, of course, was an active agent in the establishment and justification of white supremacy. Contemporary racial liberalism is different. Racist characterizations of people of color are absent, and on occasion (if not many occasions) racism is even condemned, as in Rawls's work. Nonetheless, I would claim that this new liberalism is still a racial liberalism in its evasion of the realities of race and its endorsement of the misleading periodization of the standard narrative (above). Thus we typically find, as sketched above, a sanitized history of modernity, one that erases the reality of moral inegalitarianism, denies or downplays the role of racial violence in establishing the modern world, and misrepresents this world as one of equal, symmetrically positioned individuals rather than asymmetrical racial groups in relations of domination and subordination—thereby ruling out by simple conceptual framing the structuring fact of systemic, illicit white advantage. Indeed, the most obvious and striking manifestation of the racial nature of racial liberalism has been its (non)treatment of racial oppression. The supposed universality and inclusiveness of liberal norms somehow did not extend to the analysis and condemnation of racial injustice. The "colorlessness" turned out to be colored white.

Rawls himself must shoulder a major part of the blame for this (mis)orientation of the field, though it could be argued that the overwhelming combined influence of a white tradition and a white demography would have had the same result in any event.[4] Rawls (1971: 7–9) announced from the start that he was going to be focusing on what he called "ideal theory": "[F]or the most part I examine the principles of justice that would regulate a well-ordered society . . . what a perfectly just society would be like. Thus I consider primarily what I call strict compliance as opposed to partial compliance theory." This seemingly minor methodological decision was actually hugely consequential in its philosophical repercussions. In effect, Rawls legitimated the exclusion of issues of racial justice from contemporary normative political theory. The contract apparatus—already historically predicated on the white male experience of modernity, and oriented toward its distinctive ethical-political agenda—would be employed to determine the contours of an ideal social order, without any history of injustice. It asked us, basically, to imagine what kind of society we would create if we were starting from ground zero; no history of racial subordination needed to be taken into account. In a well-ordered society of perfect justice, racism would not exist. So the crucial discussion of different possible remedies for racism and the legacy of white supremacy in our own ill-ordered and imperfect society could not even make it onto the philosophical agenda. The focus was to be distributive justice under ideal circumstances, not the obviously far more pressing issue (one would think) of compensatory rectificatory justice under nonideal circumstances. The naïve nonphilosopher assuming that discussions of racial justice would naturally be central to the normative political philosophy debates of a formerly white-supremacist polity would have been bewildered. Nowhere in the thousands of pages of Rawls's writings, the writings of the most celebrated American philosopher of social justice of the twentieth century, can even the phrase "affirmative action"—referring to the most important postwar measure of remedial American racial justice—be found, let alone any discussion of the rights and wrongs of the policy itself! What was supposedly a neutral methodological decision was really a substantive commitment to the theoretical marginalization of matters of racial redress; what was represented as a universalist and colorless choice was really a manifestation of particularist and white privilege.

Today, forty years after *Theory of Justice*'s original publication, the result is a huge secondary literature of articles and books on justice—not merely in the English-speaking world but globally, given its translation into more than thirty languages (Freeman 2007: x)—in which racial injustice, the injustice brought into existence by and peculiar to the modern world, is almost completely sidelined. Not only does none of the fourteen chapters in Samuel Freeman's (2003) edited *Cambridge Companion to Rawls* deal with race but not a single section or subsection of any of the chapters does so. And a sixty-page symposium by several authors on Rawls's legacy in a 2006 issue of *Perspectives on Politics*, one of the official journals of the American Political Science Association (Ackerley et al. 2006), has a grand total of two paragraphs on the subject. Social justice, yes; racial justice, no. What could have been one of the most powerful resources in the arsenal of those seeking a racially equitable social order—the backing of philosophy, the oldest discipline of the academy—has instead been largely absent. It has fallen mostly to philosophers of color (with a few honorable white exceptions) to raise these issues.

DERACIALIZING RACIAL LIBERALISM

What then is the appropriate theoretical response? One natural reaction would be the repudiation of liberalism in principle, both for its historical complicity with racism and for its ongoing evasions. However, as I have tried to argue elsewhere, I think this response would be mistaken (Pateman and Mills 2007). At the most basic level, liberalism is a political theory about the equitable treatment of individuals conceptualized as morally equal, whose basic rights and freedoms should be respected. The problem is that these individuals were conceived of as white, and as justifiably positioned above people of color. Thus the apparatus has been shaped from the start by these relations of domination, a shaping which has affected both the mapping of the polity and the normative orientation toward determining justice in the polity. But for me this does not rule out a revisionist liberalism that starts out from a recognition of its historic and current racialization. In other words, one would begin by rejecting the bogus colorlessness of liberalism, and situate liberalism in the demystified context of being the ideology of white supremacy. The question would then be what conceptual and normative rearticulations would be necessary to reconstitute it on a genuinely racially inclusive basis.

I have argued in greater detail in other work that one promising strategy would be to adopt what I have called the "domination contract" as a revisionist way to do contract theory. The domination contract as a concept goes back to Rousseau, the Rousseau (1997) of *Discourse on the Origins of Inequality*, though there is a sense in which he has yet to receive proper credit for it. In this 1755 book, Rousseau says bluntly—perhaps too bluntly—that social contract theory is a scam. To understand where the status inequalities of contemporary society come from, we need to understand that the real contract is not a fair arrangement to which everybody can freely give informed consent, but a deal among the rich. It is, in effect, a class contract to establish a plutocratic social order in which, behind the façade of consensus, the rich rule. Rousseau's own focus was on class inequality, but obviously the concept can be generalized to other axes of social domination. Carole Pateman's "sexual contract" and my "racial contract" can both be seen as extrapolations of this idea.

All three "contracts" represent then a theoretical challenge to the orthodox conceptions of the polity, since they all see social domination rather than social equality as the actual norm. Thus they register conceptually the demystified periodization of the second, revised account. Whether in the ancient, medieval, or modern epoch, the sociopolitical order is characterized by hierarchy, group domination, and moral inegalitarianism. The concept of the domination contract thus provides a superior theoretical starting point, descriptively and normatively, for understanding both the actual workings of the polity and what our moral priorities should be in trying to make it more just. If an unmodified contract metaphor, a racial opacity, a misleading moral economy, and a mis-orientation toward questions of justice have all been central to the architecture of racial liberalism, then these will all have to be revised. We need to formally adopt the revisionist domination contract as a metaphor, demand racial transparency about the past and present, acknowledge the actual inegalitarian moral economy, and reorient social justice discussions to nonideal theory, namely the correction of the flagrant injustices of several hundred years of racial oppression. Only through the exposure of racial liberalism for what it is can the requisite condemnation and egalitarian reconstruction of the racial state be accomplished.

2 WHITE SUPREMACY AS SUBSTRUCTURE
Toward a Genealogy of a Racial Animus,
from "Reconstruction" to "Pacification"

Dylan Rodríguez

WHITE SUPREMACY AS A SOCIOHISTORICAL FORM

The foundational orderings of white supremacy form multiple global circuits of trauma, fatality, and social disruption, each of which is central to—in fact historically determinant of—the present-tense social forms under which we live. This political logic of human domination constitutes a perpetual state of emergency of vacillating intensity for the millions who encounter white European and Euro-American civilization and nation-building as inherently hostile projects. It is the historical indelibility of this crisis condition, constituted by the material and institutional continuities of its internal logics of civilizational ascendancy, that situates white supremacy as a central analytic for the political intellectual work of radical critique and social transformation.

White supremacy requires its own activist research and theoretical trajectory—a praxis, in the fullest sense of critical thought and practice—that engages a historical tracing of its irreducible circuits of violence and social reproduction. As such, I am arguing for an analytical conception of white supremacy as an internally complex, historically dynamic logic of social organization rather than as a singular ideological or political category. In this sense, white supremacy is related to, sometimes symbiotic with, but still analytically distinguishable from the more commonly accepted social determinations or "substructures" of capitalism, empire, and patriarchy.

Thus "race," as a perpetually contested discursive structure and site of political and communal identification (and disavowal), is not the central focus of my political and theoretical concerns here, to the extent that "race" has been too frequently and carelessly dislocated from its constituting logic of white supremacist social dominance. There is no "race" outside of the histori-cal genealogies and multiple political derivations of white supremacy, and to posit race without an essential and critical engagement with its structuring white supremacist genealogies is (at the very least) a profoundly ahistorical gesture. The political and scholarly attention invested in discussions of "race" and "racialization" during the late twentieth and early twenty-first centuries pivots on a certain political-intellectual bankruptcy in the moments wherein white supremacy is erased from or rendered epiphenomenal to the ongoing productions of race as a technology of dominance, system of social ordering, and modality of subject formation.

In this context, the challenge of definition requires a theoretical approach that rubs against the empiricist tendency to neatly categorize white supremacy within a discrete and peculiar set of ideological, political, and institutional practices. To address white supremacy as a sociohistorical form is to attempt to explain the tensions and contradictions—as well as the congruencies and sym-bioses—between its animus (which seems to persist across historical periods) and its multiple mobilizations (across scales of institutionality, physiology, and phenotype). I am not dismissing the importance of the empirical realm in de-fining a sociohistorical form; to the contrary, I am arguing for a different ana-lytical premise and theoretical approach to apprehending (and thus engaging) white supremacy and its living archive.

In what follows, I concisely examine two moments in white supremacy's living archive, spanning the late nineteenth to the early twentieth centuries. The purpose of my meditation here, however, is not to exhaustively chronicle the details of each moment in the manner of a traditional historical or histo-riographic study. Rather, I am attempting to read white supremacy's mundane self-chronicling, and hence its official and quotidian self-narrations, against a critical analytic that situates white supremacy as a substructure of social formation, statecraft, and nation-building. What productive theoretical and political work might be enabled by examining this archive as a dynamic, complex, and flexible "autobiography" of a white supremacist animus? If the white supremacist animus is not merely provincial, regional, or even national in its self-conceptions and political aspirations but is in fact a *civilizational* ambition that consistently seeks the remaking and remapping of the world, how can we make sense of its internal continuities across different historical moments? I will attempt to outline a working response to these questions by tracing white supremacy's animus through two apparently disparate archival settings: the late-nineteenth-century Reconstruction-era testimonials of the Freedmen's Bureau; and the early-twentieth-century self-chronicling of colonialist "pacification" and U.S. proctored nation-building in the Philippines.

CENTRIPETAL FORCE AND WHITE SUPREMACIST HISTORICITY

It is the perpetual societal dilemma of (white) freedom, not the grueling matter-of-factness or "bare life" (Agamben 1998) of Black, Brown, or indigenous unfreedom, that situates white supremacy as the compulsory and indelible logic of the national form. In this context, we might revisit the text of the Thirteenth Amendment to the U.S. Constitution, commonly valorized as the decree that freed enslaved Africans, as a primary point of historical departure:

> Neither slavery nor involuntary servitude, *except as a punishment for crime whereof the party shall have been duly convicted*, shall exist within the United States, or any place subject to their jurisdiction. (emphasis added)

The Thirteenth Amendment, in its most immediate sense, accomplished two related shifts in the structuring of slavery's essential racist violence: (1) it nominally transferred the legally sanctioned entitlement to construct and mobilize a regime of punishment out of the collective hands of a slaveholding, white supremacist civil society, and formally (though not actually) restricted that racial entitlement to the rarified domains of the racist state. By "reforming" slavery as such, the Thirteenth Amendment *permanently inscribed slavery on "postemancipation" U.S. statecraft*. As such, the amendment defined, and deformed, the political and institutional premises on which the Freedmen's Bureau would undertake its labors of national reconstruction and racial crisis mediation; and (2) conceptually (legally) and materially (physiologically), the amendment definitively assigned the captive to the state as its property and bodily possession (Hartman 1997). As such, the convict/slave (that is, the emancipated Black) was and is more than an object of formalized carceral state violence or a subject of resistance and revolt against racial criminalization as recodified slavery, but also becomes the physical crucible of white supremacist historical agency. That is, the postemancipation convict/slave, and a fungible Black "freedom," calibrate the white supremacist state's nation-building capacities in the aftermath of civil war, and stage white civil society's exercises of social entitlement and its flexible access to state-condoned racial violence and terror. Thus, when the Thirteenth Amendment first designated the "duly convicted" as a category of (non)human available for formal subjection to the bodily punishment of slavery, it was revising and elaborating—not abolishing—the essential violences enmeshing racial chattel: disposability, exchangeability, and categorical exposure to white (state) violence for the sake of a national-racial destiny.

I am initially privileging this transitional moment in the juridical, cultural, and ideological structuring of racial slavery—the movement and vacillation between Manifest Destiny's rationalization and emancipation's recodification—in order to scrape at the surfaces of the white supremacist civilizational project and encounter the constitutive terror of white historicity itself. A genealogy of the white supremacist animus is necessarily different from an outline of white supremacy's labors of oppressive dominance or systemic and ritualized technologies of violence. While its accumulated labors and technologies do require a compilation of historical inventories, white supremacy is not reducible to its various institutional and ad hoc expressions. This is where the endemic methodological and theoretical slipperiness of trying to trace the trajectory of a social logic requires something like a speculative formulation of its historical physics.

What I am seeking to understand, in this sense, is the *centripetal force* of white supremacy's historicity. Centripetal force is what creates and sustains an orbit or circular path: a moving object remains in constant radial proximity to an identifiable center only when a tethering force (whether gravitational pull, a string, or friction) keeps that object from flying away on its own momentum (Figure 2.1). What I am attempting to begin to interrogate and calibrate here is the consistency of the centering (tethering) centripetal force that tends to

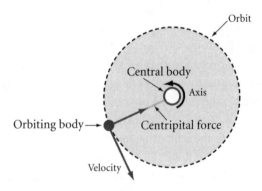

Figure 2.1 Centripetal Force
SOURCE: http://commons.wikimedia.org/wiki/Image:Centripetal_force_diagram.svg (adapted from public domain image).

harness white supremacy's variable articulations of domination and violence within a generalized "orbit" around the grand core projects of civilization and nation-building; in other words, white supremacy's most excessive and extensive violences never quite displace, or truly depart from, the massive historical ambitions to which they are attached, whether Manifest Destiny, democracy, or the making of white "modernity" itself. Rather, these violences seem to revolve or orbit around the durable projects of white supremacy's social substructure: its relations of fatal and immanently fatal dominance; inscriptions of "the human" and its historical subjectivity; distensions of genocide as both a militarized technology of extermination and a structuring logic of social formation (encompassing and exceeding the social forms of slavery, colonialism, and frontier conquest); and so forth.

I would suggest here that the material historicity of what I am calling white supremacy's animus crystallizes precisely as the centripetal force that harnesses and disciplines these orbiting violences. If the stuff of the "historical" here entails an alchemy of (racial) subjectivity, militarized and fortified collective bodily integrity, and moral amnesty from evil (which is both the pretense and outcome of the Manifest Destiny allegory), then the white supremacist animus is what dynamically orders and enables the kind of proliferated violence that characterizes particular moments in white supremacy's social articulation. Of course, while I offer this "scientific" schema as a theoretical and analytical tool, I also refrain from conceptualizing the historical physics of white supremacy as a closed, unaffected system that is immune to deformation or intervention: the centripetal force tethering the violence may be disrupted or detached; the proximity (radius) of the violence's orbit to the social substructure may rapidly change and periodically collapse; and there are always multiple violences in orbit at once, each with its own analytical specificity, volatility, and historicity (these violences may also converge and collide with one another, with both logical and unanticipated outcomes). The formulaic integrity of this physics is less important, however, than the conceptual clarity it can provide for comprehending the persistence and fluidity of white supremacy as a socially productive organization and animation of violence.

I am departing from the Thirteenth Amendment's recodification of slavery here, not only because it is a primary juridical technology of postemancipation white supremacist social formation, but also because the animus, or centripetal force, of its historical orbit implicates and enables the shared historical subject that presides over the Freedmen's Bureau and Philippine colonialist pacification. The disparate historical and geographic location of these moments in white supremacist social formation, in other words, indicates the need for an analytic of continuity, nuance, and fluidity that is capable of stretching and linking otherwise self-contained genealogies of racialization, racism, reform, and racial retrenchment/reaction. It is precisely the apparent incongruity between these archival examples that catalyzes a reading of how they might nonetheless be tethered to the substructural logic of a white supremacist historicity.

THE FREEDMEN'S BUREAU AND THE AUTOBIOGRAPHY OF WHITE TERROR

In the context of blooming white racist violence and political reaction in the aftermath of emancipation and civil war, the Freedmen's Bureau was an exercise of white governmentality that alleged to perform a feat of magic: it would protect a fictive Black (male) civil subject whose inhabitation of citizenship and civil society was essentially and organically fragile, traumatized, and terrorized; facilitate a national resuturing that accommodated and placated Confederate treason and its postbellum survivals; and breathe civic life—"freedom"—into the social body of a population whose racial enslavement had recently been recodified as racial criminalization (juridical unfreedom). W.E.B. Du Bois' account of the Bureau's inception in a 1901 essay for the *Atlantic Monthly* is instructive, to the extent that it reveals both a masculine longing for authentic Black civil subjectivity and the irreducibility of the (former) white master as the social substructure's flesh and blood:

> Here, at a stroke of the pen, was erected a government of millions of men . . . black men emasculated by a peculiarly complete system of slavery, centuries old; and now, suddenly, violently, they come into a new birthright, at a time of war and passion, in the midst of the stricken, embittered population of their former masters. (357)

Du Bois fixes historical attention on the accumulated gravity of racial slavery and white supremacist nation-building, as they radically repress the possibility of "citizenship" as a *new* Black male "birthright." Birthright, by definition, fixes a particular entitlement or privilege as a congenital inheritance; it suggests a right that persons (often first-born sons) carry or possess by virtue of their birth, rather than a right that is benevolently bestowed on them by a civil correlate or ostensible peer. According to the *Oxford English Dictionary*, "birthright" has two meanings: "1. Right by birth; the rights, privileges, of possessions to which one is entitled by birth; inheritance, patrimony. (Specifically used of the special rights of the first-born.)"; and "2. Native right; lot to which birth entitles." To "come into a new birthright," then, is the equivalent of a nonperson—one who has existed outside of and in alienation from the cultural and legal structures of rights and inheritance—suddenly encountering the reformist violence of "humanization" or, literally, species reclassification (Fanon 1967, 1968). This reformist/white humanist violence is in ample evidence throughout the archive of the Freedmen's Bureau's earliest conceptualizations.

Not only was the Freedmen's Bureau the racial substate designated to govern a (racially) illegitimate polity, but it was also inhabited by white state subjects (many of whom were former officers in the Union army) whose labors of governing could not fully comprehend or legitimate the idea of Black citizenship, much less authorize (or protect) Black existence in an emergent white supremacist civil society. Colonel O. Brown, an assistant commissioner of the Bureau, crystallizes this unsolvable dilemma in his 1865 report on the state of affairs in Virginia:

> The problem to be solved was, how to provide for the protection, elevation, and government of nearly half a million of people suddenly freed from the bonds of a rigorous control, acquainted with no law but that of force, ignorant of the elementary principles of civil government and of the first duties of citizenship . . . and entertaining many false and extravagant notions in respect to the intentions of the government towards them. (39th Congress, Session 1, Sen. Ex. Doc. No. 27, p. 144)

Locked in the conundrum of an emergent white civil modernity's confrontation with an essential Black alienation from both "government" and "civility" as such, the Freedman's Bureau (and its immediate antecedents) is best understood as a troubled managerial incarnation of white supremacist institutionality.

As a vehicle of national-political narrative, the Bureau was both the author and inheritor of white liberal racial melodrama; and as a political-bureaucratic innovation, it reformed and extended the moral architecture of the white human. Whatever restrictions it encountered in the form of Southern resistance to external "Yankee" occupation were mitigated by an autonomy of governance over the public discourse, administration, and political parameters of Black welfare. It was this direct management, disciplining, and rhetorical production of the Black proto-human that animated the Freedmen's Bureau as a primary apparatus of the Reconstruction epoch:

> We have found the freedman easy to manage, beyond even our best hopes; . . . docile, patient, affectionate, grateful, and although with a great tribal range of intellect from nearly infantile to nearly or quite the best white intelligence, yet with an average mental capacity above the ordinary estimates of it.
>
> We have no doubts of the aptitude of the slave for freedom under any fair circumstances. But we see that his circumstances must be inevitably unfair . . . and that, independently of a great and paternal care on the part of the government, they will be so bad as to wring cries of shame and indignation from the civilized world. (Sen. Ex. Doc. 1, [serial 1176], 38th Congress, Session 1, No. 1, p. 2)

According to historian Paul S. Peirce's venerable 1904 study, the essential task of the Freedmen's Bureau, as decreed by Commissioner (and Union General) Oliver Howard, was to fulfill a racial client-relation, that is, "to supply the wants and guarantee the freedom of the negroes" (Peirce 1970 [1904]: 50). It is the conceptual premises and assumptive logic enabling this bureaucratic module of white civil (and civilizational) historical agency, the institutional and narrative projection of "negro" desire ("wants"), and the overarching political invention and reproduction of the racial client-relation at the heart of the "freedom" nexus that I wish to interrogate within the historical archive of the Freedmen's Bureau.

Importantly, the fulfillment of the Bureau's stated duties was structurally undermined and politically vexed from its very inception: in 1866, President Andrew Johnson twice vetoed congressional bills intended to sustain the Freedmen's Bureau beyond its first year, and the second veto had to be overridden by Congress. Yet, the contestation of its political scope actually seems to reflect the Bureau's significance to the social—and narrative—productions of a white civil subjectivity struggling to cohere through a moment of profound national rupture. As "the principal expression and extension of federal authority in the defeated South" (Cimbala and Miller 1999: ix), which conceivably "embodied what the Union would have freedom mean—in constitutional, ideological, and practical terms" (R. Miller 1999: xv), the Bureau's most historically valorized functions included legal advocacy and ostensible civil protection for emancipated Southern Blacks, the construction of public schools for the newly freed population, and mediation of "free labor" contracts between the formerly enslaved and their formerly slaveholding white employers (Du Bois 1901: 359). As is widely noted by historians of the Recon-struction era, the seven-year life of the Bureau was marked by a lack of clarity regarding the political scope of its executive authority and the parameters of its institutional responsibilities.

Yet, rather than characterizing the Freedmen's Bureau as symptomatic of a "failed" Reconstruction or as prima facie evidence of the federal government's "sellout" of a Black population newly (and in fact involuntarily) designated with citizen or free status though still vulnerable to economic exploitation, physical violence, and socialized racial terror, it may be more useful to reex-amine the Bureau as a therapeutic moment in the autobiography of the white supremacist animus. That is, its very (planned) bureaucratic failures, insuffi-ciencies, and corruptions—from the infrastructural problems of underfund-ing and understaffing to the virtual political impossibilities of "governing" a Black citizenry/polity within white supremacist civil society—point in the direction of a rather understudied (and profoundly undertheorized) aspect of the Freedmen's Bureau archive.

While its stated duties encompassed the work of Black civil assimilation and national reunion, what arguably became the Freedmen's Bureau's most lasting and critical political labor (alongside its attempted administration of public schooling) was its chronicling—or, more precisely, liberal white na-tionalist narration—of racist violence and white racial terror (Foner 1988; Litwack 1979). Huntsville, Alabama, Freedmen's Bureau agent and disburs-ing officer John J. Wagner offers one description of the mechanics of this chronicling/narration in his 1871 congressional testimony:

> *Question:* Have you kept a memorandum of the outrages committed since you have come to this place—Huntsville?
>
> *Answer:* I have kept a kind of a memorandum when anybody came to me. I thought the best way to do, where the outrages were of a very serious nature, was to write their statements out and have them sworn to, either before Judge Douglass, probate judge, or the clerk of the circuit court, and some copies of these I kept and gave to Mr. Lakin, and some copies I forwarded to General Crawford. Most of the valuable testimony I had I transferred to General Crawford's hands, in the shape of affidavits. (Sen. Rpt. 41, pt. 9, 42nd Congress, Session 2 [Serial Set Volume No. 1492], p. 927)

While this account provides insight as to the selective and endemically subjec-tive nature of the gathering of testimonial evidence of racist terror, another contextualization of the Bureau's methodology of reportage more clearly locates it within the climate of white supremacist endangerment that pervaded the Reconstruction South. An 1868 investigation of white racist violence in St. Bernard Parish, Louisiana, reveals the difficulty of engaging Black respondents under conditions of amplified white terrorism:

> At first I found the freed people hesitating and diffident in giving me information, and it was only under promise that they would not be brought into trouble by telling me facts of which they were personally cognizant.
>
> This is manifestly the result of intimidation by the whites in the parish, and there are but few of the freed people who do not live in continual dread and fear of being abused and killed on the slightest pretext. (Sen. Ex. Doc. No. 15, 40th Congress, Session 3, p. 19)

It is not speculation to suggest that the existing archive of white supremacist terror, as composed by the Freedmen's Bureau, is a relatively minimal refraction—and not a remotely accurate or "objective" detailing—of the frequency, intensity, and geographic breadth of racist violence in the immediate aftermath of emancipation and civil war. Yet, as the voice of postbellum, enlightened white civil society's official outrage against the racial terrorism of a feudal or premodern Southern whiteness, the Freedmen's Bureau's testimonies of white supremacist violence[1] refract the core argument of my prior meditation on the Thirteenth Amendment's rearticulation and reproduction of the slavery relation.

The profoundly intimate, physical structuring of slavery's relation of dominance and subjection both foreshadowed and significantly facilitated the ritualized, systemic—and seemingly exaggerated—civil violence (white mobbing, lynching, kidnapping, torture, murder) that the Bureau documented. To the extent that a dynamic and complex regime of white supremacist violence was constitutive of the antebellum plantation South, the sedimentations and grassroots remobilizations of this regime were central to the dynamics of white Reconstruction, and as such the work of the Freedmen's Bureau significantly encompassed the discursive labor of rationalizing and politically externalizing these remnants of the white supremacist premodern.

Having lost its formalized racial monopoly on both "citizenship" and "freedom," the white world was on the cusp of implosion: its capacity for racial self-actualization and self-recognition was structurally undermined at the moment of abolition, emancipation, and "Black citizenship." What made this world intelligible to itself once again—the fundamental practice that rewired its circuits of cohesion and rewrote its very legibility in the midst of "Black freedom's" immediacies—was its revision of how Black bodies were to be regularly subjected to violent white will. This ideological, (para)militarized, and deeply cultural reforming of the circuits of anti-Black violence reflects the paradigmatic and indelible structural location of anti-Blackness within the white civilizational (and nation-building) project, often convergent with but not reducible to the social and state formations of white supremacy (Sexton 2010; Wilderson 2003).

While this anti-Black violence necessarily entailed a modification of white racist homicide's (and proto-genocide's) relation to the state (which was itself undergoing a massive suturing in the wake of civil war), the material template through which postemancipation white supremacy was altered and enlivened was located in the Thirteenth Amendment's recodification of the slave rela-tion, and the Fourteenth Amendment's articulation of "equal protection." Herein we can read Thomas Smith's characterization of Shongalo's (Missis-sippi) racial climate as an enunciation of white social truth:

> Threats of burning out the colored people had been made at different times by the white people. The reason they assigned was that they would break up the free niggers. (Sen. Exec. Doc. No. 27, 39th Congress, Session 1, p. 32)

The political linking and violent affiliation of, and conflation between, burned Black bodies with "free" Black bodies works to amplify (and in fact render historically possible) the structuring social logic of white suprema-cy, to the extent that it locates pain, terror, and fatality within the categori-cal condition (the "racial profile") of the Black post-slave. To be threatened with "burning out" is the condition of "free nigger" existence, and it is pre-cisely the narrative (hence political) reification—the liberal racist taken-for-grantedness—of white civil life's *nonequivalence with*, and essential ascendan-cy over, the *systemic fragility of Black bodily integrity* that resonates throughout the Freedmen's Bureau's archival chronicling/narration of white supremacist violence. In this context, the literal ledgering of fatal and near-fatal anti-Black racism throughout the archive, which selectively plots the casualties of white supremacist violence onto rudimentary data/incident tables that fabricate an appearance of social scientific rigor, seems to mark a white familiarity with Black death and subjection that recodes the experiential terror through nu-merical abstraction and pseudoscientific description (see Figure 2.2).

Recapitulation of casualties.

Name and designation.	Nature of casualty.	Date of casualty.	Remarks.
Felio Pablo*	Killed	Oct. 25, 1868	By Andy Mayo, Thompson Morgan, and other freedmen.†
One white man, (Dem. club.)	Wounded	do.	By Eugene Loch.†
Mike Curtis*	Killed	do.	By Ryco John Beuf.
Eugene Loch†	do.	do.	By Valivey Veillon.
Thompson Morgan†	do.	do.	Supposed by Pablo Felio, and body consumed in burning house.
Josiah Johnson†	Wounded	do.	By Pablo Felio.*
Little Jacob†	do.	do.	Do.
John Proctor†	do.	do.	Do.
Billy Smith†	do.	do.	Do.
Henry Sterling†	do.	do.	By Democratic procession.
Spencer Jones, (aged 50 years.)†	do.	do.	By Valivey Veillon.*
Pierre Golet†	Killed	Oct. 26, 1868	By Julian Serpas.*
Res Voltaire†	do.	do.	By Felio, Leone, Porter, & party.
Baptiste Clemer†	do.	do.	Do. do.
Emile Azenor†	do.	do.	Do. do.
Francis ——— †	do.	do.	Do. do.
Henry ——— †	do.	do.	Do. do.
Joseph Cole†	do.	do.	By Valivey Veillon.*
Felix Thomas, (freed woman,)	Wounded	do.	By Alma Marshal *
William Froleck†	do.	do.	By Philip Goodyear.*
David Jones†	do.	do.	Do.
——— Marshal†	do.	do.	By Julian Serpas.*
Alfred Lee †	do.	do.	By parties unknown.
Two freedmen, Decro x place	do.	do.	Do.
Nelson ———, (aged 90 years,)†	Killed	Oct. 27, 1868	Do.
Sophia Marshal, (freedwoman,)	Wounded	do.	By Julian Serpas.*
Eugene Joseph†	do.	Nov. 1, 1868	By Sarapio Yona.*
——— Arnold †	Killed	Nov. 3, 1868	By parties unkown.

* White.   † Colored.

Designation.	Killed.	Wounded.	Total.
Whites	2	1	3
Freedmen	9	14	23
Freedwomen		2	2
Aggregate	11	17	28

NOTE.—One of whites killed by democratic procession; Mike Curtis, the policeman.

The above embraces all casualties as far as ascertained, but I am of the opinion that there are others not yet made known.

Figure 2.2 "Recapitulation of Casualties," Printed in Testimony of First Lieutenant J. M. Lee, October 4, 1868, Sen. Ex. Doc. No. 15, 40th Congress, Session 3, p. 34

In fact, the ritualized, culturally codified racist terror of the immediate postemancipation period was so mundane in its consistency, so transparent in its social mandate, that the Freedmen's Bureau's official congressional reports and testimonies frequently assume the voice of ethnographic detachment. White racist violence, and its layered productions of Black vulnerability to repression, bodily disintegration, and social terror, are empirically and anecdotally catalogued under the rubric of "outrages," and are often detailed through a month-by-month accounting of notable incidents in specific cities, counties, and regions. A small portion of an 1868 report on "Freedmen's Affairs in Kentucky and Tennessee" is typical in this regard.

Detailing "outrages" in Kentucky during the month of January 1868, the section reads:

> On the 29th of January, at Frankfort, the capital of Kentucky, a mob of white citizens took a negro from the jail and hung him until he was dead. This negro had been arrested and placed in jail charged with raping a white girl. Sufficient information has been received since to establish the fact that the man was innocent. . . . A colored man—name unknown—was shot and killed at Newton, Scott county, on the night of the . . . day of January. A colored woman named Betsey was unmercifully whipped at Georgetown, Kentucky.
>
> On the 30th day of January, Wm. Scorggins, a small negro boy, was stabbed by Mr. Scroggins, (white,) while working in a hemp field. Two freedmen were shot and dangerously wounded at Central Furnace, western Kentucky. . . .
>
> Two colored men were waylaid and shot in Henry county, Kentucky, near the Trimble line, by "regulators." Another colored man was also shot and dangerously wounded in the Louisville sub-district. . . .
>
> A little girl, aged nine years, was, on the 17th day of January, brought to the freedmen's hospital by a man named Bull. Upon examination it was found that her hands and feet were frozen dreadfully. Her back was scarred all over, the stripes having probably been inflicted with a cowhide. Upon investigation it was ascertained that the whipping was done by the wife of Mr. Bull, and the child was frozen by being compelled by Mrs. Bull to sleep in the coal-house. All of the child's toes were amputated. This happened in the law-abiding city of Louisville. (H. Rep. Doc. No. 329, 40th Congress, Session 2, p. 4)

Such accounts prevail throughout the Freedmen's Bureau archive, and the sheer accumulation of scenarios exceeds summary characterization. In the process of examining archival testimonies and reports covering the states of Louisiana, Kentucky, Tennessee, Missouri, Arkansas, Mississippi, South Carolina, Georgia, Florida, and Virginia for the purposes of this chapter, it became clear that the crucial political-intellectual challenge is not necessarily to uncover or reveal the socially constituting presence of white supremacist violence in this period—in fact, Bureau officials frequently frame this violence as a durable facet of the overarching Southern social condition—but rather to situate this violence against the grain of the Freedmen's Bureau's "official"/narrative discursive regime. Again, I am less concerned with the descriptive content of these archival accounts and the question of whether they precisely and adequately illuminate a period of proliferating white supremacist social terror; flatly "reading" and historicizing racist violence through such official catalogues runs the risk of collapsing the political scope and historical depth of white supremacist violence to identifiable or verifiable events.

Rather, I wish to focus on the critical problem of how to conceptualize the periodic political antagonisms *between* multiple and coexisting white supremacist social and institutional forms. I am especially concerned with the tense, and often sustained, historical overlap between different (and seemingly contradictory) white supremacist social forms—in this case, between racial slavery and Reconstructionist white nation-building—and with the contestation for dominance that ensues as each social form asserts its capacity and moral adequacy to assume the civilizational as well as national burden of materially remaking and discursively rewriting white civil and biological life as the template of social coherence and rational politicality.

As something like a social force of nature, white supremacist violence is positioned by many Freedmen's Bureau testimonies as an overwhelming social condition rather than a panoply of controllable or disciplinable incidents. The problem of reconstituting a white national subjectivity in the aftermath of civil war, in this case, is partly reconciled through anecdotal and empirical assertions of postemancipation white supremacist violence as uncontrollable, unpredictable, and irrational, and thus outside the parameters of both an emergent modernist white politicality and the pragmatic capacities of white liberal political agency. Abundant Freedmen's Bureau testimonies allege the generalized incapacity of white Southerners to either politically apprehend or socially accept Black freedom, and illuminate the consistency with which this ethic of white supremacist civil disobedience found its primary modality in exercises of racist bodily violence and psychological warfare.

The Freedmen's Bureau archive of racist violence is a multifaceted narrative-in-progress—a gathering of political rationalization, ideological brainstorm, and editorialized *Bildungsroman*. The archive is not simply a compilation of the "primary" and "secondary" evidence of white supremacy's historicity, it is also a "live recording" of the liberal white subject's (reluctant) proximity, familiarity, and tragic coexistence with sustained Black suffering and death in the epoch of postemancipation white supremacy. The extensive accounts of otherwise devastating scenes of racist homicide, kidnapping/hostage-taking, and white supremacist terrorism are rather mind-numbing in the density of their accumulation and the disinterested matter-of-factness of their testimonial and correspondent chronicling.

A sense of helplessness and unaccountability threads throughout the Freedmen's Bureau reports and testimonials of racist violence in the Reconstruction South: "I am powerless to accomplish anything without soldiers" (Sen. Ex. Doc. 27, 39th Congress, Session 1, p. 10); "While I remain in the position I desire the power to protect the poor, the weak, and the ignorant, who confidently look to this bureau for the protection which the State, made rich by their unrequited toil, yet fails to afford them" (Sen. Exec. Doc. 27, 39th Congress, Session 1, p. 12); "Outrage and disorder is the rule. . . . The officers of the bureau in that district have been active and energetic, but they have met with but little success in their efforts" (H. Rep. Ex. Doc. 329, 40th Congress, Session 2, p. 11); "I would but say that it has long been my conviction that for a freedman to attempt to have himself righted before the civil courts of this State, outside of a few of the principal cities, is a farce. Magistrates, constables, and attorneys dare not, if they were so inclined, do justice to a colored man where his opponent is white. On their lives they dare not" (H. Rep. Ex. Doc. 329, 40th Congress, Session 2, p. 38). This vernacular of resignation and overwhelmed bureaucratic, juridical, and martial impotency is not simply the lament of a frustrated and arrested Reconstructionist white nation-building, it is the organic articulation of a critical—and ultimately transformative— moment in the autobiography of white supremacy.

Beyond its constant assertions of institutional incapacity (such as insufficiency of administrative and military personnel, and lack of an adequate federal mandate) to exert effective governmental, police, and martial control over the white South's litany of "outrages" against the freed population, the Bureau arrives at a generalized understanding of its own historical agency as alienated from the peculiar incorrigibility of the white racist reactionary. *This is the political-discursive moment in which the white supremacist animus must renovate, reform, and finally revivify.* The premodern, plantation-attached Southern white Confederate subject is the autobiographical Other of the emergent liberal modern white national/Reconstruction subject, who throughout this archive is attempting to author proper Black civil existence and, inseparably, rewrite white Americana's enlightened democratic telos.

The necessarily experimental work of constituting postemancipation white politicality through the Freedmen's Bureau was, in this sense, much more than a utilitarian state mobilization intended to facilitate the reunion of the white nation, over and through the putative civil and citizen status of the freed Black population. "Pacification," then, can be understood as the conceptual and practical bridge between seemingly contradictory white su-premacist institutionalities and violences. In this context, tracing the state-craft of pacification from the Reconstruction era to the U.S. colonialist occu-pation of the Philippines in the early twentieth century geographically and theoretically stretches the parameters of white supremacy as a logic of social organization and historical animus.

PHILIPPINE PACIFICATION AND THE REMAKING
OF WHITE SUPREMACIST CIVIL SOCIETY

"Pacification" always implies the *possibility* of the alienated racial other's (newly or recently) historicized humanity and labored adequacy for civil sub-jectivity, while its fundamental processes occur through the agency of the white historical subject. It is this white subject—along with its ("nonwhite") derivatives or correlates—that possesses the wisdom, rationality, and prag-matic wherewithal to actually pacify people, places, and crises, and thus to sufficiently engage the perpetual epochal duties of making civil society in the wake of land conquest, enslavement, and colonialist domination. The case of Philippine pacification, as another moment of autobiographical revelation for white supremacy's animus, emerges from three broad, overlapping national-racial crises: (1) the putative attainment of Manifest Destiny's continental frontier limits; (2) the troubled nexus of emancipation, slavery recodification, Southern Reconstruction, and post–civil war national resuturing; and (3) the vexed formation of post-1898 U.S. racial colonialism.

I have examined the genocidal dimensions of the U.S. colonialist conquest of the Philippines elsewhere, and will not here revisit the systemically mas-sive violences and fatalities of the turn-of-the-century American "pacifica-tion campaigns" in the archipelago (Francisco 1973; S. Miller 1982; Pomeroy 1967). Rather, my point of departure will be from historian Warwick An-derson's insightful examination of the U.S. colonial project's foundational diagnosis of "Filipinos as infantile, immature subjects, unready yet for self-government of body or polity—as *formes frustes* [incomplete manifestations of disease] stalled on the trajectory from native to citizen" (W. Anderson 2006: 3). (In one of the most notorious statements in the archive of U.S. em-pire, Senator Albert Beveridge expressed support for Philippine colonization on the floor of Congress in 1900 by stating that "the common people in their stupidity are like their caribou bulls. . . . They are incurably indolent. . . . They are like children playing at men's work" [*Congressional Record*, 56th

Congress, Session 1, Vol. 33, p. 709].) This clinical and vulgar metaphorical association of Filipinos with the projected pathologies of childhood, adolescence, beasts of burden, and disease—a grammar that both presumes and anticipates the endemic maturity and healthfulness of the white subject—is precisely what implied the racial necessity of the cultural (read civil society-building) work of "Americanization" and the compulsory pedagogical form of the U.S. colonialist nation-building regime in the aftermath of the U.S. conquest of the archipelago.

The institutional logic of the U.S.-proctored transition from postwar colony to independent Philippine neocolony is sharply analyzed in Philippine nationalist historian Renato Constantino's famous polemic "The Miseducation of the Filipino" (Constantino 1970), a piece that explicitly echoes the critical race analysis of African American educator Carter G. Woodson in his classic book *The Miseducation of the Negro* (1998 [1933]). (Significantly, Woodson's text was itself influenced by the radical political disillusionment that derived from his encounters with colonialist white supremacy during his time as a high-level administrator of the U.S.-created public school system in the Philippines.) Constantino (1970: 24) outlines this phase of colonialist pacification as such:

> The first and perhaps the master stroke in the plan to use education as an instrument of colonial policy was the decision to use English as the medium of instruction. . . . With American textbooks, Filipinos started learning not only a new language but also a new way of life, alien to their traditions and yet a caricature of their model. This was the beginning of their education. At the same time, it was the beginning of their mis-education, for they learned no longer as Filipinos but as colonials.

Following Constantino, my concern here is with the postconquest civil society and colonialist nation-building projects of American pacification in the Philippines, which culminated in the United States disposing of its colonialist status through a proctoring of neocolonialist Philippine independence.

This era of colonial pacification, between 1904 and 1946 (the period of U.S. colonial occupation that followed the intensified military-conquest mobilizations of the "forgotten" Philippine-American War of 1899–1902 [Agoncillo 1990; Schirmer 1972; Shaw and Francia 2002; Constantino 1975]), both relied on and elaborated the template of reformist white supremacist proctorship that animated the political work—and archival authorship—of the

Freedmen's Bureau. That is, if the crisis disrupting white supremacy's internal coherence—if the contradictions that destabilized its autobiographical equilibrium and political identity—during the late-nineteenth-century Reconstruction entailed the discursive conflict between a "barbaric" (feudalist, enslaving) white supremacy and an emerging modern, civilized, reformist white supremacist national pedagogy, then this antagonism was partly reconciled through the racial colonialist project of making the independent Philippine nation-state, thereby symbolically and momentarily dispersing the constitutive racist violence of slavery, conquest, and colonization. I should be clear that I am not suggesting the material disappearance—or even the historical ebbing—of grassroots white supremacist violence in this historical period, whether in the form of accelerated white mob violence, lynchings, or emergent U.S. apartheid. Rather, I am paying attention to the changing comportment of the white supremacist animus, and am attempting to elaborate how shifts in its self-articulation and self-comprehension service the diversification and nuancing of a fundamentally coercive social regime.

It is within such a critical framing that we might revisit Beveridge's articulation of the white supremacist premises of the American colonial project:

> The Philippines are ours forever, "territory belonging to the United States," as the Constitution calls them. . . . We will not repudiate our duty in the archipelago. . . . We will not renounce our part in the mission of our race, trustee, under God, of the civilization of the world. . . . He has marked us as His chosen people, henceforth to lead in the regeneration of the world. . . .
>
> [The Filipinos] are not capable of self-government. How could they be? They are not of a self-governing race. They are Orientals, Malays, instructed by Spaniards in the latter's worst estate.
>
> They know nothing of practical government except as they have witnessed the weak, corrupt, cruel, and capricious rule of Spain. . . . What alchemy will change the Oriental quality of their blood and set the self-governing currents of the American pouring through their Malay veins? How shall they, in the twinkling of an eye, be exalted to the heights of self-governing peoples which required a thousand years for us to reach, Anglo-Saxon though we are?
>
> Let men beware how they employ the term "self-government." It is a sacred term. It is the watchword at the door of the inner temple of liberty, for liberty does not always mean self-government. . . . Self-government is no base and

common thing to be bestowed on the merely audacious. . . . Savage blood, Oriental blood, Malay blood, Spanish example—are these the elements of self-government? (*Congressional Record*, 56th Congress, Session 1, Vol. 33, pp. 704–8)

While Beveridge's oration is well known as an enunciation of white nationalist arrogance and is often read as a primary document of "classical" racist ideology, the speech has generally been conceptualized as a discursive artifact of a U.S. national-racial past. In contrast to this analytical impulse, I consider Beveridge's discourse of Anglo-Saxon civilization—which invokes and extends the classical cultural geographies and political tropes of genocidal Manifest Destiny (Horsman 1981)—as a paradigmatic, commonsense articulation of a fundamental and structuring *epistemological* condition that is not isolatable from its white supremacist ideological and institutional precedents and derivatives. Hence, we should understand that the civil and pedagogical projects of colonialist "pacification" can only occur in a climate that is already presumed to be restless, disorderly, and immanently warlike; this indelible connection illustrates how white supremacy, as a flexible and creative logic of domination, is as nuanced as it is deadly.

In what follows, I will depart from the Freedmen's Bureau's archive of racist violence through a concise rereading of the archival moments that contextualized and produced Philippine "emancipation," a period from 1934 to 1935 in which an unsettled white supremacist politicality undertook a peculiar racial statecraft of national independence that rearticulated colonialist occupation as liberal democratic nation-building. While formal Philippine independence was meticulously and famously scripted for debut on July 4, 1946, its inscription through the white supremacist animus of the Philippines Independence Act of 1934—more commonly known as the Tydings-McDuffie Act—is substantially undertheorized, and the context of its enunciation as a global racial protocol is not well understood.

Traced through the overlapping racial-pedagogical genealogies and institutional formations of the Bureau of Indian Affairs and the Freedmen's Bureau, the U.S. colonial administration of Philippine independence was the organic twentieth-century political offspring of white supremacist civilization expansion. President Franklin D. Roosevelt's 1934 missive to Congress—tantamount to an executive letter of recommendation attesting to the successful maturation of the Filipino civil subject—composes a rather stunning vernacular and historical revision (or perhaps erasure) of colonialist conquest, and appears to displace the statecraft of racial dominance with a global government of and for "sovereignty." Herein lies a critical, transformative moment in the life of white supremacist social formation: the innovation of a transposition between the layered technologies of civil, social, and biological death (slavery, frontier conquest, and militarized colonialist occupation) and the proctoring of political sovereignty for racial subjects unfamiliar (and generally incompatible) with white politicality.

> To the Congress:
> Over a third of a century ago the United States as a result of a war which had its origin in the Caribbean Sea acquired sovereignty over the Philippine Islands. . . . *Our Nation covets no territory; it desires to hold no people over whom it has gained sovereignty through war against their will. . . .*
>
> For 36 years the relations between the people of the Philippine Islands and the people of the United States have been friendly and of great mutual benefit. . . . After the attainment of actual independence by them, friendship and trust will live. (H. Rep. Doc. No. 272, 73rd Congress, Session 2, pp. 1–2; emphasis added)

This white supremacist transposition between genocidal conquest and announced respect for sovereignty, between violent colonialist occupation and "friendship," is as much an institutional matrix as it is a narrative strategy. The movement of white politicality is disciplined by a comportment of democratic adaptibility that is, itself, irreparably entwined with the assumptive ethicality of the white political body.

Put differently, Roosevelt's letter of racial recommendation positions the colonialist statecraft of white supremacy as having held dear *all along* the best interests of the colonized, whose political destiny is, in turn, always contingent on the civil pedagogy of the white state subject and its multiple juridical, military, and bureaucratic forms. This explains why the presidentially appointed Philippine Commission, which investigated social conditions, made executive recommendations, and initiated a comprehensive governmental-juridical overhaul during the early years of occupation (1900–1916), was so concerned with administering and managing Philippine state and civil society into existence. In its first four years, in addition to a panoply of other bureaucratic accomplishments, the commission passed more than twelve hundred pieces of legislation addressing everything from the reorganization and modernist streamlining of Philippine "municipalities," purchases of individual land tracts and buildings, the rationalization of a coinage, erection of public schools, and the organization of tax collection (H. Rep. Doc. No. 2, 58th Congress, Session 3).

The 1909 Philippine Commission Report, as with the others preceding and following it, is a generally tedious, mundane document. Its detailing of legislative acts, school and hospital development, and other colonialist modernization projects tells a rather typical story of underdevelopment such that the fabrication of a Philippine civil society seems to clearly work according to the vested interests of U.S. corporate and military interests. Concerns over both the capitalist development and global sovereignty of the colonialist nation-state inflect the report's textual organization, and structure its alternation between rhetorics of explanation and advocacy; in this, the U.S. colonial project reflects the classical political-economic motives of an expanding industrial capitalism and emergent imperialism. For example, criticizing what it sees as the U.S. government's interference with the accumulation and concentration of private American business interests in the Philippines, the commission report contends,

> The fact that no large tract of land has been purchased of the government, and that no single large enterprise has been undertaken for the development of agriculture, in our judgment proves conclusively that the limitations placed by [the U.S.] Congress on the quantity of land which one corporation or individual may acquire from the public domain has had the deterrent effect of preventing capital from coming here, which could not but prove beneficial, not only to the capitalist, but also to the Philippine Islands from the development of their latent resources and the opportunity for employment and better conditions of living which it would bring to the inhabitants. (*War Department Annual Reports, 1909,* Vol. VII, p. 49)

On the one hand, such early texts of the Philippine pacification project clearly demonstrate the strategic, bureaucratically managed conflation between the pathways of eventual Philippine independence—production of a viable civil society, facilitation and political-military protection of foreign and U.S. capital, construction of modern governmental apparatuses, and so on—and the ambitions of a neocolonialist U.S. global (or at least trans-Pacific) hegemony. On the other hand, this archive also reveals the inseparability between the overarching social imagination of pacification and the structural animus of a white supremacist sociality. To be clear, I understand pacification's social imagination to be entirely structural, institutional, and material in the modality of its inspiration and political guidance of a peculiar American colonialism that was fixated almost from its inception on a proctored yielding of formal sovereignty to the natives. The durable link between the pacificationist social imagination and its white supremacist substructure, however, is most evident in the textual-ideological moments of the colonial archive that appear to confuse, confound, or depart from the clinical sterility and descriptive tedium of the official records.

This departure from empirical tedium and narrative cleanliness is most marked in the textual moments that reveal (1) the persistence of Philippine civil discord, most notably resistance to and armed insurrection against U.S. colonial occupation among the Muslim and non-Christian indigenous minorities; and (2) the multiple pestering failures, insufficiencies, and lingering pathologies pocking the Philippine civilizational substructure—here, the custom, culture, and physical comportment of the Filipino native are not simply the collective object of cosmetic (or even "superstructural") reform for pacification's white supremacist proctorship and civil pedagogy; indeed, they compose an essential focus of U.S. colonialism's logic of social makeover.

The tale of pacification begins to burst at its narrative seams when the commission describes the "Conditions as to Peace and Order." In the immediate aftermath of a genocidal military conquest in which the U.S. military—following in the direct genealogy of the continental campaigns against North American indigenous peoples—permanently dislocated native cultural and political economies, exterminated one to two million people, and destroyed countless homes, villages, and sacred objects, the mere existence of indigenous resistance to U.S. occupation amounts to a significant disruption of pacification's white supremacist benevolent desire (that is, white benevolence must turn punitive, deadly, repressive). Perhaps most significant in this archive is its utter silence around the widespread death and social trauma wrought by the first decade of the colonialist conquest and occupation, a legacy that accompanied and impacted the latter phase of the colonial project. It is as if the commission's treatment of surviving indigenous insurrectionists presumes the prior years of genocidal violence as a natural (unavoidable? ordinary?) feature of the social and historical span, and thus the insurgency against U.S. authority is not evidence of an ongoing anticolonial (or civil) war but is a disparately located rupturing of an extant social peace.

In short, colonialist repression assumes the role of civic policing on behalf of the Filipino colonial/civil subject.

> We believe it is safe to say that never before in the history of the islands has public order been as well preserved as it is to-day. . . .
>
> This statement, however, does not hold good of the island of Mindanao, where during the year there have been several serious infractions of public order. The first of these resulted in the punitive expedition by the constabulary against certain Moros inhabiting the country between Lake Lanao and Cotabato Valley, known as the Buldong country. The second were depradations of a band of pirates under the leadership of a man by the name of Jikiri. (*War Department Annual Reports, 1909*, Vol. VII, pp. 41–42)

Equally disruptive to the pacificationist social vision is the racial incorrigibility of Filipino social comportment, which stubbornly fails (or refuses) the tutorship of a white supremacist cultural modernity. The commission insists, for example, that the dismantling and reforming of Filipino eating habits become a focal point of U.S. colonial statecraft:

> Another change toward which the energies of the government should be bent, but one fraught with much more difficulty and one in which any general progress can not be expected except during the lapse of a considerable number of years, is teaching the people to eat with knives and forks and to discontinue the present custom of eating with the fingers, which prevails among the lower classes throughout the archipelago. (*War Department Annual Reports, 1909*, Vol. VII, p. 44)

In addition to the notion that eating with the hands is a trait so ingrained that it requires a "considerable number of years" of racial training to undo, this passage gestures toward a generally undertheorized, speculative—though no less practical—dimension of white supremacist colonialism. The endemic failure of the colonial native to inhabit the raciality of the white modernist civilizational telos marks the permanent and productive failure of pacification's social dream, a dream in which the white supremacist substructure reproduces through the vexing difficulty—if not the outright incapacity—of the native's reform as an imperfectible object-subject of white civil society's political, cultural, and physiological architecture. It is not merely the native's "custom" of eating that disturbs and disrupts the reformist white supremacy of colonial pacification; it is the very gesturing of the native body, its epidermal and physiological nonassimilation to white civilizational expectation, and finally its lurking susceptibility to racial regression to pretutorial mores, that constitute a permanent threat of betrayal to the white civilizational project.

This genealogy of pacification as both a narrative of civilizational fulfillment and productively failed racial reformism opens up a theoretical conception of white supremacy as a social logic of multiple registers, which may generally work in concert but might also periodically work in contradiction and tension. The aggressive bureaucratic fabrication and management of Filipino civil society yields a certain surgical and procedural cleanliness—"It is fortunate that the Philippine people themselves appreciate the value of pure water. . . . This most encouraging feature of the work indicates that it will not be difficult to persuade the Filipino to make use of other sanitary facilities when offered" (*War Department Annual Reports, 1909*, Vol. VII, p. 44)—that is consistently sullied by the racial ward's inaptitude, stubborn disobedience, or phenotypic betrayal of white politicality and its civic template.

The archival texts of Philippine national emancipation, then, are both a rationalization of the "outcomes" of pacification and a rescripting of white supremacist subjectivity that departs from a narrative foreclosure of Filipino raciality. The discordances, incompatibilities, and incorrigibilities endemic to the postconquest Philippines—a complex social and political geography that according to this archive's own account suggests a proliferation of multiple racial subjects rather than a singular "Filipino" raciality—are strategically foreclosed, sacrificed to a mythology of political independence and national sovereignty that rearticulates (and ultimately reasserts) the civilizational progress of trans-Pacific Manifest Destiny. Representative Millard E. Tydings's 1934 report on "Philippine Independence" thus defines the racial genealogy of the Philippines, and by extension situates "Moro," "Mohammedan," and "Pagan" difference as relatively inessential rifts within an otherwise appropriately racially unified modern national Filipino subject.

> Ninety-two percent of the approximately 13,500,000 inhabitants of the Philippine Islands are Christians. Four percent are Pagans and 4 percent Mohammedans. These Mohammedans are the so-called "Moros." The Mohammedan, the Pagan, and the Christian Filipinos are racially identical. Their history and tradition are the same. The Mohammedan and Pagan Filipinos have for a long time acquiesced in the government of the islands by the Christian majority. . . .

There is no substantial evidence that these Moros and others have protested against Christian preponderance in the government. (Sen. Rep. No. 494, 73rd Congress, Session 2, p. 13)

While it is inconceivable, given ample evidence of revolt and armed insurrection in different parts of the archipelago during this period (Majul 1985), that Tydings and the rest of the Committee on Territories and Insular Affairs could have possibly believed that the Moro and non-Christian minorities passively consented to the veritable governmental monopoly of Christian Filipinos, the purpose of this report was to suture any remnant fissuring, to rationalize and minimize sociopolitical antagonism, not to "objectively" describe it. The report's flimsy explanation of religious, tribal, and regional difference, and its clumsy conflation of all "inhabitants" into a racial, historical, and traditional "sameness," is central to its conceptual apparatus of proctored sovereignty. Speaking to the period preceding U.S. colonialism, the report suggests the preparedness of Filipinos for appropriately modern white racial mentorship:

The Filipino people are the beneficiaries of several centuries of civilization. Long before the Spanish conquest of the islands in the latter half of the sixteenth century, the inhabitants possessed a certain degree of culture, including written languages, characteristic arts, and industries. . . . This civilization and culture were, like the people themselves, of Malay origin, but with Indonesian and Mongolian elements.

Spanish occupation of the islands for more than 3 centuries introduced and established Christianity, European jurisprudence, language, and customs. It centralized authority and tended thereby to unify the country. (Sen. Rep. No. 494, 73rd Congress, Session 2, pp. 6–7)

The vindication of white supremacist reform, that is, the success of its pacification project, pivots on the outcome of its labored production/proctorship of racial wards capable of assimilating enough of the mechanics, rituals, rhetorics, and institutional forms of white politicality to merit emancipation. This was allegedly, for the Filipino, tantamount to "a practical apprenticeship in self-government" (Sen. Rep. No. 494, 73rd Congress, Session 2, p. 8).

In fact, it is the integrity of white subjectivity—specifically, the ascendancy of its political habitus and embodiment—that is at stake in this venture, as it is in other civilizational labors in which a version of white supremacist pedagogy and politicality is forwarded as the template for building and remaking a (national, sovereign) civil society. In this sense, Tydings's report (an almost identical version of which was submitted to the Senate by Senator John McDuffie) (H. Rep. No. 968, 73rd Congress, Session 2) offers another definitive moment in the autobiography of the white supremacist animus. It is as much an archival statement about the historical nuance of white supremacy's sociohistorical logic as it is about the perception and projection of a putative Filipino raciality. The transparency of white historicity, its endowment—at once divinely ordained and rationally cultivated—with the capacity to arbitrate access to sovereign governmentality, is the keystone of Philippine emancipation as a grandiose racial-political gesture:

> The people of the islands are not unmindful of our efforts at the cost of our blood and large expenditures of our public funds for their progress and development, and to give them their place in the sun. . . . From a standpoint of education, the administration of justice, and a capacity to maintain their economic progress, it is not doubted that the Filipino people are fully competent to set up and maintain a free and independent government. (Sen. Rep. No. 494, 73rd Congress, Session 2, p. 4)

> Every step taken by the United States since the inception of American sovereignty over the Philippines has been to prepare the Filipino people for independence. As a result, they are now ready for independence politically, socially, and economically. (p. 5)

White supremacist pedagogical agency forms a global, epochal spatial-temporal bridge that spans entry to the privileged reaches of the free world, and defines the parameters of civic life, even and especially as the purported departure from a white supremacist violence that initially coerces the subordination and extinction of the native subject. This pedagogy frames Philippine independence as a definitive achievement of white supremacist modernity, and displaces any notion of "modernity" that does not center the violence of white supremacy in its conceptualization of political economic and military hegemony.

CONCLUSION: THE PROBLEM OF DEFINITION

To attempt to define and describe white supremacy in an absolutist, ironclad, transhistorical manner is not a useful exercise: its matrices of institutional mobilization, conceptual apparatuses of civilizational, national, and subjective ordering, and grammars of articulation (both as a rhetoric of power and commonsense arrangement of everyday rule) too quickly flex and change in response to the political expediencies and social crises composing certain historical conjunctures.

As a layered, textured matrix through which sociality has formed, the global permutations of white supremacy overdetermine our very conceptions of politicality itself. Contestations over the means and principles through which the social form should be organized and "ruled" are assumptively and inescapably shaped by the multiple (though no less singularly identifiable) politicalities of the white civilizational animus, from bourgeois republicanism and militarist fascism to derivative "democracies" and socialist governmentalities. White politicality—as it encompasses notions of viable and legitimate political subjectivity, social movement, "revolution," government, and statecraft—forms a premise of political discourse as well as articulating multiple concrete prototypes through which political discourse manifests in rule and transformation.

This historical framing provokes a key theoretical question: What are the political and conceptual premises of coherence, the grammars of articulation, through which this continuum of white supremacist civilizational articulation obtains its currency, common accessibility, and generalized acceptability? At stake here is a reconsideration of white supremacy's flexibility and durability as a social logic and historical telos, as well as a critical reflection on the animus that persistently reveals itself across the specificities of institutional mobilizations, rhetorical shifts, and transformations of white social subjectivities.

Here I will suggest a few points of departure for such a reconsideration, points which address the problem of definition by offering a framing conceptualization of the white supremacist animus. The conceptual architecture of this animus, I would suggest, does not amount to an adequate singular definition of white supremacy but instead facilitates multiple historically situated and politically contextualized definitions of white supremacy that can still be apprehended in a genealogical relation to one another. There seem to be three overarching registers of the white supremacist animus that structure the particular ideological and institutional articulations of white supremacy in given historical moments and political geographies:

1. This animus constitutes a *narrative indelibility* that concretely shapes the political and cultural discourses as well as the material social worlds which it seeks to both represent and produce; for example, white supremacy differently constitutes the narrative structures of nation-building, citizenship, rationality, civilization, and the "human" in different times

and places. What remains consistent is that white supremacy's mobilizations of power and dominance do not simply "speak for themselves," nor are they characterized and represented by external cultural agents but are fundamentally occupied with the elaboration (and naturalization) of these narrative structures: white supremacist power and dominance *cannot make sense otherwise.* It is in the moments when the apparatus of sense-making fails to accommodate the concreteness of white supremacist violence that narrative structures erode and reconfigure.

2. The white supremacist animus summons an *assumptive politicality* that forms the historical and institutional framework through which struggles over social power are disciplined, articulated, and ultimately rendered intelligible. The ascendancy and fabricated transparency of the normative white political subject, for example, composes the matrix against which the comportment, fashioning, and self-enunciation of political actors in general are apprehended, judged, and measured. This calibration of "the political" is often so inherent to the social form— akin to the genotype of the organic political body that it nourishes— that white supremacist politicality is effectively outside the parameters of critical engagement: put differently, this politicality becomes densely, gravely taken for granted.

3. An apparitional—but no less social and material—effect (Gordon 2008) both guides and follows the nuanced movements and transitions of white supremacy's animus across historical moments: the ascendancy of white life, as both a civilizational imperative and affective structure (that is itself not exclusive to "white people"), is preceded and accompanied by a profound familiarity with coordinated human subjection and an intimacy with systemic human fatality. This is how the death of the slave, the native, and the human Other becomes symbiotic with the white subject's socially produced presumption of entitlement to physiological and spiritual integrity: that death, their death, is tolerable though tragic; it is not cause for emergency even as it suggests disaster; and it finally restates the sanctity of white existence as the earthly project of transcending the condition of unexpected fatality. The animus of white supremacy seems to constantly invoke and reinvent this relation of tolerance, acceptance, and comfort with the other body's disintegration, the other subject's degradation.

In the context of this provisional framing, white supremacy is not a problem to be decisively "solved" or escaped but rather forms a condition of antagonism—a sociohistorical substructure—that is politically productive to the extent that it is constantly, critically, and radically confronted and opposed rather than obscured or reified. Put differently, white supremacist politicality is constitutive of the generalized condition of political discourse itself, and composes the premises of dominance against which other politicalities must somehow self-position. Effectively, a liberated politicality can only organically emerge from a praxis of white supremacy's—and perhaps the white (political) body's—abolition as such, a political imagination that requires an extended theorization of its own.

GOVERNMENT DOCUMENTS CITED

Acts of the Philippine Commission and Public Resolutions, Etc. (Volume XIV): from September 24, 1900, to August 31, 1904, Annual Report of the War Department for the Fiscal Year Ended June 30, 1904, H. Rep. Doc. No. 2, 58th Congress, Session 3.

Letter to General Fisk by J. Stewart (Bradenburgh, KY), January 4, 1866, Sen. Ex. Doc. 27, 39th Congress, Session 1.

Report No. 9, "Reports of Assistant Commissioners of the Freedmen's Bureau," Sen. Ex. Doc. No. 27, 39th Congress, Session 1.

Report of Assistant Commissioner's Office for the month of March 1868, Kentucky, April 10, 1868, H. Rep. Ex. Doc. 329, 40th Congress, Session 2.

Report of Assistant Commissioner's Office, Kentucky, February 15, 1868, H. Rep. Doc. No. 329, 40th Congress, Session 2.

Report of Assistant Commissioner's Office, Maj. Gen. (Assistant Commissioner) Clinton B. Fisk, Nashville, TN, February 14, 1866, Sen. Exec. Doc. 27, 39th Congress, Session 1.

Report of the Philippine Commission. 1910. War Department Annual Reports, 1909 (Vol. VII). Washington, DC: Government Printing Office.

Report on Philippine Independence, submitted by Rep. John McDuffie, March 13, 1934. H. Rep. No. 968, 73rd Congress, Session 2.

Report on Philippine Independence, submitted by Sen. Millard E. Tydings, March 15, 1934, Sen. Rep. No. 494, 73rd Congress, Session 2.

Report on St. Bernard Parish (Louisiana), November 27, 1868, Sen. Ex. Doc. No. 15, 40th Congress, Session 3.

Roosevelt, Franklin D. "A Recommendation That Legislation Be Enacted to the Effect That the Philippine Islands Shall Be Granted Their Independence." March 2, 1934, H. Rep. Doc. No. 272, 73rd Congress, Session 2.

Statement of Freedmen's Bureau official William Goodloe, Report of Assistant Commissioner's Office, Nashville, TN, February 14, 1866, Sen. Ex. Doc. 27, 39th Congress, Session 1.

Summary report of Virginia, by Colonel O. Brown, Assistant Commissioner, November 31, 1865, 39th Congress, Session 1, Sen. Ex. Doc. No. 27. Testimony of First Lieutenant J. M. Lee, October 4, 1868, Sen. Ex. Doc. No. 15, 40th Congress, Session 3.

Testimony of Freedmen's Bureau Agent J. C. McMullen, Report of Assistant Commissioner's Office (Tennessee), April 14, 1868, H. Rep. Ex. Doc. 329, 40th Congress, Session 2.

Testimony of John H. Wagner before Congressional Joint Select Committee to Inquire into the Condition of Affairs in the Late Insurrectionary States (Alabama), October 14, 1871, Sen. Rpt. 41, pt. 9, 42nd Congress, Session 2 (Serial Set Volume No. 1492).

3 ON (NOT) BELONGING

Why Citizenship Does Not Remedy Racial Inequality

Eduardo Bonilla-Silva and Sarah Mayorga

We begin this chapter by acknowledging that we are not citizenship studies scholars per se. Citizenship has never been a central category of analysis for us because we know conceptually and experientially that the racial status of individuals trumps their citizenship standing in *any* polity. As a Black Puerto Rican, for example, the first author is a member of two communities for whom citizenship has always been suspect in the United States. Blacks, even after the election of Barack Obama as the forty-fourth president of the country, remain collectively in a second-class condition. Puerto Ricans, who became citizens of the United States in 1917, remain colonial subjects on the island as well as when they walk "down these mean streets" of America (P. Thomas 1997).

To highlight the problematic connection between citizenship and race, we begin with two very personal stories, narrated by Eduardo.

The first story is about an old, rich, and quite liberal Jewish female acquaintance of mine. She told me that at a recent attendance at an opera in Washington, D.C., she was seated by the presidential box seat. Condoleezza Rice was seated in the box that night, a fact that fascinated many in the audience. But my acquaintance was not impressed; she told me and my wife, "I do not know why people get all excited about seeing her. She is still a Nigger, isn't she?" And then she laughed!

The second story is of a recent incident. As I returned home from work one day, I realized that a car wreck had taken place by the entrance of my community. After I got into my house, I decided to walk down my long driveway to check out the accident. As I approached my mailbox, I realized that the accident had been cleared but that a few police cars were entering my community. I kept walking towards my mailbox and saw that two police cars had parked by it. I approached the officers to inquire about the accident, when all of a sudden a white police officer stepped out of his vehicle and said to me, "What's up, man?" I thought this was a rather unprofessional expression but proceeded to ask him about the accident. The officer told me the accident had been cleared and then asked me, "Where do you live? ... Sir." I told him, somewhat puzzled by the officer's question and tone, "Right here in this house." The officer then asked him, "What's your house number, sir?" I was angry and, honestly, somewhat shaken by this interaction and told the officer to look at the number on my mailbox. At that moment, an officer from the second car stepped out and asked me again, "What's your house number, *Sir*?" When I began to answer, one of the officers seemed to have realized something. He looked at the other officer and said to him, "He's not ... "—he did not finish the sentence—and then said to me, "Sorry, Sir, we are dealing with a police matter here." All of the officers then got into their vehicles and sped away. Had I been the victim of racial profiling in my own home, or was I being "hypersensitive," as so many whites think we are when things like this happen to people of color? Evidence I gathered thirty minutes later confirmed my suspicion: I had been profiled.[1]

The "success" of conservative Black individuals such as Condoleezza Rice does not exempt them from their Blackness. The first author's success, if any, means very little in the "mean streets" of America (even in his driveway), as he still is, as Fanon said, "overdetermined from without." Whites still see dark people of color and say, "Look ... a Negro," as Fanon wrote in *Black Skin, White Masks* (1967). These two stories anchor this chapter because they capture the essence of our arguments. So long as polities in the modern world are "racial states" (D. Golberg 2002), juridical-political categories such as "citizenship" will not confer full equality. These categories were racialized from their inception and thus belonging to a polity is deeply conceived and practiced as a racial privilege (Olson 2004). To telegraph our punch line, whatever degree of "equality" people of color have attained in America, it has been through collective struggle. That has been, and will continue to be, the road to full and real equality!

In this chapter we will do three things. First, we examine briefly how people of color were viewed by central figures of the Enlightenment, that is, those who produced the foundational ideas in the discourse on citizenship. Second, we review central moments in the history of the United States and contemporary "data" that show the lower standing of people of color. We focus our attention, however, on contemporary matters that clearly reveal the second-class nature of citizenship for people of color. Last, we discuss the limitations of citizenship as a category and how citizenship is monitored through state and nonstate actors alike. We conclude by addressing the burning question of what can be done.

THE FRUITS OF ENLIGHTENMENT (FORBIDDEN FOR SOME)

We are fascinated, albeit not surprised, by how many scholars of citizenship, human rights, and democracy—the humanistic discourses of modernity—ignore the centrality of race, then and now. Most romanticize Enlightenment figures such as Hobbes,[2] Voltaire, Montesquieu,[3] Rousseau, Kant, Hume, and Locke[4]; most universalize the ideas produced by the French and the American revolutions when neither intended this to be the case; and too many read words such as *men, liberty,* or *citizen* as all-inclusive terms, even though they were not intended as such.[5]

To refresh the reader's memory on the racial views of the men of the Enlightenment, a few quotations should suffice. David Hume, for instance, one of the famous Scottish Moralists, wrote in his 1753 *Of National Characters*:

> I am apt to suspect the negroes . . . to be *naturally inferior to the whites.* . . . There are Negro slaves dispersed all over Europe, of which *none ever discovered any symptoms of ingenuity*; . . . In Jamaica . . . they talk of one negro as a man of arts and learning; but it is likely he is admired for very slender accomplishments, *like a parrot who speaks a few words plainly.* (Goldberg 2002: 57)

Kant, father of modern moral theory and canonized by contemporary liberal theoreticians such as Norberto Bobbio and Jürgen Habermas for his ideas on "universal civil society" and "cosmopolitanism," also wrote racist essays such as *The Different Races of Mankind*. An example of Kant's racist views appears in his *Observations on the Feelings of the Beautiful and the Sublime* where he stated that "So fundamental is the difference between [the black and white] races of man . . . it appears to be as great in regard to mental capacities as in color," so that "a clear proof that what [a Negro] said was stupid" was that "this fellow was quite black from head to toe" (cited by Mills 1997: 70).

And let us never forget that enlightened liberals on the American shore used to own people. Have we forgotten that ten presidents of the United States (Washington, Jefferson, Madison, Monroe, Jackson, Tyler, Taylor, Polk,

Johnson, and Grant) "at some point [in their lives] enslaved black Americans"? (Feagin 2006: 12). Have we forgotten the racist views of Thomas Jefferson, who though condemning the institution of slavery in his *Notes on the State of Virginia* (Jefferson 1982), also produced one of the earliest tracts of "American scientific racism"? (Klinker and Smith 1999: 23). In *Notes*, Jefferson wrote that the color of Blacks "is fixed in nature" and answered his question, "And is this difference of no importance?" in the affirmative. According to Jefferson, Blacks were, among other things, ugly, smelly, unneedful of much sleep, highly sexual (but unable to truly love), lacking in imagination, and none too smart. Hence, as Charles Mills has argued, the so-called social contract of modernity was also a *racial contract*. Blacks—the wretched of the earth—were not deemed subjects worthy of inclusion in this contract. Rousseau himself, father of the notion of the social contract, stated that after years of Europeans "swarming all over the world," he was convinced that "we have known no other men than Europeans" (Castles and Davidson 2000: 48).[6] This racist foundation of modernity is rationalized, covered up, or ignored by contemporary citizenship scholars as well as by most whites who keep writing about the "founding fathers" and the great thinkers of the Enlightenment.

SECOND-CLASS CITIZENSHIP AND THE RACIAL "ORDER OF THINGS"

If we turn our attention to the citizenship standing of Blacks in the Dis-United States of Amerika the overview begins in 1776.[7] Before the abolition of slavery, the debate about the majority of Blacks (that is, enslaved Africans) was mostly about their standing either as "slaves" or "free men." However, nothing in that debate addressed their citizenship standing because property "was neither alien nor citizen" (Kettner 1978: 297).

Potentially, however, a debate about the standing of Black citizenship could have taken place via a discussion of the standing of free Blacks. Even though the courts exhibited some ambivalence, and states such as Pennsylvania, Massachusetts, and Vermont[8] regarded free Blacks as citizens, in states and courts in the North and South free Blacks were nevertheless treated as subjects with a lower standing. For instance, in a Pennsylvania decision from 1853 dealing with voting rights, the court upheld that "the black population of Africa [had not yet been admitted] into political partnership" and added that although Blacks might be citizens, they could not yet aspire to "exercise . . . the effective franchise, or to the right to become our legislators, judges and governors" (Kettner 1978: 316).

In the nineteenth century, state after state closely followed New York State's discussion on the disenfranchisement of Blacks. A delegate from its 1821 constitutional convention bluntly justified this policy along these lines: "But it was said that the right of suffrage would elevate [Blacks]. I would ask whether it would elevate a monkey, or a baboon, to allow them to vote" (Klinker and Smith 1999: 35).

In 1851 the legislature in Iowa enacted a law barring the immigration of free Blacks into the state. A newspaper at the time editorialized on this policy as follows:

> We have always been taught to believe, and it is hard for us to forget it, "that all men are created equal." But according to modern ethics the quotation should read "all men (*except niggers*) are created equal." (Klinker and Smith 1999: 38)

In the Southern states, the secondary standing of free Blacks was stipulated in a more forceful way as states and courts alike refused to extend to them even the *formal* status of citizen. In decision after decision, free Blacks were regarded as "a degraded race" or as a "third class" (Kettner 1978: 320). This lesser standing of Blacks was codified as the law of the land in the Dred Scott decision of 1857. When Chief Justice Taney wrote that the word "citizen" and "people of the United States" were synonymous, he was reflecting whites' common sense about America; that is, Justice Taney imagined the nation (the "people of the United States") as white. In his words,

> [T]hose men who created the Union in 1789 formed a closed community in which membership was restricted to the descendants of the founders and to aliens co-opted by the process of naturalization. [We can be] absolutely certain that [those of] the African race were not included under the name of citizens of a State, and were not in the contemplation of the framers of the Constitution when these privileges and immunities were provided for the protection of the citizens in other States. (Kettner 1978: 327)

Before we move forward, we must underscore that we do not believe citizenship is a purely juridical matter. We follow the view of Evelyn Nakano Glenn, who in her book *Unequal Freedom* states that

> Citizenship is not just a matter of formal legal status; it is a matter of belonging, including recognition by other members of the community. . . . Formal law and legal rulings create a structure that legitimates the granting or denial of

recognition. *However, the maintenance of boundaries relies on "enforcement" not only by designated officials but also by so-called members of the public.* (2002: 52; our emphasis)

Therefore, even when people of color have had "formal" citizenship, their substantive citizenship experience has always been diminished by state-actors, by the courts, and more fundamentally, by the white citizenry. The white masses had a collective investment in making sure democracy and citizenship were prerogatives of whites (Olson 2004). Hence, as Glenn argues, during the Jim Crow era, "all whites were deputized to interpret and enforce segregation laws, while police and courts used their formal authority to back up white civilians" (2002: 243). We further address Glenn's framework later in the chapter, along with how the state empowers the white citizenry to police and, ultimately, maintain the "(racial) order of things" (Foucault 1970).

To move our argument forward, we will here make a historical jump from nineteenth-century judicial decisions to current events in order to discuss race matters in a period when most whites believe "Amerika" has become a color-blind nation. Although we could have illustrated the lower standing of people of color through quotations from white respondents from Bonilla-Silva's 2006 book *Racism Without Racists* or marshaled socioeconomic indicators to make our point, we have chosen a different path. We hope to illustrate the standing of people of color in contemporary America with "data" that academics hardly ever regard as evidence of inequality in citizenship. We hope this seemingly odd data will hit your heads as well as your hearts!

Let us first discuss child abductions.[9] We all know the names Elizabeth Smart, from Utah; Jessica Lunsford, from Florida; or Shawn Hornbeck and Ben Ownby, from the recent case in St. Louis, Missouri. But who among us recognizes the names Alexis Patterson, Laura Ayala, or Jahi Turner? These are the names of minority children abducted in the last few years. Only the case of Alexis, the Milwaukee girl abducted five years ago, received any serious media attention. The abduction of Elizabeth Smart, which happened at the same time as Alexis's, received *six* times more news coverage (McBride 2000).

Is this because minority children are not likely to be kidnapped? Actually, 19 percent of all "stereotypical child kidnappings" involve minority children (Glassner 2000); therefore, one would expect about one out of every five child-abduction news stories to involve minority children. Of course, some of the observed disparity in coverage is due to class (the media loves to show the pain of middle- and upper-middle-class people); yet, we remind readers that the white children in the Missouri and Florida cases came from poor families.

To sum up, we cite Alexis Patterson's stepfather, who said in a desperate tone before the 2002 National Association of Black Journalists' convention:

> We have nothing against the other kids that have been missing. . . . We know their parents hurt the same way we do and are grieving the same way. We want the same attention for our child so we can have just as much a chance of getting [Alexis] back as they do. (Sykes 2002)

Let us now highlight another issue that shows minorities' diminished standing as citizens in this country. As we all know, the single most important asset for average Americans is their house. We all want to own our homes and own them in areas where they will appreciate over time. But for Blacks, getting a piece of the American Dream was a nightmare during the Jim Crow era, as they were excluded from many neighborhoods through covenants, intimidation, bombs, and other overt strategies.[10] In the post–civil rights era the courts have made most of these practices illegal. Yet residential segregation remains almost as high today as it was fifty years ago.[11] This high level of segregation is not the desire of people of color to "self-segregate," as so many whites believe. In fact, researchers consistently find that people of color express a preference for living in mixed neighborhoods. Residential segregation remains high because discrimination in the housing and lending markets remains high. Period.

In a recent report issued by the Civil Rights Project at Harvard, the authors noted that "affordability alone cannot explain the existing pattern of segregation (in Massachusetts)," adding that "the main reasons for continuing segregation include steering by realtors, subprime loans given disproportionately to Blacks and Latinos, and a lack of action by the area's cities and towns" (Harris and McArdle 2003). Another report, issued in 2006 by the Fair Housing Center of Greater Boston, indicated that their Black and Latino testers experienced discrimination in 45 percent of cases; Blacks alone experienced discrimination 50 percent of the time in renter cases.[12] The report also indicated that besides steering by realtors, the exclusionary tactic most often used was providing differential information to minority applicants about availability. All in all, they found that whites were five to six times more likely to be told about available units than were minority applicants. The report told of one Black tester who was advised that the apartments she had seen were not available until January 1, while the white tester was told December 1. In another case, a Latino tester and a white tester both e-mailed an agent and left voice messages. The white tester received a return e-mail including photos of an available apartment, and made an appointment to see it. The Latino tester received no response from the agent. Another agent quoted a monthly rent to a Latino tester that was seventy-five dollars higher than the rent quoted to a white tester.[13]

If we turn to the banking industry, the Center for Responsible Lending released a study in 2006 based on about 177,000 loans processed in the state of North Carolina in 2004. After controlling for all sorts of factors, the study found that "African American borrowers were 31 percent more likely [than whites] to receive a higher-rate loan on fixed rate purchases" (Bocian, Gruenstein, Ernst, and Li 2006: 16).[14] This means that banks, after years of studies showing their discriminatory practices and after years of lawsuits, still discriminate.[15] In 2006 African Americans in Chicago were five times more likely to be denied a conventional mortgage to purchase a home than whites (Street 2005). Is this due to class ("Black folks are poorer than whites, and that's why banks regard them as not fit for loans"), as so many whites believe? A 2009 study from the University of Minnesota Law School noted that "Lenders are substantially more likely to deny loans to people of color, regardless of their income. For instance, high-income Black, Hispanic and Asian applicants have higher denial rates for home purchase and refinance loans than low-income white applicants." In fact, "The denial rate for blacks with incomes above $157,000 was 25%, while it was just 11% for Whites making less than $39,250" (Institute on Race and Poverty 2009). This means that differences in lending between whites and nonwhites are clearly not about class but about race.

The above findings can be illustrated with a case that aired in Paula Zahn's show on CNN on February 1, 2007. She had a Black woman named Nannette, from Detroit, on the show, who had discovered, thanks to an investigation by the Housing and Urban Development Department, that "at the same time [she] was turned down for a loan [by Fifth Third Bank], people with similar or even weaker financial histories were approved by the bank, and nearly all of them were white." (In the post–civil rights era, it is very hard to detect and document discrimination, as most of it occurs in a "now you see it, now you don't" fashion (Bonilla-Silva 2001).

Let us now address the burning matter of racial profiling: of driving while Black or Latino ("DWB/L"), walking while Black or Latino, shopping while Black or Latino, or simply breathing while Black or Latino. A recent case in San Antonio, Texas, illustrates how citizenship inequality works in this area. Joseph Fennell and Coby Taylor, two Black men in their twenties, were walking along a sidewalk toward their respective jobs at Tom's Ribs and Momma's Café when a marked San Antonio police car veered into their path. The officer in the driver's seat, Robert Rosales, ordered both men to put their hands in the air and move toward a fence. Believing Fennell had a handgun, Rosales then fired his weapon, grazing Fennell, who was twenty-four, in the forehead, police said. Fennell had been holding his keys. The afternoon shooting was "a mistake," said police spokesman Gabe Trevino. Rosales had been investigating a string of armed robberies in the area, and both Fennell and Taylor fit the description of the robber: a short Black man in his twenties. That explanation did not appease Taylor, twenty, who said the officer already had his gun drawn when he drove up (Chasnoff 2006).

The rationale given by the officer is the crucial issue for our analysis: for whites—and "honorary whites" (chap. 8 in Bonilla-Silva 2006) like Mr. Rosales—people of color always fit the description. Whether they are tall or short, have money or not, drive a fancy car or a "ghettomobile," they always "look suspicious" and thus fit the proverbial description; they must, as Smith, Allen, and Danley (2007) put it, "assume the position." Accordingly, the rights of people of color can be individually or even collectively violated without much concern from white citizens. For instance, the employment of DNA-dragnet tactics[16] in places such as Miami, Charlottesville, Louisiana, and Los Angeles, and in the infamous 1994 case in "liberal" Ann Arbor, Michigan, all show how minorities can suffer from collective punishment with impunity for the perpetrators.[17]

School shootings are another example of the lower standing of people of color in this polity. Although nine out of ten children killed in schools die in urban schools, and although violent acts (murder, suicide, and so on) are 11.5 times more likely in urban than rural and suburban schools, white America is morally distraught by tragedies such as the one in suburban Columbine. Eugene Kane, a writer for the *Milwaukee Journal Sentinel*, best accounted for this in a 2006 piece after a shooting in Cazenovia, Wisconsin, and an alleged plot in Green Bay:

> When tragedy hits a small town or city, the sympathy swells up for all involved. When young people die in Milwaukee's central city, too often the reaction from outsiders is to point fingers and blame residents for tolerating the violence.

He then added,

> Suburban and rural white students caught in gunfire get immediate grief counselors dispatched to the scene. Black and brown city kids surrounded by violence have to resolve their emotional issues all by themselves. (Kane 2006)

For readers who believe these shootings are in fact different events and thus ought to be treated differently,[18] we urge them to read the 2001 paper by Menifield and colleagues in *Deviant Behavior*. These researchers document that even when one compares similar types of school shooting incidents, the media coverage is disproportionally toward white schools. More significantly, the authors found the tone of the coverage to be completely different: articles dealing with shootings in white schools report the news in ways that elicit the sympathy of their readers, but articles dealing with shootings in urban schools convey the idea these were more examples "of the usual violence" and betray a concern with accountability, that is, a concern about minority parents not supervising their youngsters properly (Menifield, Brewer, Rose, and Homa 2001).

Further, if the (racialized) imagination of some readers is telling them, "Well, I am not a racist, but . . . aren't minority kids more likely to be involved in drugs, alcohol abuse, and to bring weapons to schools than white children, therefore . . . ?" they are in for a surprise. Antiracist activist Tim Wise, citing data from the Centers for Disease Control and Prevention, writes:

> [W]hite high school students are seven times more likely than blacks to have used cocaine; eight times more likely to have smoked crack; ten times more likely to have used LSD and seven times more likely to have used heroin. . . . What's more, white youth ages 12–17 are more likely to sell drugs: 34% more likely, in fact than their black counterparts. And it is white youth who are twice as likely to binge drink, and nearly twice as likely as blacks to drive drunk. And white males are twice as likely to bring a weapon to school as are black males. (Wise 2001: 3–4)

These sobering facts led Wise to state, "I can think of no other way to say this, so here goes: white people need to pull our heads out of our collective ass" (Wise 2001: 3). Although we like Wise's cute statement, we believe it is sociologically flawed. "Facts" matter very little with the things we have been discussing in this chapter. What ultimately counts in the real world—which is partially woven with the thread of race—is whites' perceptions of Blacks, their perception of Black men as "criminalblackmen" to use the term coined by Katheryn Russell (1997).

We now shift the discussion to the matter of immigration, and how the white national mood and the draconian measures being contemplated by many cities are affecting the citizenship standing of people who have brown skin and speak English with a Latino accent. For example, Farmers Branch, a Dallas suburb, passed an ordinance banning the rental of apartments to undocumented workers. Elizabeth Villafranca, a member of a group opposed to the ban, stated that "They're trying to send a message that minorities aren't welcome," and added that although she was born in the United States, she has been told to "go back to Mexico" (Feldman 2006).

As of this writing, sixty local governments in twenty-one states have considered ordinances to drive immigrants away; fifteen governments have passed such measures. Some localities have enacted measures even though they do not have a so-called immigrant problem. For example, Altoona, Pennsylvania, has passed such legislation; Joe Rieker, a city councilman, defended the action as follows: "We don't have a problem here with immigrants. . . . But we want to stay ahead of the curve" (Hamill 2006).

Since the white masses have all but declared open season on Mexican immigrants, it is not surprising to learn that in 2006 a high school principal in Georgia called her Hispanic ninth- and tenth-graders to a meeting in the cafeteria, accused some of them of being gang members responsible for recent off-campus fights, and told them she would call the police and immigration officials into the school the next time a Latino student caused a problem. Although she was suspended, her initial reaction was condoned (Reid and Varela 2006).

The final matter we wish to discuss is voter disenfranchisement. Voting is regarded as the most fundamental right of citizenship since it potentially leads to the expansion of social, civil, and even economic rights. The Fifteenth Amendment and the 1965 Voting Rights Act presumably removed all barriers to the right to vote for people of color. In 2000 and 2004, however, the right to vote of many Black and Latino citizens went down the drain.

The Select Task Force Commission created by Governor Jeb Bush in Florida (this commission was forced on him) to examine voting irregularities in his state in the 2000 election concluded:

> Accordingly, the Commission is duty bound to report, without equivocation, that the analysis presented here supports a disturbing impression that Florida's reliance on a flawed voter exclusion list, combined with the state law placing the burden of removal from the list on the voter, had the result of denying

African Americans the right to vote.... Based on the evidence presented to the Commission, there is a strong basis for concluding that section 2 of the VRA was violated.

The commission found that the percentage of a county's population that was Black explained 25 percent of the variance in ballot rejection rates in Florida, which in that state alone amounted to the disenfranchisement of ninety thousand Black voters.[19] How was this disenfranchisement accomplished in a nation that claims to be color-blind? It was accomplished through white precinct workers "faking the funk" with Black voters (that is, being nonresponsive, asking for multiple forms of identification, and so on), police intimidation,[20] and the erroneous inclusion of Black voters on ineligible-voter lists.

Despite the 2000 fiasco, voter disenfranchisement happened again in 2004 and in 2006. Most whites did not care about it too much these times, however, because it presumably did not affect the overall outcome of these elections (not a very principled position). Once again, many Black voters experienced voter intimidation by police[21] and by white citizens alike at polls, some wearing T-shirts that read "U.S. Constitution Enforcer." Other Black voters received calls telling them they could not vote or instructing them to vote on a different day (National Network for Election Reform 2007).

The reason all these things stand with impunity is because people of color are still regarded as lesser beings, as lesser humans, as lesser citizens of the United States. We ask readers to imagine what would happen if we truly had reverse discrimination in this nation and whites were the ones getting the death sentence four to fifteen times more often than Blacks, or not having their abducted children discussed by the media; or if whites' sacred right to vote were taken away? Would the nation continue with a "business as usual" attitude, or would we have a (white) revolution? We argue that because these violations happen to people of color, the nation "keeps on trucking," and those of us who complain are told, "It is not race," "You guys are hypersensitive," or "It is not as bad as you paint it!"

LIMITATIONS OF THE CATEGORY "CITIZENSHIP"

Our review of the historical origins of the category "citizenship," how the category was implemented in the United States, and how it operates nowadays clearly points out that citizenship was never intended as a neutral category and, as such, bears the mark of whiteness. The "universal" in the categories of modernity (e.g., democracy, human rights, and citizenship) was "white" and still is. We now enumerate the limitations of citizenship as a category and articulate a political path for people of color to overcome it.

1. Citizenship scholars are stuck in the bourgeois liberal individualism that created this category and, accordingly, reject group-based claims.[22] This stance, as Guinier and Torres (2002) suggest in *The Miner's Canary*, provides a cover for dominant identities, which are subsumed in so-called universal categories.

2. Citizenship is a category that is bound to the nation-state. However, being a citizen is not the same as belonging to a nation-state, because nation-states are also "racial states" (D. Goldberg 2002). Hence, belonging to a nation-state has historically been a racial prerogative for those emblazoned in the body politic.

3. Citizenship scholars favor democracy as the main tool for social progress and scorn militant tactics because they harm "free individuals" and hinder what Habermas (1992) has called "communicative action." These analysts forget, however, that without the struggles of people of color, workers, and women, democracy would have been for the elite and the "communicative action" would have taken place among a few rich white men.

   More significantly, scholars of citizenship ignore that democracy has been used as a strategy of "social closure" by white citizens. Whites have voted historically to enforce their right to a *Herrenvolk* democracy. Nowadays, for example, whites are voting against affirmative action, as they did in Michigan in the 2006 election, and are supporting candidates who advocate drastically reducing the size and reach of the welfare state because it presumably benefits minorities and immigrants the most.

4. Citizenship scholars treat citizenship as if it were a mere juridical-political category. By doing this, they ignore (a) that citizenship is also a practice, (b) that it entails a sense of and a claim to belonging, and (c) that citizenship is always a local rather than national or international experience. On this latter point, the national or international ratification of treaties or agreements extending this category of human rights to people of color, as important as it may be in the struggle for equality, is never equivalent to equality of treatment within local communities. Citizens of color can still experience racial profiling and discrimination in their own driveways.

.   .   .

What is to be done? First, we must challenge the "abstract liberal" (Bonilla-Silva 2006) stance of the citizenship paradigm. Because people of color are valued differently in "Amerika," they have the right of insisting on group-level remedies such as a "Marshall Plan" for urban America and even reparations. Individual-level strategies will not save them.

Second, since people of color are not only valued but also treated differently from whites, they must demand not "equal opportunity" but either "equality of outcomes" or "preferential treatment"—at least until they reach parity with whites (who have received preferential treatment for centuries, and still do) (Katznelson 2005). They also must make sure antidiscrimination laws are enforced against old-fashioned as well as against the "smiling-face" discrimination that has become so typical in the post–civil rights era (Robert Smith 1995).

Third, people of color must make their demands loud and clear. This does not mean that violent struggle is the only path for redemption; violence, however, must be one of the options in the repertoire of the "wretched of the earth." On this the research is clear: social protest works and is an efficient political tool to advance the political interests of excluded groups (Fox-Piven 2006).

Finally, the category "citizen" may be used in the struggle to attain ultimate equality, but people of color must be cognizant that categories do not liberate people or make them equal in the eyes of others.[23] Tactically, they may use citizenship to showcase the contradiction between the theory and the practice of the nation the way they did during the civil rights era when they exposed the fallacy and the folly of America's self-portrayal as a liberal and democratic country. However, people of color must never confuse the tool with the end, as the car that takes one on the road to equality is not equality itself! We conclude with a quotation by the always essential Fanon, who wrote in *The Wretched of the Earth*:

> From the moment that you and your like are liquidated like so many dogs, you have no other resources but to use all and every means to regain your importance as a man [or woman]. You must therefore weigh as heavily as you can upon the body of your torturer in order that his soul, lost in some byway, may finally find once more its universal dimension. (1968 [1961]: 295)

Please know then that men and women of color will weigh heavily on their torturers to make sure their souls become truly universal. Then citizenship will become a largely irrelevant matter, as we will all be equal partners in the community of humans.

POLITICS OF PRIVILEGE AND PUNISHMENT Part 2

4 THE BEST EDUCATION FOR SOME
Race and Schooling in the United States Today

Amanda E. Lewis and Michelle J. Manno

Our national school system has always been deeply shaped by the color line (Anderson 1988; Chesler, Lewis, and Crowfoot 2004; Litwack 1998; Woodson 1998 [1933]). Before Reconstruction, Black children were subjected to a "system of compulsory ignorance" (Weinberg 1977: 11) in which white interests in maintaining a subordinate class of Black slaves and laborers led to a systematic denial of access to education. White dominance of schooling is less overt today but no less real. Intergenerational transmissions of racial resources provide whites in the United States far greater access than non-whites to quality education (Johnson 2006; Shapiro 2004). These are "racial" resources because they were originally accrued largely through a combination of discriminatory private practices and the operation of racist federal, state, and local laws (Feagin 2000; McKinney and Feagin 2003; Guglielmo 2003; Katznelson 2005; Lipsitz 2006; Massey and Denton 1993; Quadagno 1994; Shapiro 2004). The benefits resulting from "the moment not long ago when affirmative action was white" (Katznelson 2005: xv) continue to be passed on to successive generations. This enduring legacy includes powerful social networks, wealth accumulated in homes purchased before fair housing laws, seniority accrued in previously segregated employment sectors, and alumni status (which provides advantage to offspring as "legacy admits") at previously all-white colleges and universities.

Such resources are concentrated within particular communities, not by accident but as a result of centuries of formal, state-supported racial domination in all arenas, including education. According to Walters (2001: 35), "racial inequality in educational funding and other forms of educational opportunity were explicit policies of the state throughout the country." And as Mickelson (2003: 1070) points out, though less obvious than during the periods of slavery and Jim Crow, state participation in the production of unequal education continues:

> State actors site schools and draw attendance zones that assist or hinder desegregation; they design and operate systems of ability grouping and tracking; they operate schools and school systems so as to permit middle class white parents to activate their race and class privileges . . . they generate reforms— such as high stakes testing—whose harsh accountability outcomes affect whites, Blacks and Latinos disparately, in part because these state actors often fail to ensure equitable distribution of opportunities to learn the materials covered on the tests.

Thus, even when not directly or explicitly involved, the state enables elite groups (whites) to resist efforts to curtail their relative educational advantages. Today school segregation levels are high and getting higher (Orfield and Gordon 2001; Orfield and Yun 1999). Whites are the most racially isolated group in our country's educational institutions, attending schools with the highest levels of resources (Kozol 1991; Mickelson 2003; Orfield and Gordon 2001; Orfield and Yun 1999). Blacks and Latinos are not only more likely to attend high-poverty schools (that is, greater than 50 percent poor; see Orfield and Lee 2005) but more likely to attend schools with fewer resources. Overall, majority minority schools have fewer qualified teachers, less access to technology, less access to advanced curricula, lower-quality facilities, and less availability of instructional materials (Darling-Hammond 2003; Institute for Democracy, Education, and Access 2004; Mickelson 2003; Oakes 2003). Schools with high minority enrollments are also less likely to have Internet access in the classroom; they have more students per available computer, and are less likely to provide access to computers in the early grades (U.S. Census 2001). Schools with Black majorities are much more likely to have underqualified instructors or to use long-term substitutes to fill teacher vacancies (Darling-Hammond 2003; Nettles and Perna, 1997). Recent studies have also shown that Black and Latino students are less likely to have access to college preparatory curriculum and advanced placement courses, and are less likely to take either the SAT or ACT (Allen, Bonous-Hammarth, and Ternishi 2002; Oakes 2003; U.S. Census 2001).

Inequalities in school resources are not a result, as they were in the past, of explicit segregation and direct action to limit minority access to quality education. Instead these inequalities typically are the direct result or indirect outcome of a number of school and nonschool processes such as the segregation of communities, concentration of poverty, the dependence on local property taxes to fund schools, and white aversion to sending their children to minority schools (Denton 1995–96; Kozol 1991; Saporito and Lareau 1999; Shapiro 2004; Wells, Home, Revilla, and Atanda 2009). Some of these processes involve seemingly "race-neutral" public policies (for example, local funding of schools), and some involve private practices (such as a family's process for choosing a school). Their cumulative impact, however, is unquestionable. For example, in 2002–3 over 80 percent of white students nationally attended schools with poverty rates below 10 percent, while only 5 percent of Black students and 7 percent of Latino students did. At the same time, Black and Latino students "comprise 80 percent of the student population in extreme poverty schools (90 to 100% poor)" (Orfield and Lee 2005: 21).

Differences in educational quality are receiving growing attention because of the persistence in racial gaps in school achievement. Though the gaps narrowed in the 1970s and 1980s, they have leveled off or increased in the 1990s (Lee 2002). There are competing explanations for gaps in school achievement. Individual-level explanations include those emphasizing innate or genetic factors (for example, Herrnstein and Murray 1994) and those pointing to community or family factors (for example, Coleman et al. 1966). Currently, there is a considerable debate about whether students of color (particularly Blacks and Latinos) have a "culture of opposition" that might explain their underperformance. While Ogbu (1978, 2003) and Fordham and Ogbu (1986) have received much attention for these arguments, substantial recent research questions the utility of oppositional culture for explaining school outcomes and suggests that school practices, personnel, and institutional cultures—rather than student cultures—might be more important factors in determining achievement levels (Ainsworth-Darnell and Downey 1998; Carter 2005; Harris 2006; Harris and Robinson 2007; Horvat and O'Connor 2006; Mickelson 1990; Noguera and Wing 2006; O'Connor 2001; O'Connor, Lewis, and Mueller 2007; Perry, Steele, and Hilliard 2004; Tyson 2002). Like other school-level or structural explanations, this work has focused on how schools function to support some students and families more than others; how resource differences across schools or communities shape different outcomes (Card and Kreuger 1996; Conley 1999; Hanushek 1994; Kozol 1991); and how racial dynamics play out in teacher expectations, home-school relations, rewards for cultural resources, and school discipline (Ainsworth-Darnell and Downey 1998; Delpit 1995; A. Ferguson 2000; Ferguson 1998a, 1998b; Lareau and Horvat 1999).

Related to these school-level practices and institutional dynamics is research that shows how the culture of schools also contributes to making many of them white places (Delpit 1995; Gould 1999; Ladson-Billings 1994; Nieto 2001). "School problems," Mickelson asserts, "are linked to the failure of white-controlled educational institutions to incorporate non-dominant cultures into school culture, curricula, pedagogy, or structures" (2003: 1067). Raced and gendered ideas (for example, stereotypes about inherent ability, criminality, and family dysfunction) penetrate deeply into schools and fundamentally shape everyday encounters between school personnel and students and their families (A. Ferguson 2000; Lareau and Horvat 1999; Lewis 2003). Educational anthropologists have documented the ways in which dominant cultural frameworks read students of color as deficient (Au 1980; Cazden 1988; Cazden, John, and Hymes 1972; Philips 1972). Ferguson's (2000) work demonstrates how school personnel interpret similar behaviors by male students differently, depending on whether the boys are white or Black. Lareau and Horvat (1999) and Roscigno and Ainsworth-Darnell (1999) show that resources children and families bring with them to school are differentially valued by teachers. This is the kind of institutionalization of dominant forms of whiteness Gould (1999: 172) describes:

> When the major institutions in society are constructed within the culture and in the interests of one group instead of another, even when the subordinate group is included within those institutions, its performance will be, on average, less proficient than the dominant group. Organizations may systematically favor the culturally constituted performances of one group over the developmentally equivalent, substantively different, performances of another group.

Students from racial and ethnic minority groups who attend schools that appear on the surface to be culturally neutral but which in fact privilege certain cultural attributes and devalue others are systematically disadvantaged. White cultural hegemony, including the institutionalization of white cultural norms and the demographic dominance of white middle-class teachers in schools, sets the context for much of what takes place in public schools (Delpit 1995). Cultural differences in styles of interaction, modes of expression, and ways of handling conflict (Kochman 1981) have significant effects on students' school experiences (Delpit 1995; A. Ferguson 2000; Fordham 1996; Ladson-Billings 1994; Lewis 2003; Nieto 2001).

In addition to the impact of the material and cultural components of racial hierarchies on educational outcomes, white skin itself provides certain advantages. This kind of "symbolic capital" has been documented across a range of social institutions (for example, health care, employment, service industry, criminal justice) and is one form of what Du Bois (1999) termed the "wages of whiteness."

In this chapter we take a closer look at some of the ways race shapes educational experiences in the United States. Public education systems in the United States are the main focus of this chapter and of the research from which we draw. Although education is not provided for in the federal Constitution, and remains primarily a responsibility of state and local governments, the education of children is a regular point of national discussion, debate, and legislation. Public schools, while not the only organizations providing educational experiences to children in the United States, are charged as state institutions with providing education for all. As we outline here, however, broad patterns of inequality persist in our educational systems along several key dimensions. Schools, in many ways, continue to play a role in the reproduction of racial hierarchies. Throughout the history of the United States, educational institutions have at times reproduced, maintained, or indeed even challenged racial inequality. From the systematic denial of education to Black slaves, Japanese field workers, and Mexican laborers to the provision of distinctly separate but equal schools in the South, to the development of freedom schools (Anderson 1988; Franklin 2000; Montejano 1987; Takaki 1989), education has been a key arena in which racial hierarchies have been negotiated and contested (Walters 2001). However, while they are in some moments instruments of challenge or change, for the most part schools remain highly racialized and highly unequal. Moreover, while schools are no longer legally segregated, a range of structural, institutional, and interactional mechanisms today produce a public school system that remains highly segregated and unequal (Kozol 1991; Lewis 2003; Lewis, Krysan, Collins, Edwards, and Ward 2004; Orfield and Gordon 2001; Orfield and Yun 1999). While it was easy to label de jure segregated school systems as deeply racist organizationally and in practice, separate and unequal schools today are no longer defined in explicit racial terms. Instead schools are defined geographically, believed to belong to discrete local (often segregated) municipalities. In the place of Jim Crow practices and ideologies of the past, new racial structures and logics have emerged. Part of a larger phenomenon variously labeled by different scholars, this new racism includes persistent high levels of racial inequality across a range of social institutions within an ideological frame that denies the continuing relevance of race (Bonilla-Silva and Lewis 1999; Forman 2004; Forman and Lewis 2006; Gould 1999). As we outline below, however, while the forms have changed, deep structures of racism still pervade our educational systems, shaping how schools are organized, the culture of schools, beliefs about who is and is not intelligent, and the treatment of students based on race. The results of structures of racism, we will show, continue to have profound, negative consequences for the educational outcomes of minority students.

RACIAL INEQUALITY IN SCHOOL FUNDING

In the United States schools receive resources from federal and state sources, but they are primarily funded through local property taxes, which compose half of the total revenue for public schools. In 2003, for example, 44 percent of all school funds came from local property taxes; state support provided about 49 percent on average; and federal support reached only about 7 percent (Biddle and Berliner 2003; Karp 2003; UCLA/IDEA 2004). One result of the way public schools are financed is that there are stark differences between schools in affluent neighborhoods and schools in poor neighborhoods (Kozol 1991). The reliance on property taxes means that there are differences not only between states but also between school districts within the same state (Biddle and Berliner 2003; Kozol 1991; Liu 2006; Campbell, Cunningham, Nystrand, and Usdan 1990). Schools in many wealthier communities have over $15,000 available per student, while those in less affluent and poor communities often have $5,000 or less per student each year (Biddle and Berliner 2003).

Unequal funding for public schools in this country has far-reaching consequences both inside of the classroom and out. Achievement levels, quality of school buildings, number and quality of facilities, curricula, availability of equipment for classroom instruction, retention of experienced and credentialed teachers, and class size are all impacted by the amount of funding available for each school (Biddle and Berliner 2003; Orfield and Lee 2005; UCLA/IDEA 2004). Moreover, higher-income communities that can generate more money, often through private funds but also through property taxes, can put more resources into school construction and improvement, and can modernize buildings as well as contribute to the creation of libraries and art programs (UCLA/IDEA 2004).

The development and persistence of racial residential segregation coupled with the very way that public school funding is structured in this country results in deep racial inequalities in school funding. Because cities and suburbs tend to be segregated and because white Americans have access to higher incomes and wealth than minorities, the obvious consequence of funding public schools primarily on the basis of local property taxes is racial disparity in access to well-funded schools. These types of inequalities accumulate over years leaving many poor and minority students without basic essentials such as textbooks, let alone modern buildings, computers, or libraries.

TEACHER QUALITY

Partly related to school funding differences, low-income and minority students are disproportionately likely, when compared to their white peers, to be taught by lower-quality or uncredentialed teachers (Center for the Future of Teaching and Learning 2008; Clotfelter, Ladd, and Vigdor 2004; Darling-Hammond 2001; Murnane and Steele 2007). Teachers of minority and poor students are less prepared and less experienced (many being novice teachers) than teachers of middle- and upper-class white students (Jacob 2007; Murnane and Steele 2007). Moreover, schools with large populations of poor and minority students experience higher rates of teacher turnover than schools populated with white students (Murnane and Steele 2007), and teachers in poor urban schools are often uncertified for the classes they teach (Center for the Future of Teaching and Learning 2008; Jacob 2007). Even within schools, teachers with higher credentials tend to teach more affluent students (Clotfelter, Ladd, and Vigdor 2004).

The fact that urban school districts face teacher shortages could explain why, in many cases, poor and minority students are often taught by inexperienced and ill-equipped teachers. There are other explanations, however, for the presence of poor teacher quality in these schools (Ladson-Billings 1994). Some suggest that urban schools have difficulty in attracting well-qualified, experienced teachers or that these schools might not be effectively hiring the most qualified and experienced teachers (Jacob 2007). If urban schools cannot offer teachers the salaries that suburban schools can, or cannot provide comparable school environments, teachers are more likely to gravitate towards suburban schools (Clotfelter, Ladd, and Vigdor 2004). The racial composition of the student bodies, however, does play a role in determining the distribution of highly qualified, experienced teachers across schools and school districts. Jacob (2007) points out that as the number of African American and Hispanic students in schools increased, white teachers were more likely to leave. In Texas, for example, public schools that have large portions of African American and Hispanic students lose a significant number of their teachers either because they move to other public schools or drop out of the school system completely (Hanushek, Kain, and Rivkin 2004). If given a choice between teaching in schools or school districts with advantaged students or disadvantaged students, most teachers would prefer to teach already advantaged students (Clotfelter, Ladd, Vigdor, and Diaz 2004).

Another mechanism that contributes to the lack of high-quality teachers in poor and minority schools is the tendency for white middle-class parents to demand that their children be taught by high-quality, experienced teachers (Clotfelter, Ladd, and Vigdor 2004). The combined effects of teachers seeking out schools with better working environments and parents of high-achieving students demanding high-quality teachers (or seeking out schools that can provide such teachers) result in school environments in which high-achieving students are typically taught by highly qualified teachers (Clotfelter, Ladd, and Vigdor 2004). The fact that poor and minority students are often being taught by inexperienced and underqualified teachers while affluent white students are taught by experienced and well-qualified teachers serves to exacerbate the Black-white achievement gap (Clotfelter et al., 2004; Darling-Hammond 2001).

TEACHER EXPECTATIONS

Distinct from research on the quality of the teaching staff at different schools is research on interactions between teachers and students within schools and classrooms. Research demonstrates that teachers perceive students of color and low-income students to have lower academic capabilities than white and high-socioeconomic-status students (Diamond, Randolph, and Spillane 2004; Farkas 2003) and that they have lower expectations in general for minority students than for white students (Tenenbaum and Ruck 2007). However, more than just having differing levels of expectations, teachers, argue some scholars, make more positive referrals and offer more positive and neutral speech for white students than for African American and Latino students (Tenenbaum and Ruck 2007). In regard to certain subjects, particularly upper-level mathematics, few African American and Latino students are enrolled in such courses at least in part because few receive opportunities (Walker 2007).

Scholars offer differing yet overlapping explanations for why teachers tend to hold lower academic expectations for minority students than for white students. Minority students are often perceived to have less academic capability than their white peers (Diamond et al. 2004; Roscigno and Ainsworth-Darnell 1999) largely because of students' race and class backgrounds (Diamond et al. 2004; Lewis 2003). These perceptions can dramatically influence the curriculum, teacher instruction, and teacher assessment of students (Walker 2007). Perceptions of capability, or the lack thereof, of minority students not only affects students by keeping them out of challenging courses but also influences whether advanced mathematics courses are offered, the kinds of textbooks the school purchases, where students are tracked, and the assignment of teachers to certain groups of students (Walker 2007).

Recent research on teachers' perceptions of minority students points out that cultural differences between teachers and students, especially minority students and white teachers, lead to inaccurate perceptions of ability in the classroom. Students who align their classroom behavior with mainstream educational values such as competitiveness and individualism are often viewed as "significantly more motivated and achievement-oriented" than students who display communal types of classroom behaviors (Tyler, Boykin, and Walton 2006: 1003). Given that the culture of mainstream education resembles white culture, minority students who display opposing, culturally based classroom behaviors could potentially be perceived as less competent, and thus have less expected of them from their teachers (Delpit 1995; Gould 1999). Research on teacher expectations of minority students also highlights the way in which self-fulfilling prophecies emerge, as students begin to spend less effort in classes where they know that not much is expected of them (Diamond et al. 2004; Oakes 2005). Racism and racial stereotyping influence teachers' perceptions of students' capabilities, with Black students perceived to be innately less intelligent than their white counterparts (Diamond et al. 2004; Fordham 1996; Perry et al. 2004). Abundant research on "stereotype threat" shows that Black students are aware of negative perceptions about their intelligence and that such ideas depress their performance (Steele 1997; Steele and Aronson 1998).

Beyond simply examining teacher-student interaction as the basis for the development of certain expectations, some have argued for a closer look at the role of school organizational factors in expectation development, particularly "teachers' sense of responsibility for student learning" (Diamond et al. 2004: 76). School organizational context, when coupled with teachers' expectations, becomes especially relevant in low-income and African American schools, where teachers focus on the deficits of students and thus have less of a sense of responsibility for their academic success (Diamond et al. 2004). The consequences of lower teacher expectations for minority students are just as obvious as they are detrimental.

RACIAL PATTERNS IN TRACKING

Ability grouping or tracking takes several forms, from fixed academic levels that shape all course-taking in secondary schools, to flexible programs that allow course-taking at different levels across subject matter, to ability grouping or grouped instruction within classes for math or reading in elementary schools. While the forms of ability grouping vary, all indicators are that a majority of schools nationally include some form of ability grouping (Condron 2007, 2008; Oakes 2005).

Virtually every study shows poor and minority students disproportionately placed in the bottom groups or lower tracks. This is sometimes referred to as second-generation segregation; in racially mixed schools, Black and Latino students are underrepresented in high tracks and overrepresented in low and vocational tracks (Ansalone 2006; Clotfelter 2004; Lucas 1999; Lucas and Berends 2007; Meier, Stewart, and England 1989; Mickelson 2001; Oakes 2005; Orfield and Eaton 1997; Wells et al. 2009). In addition, predominantly minority schools have fewer high-track classes and are more likely to have less rigorous courses and less qualified teachers (Oakes 2005).[1] These patterns are troubling on a number of counts but are especially problematic given the research on placement into tracks and on the consequences of tracking for learning and achievement.

Studies on tracking have found a great deal of potential for discrimination in placements, including subjective assessments of ability, parental influence, and irrelevant or narrow evaluations (Oakes 2005). For example, research shows that even high-scoring Black and Latino students are less likely to be in high-track classes (Lucas and Berends 1997; Mickelson 2001; Oakes and Guiton 1995). This work shows that race and ethnicity was significant for predicting track placement over and above measured achievement: Black and Latino students were more likely to be placed in lower tracks than their similarly scoring Asian American and white peers. Ethnographic work echoes these studies, raising a number of questions about how ability group placements are made (Lewis 2003; Rist 1970).

Research has consistently found that different tracks teach different material and use different techniques (Ansalone 2006, 2003; Oakes 2005; Wheelock 1992). Low-track classes tend to offer a more watered-down curriculum; less effective and challenging pedagogy; more focus on basic skills; fewer experienced teachers, who are more often uncertified in the specific area or have less preparation; and generally fewer opportunities to learn. Using national data, Condron (2007, 2008) found differential placement in high reading groups by race, socioeconomic status, gender, and family structure. He found that 70–75 percent of first graders nationally are sorted into ability groups for reading instruction and that placement is based on academic, social, *and* behavioral skills. Compared to ungrouped students, high-group students learn more and low-group students learn less. Grouping thus exacerbates preexisting inequalities (Condron 2007, 2008). As Sorenson and Hallinan (1986: 519) put it:

> Grouping is not neutral with respect to inequality of educational opportunity. ... Since less material is also taught in grouped classes, and since Black students in this sample tend to be in grouped classes more often than whites, race differences are increased by grouping according to ability. Finally, grouping appears to increase inequality of educational outcomes. Students assigned to high groups are taught more than students in low groups.

Tracking leads to different expectations for achievement, different access to content and subject matter, different opportunities to learn, different teaching quality, and different educational resources; the result is that low-track students fall behind. Unsurprisingly, then, the achievement gap between students placed in high and low tracks grows over time (no matter where students begin in terms of their test scores). Those placed in low tracks learn less and show fewer gains over time than similarly situated high-track students. High-track students benefit from the enhanced curriculum and special resources and supports. Everyone, regardless of prior achievement, benefits from being placed in high-track groups because of the enhanced educational experience there provided.

While research shows benefits to high-achieving students being in tracked classes, no studies show benefits to those placed in low tracks. In addition, there is plenty of evidence that students placed in low tracks lose out considerably both academically and nonacademically (for example, costs to self-concept, academic identity). Moreover, while there is good evidence that tracking negatively effects learning outcomes for many, there is not much evidence that heterogeneous or nontracked instruction is bad for anyone. A recent series of international studies in fact shows benefits of heterogeneous grouping over grouped instruction (Boaler 1997; Hanushek and Wößmann 2006; Linchevski and Kutscher 1998). Why then does tracking remain pervasive despite clear evidence that it exacerbates educational inequality? Clearly, as Ansalone (2006: 1) noted, "the idea of tracking is deeply imbedded in cultural assumptions about the nature and meaning of intelligence, ability and equity" and tied to specifically racialized ideas about intelligence (Diamond et al. 2004; Fordham 1996; Oakes 2005; Perry et al. 2004). These kinds of racialized ideas about intelligence—a legacy of scientific racism—remain pervasive, even if rarely explicitly articulated. Such racial ideologies help "make sense" of the otherwise unjustifiable demographic reality of many schools today, in which Black and Latino students attending the same schools as white students remain internally segregated, in separate classes.

RACIAL INEQUALITIES IN SPECIAL EDUCATION

Similar to the sorting of students that happens in ability grouping are processes of labeling students for special education. Across all states and categories of disability, African American students (when compared to other racial/ethnic groups) are more likely to be labeled with a disability (Harry and Klinger 2006; Skiba et al. 2008). Black students are more likely to be overrepresented in "soft" disability categories such as mental retardation, emotional disturbance, and learning disability rather than "hard" categories such as hearing or visual impairment (Harry and Klinger 2006; Losen and Orfield 2002; Skiba et al. 2008). African Americans with disabilities are also more likely than their peers with the same disability (in four out of five disability categories) to be overrepresented in restrictive educational settings and underrepresented in general settings (Fierros and Conroy 2002; Losen and Orfield 2002; Skiba et al. 2008).

The fact that minority students, and particularly African American students, have a higher rate of receiving special education designations that depend on clinical judgment rather than biological data (Harry and Klinger 2006; Skiba et al. 2008) has led to a continuous examination into the reasons underlying their disproportionate placement (based on race). Despite the fact that federal law requires students to be placed in the least restrictive environment, minority students in special education are typically placed in more restrictive classrooms that take them away from mainstream curricula as well as their nondisabled peers (Perez, Skiba, and Chung 2008). Placement in special education and in restrictive classroom environments remains of high concern precisely because special education leaves so much to be desired (in most incarnations it remains far from "special"). For many, placement in special education results in poor academic achievement (Fierros and Conroy 2002; Gottlieb, Alter, Gottlieb, and Wishner 1994; Perez et al. 2008).

Contrary to the overrepresentation of African American students in special education programs, Latino students have largely been underrepresented in those programs (Skiba et al. 2008), particularly in regions such as the Midwest and Southeast (Perez et al. 2008). However, similar to African American students, Latino students who receive a special education designation are more often placed in restrictive classroom settings than other students with disabilities (Perez et al. 2008). The underrepresentation of Latino students in special education, particularly when compared with other students of color, may partially be explained by the fact that many Latino students are English language learners. That is, it may be difficult to identify whether a student is having trouble because of a learning disability or struggling to learn a new language. It is also possible that the criteria staff use to initially identify students as well as the tools they then use to assess students for special education are limited when attempting to assess students who are learning a new language (Barrera 1979; Perez et al. 2008). Finally, Latino students may be underrepresented in special education since in an attempt to take language acquisition seriously, school personnel only consider Latino students for special education after services offered for English language acquisition have been exhausted (Perez et al. 2008).

Accounting for the overrepresentation of African Americans in certain special education designations, however, proves more challenging. Researchers have documented a variety of mechanisms that may be able to account for racial disparities in special education placement. For example, research demonstrates that disability categories are ambiguous and that their use has changed over time (and across states) in some ways because of differential levels of stigmatization for certain disabilities (Harry and Klinger 2006).[2] While most of the literature has argued against cultural bias in standardized testing, there is some evidence of bias (for example, item bias, examiner bias) that may account for overrepresentation of minorities in special education (Losen and Orfield 2002; Skiba et al. 2008). The examination of sociodemographic factors linked to poverty (for example, neighborhood and housing stability, home environment, family health care, geographic location) have also been important in explaining racial disparities within special education (Skiba et al. 2008).

Minority students also get referred to special education for behavioral rather than academic reasons more often than white students (Gottlieb, Gottlieb, and Trongone 1991). Teachers are more likely to refer African American students to special education because they are "difficult" (Bahr and Fuchs 1991) or for "behavioral" reasons (Gottlieb et al. 1991; MacMillan, Gresham, Lopez, and Bocian 1996). Similarly, research has suggested that overrepresentation of African Americans in special education may result from bias in the referral process on the part of teachers who may mistake cultural differences for cognitive or behavioral disabilities (Harry and Klinger 2006; Losen and Orfield 2002; Skiba et al. 2008). The cultural gulf that exists between mainstream educational culture and "cultural orientations of communities of color" (Skiba et al. 2008: 277) often leads to clashes between teachers and students and consequently to disproportionate referrals to special education. The educational system "reflects the knowledge, values, interests, and cultural orientations of white, middle-class, cultural groups" (Delpit 1995; King 2005; Skiba et al. 2008) and thus poses particular challenges for students and teachers who do not share similar cultural starting points. While seemingly race-neutral, the processes used to assign disabilities to students are infused with race (and racism), thus resulting in the unequal placement of students of color into programs that too often only serve to further disadvantage them.

RACIAL DISPARITIES IN SCHOOL DISCIPLINE

Related to the processes that lead to disparities in minority referral to special education are processes involved in dramatic differentials in school disciplinary rates (Ayers, Dohrn, and Ayers 2001; Ferguson 2000; Johnson, Boyden, and Pittz 2001). Linked at least figuratively to the criminalization of minority communities generally, students of color are being increasingly targeted for punishment and excluded from school.

Research on school discipline shows consistent disproportionality in the amount of discipline students receive but also in the processes whereby discipline is meted out. Scholars have noted inequities across lines of race, socioeconomic status, and gender such that students of low socioeconomic status, boys, and students of color—particularly African American students—are overrepresented in school suspensions and other disciplinary consequences (Ferguson 2000; Skiba, Michael, Nardo, and Peterson 2002). While whites make up 61 percent of students enrolled in public schools nationally, they compose only 15 percent of suspensions. Conversely, African Americans and Hispanics, who compose 17 and 16 percent of those enrolled in public schools, respectively, make up 35 and 20 percent of suspensions (Reyes 2006). Recent research in the San Diego city school district found that students of color are dramatically overrepresented in suspensions and expulsions compared to white students. In the academic year 2000–2001, African American and Latino students composed 53 percent of the district's total enrollment but approximately 70 percent of all suspensions and expulsions (Skiba and Leone 2002). Qualitative research in individual schools and communities has found similar patterns (Ferguson 2000; Lewis 2003; Morris 2005).

Research has documented the existence of racial disproportionality in both the number of students from different racial groups who receive disciplinary consequences and the severity of that discipline; students of color not only are disciplined more frequently than their white counterparts but are punished more severely as well (Reyes 2006). For example, Black boys are many times more likely than white females to receive severe punishment (for example, corporal) for disciplinary infractions (Skiba et al. 2002). At the state level, data for Texas highlight that while minorities are overrepresented in all discipline categories, disparities between white students and students of color are most pronounced in the subjective and severe discipline categories, such as out-of-school suspensions and expulsions (Reyes 2006).

In recent years some of these patterns have been exacerbated with the implementation of zero-tolerance policies across districts nationally (Ayers, Dohrn, and Ayers 2001). Generally these policies have been found to be unequally applied to at-risk, low-income, and minority students—further exacerbating existing disparities in discipline. The unequal distribution of zero-tolerance policies that disproportionately affect students of color has profound implications for their future learning opportunities; thus students face further disenfranchisement in an educational system that already puts them at risk. Suspensions and expulsions take students out of the classroom, away from their peers, and perhaps most importantly, disengage them from instruction and assignments, which results in a decrease in their overall academic achievement (Reyes 2006). The negative consequences for minority students paying a higher price for disciplinary infractions—mostly in the form of out-of-school suspensions and expulsions—not only lead to lower academic achievement but also contribute to higher drop-out rates for these students of color (Reyes 2006). In short, the subjective nature of disciplinary practices leads to the unequal application of zero-tolerance policies that in turn affect students of color at levels disproportionate to their enrollment (Reyes 2006).

While on the surface zero-tolerance policies appear race-neutral, the reality is that students of color, at-risk students, and low-income students are affected, not because they misbehave more often than white students but because zero-tolerance policies open the door for discretionary and subjective teacher referral. Research has demonstrated that greater disparities exist among subjective discretionary removals (such as dress code violations, classroom disruption) than among objective mandatory removals (drug or weapons possession) (Reyes 2006). Subjective interpretations of (mis)behavior by students of color also allow for cultural differences in communication and presentation to result in discriminatory applications of zero-tolerance policies (Ferguson 2000).

CONCLUSION

In this chapter we have outlined just some of the many different ways race shapes educational opportunities and experiences, including where children go to school, what kinds of expectations staff have for students, how children are disciplined, which courses they enroll in, and how educational resources get divvied up. Historically, schools were deeply linked to larger efforts to control racial minorities by providing both less and lesser education. While explicit and formal efforts of this kind have since been outlawed, the countereffort to close what were for much of our history intentionally produced gaps in educational opportunities has been at best intermittent, sporadic, and uneven such that it is hard to name a time when the United States was ever providing all children with equal educational experiences. Today is clearly not such a time.

One of the largest remaining barriers to the transformation of educational institutions in the United States is the dominance of very limited notions of equality. Michael Apple (1988) has termed this the support of negative freedom, a freedom *from* inhibition in the free-market sense (what Bobo, Kluegel, and Smith [1997] call laissez-faire racism), rather than positive freedom, a freedom *of* access to the resources necessary for a dignified life. For example, unlike most industrialized nations, which fund schools nationally, schools in the United States have been historically funded at the local level, resulting in a great deal of disparities (Kozol 1991). As state lawsuits contesting this funding scheme have demonstrated, support for universal education has repeatedly come up against the even stronger force of parental desire for advantages for their own children (Hadderman 1999). As James Coleman (quoted in Kahlenberg 2001: 64) put it, "The history of education since the industrial revolution shows a continual struggle between two forces: the desire by members of society to have educational opportunity for all children, and the desire of each family to provide the best education it can afford for its own students." The second of these competing forces has been the historic winner in the United States. If we judge schools' success on whether they "reduce the dependence of a child's opportunities upon his social origins" (Coleman, from Kahlenberg 2001), then our school systems are failing miserably. As survey data have repeatedly shown, this situation is not likely to change as long as we continue to support only abstract principles of racial equality without committing to the implementation of such principles (Schuman, Steeh, Bobo, and Krysan 1997).

Obviously, there are individual teachers, schools, and school practices that provide good educational experiences to students of color (see, for example, Conchas 2006; Foster 1997; Ladson-Billings 1994). We can use such examples to learn how to help students succeed within a world that too often is not structured to help them do so. It is, of course, also true that many students of color manage to succeed despite the barriers; but these students are not the rule. It is their success that needs explaining, not the fact that so many other students are not living up to their own full potential.

Schools are not merely neutral institutions conveying education to all who show up. They are what Loïc Wacquant (2002: 54) has labeled "race-making institutions." As he elucidates, "they do not simply process an ethnoracial division that would somehow exist outside of and independently from them. Rather each *produces* (or co-produces) this division (anew) out of inherited demarcations and disparities of group power." Elsewhere, the first author has written about the role schools play in shaping children's racial understanding and identities (Lewis 2003). But schools do not merely produce racial subjects; they produce racial disparities in life outcomes.

School reforms alone will not be enough to address racially unequal school outcomes. If our goal is racial justice broadly, school reforms need to be undertaken in conjunction with larger struggles. As long as racial injustice persists, and as long as racial ideologies continue to justify these inequalities and suggest that disadvantaged groups are to blame for their failures, it is hard to imagine these kinds of progressive changes happening.

5 SEPARATE AND UNEQUAL

Big Government Conservatism and the Racial State

George Lipsitz

On June 28, 2007, the Supreme Court, overturning lower court decisions and ignoring decades of legal precedent, declared that modest school desegregation programs in Seattle and Louisville deprived white children and their parents of their Fourteenth Amendment rights to equal protection of the law. In a mendacious and mean-spirited opinion, the Court mobilized the full power of the federal government against local school boards seeking to ensure that rampant housing discrimination in their cities does not deny Black children access to high quality schools.

The Court's decision sounds the death knell for the desegregation paradigm that started with *Brown v. Board of Education* in 1954, and it reveals even more somber realities about the United States. In this country, the nation-state is a racial state. The privileges of whiteness are protected zealously in the legal system. One hundred and fifty years after the *Dred Scott* decision, Black people still have no rights that whites are obligated to respect.

The Court's findings in the *Parents Involved in Community Schools v. Seattle School District No. 1 et al.* cases clearly contradict the pledges made by Justice Roberts and Justice Alito during their confirmation hearings to uphold precedent and avoid legislating from the bench. The decision mocked the principles of federalism celebrated by conservative justices in previous desegregation decisions dating back to *San Antonio v. Rodriguez* in 1973 and *Milliken v. Bradley* in 1975, and articulated as recently as *Missouri v. Jenkins* in 1995. While claiming to uphold tradition and legal precedent, both the plurality opinion by Justices Roberts, Alito, Scalia, and Thomas and the concurring opinion by Justice Kennedy directly disavow explicit precedents in previous rulings by the Supreme Court about school desegregation in Charlotte, Columbus, Los Angeles, Denver, Fort Wayne, and Pontiac.

The plurality and concurring opinions follow what philosopher Charles Mills (1997: 18) calls an "epistemology of ignorance." The Court suffers less from an inability to know than from a firm determination not to know. In order to render this decision, the plurality and Justice Kennedy embrace a series of fictions as if they were facts. The plurality pretends that *Brown v. Board* addressed only the abstract question of whether school boards could recognize race in assigning students to schools. Yet the Warren Court ruled in 1954 that segregated schools deprived Black children of the right to an equal education because segregation composed part of a racial caste system rooted in slavery, and because the all-Black schools that resulted from segregation suffered from the stigma of inferiority even in the unlikely event that their facilities, curriculum, and teachers were equal to those in white schools. The Roberts Court rewrites this history to find the essence of *Brown* to rest in banning the use of racial identities as a consideration in assigning students to schools. It therefore holds that recognizing the race of a student in order to desegregate schools is the same thing as using race to keep schools segregated.

With this decision the Supreme Court that previously found it improper to intervene when local district officials routinely used patterns of residential segregation to draw attendance lines and to locate new schools in places that guaranteed whites privileged access to better education—this same Court now outlaws actions by educators trying to respond conscientiously to *Brown*'s mandates to end racial isolation and equalize educational opportunity. Closing their eyes to the history of *Brown* and the Fourteenth Amendment as measures designed to correct the injuries done to Black people by the legacy of slavery, the Court pretends that the Fourteenth Amendment and *Brown* justify protection of the hereditary privileges that whites derive from past and present racism, and puts the full power of the federal government behind that protection. As Justice Stevens notes in his concurring dissent from the plurality opinion in *Parents Involved*, it was racial injustice rather than racial recognition that motivated the plaintiffs in *Brown*. In all the years before the *Brown* decision, no white student ever came to the courts claiming to be stigmatized as inferior for having to attend all-white schools. The white plaintiffs in Seattle and Louisville were not relegated to schools widely known to be inferior. On the contrary, they sought to avoid sending their children to schools that they believed were plenty good for Blacks.

Moreover, as Justice Breyer argues in his dissent (joined by Stevens, Ginsburg, and Souter), the Supreme Court has held repeatedly that recognizing race is one of the few ways to desegregate schools successfully, a view clearly articulated in opinions by the Court in *Green v. New Kent County* in 1968 and *Swann v. Mecklenberg* in 1971. Speaking for a unanimous court in the *Swann* case, Chief Justice Warren Burger expressly gave school districts the right to desegregate by using a prescribed ratio of Black and white students. In *Bustop v. Board of Education of the City of Los Angeles* in 1978, Justice Rehnquist declared that local school boards had the right to adopt race-conscious measures to desegregate schools even where no violation of *Brown* had taken place. Yet this entire history is erased or distorted in the *Parents Involved* opinions.

Justice Thomas takes the revision and distortion of the history of *Brown* to an unprecedented level. He contends that "segregation" only refers to a setup where a school board operates a dual system in which one set of schools is assigned by law to whites and the other to Blacks. Thus, even if every Black student in a district attended all-Black, underfunded, underequipped, and educationally inferior schools and every white student attended all-white, well-funded, well-equipped, and educationally superior schools, there would be no segregation from Thomas's perspective. Yet it was precisely concerns about residential segregation, racial isolation, and racial inequality in schools that decided previous desegregation decisions in Denver, Columbus, Boston, and many other cities which never had the kinds of dual systems Thomas claims are a prerequisite for court action.

Despite its flagrant disregard for legal precedent, the Court's decision in *Parents Involved* does continue one tradition of Supreme Court jurisprudence about desegregation: it elevates the convenience and comfort of white people over the constitutional rights of Blacks. Thus when decisions by local school boards have benefited whites, the Supreme Court has been an ardent defender of local control. In school desegregation cases where nonwhite parents and children in San Antonio, Detroit, and Kansas City demonstrated that local school boards deprived minority children of equal educational opportunity, Supreme Court decisions went against them because the Court claimed that local control of public education was an overriding public good, a precious principle worthy of constitutional protection. Yet when confronted in the *Parents Involved* cases with local school boards in Louisville and Seattle and their actions to help minority children, the Court simply jettisons the principle of local control. Chief Justice Roberts's opinion goes so far as to claim that deference to local school boards "is fundamentally at odds with our equal protection jurisprudence" (2007: 37).

Deference to local control that benefited whites, however, has previously been held by the Court to be virtually sacrosanct. In the 1973 *San Antonio v. Rodriguez* case, Mexican American students and parents demonstrated that decisions by local school authorities relegated them to inferior schools. The Court did not dispute their assessment of unequal educational opportunity but held that education was not such an important commodity that the city and state had to provide Mexican Americans with a good one. As long as the city and state gave Mexican Americans any education at all, the Court ruled, they upheld their responsibilities. The San Antonio parents complained that state-drawn district lines and state-mandated reliance on the property tax left them isolated in a district with inadequate resources. The Court, in effect, told them to accept their second-class status, declaring that "any scheme of local taxation—indeed the very existence of identifiable local governmental units—requires the establishment of jurisdictional boundaries that are inevitably arbitrary" (Tribe 1978: 53–54). The Court's decision not only tolerated these "inevitably arbitrary constructions" in San Antonio, it endorsed them as the essence of democratic government. The majority opinion in that case held that local entities should determine how local tax monies are spent, celebrating the fact that "each locality is free to tailor local programs to local needs" in a system of pluralism that would enable "experimentation, innovation, and a healthy competition for educational excellence" (Breyer 2007: 48). San Antonio's "experiment" of depriving low-income Mexican American students of an equal education met with the approval of the Supreme Court. Yet efforts by Seattle and Louisville to make it possible for Black students to attend high-quality schools drew condemnation from the Court as a violation of the Fourteenth Amendment rights of white students, rather than as a worthy experiment enabled by our pluralist system.

The Court established additional precedents honoring local control in *Milliken v. Bradley I and II*, the 1974 and 1975 Detroit school desegregation cases. Lower courts had found that city, county, and state officials designed school district boundaries to provide white students with access to superior schools in the city and in suburban Detroit. Federal District Court judge Stephen A. Roth ruled that segregation in Detroit city schools stemmed from deliberate decisions to build new schools in the center of neighborhoods known to be largely white or largely Black and to permit white students to transfer out of majority Black schools while denying requests by Black students to transfer to majority white schools. Roth noted that the state of Michigan rather than the city of Detroit bore responsibility for these decisions because the Supreme Court of the state repeatedly ruled that education in Michigan "is not a matter of local concern but belongs to the state at large" (Irons 2004: 238).

Judge Roth found the city, its suburbs, and the state guilty of violating the Fourteenth Amendment rights of Black children. He ordered an interdistrict busing plan that encompassed the city and its suburbs as a remedy. Recognizing that nearly three hundred thousand children in the three-county area covered by his ruling already rode buses to school, he reasoned that riding the bus for purposes of desegregation should be no more onerous than riding the bus for purposes of segregation. Yet a public outcry against his decision attracted support from political leaders of both major parties, and eventually persuaded the Supreme Court to overturn Roth's decision (Irons 2004: 242–43).

The citizens who brought the initial suit to desegregate Detroit's schools included white parents who believed that their children were harmed by state actions that deprived them of an integrated education. Their concerns were dismissed by the Supreme Court, even though they and their Black allies had introduced extensive evidence persuading Judge Roth that private sector actions in real estate and home lending shaped the patterns of school segregation, and that these patterns led residents of Detroit to assume routinely that whites had a right to expect their children's schools to be better funded and better equipped than schools with a majority Black student body.

The Supreme Court overruled the Detroit desegregation plan by a 5–4 margin, invoking the sanctity of local control over schools as a guiding principle. "No single tradition in public education is more deeply rooted than local control over the operation of schools," the Court held, noting that "local autonomy has long been thought essential both to the maintenance of community concern and support for public schools and to quality of the educational process" (Breyer 2007: 48). Yet the very local control honored so effusively in *Milliken* was dismissed blithely in *Parents Involved*. This "tradition" of local control invoked in the Detroit case was invented for the occasion, saluted only because it offered an excuse for protecting white privilege. As Justice Thurgood Marshall argued in his dissenting opinion, existing school district boundaries covered by the *Milliken* case did not follow neighborhood or even municipal boundaries. The state of Michigan configured school districts so that the Detroit metropolitan area contained eighty-five different administrative units. Some suburbs contained as many as six different school districts. One school district covered five different cities. Seventeen districts extended across two counties, and two districts encompassed three counties. There was no tradition of local autonomy to uphold in Detroit. White privilege rather than local control accounted for the true reason for the Court overturning Judge Roth's ruling.

The majority opinion in *Milliken* contained another blatant fiction about housing segregation that subsequent decisions, including *Parents Involved*, have perpetuated. The court record in *Milliken* contained evidence of repeated and pervasive violations of state and federal fair housing laws, a pattern of law-breaking responsible for the existence of largely Black cities and largely white suburbs. Yet Justice Potter Stewart's majority opinion ignored this extensive body of evidence, contending that segregation in Detroit and its suburbs stemmed from "unknown or unknowable causes" (Patterson 2001: 178–81).

By banning interdistrict busing, however, the *Milliken* decision itself became one more in a long list of completely known and knowable causes of segregation. The decision solidified the economic advantages of housing segregation for whites. As Jamin Raskin notes, cogently, the decision told whites that it made sense to move to segregated suburbs. It gave "judicial impetus and imprimatur to white flight" (Raskin 2003: 160). *Milliken* rewarded those whites who resisted integration and punished those who supported it. The majority opinion provided rewards for racism and massive subsidies for segregation, granting suburbs that excluded Blacks from residence immunity from school desegregation. It told white parents that the way to secure an optimal education for their children—and in the process deny it to children of color—was to move away from areas where Blacks resided.

Protecting whites from the possibility of unfavorable competition with minorities guided the Court in *Parents Involved*. The guardian of kindergarten student Joshua McDonald sued the Louisville school board because the board had rejected McDonald's application to transfer to a school of his choice. In fact, McDonald missed the transfer request deadline because he had moved into the district after the application had to be submitted. The school board interpreted his application as an attempt to transfer the next year when he would have been in the first grade. They turned him down because the transfer he requested would have had an adverse impact on desegregation in the majority white school into which he wished to enroll. When the district realized that McDonald wished to transfer immediately, however, they granted his request. The Louisville board questioned whether McDonald had suffered an injury in this case worthy of Supreme Court review. He had asked for a transfer, and he had received it. The Court ruled, however, that getting into the school McDonald wanted to attend was not sufficient. The Court held that the racial integration system the school board used might *one day in the future* work to McDonald's disadvantage, for example, when he entered middle school or high school. Thus the "injury" in this case that justified the Court's overturning a successful program devised by a local board was the mere possibility that sometime in the future Joshua McDonald might be disadvantaged in competing for a slot in a majority white school. Yet the routine exclusion of Mexican and Black students from majority white schools in San Antonio, Detroit, Louisville, or Seattle raised no similar question of equal protection for the Court.

The Court's decision in *Parents Involved* offered no opinion on why white students are concentrated on the north side of Seattle or why Louisville was able to integrate successfully only by including the entire metropolitan area in one school district. To the plurality and Justice Kennedy, systematic residential segregation in Seattle and Louisville has no known or knowable causes. Yet the segregated neighborhoods of these cities are actually prima facie evidence of widespread defiance of the 1968 Fair Housing Act. Justice Thomas (2007: 3) proved especially creative in evading this fact in his concurring opinion in *Parents Involved*. Deploying the stupefying, insouciant malevolence that characterizes many of his writings, Thomas writes in his concurring opinion that while "presently observed racial imbalance might result from past *de jure* segregation, racial imbalance can also result from any number of innocent private decisions including voluntary housing choices."

Although the Burger Court recognized in the 1971 *Swann* case that segregated and unequal schools shape housing choices, most subsequent rulings have attempted to deny that link out of hand (Days 2001: 159–81). While holding the Denver school system responsible for policies that intentionally segregated Black and Latino students in the 1973 *Keyes* decision, for example, Justice Powell absolved the district of responsibility to remedy "geographical separation of the races" that "resulted from purely natural and neutral non-state causes." In a 1976 decision on segregation in Austin, Texas, Justice

Rehnquist likewise asserted (without proof) that "economic pressures and voluntary preferences are the primary determinants of residential patterns." He expanded on that theme in reviewing the Columbus, Ohio, case in 1977, claiming that residential segregation in the region resulted from a "mélange of past happenings prompted by economic considerations, private discrimination, discriminatory school assignments or a desire to reside near people of one's own race or ethnic background" (Days 2001: 175). Rehnquist mentions private discrimination and discriminatory school assignments only to dismiss them, to relegate them to less importance than the desire by whites to live in segregated neighborhoods, which apparently in his view is a constitutional right protected by law even though it violates the letter and spirit of the 1968 Fair Housing Act.

In attributing residential segregation to "natural," "neutral," "voluntary" desires, the Supreme Court has written into law the fictions advanced by guilty defendants in desegregation cases. Attorney James P. Gorton, who represented school districts in suburban St. Louis and Atlanta against desegregation orders, boasted to a reporter that he and his colleagues had established that "people live in specific school districts and urban areas based on job needs, personal preferences, and other factors—not because of race" (Wells and Crain 1997: 259). Yet an enormous body of unchallenged and uncontradicted evidence demonstrates the contrary. Researchers have found consistently that the racial composition of a neighborhood is more important to whites than housing quality, levels of crime, environmental amenities, and location (Taub, Taylor, and Dunham 1984; St. John and Bates 1990: 47–61). Even putatively nonracial considerations such as the reputation of local schools often contain perceptions about the racial identities of the student body (Shapiro 2004: 271).

In the early years of school desegregation cases, judges drew upon this overwhelming evidence to rule that residential segregation stemmed from a combination of private discriminatory acts, including mortgage redlining, real estate steering or blockbusting, and discriminatory public policies such as urban renewal programs that concentrated minorities in overcrowded neighborhoods by offering relocation housing only in those areas, by allocating Section 235 funds only to ghetto and barrio neighborhoods, and placement decisions about public housing projects, subsidized developments, and schools (Bryant 2001: 56–58). As late as 1987, a circuit court established a mutually constitutive relationship between housing and school segregation

in Yonkers, New York, fashioning a remedy that required integrated housing as well as integrated schools (Bryant 2001: 58). In St. Louis, the federal
courts ordered the state of Missouri to develop plans for encouraging integrated housing. Yet the Rehnquist Court, and now the Roberts Court, have
consistently massaged the facts in order to excuse and enable systematic discrimination in housing. According to this line of reasoning, the existence
of segregation in housing is attributed to nonracial causes. It argues that no
whites move away from municipalities to secure the benefits they gain from
neighborhoods and schools that are prohibited to Blacks. Existing segregation
is instead attributed to race-neutral causes, beyond the concern of the courts.

When it comes to school desegregation plans, however, the Court rejects
them because they might cause white flight—the very white flight they claim
does not exist and cannot account for segregated housing patterns. Maintaining that Blacks live in ghettos because they "choose" to live near other
members of their race, the Court views white flight as a tragedy provoked by
plans to desegregate schools. Whites are thus judged to be not currently race
conscious in their selection of neighborhoods and schools, but they might
become so, the Court complains, if faced with desegregation (Orfield 1996a:
96). Perhaps the most honest expression of the judiciary's evolving attitude
toward school desegregation came in the 1979 resolution of the *Armour v. Nix*
case. This litigation was filed by the American Civil Liberties Union on behalf of a group of impoverished Black women from Atlanta as a rival to the
successful *Calhoun* case, which was settled in private outside public scrutiny
through the legally questionable intervention of sitting circuit court judge and
later U.S. attorney general Griffin Bell. The plaintiffs proposed remedies far
more radical than the settlement reached in the *Calhoun* case. They assem-
bled an enormous compendium of evidence proving that repeated actions by
city, state, county, and federal governments concerning housing, transportation, and neighborhood development had led to permanent and seemingly
intractable residential segregation in the Atlanta area. Judge William O'Kelly
conceded that the region's residential segregation had been "caused in part
by the actions of government officials," acknowledging eighteen separate actions, including racial zoning laws, racially based selection of public housing
sites, racial designation of schools, and segregated relocation from neighborhoods cleared for urban renewal. Yet he ruled that because the schools had
not *caused* residential segregation, they should not be desegregated *because*
of it. Nor would O'Kelly consider systematic violations of fair housing laws

a proper matter for adjudication in the courts, declaring that "to change the residential patterns which exist it would be necessary to rip up the very fabric of society in a manner that is not within the province of the federal courts" (Orfield 1996b: 301).

O'Kelly's ruling at least had the virtue of a certain honesty. Apparently the injury done to Blacks in Atlanta was so systematic and so successful that remedy was now seen as beyond the power of the federal courts: to challenge the group position that whites secured from segregated housing would be to challenge the very fabric of society.

Judge O'Kelly found the proposed remedies in Atlanta too all-encompassing. In contrast, Chief Justice Roberts and the plurality of the Court in *Parents Involved* dismissed the Seattle and Louisville desegregation plans because they judged their impact to be too mild. After decades of being told that whites did not oppose desegregation but only reacted negatively to allegedly "harsh" remedies like busing, the Seattle and Louisville school boards created desegregation plans that minimized inconvenience to whites. The white plaintiffs in the Seattle case would have been affected personally by the desegregation plan for only one year, and then only if their children sought enrollment in a majority white high school that had too many applicants for the available spaces. Moreover, race was not the main factor in determining assignments but was instead a "tiebreaker" used to decide among equally qualified applicants. The district demonstrated that at most only fifty-two students would be affected in any given year by the plan. The Louisville plan had a similar minimal impact. Yet instead of the modesty of the programs counting in their favor, the Court held it against them. With so few students affected, the Court ruled that the gains from the program could only be small and that educational diversity could probably be achieved by means (which the Court failed to specify) other than through "odious" recognition of race.

The *Parents Involved* decision uses contradictory logic and language in explaining why school boards in Seattle and Louisville may not use race as a factor in making school assignments. In the Seattle case the plurality opinion notes that the district had never been found guilty of de jure school segregation and therefore could not be subject (even voluntarily) to remedies designed for districts covered directly by *Brown*. Yet the findings in this case by the Ninth Circuit Court reveal that Black parents in Seattle had long charged the school board with locating schools deliberately in neighborhoods where their population would consist only of members of one race and with allowing white students to transfer out of schools but making it nearly impossible for Blacks to do so. Yet because the school district settled with these parents (to avoid litigation where the system would likely have been found guilty of deliberate de jure discrimination), the Court rules that these charges have not been proven in court and therefore must be treated as if they do not exist. In contrast, in the Louisville case, the Court acknowledged that the district had been found guilty of deliberate de jure discrimination and as a result had implemented desegregation programs including plans like the one under review. Because these programs proved to be successful, however, the district court in 2000 declared Louisville schools to now be unitary and dissolved all desegregation orders. Although Louisville was no longer obligated to desegregate, the district continued to do so because it found integrated schools to be educationally and socially beneficial to the community as a whole. One study found that desegregation played an important role in reducing the Black-white achievement gap in the district. In declaring this to be illegal, however, the Court said not only that Louisville was no longer obligated to desegregate but that it was no longer *permitted* to desegregate in this way because the district court ruled in 2000 that the school district had corrected the harm done by its previous policies. Thus the Seattle school board could not desegregate because it had never been found guilty of deliberate segregation, while the Louisville school board could not desegregate because it had been found guilty of deliberate segregation and taken remedial action. It was no longer permitted to take the kinds of remedial action that had made it sufficiently integrated to no longer be covered by mandatory desegregation orders. Desegregation in this view is only a temporary punishment for whites, not a guarantee of constitutional rights for Blacks.

In both Seattle and Louisville, school boards had made concession after concession to white parents over the years. They had constantly refined their desegregation programs to minimize white inconvenience, to limit busing, and to use neighborhood location as an important factor in making school assignments. Rather than rewarding these school boards for their conciliatory efforts, the Supreme Court at each stage condoned, encouraged, and then supported white resistance, refusal, and renegotiation of previously agreed upon settlements. Consistent with the administrative and judicial policies of the racial state with respect to employment and housing discrimination, the Supreme Court has generally responded to school desegregation suits by exaggerating white injuries and treating antidiscrimination efforts as more-egregious civil rights violations than the acts of discrimination by whites that made these efforts necessary in the first place.

With shameful hyperbole, the plurality and Justice Kennedy equate the minor inconveniences faced by the white plaintiffs in the Seattle and Louisville cases with the injustices corrected by *Brown*. The Court compares the harm done to Linda Brown and her coplaintiffs in the 1954 *Brown* case to the linked fate of the white plaintiffs in *Parents Involved*. In Justice Thomas's words, "what was wrong in 1954 cannot be right today" (Thomas 2007: 33). What was wrong for Linda Brown and Black children all across the nation in 1954 was that a caste system dating back to government-supported slavery relegated them to inferior segregated schools, which stigmatized them as inferior people being trained to settle for unequal and unjust futures. The harm claimed by the white plaintiffs in Seattle was that a complicated chain of circumstances might possibly make some of them have to spend one year in a high school they might not have listed as either their first or second choice. As Ninth Circuit Court judge Alex Kozinski observed about the Seattle plan: "That a student is denied the school of his choice may be disappointing, but it carries no racial stigma and says nothing at all about that individual's aptitude or ability" (Breyer 2007: 35). The injury claimed by the plaintiffs in the Louisville case was that they might be denied admission to the precise educationally advantaged schools of their choosing, a complaint that pales in comparison to the obstacles facing not only Linda Brown in 1954, but Mexican American students in San Antonio in 1973, Black students in Detroit in 1975, and most Black students in Seattle and Louisville today.

The decision by the Court in *Parents Involved* exemplifies the Supreme Court's consistent support for the "3Rs," not "readin', (w)ritin', and 'rithmetic" but the pattern of resistance, refusal, and renegotiation that permeates state support for white supremacy in the United States (Lipsitz 2006: 24–47). Even the original *Brown* decision entailed an invitation for whites to break the law. Constitutional rights in the U.S. system are generally "personal and present"; their violation is a matter of the greatest importance, requiring immediate redress and remedy. The *Brown* decision, however, undermined its mandate for desegregation by specifying that corrective actions were to be taken with "all deliberate speed" rather than immediately. This left both the pace and the parameters of desegregation up to the comfort and convenience of those doing the discriminating (Patterson 2001: 113; Ogletree 2004: 25,

33, 44, 128, 143, 256, 294; Harris 1993: 1735). Thus, the Court's own ruling incited defiance and invited delay. As many commentators have observed, the Court's injunction to school districts to proceed "with all deliberate speed" produced much more deliberation than speed.

In *Brown*, the Court unanimously overturned *Plessy* as the law of the land. Yet as Derrick Bell reminds us, *Plessy* "is only fortuitously a legal precedent. In actuality, it is a judicial affirmation of an unwritten but no less clearly understood social compact that is older than the Constitution, was incorporated into that document, and has continually been affirmed" (Bell 2002, p. 185). That compact entails a possessive investment in whiteness and protections for the group position of whites in perpetuity, a systematic and structured advantage (Lipsitz 2006). In her brilliant analysis of whiteness as property, Cheryl I. Harris explains that both before and after the passage of comprehensive civil rights laws, the U.S. judiciary has honored this compact, recognizing "implicitly or explicitly, the settled expectations of whites built on the privileges and benefits produced by white supremacy" (Harris 1993: 1731).

Even though the Supreme Court disavowed *Plessy* in 1954, five decades of court-supported "getting around *Brown*" have produced a situation that is even worse. The wording of the *Brown* decision and its interpretation by subsequent judges has allowed school boards and state governments merely to declare nondiscriminatory intentions, but not undertake nondiscriminatory actions. Consequently, unlike the regime that prevailed under Plessy, school boards today can operate racially unequal schools without the costs of operating dual school systems. They can, and do, reserve superior educational settings and resources for white children. School boards now have federal permission to do what even *Plessy* could not countenance openly, namely, run schools that are both separate and unequal.

Because whites resisted *Brown*, the Supreme Court was forced to issue *Swann v. Mecklenberg*, which allowed busing as an instrument of desegregation. When white opposition to *Swann* took violent forms in Pontiac, Michigan, and Boston, Massachusetts, liberal and conservative white politicians took steps to limit desegregation, and the Supreme Court supported them by issuing *Milliken v. Bradley* banning interdistrict busing. The one concession made to Blacks in the Detroit decision came in the form of permissible educational enhancements for minority victims of exclusion. Yet the Court ruled in *Missouri v. Jenkins* in 1995 that these "sweeteners" could not be made so valuable that they made whites desire them, because then they would serve as an incentive for suburban whites to attend inner-city schools—which the Court held violated the ban on interdistrict busing enunciated in *Milliken*. When whites claimed that the busing remedy identified by *Swann* was offensive, the Supreme Court responded with *Milliken*. When schools in Kansas City, Seattle, and Louisville tried to follow the mandates of *Brown* and *Swann* without using the busing outlawed by *Milliken*, the Court punished them for it.

Missouri serves as microcosm of the half century of resistance, refusal, and renegotiation central to the racial state. City and state officials in Kansas City resisted desegregation and refused to implement *Brown*'s mandates for twenty-three years until they were successfully sued in 1977. They did not come up with a desegregation plan until the courts mandated one eight years later, in 1985. The plan was not implemented until 1988, a further three years of delay. Yet a mere seven years later, the Supreme Court ruled in *Missouri* that racial inequality in education in the Kansas City area no longer stemmed from segregation but from "voluntary" and "natural" decisions about where people live. The Court claimed, in all seriousness, that residential choices in Kansas City had nothing to do with the legacy of segregation, even though these purportedly innocent and independent decisions concentrated white people in affluent suburbs with well-funded schools while relegating Blacks to poverty-stricken inner-city neighborhoods where schools were literally falling apart (Morantz 1996: 241–63). As soon as the majority of the school population became Black in Kansas City, the white majority of the electorate failed to pass a single bond issue or tax levy to support the schools (Shaw 2001: 263). In her dissenting opinion in *Missouri*, Justice Ginsburg pointed out that the Court majority had decided that remedial programs had effectively countered in only seven years the legacy of discrimination that started in Kansas City with the proclamation of the Code Noir by King Louis XV of France in 1724, a legacy that included slavery, state laws prohibiting public education for Blacks, mandatory Jim Crow segregation, and thirty-four years of resistance to the *Brown* decision (Ginsburg 1995: 53).

Missouri also broke with stare decisis while purporting to uphold it. Conservatives on the Court from the Nixon years through the present have claimed that liberal judges legislate from the bench while conservatives respect judicial precedent by letting legally settled matters stay settled. But as cases like *Missouri* and *Parents Involved* demonstrate, the conservatives in fact throw out precedents in civil rights case routinely. As Justice Souter proved in his dissenting opinion in *Missouri*, the Court was so eager to end Kansas

City's seven-year-old desegregation program that it overruled "a unanimous constitutional precedent of twenty year standing, which was not even addressed in argument, was mentioned merely in passing by one of the parties, and discussed by another of them only in a misleading way." Souter concluded that "the Court's failure to provide adequate notice of the issue to be decided (or to limit the decision to issues on which *certiorari* was clearly granted) rules out any confidence that today's result is sound, either in fact or in law" (Souter 1995: 35).

Like the San Antonio and Detroit desegregation decisions, the Supreme Court's ruling purported to support the principle of local school board autonomy. The majority declared that returning the Kansas City schools to local control was the issue of overriding importance in the case. Yet local authorities had been forced to surrender that control only because federal courts found them in criminal noncompliance with constitutional law. The Rehnquist Court argued for the necessity of reining in federal power and respecting traditions of local governance when it terminated the Kansas City school desegregation plan. The Court took the opposite position, however, when it freely deployed federal power to overturn the minority set-aside program for city contracts approved by the Richmond, Virginia, city council in the *Croson* case; and to void the North Carolina legislature's decision to create a congressional district with a slight majority of Black residents in *Shaw v. Reno*. The principle of local control that purportedly loomed large for the Court in *Missouri* disappeared in *Croson*, in *Shaw*, and in *Parents Involved*.

In *Shaw*, Justice O'Connor argued that the creation of one of the most integrated congressional districts in the nation by the North Carolina legislature was a form of racial apartheid that directly contradicted the constitutional obligation to meld different groups together into a unified totality. Yet O'Connor did not object to legislative districts drawn to ensure the election of white candidates in all-white districts made possible by residential racial segregation, or to the hypersegregation of Black and Latino students in underfunded ghetto schools.

The Rehnquist Court ruled in *Shaw* and *Miller v. Johnson* that whites are protected by the Fourteenth Amendment from dwelling in districts with irregular boundaries that have African American or Latino majorities. The Court recognizes no parallel right of African Americans and Latinos to be free from living in districts with irregular boundaries and white majorities (Raskin 2003: 3, 167; Morantz 1996: 241–63; Carter 1993: 86, 88). Justice

Thomas supported the dismantling of the majority Black congressional district in North Carolina because of the "stigma" that would purportedly attach to the district, but he argued in *Missouri* that majority Black schools in impoverished areas are a good thing—so good, he claimed, that the lower courts who tried to desegregate the Kansas City schools must have acted out of the belief that Blacks are inferior. Thus a majority Black congressional district offends the equal protection rights of whites, but a majority Black school population in an underfunded and underequipped school passes constitutional muster. Educators who want to desegregate education in Kansas City become portrayed by a Black Supreme Court Justice as white supremacists who believe in Black inferiority.

Over the years the Rehnquist Court fashioned a narrative about itself as a defender of federalism, a respecter of local government, and a counterweight to unwarranted judicial activism by liberal judges. Yet its fidelity to federalism (a word that does not appear anywhere in the Constitution) did not manifest itself in civil rights cases. That Court did not mind intervening in local matters when white firefighters protested against a court-approved affirmative action hiring program in Birmingham, Alabama, in *Martin v. Wilks*, or when white teachers litigated against a voluntary collective bargaining agreement between the teachers' union and the school board in Jackson, Michigan, in the *Wygant* case. The Michigan agreement protected recently hired Black teachers from budget-related layoffs because seniority-based firings would have unfairly harmed minority teachers, who had less seniority only because of the district's history of discriminatory hiring (Lipsitz 2006: 44). The plan overruled by the Court in the *Wygant* case would have protected more white jobs than random layoffs would have, but the Court intervened to protect the seniority white teachers had accrued through an openly discriminatory hiring process, in effect enabling them to hold on to the benefits of past illegal discrimination as a constitutional right.

The Rehnquist Court displayed a double standard in defense of white privilege when it came to questions of legal standing as well. In the 1984 *Allen v. Wright* case, the Supreme Court decided against Black parents who had sued to force the Internal Revenue Service to follow its obligation to enforce the law by withdrawing tax exemptions from private schools having racially discriminatory policies. Speaking for the majority, Justice O'Connor ruled that citizens do not have the right to require the government to obey the law. She claimed that the plaintiffs were not personally harmed by the actions they protested simply because they were Black. She contended that to have standing to sue in the courts, the plaintiffs would have to prove that they suffered a concrete personal injury, not just an "abstract stigmatic injury" (Raskin 2003: 14). Yet in *Shaw* O'Connor ruled that white plaintiffs had the right to have the North Carolina congressional district boundaries redrawn because living in a majority Black district "reinforces racial stereotypes and threatens to undermine our system of representative democracy by signaling to elected officials that they represent a particular racial group rather than their constituency as a whole" (Kousser 1999: 242). Thus whites suffered a personal injury and stigma by living in a majority Black congressional district, but Blacks suffered no corresponding stigma or injury when the federal government improperly granted tax exemptions to private schools when they violated the law by discriminating against Blacks. The question of standing was handled in a far different way, however, in the Court's disgraceful ruling in *Bush v. Gore.* In that case, the Court did not ask how Texas resident George W. Bush had standing to contest alleged denials of equal protection to an unidentified group of Florida voters. Justice Scalia and Justice Thomas joined the majority opinion, upholding Bush's claims without recusing themselves, even though one of the law firms representing Bush employed Scalia's son, and though Justice Thomas's wife had been charged by her employer, the Heritage Foundation, to begin collecting curricula vitae to advise the incoming Bush administration on potential appointees (Raskin 2003: 14, 27).

Thus while defying crucial precedents embedded in civil rights law, the Supreme Court's decision in *Parents Involved* does adhere to a well-established pattern. Following the lead of the Rehnquist Court, the Roberts Court breaks with stare decisis precedents freely, choosing to support or oppose local control on the basis of whether whites benefit from it. The Court systematically uses laws and rulings intended to end segregation in order to preserve it. In his deciding opinion, Chief Justice Roberts dismisses evidence about these previous decisions that contradicts his claims, calling them mere "dicta." Yet Judge Thomas's concurring opinion uses exactly such "dicta"—in this case two less than memorable quotes from himself from the *Adarand* and *Grutter* cases— to assert as legal "precedent" an approach that no court has yet followed and which even Justice Kennedy refused to endorse.

The *Parents Involved* decision has its roots in some of the weaknesses written into the original *Brown v. Board* decision. But the decision also inherits the pernicious tradition dating back to the nineteenth century of transforming the antisubjugation intentions of the Fourteenth Amendment into anti–racial recognition principles. This transformation makes meaningful enforcement of civil rights laws impossible. Previous decisions arguing that local, state, and federal authorities did not have to remedy racist wrongs in civil rights cases unless the state committed them in the first place, have now evolved into a doctrine holding that local governments may not remedy problems they claim they did not cause, even if enormous amounts of evidence indicate that they actually did play a major role in causing them.

In the minds of the dominant bloc in the Court, the Fourteenth Amendment now only restrains the state from recognizing race. They dismiss private acts of racist discrimination as unfortunate but beyond the reach of the state. Yet no racial inequality in this country is not rooted at least in part in state action in support of white interests in the private sector. White property remains more valuable than Black humanity in this society because the racial state has unfailingly provided rewards for racism. For example, federal home mortgage loans made on an openly and expressly racially discriminatory basis built equity in the estates of more than thirty million white families between 1933 and 1978 (Jackson 1985: 216). Forty-six million white Americans can trace their family wealth to the Homestead Act of 1862. This bill allocated valuable acres of land for free to white families while excluding Blacks from participation (Shapiro 2004: 190). Tax codes today that allow homeowners to deduct mortgage interest make the profits of past and present discrimination even more valuable than before and "lock in" for whites living today the value of assets they inherit from previous generations whose discrimination in home sales, mortgage lending, and insurance was openly proclaimed. Cuts in inheritance taxes and capital gains taxes give special preferences to the white beneficiaries of past and present housing discrimination, while the deductions allowable for local property taxes produce massive federal subsidies for school taxes in largely white suburbs (Rothstein 2001: A-17).

The racial state supports and subsidizes white opposition to desegregation. State power prevents meaningful efforts to equalize opportunity while dismissing systemic discrimination in education, housing, and employment as private actions without public causes or consequences. The racial state stands behind whites as they preserve and augment advantages crafted by overt discrimination in the past and by only slightly less overt acts of exclusion in the present. When it comes to schooling, as Gary Orfield argues, the superiority of suburban schools is taken for granted as a right attendant to home ownership, while desegregation is viewed as a threat to a system that passes racial advantages from one generation to the next. In Orfield's words, "Whites tell pollsters that they believe that blacks are offered equal opportunities, but fiercely resist any efforts to make them send their children to the schools they insist are good enough for blacks." At the same time, "the people who oppose busing minority students to the suburbs also tend to oppose sending suburban dollars to city schools" (Orfield 1993: 245, 240).

The U.S. state is a racial state. The legal system zealously protects the privileges of whiteness. One hundred and fifty years after *Dred Scott*, Blacks have no rights that whites are bound to respect. The injuries of the racial state require race-conscious state remedies, but the racial state will not reform itself. Racial justice depends today, as it has always depended, on grass-roots action, on the kinds of confrontational, participatory politics that created Abolition Democracy in the wake of the Civil War and that mobilized the Black freedom movement in the middle of the last century. We need to find ways to promote enforcement of civil rights laws and to increase penalties and extract appropriate damages from those who violate them. We need to promote asset-building efforts in minority communities and pay for them by increasing taxes on those forms of income most directly connected to the rewards of past discrimination. Most importantly, we need to develop new strategies, raise new demands, and develop a new political culture based on realizing the unfulfilled promises of Fourteenth Amendment egalitarianism by creating new democratic practices and institutions.

At the federal level, Jamin Raskin proposes a constitutional amendment to undo the pernicious history of discrimination legalized by *San Antonio v. Rodriguez* and *Milliken v. Bradley*. He proposes that we make explicit the implicit equal protection promises of the Fourteenth Amendment by declaring that "All children in the United States have a right to receive an equal public education for democratic citizenship." This would outlaw vast differences in learning conditions between cities and suburbs, and prevent privileged neighborhoods from monopolizing educational resources and opportunities. At the state level, community groups have brought successful lawsuits in state courts in California, Texas, and New Jersey, demanding remedies for the formulas that funnel funds toward wealthy districts while denying equal resources and opportunities to the neediest students. While state legislatures and educational officials have consistently resisted the implementation of these court orders, in some cases they have nonetheless transferred millions of dollars of resources to needy students. At the municipal and county levels, fair housing groups have started to develop new strategies to combat rampant discrimination by mortgage lenders, real estate brokers, insurance agents, and landlords. Functionaries in the housing industry violate the 1968 Fair Housing Law as a matter of course because the penalties are so small and the profits derived from discrimination so large. The fair housing groups have started to pursue creative strategies to educate the public, city officials, and judges and persuade them to assess larger penalties based on concepts from other areas of law like the "lock in" model from antitrust litigation and cumulative risk assessment from environmental law. They have explored lawsuits aimed at holding mortgage lenders, insurers, and real estate brokers liable for damages to inner-city neighborhoods much in the way that tobacco manufacturers have been held liable for the profits they made from damaging public health.

These measures will surely face ferocious opposition from whites threatened by the actual prospect of the "level playing field" they frequently affirm exists already. These opponents would no doubt receive the full support of the present majority on the Supreme Court, a Court that with its decision in *Parents Involved* has made it clear that it will decide whether to support legal precedents, federalism, or counting by race on the basis of whether whites benefit from its decisions. Yet actions initiated all across the country by antiracist opponents of school segregation and housing discrimination today demonstrate a lasting constituency for justice, a constituency eagerly awaiting the right combination of education, agitation, legislation, and litigation.

6 NEOLIBERAL PATERNALISM

Race and the New Poverty Governance

Sanford F. Schram, Richard C. Fording, and Joe Soss

In the decade or so since federal welfare reform passed in 1996, poverty in the United States has largely vanished from public view. The political arguments that once castigated "the underclass" and "welfare dependency" have now largely fallen quiet. In their absence, however, no upsurge of public support for the poor has materialized (Soss and Schram 2007), and serious proposals to reduce poverty have continued to receive scant attention even during the recent "Great Recession" (Hacker 2004; Handler and Hasenfeld 2006). Thus on the surface, the turn of the twenty-first century appears to be a period of little moment in American poverty politics, an insignificant lull between historic developments. Yet if one delves deeper, beneath the veneer of public discussion and into the actual operations of state welfare policies, a very different story line comes into view.

In the United States today, we are witnessing the crystallization of a neo-liberal-paternalist approach to poverty governance that is transforming poor communities and rewriting the social contract for low-income Americans. The emerging approach resuscitates a variety of past practices used to regulate the social, economic, and political lives of the poor (Piven and Cloward 1993, 1998); yet, it is not just a return to old ways. Under contemporary poverty governance, older methods of social control are being linked to, and transformed by, more recent developments associated with neoliberal principles of organization and paternalist-custodial approaches to discipline. The result is a distinctive approach to poverty governance that can easily be mistaken for a clean break with the past or, inversely, as nothing more than a return to old form.

By speaking of changes in poverty *governance* (Bevir 2007), we intend to signal three important starting points for our analysis. First, even in periods when political attention is focused elsewhere, socially marginal populations cannot be safely ignored for long; they must be governed. Located in the twilight space between inclusion and exclusion, normalcy and deviance, compliance and disruption, the people and problems at society's margins must be monitored, managed, and controlled (Schram 2006).

Second, although these sorts of control functions are carried out by diverse actors and institutions (Cohen 1999; Piven 1981), we focus on the roles played by government policies and the organized practices that define their operation. Such practices extend beyond the state itself to the full array of nongovernmental actors who are integrated into policy processes (and therefore need to be governed) as collaborators in hybridized systems under the "new public management" (Salamon 2002; Kettl 2002, 2005). Third and finally, by governance we refer not only to managerial practices and the exercise of coercive authority but also to the ways that policy tools are used deliberately to transform human subjectivities—that is, to change individuals' understandings and desires so they will be more likely to *govern themselves* in ways that produce preferred behaviors (Dean 1999; Schram 2006).

Poverty governance in the United States today reflects both the resurgence of old practices of social control and the emergence of new governing technologies and organizational forms. On one side, a sharp turn toward more paternalist and custodial approaches to poverty has placed greater emphasis on directive, supervisory, and punitive policy tools. This shift is exemplified by changes in the American criminal justice system beginning in the 1970s that have produced an era of mass incarceration unprecedented in world history (Western 2006). In this same period, welfare programs for poor families became more restrictive and demanding, and eligibility for aid became conditional on compliance with behavior modification efforts and work-related requirements (Mead 2005; Schram 2006). This paternalist turn is in many respects a return to older forms of social control. But it also marks an important shift in how public policies are used to govern social marginality. Contemporary poverty governance expresses a loss of faith in the belief that market incentives, state supports, and social-group norms can be sufficient in moving the poor toward full societal incorporation. Governance today favors direct administrative oversight of the poor, official statements of behavioral standards, and enforcement of these standards through disciplinary actions and custody (Wacquant 2001; Mead 1997).

The paternalist turn has intersected with a second and equally important stream of development: the reorganization of governance along neoliberal lines. The neoliberal turn has been ushered in by a resurgence of market fundamentalism, emphasizing the superior efficiency and effectiveness of market forms and the primacy of market values and obligations (Somers and Block 2005). Yet as Wendy Brown (2003) has emphasized, neoliberalism in the current era of globalization should not be misconstrued as a return to laissez-faire doctrines that would constrain the state's tendency to impede the natural flourishing of markets. To the contrary, neoliberalism marks a shift in market fundamentalism toward two distinctive principles. Rather than having faith that markets will thrive if states merely get out of the way, neoliberalism holds that the state must actively engage the twin projects of building markets and promoting market-supporting behaviors. Likewise, rather than viewing the state and market as separate and opposed entities, neoliberalism seeks to use neoclassical understandings of markets as a model for transforming the state itself.

The first of these neoliberal principles, of course, dovetails neatly with the more hands-on, work-oriented behavioral stance favored by the renewed paternalism in welfare policy. The second principle, however, has more complex implications for how paternalist poverty governance gets organized and practiced. Over the past several decades, core state functions related to social welfare provision and criminal justice have been contracted out to private providers, devolved to lower jurisdictions, and restructured along competitive market lines (Smith 2002; Ogle 1999). Thus, under the new poverty governance, the state has not only become more directive and supervisory in the sense described by Mead (1997, 2005); it has also become more "hollow" in the sense described by Milward and Provan (2003), Jessop (1994), and others. The result is a distinctive mode of poverty governance that is, at once, more muscular in its normative enforcement and diffuse and diverse in its organization. It is a mode of governance that puts disciplinary practice at the center of a system defined by collaboration and competition, organizational variation, and performance-centered evaluation and accountability.

RACE AND NEOLIBERAL PATERNALISM

In principle, one can reasonably argue that there is no logical or necessary connection between neoliberal paternalism and race. The neoliberal project is fundamentally about making the operations of the state conform to market logics and priorities (Brown 2003). In this sense, it is neither an overtly racist ideological project, nor is its internal logic dependent on racial premises. Likewise, paternalism today does not, in principle, deploy race as an explicit criterion for the application of supervisory schemes, rewards and penalties, or behavior modification efforts (Mead 2005). Taken in the abstract, then, neoliberal paternalism may be thought of as a race-neutral ideology for the transformation of governance.

Yet in practice, neoliberal paternalism in American poverty governance has been deeply entwined with race. Indeed, it is hard to imagine how it could have been otherwise. Race in the United States remains a potent "principle of vision and division" in social and political life (Bourdieu 1990), and nowhere is this more the case than in the areas of poverty, welfare provision, and criminal justice. Racialized understandings of the poor were integral to the "conditions of possibility" that enabled the shift toward a neoliberal-paternalist system of poverty governance. The path to welfare reform in the 1990s was facilitated by a "politics of disgust" rooted in a steady parade of images portraying an undeserving, irresponsible minority underclass (Gilens 1999; Hancock 2004). By capitalizing on, reinforcing, and supplementing race- and class-based segregation in the United States, such images bolstered public tolerance for tough new governance approaches by making them seem irrelevant to "Americans who play by the rules"—that is, restricted to "others" whose deviance and irresponsibility called for tougher measures. Against this backdrop, it is hardly surprising that since 1996 the racial composition of welfare caseloads has been a strong predictor of state decisions to adopt more paternalist welfare rules (Soss, Schram, Vartanian, and O'Brien 2001) and to implement more neoliberal modes of governance such as state-to-local policy devolution (Soss, Fording, and Schram 2008).

So long as race remains integral to the operations of U.S. politics and markets, one should hardly be surprised to find that it shapes the practice of welfare provision (Piven 2003). Yet just as social control may operate in new ways under neoliberal paternalism, race too must be approached as a dynamic feature of poverty governance. During the first half of the twentieth century, welfare in the United States was implemented in a racist manner that emphasized decentralized social control (Piven and Cloward 1993; Lieberman 1998; Brown 1999). Yet the overt logics of domination and discrimination that shaped welfare provision in this earlier period provide an unreliable guide to racial dynamics in our current era of poverty governance. Under a system of "advanced marginalization" (Cohen 1999), racial minorities are increasingly incorporated into mainstream institutions and figure as important actors in the production of racialized social control. Racial classifications guide practice in ways that are subtle and implicit rather than overt (Mendelberg 2001), and racial minorities cannot be singled out as the exclusive targets of neoliberal-paternalist governance. Yet as race has changed as a feature of the social landscape, it has continued to function as a powerful determinant of poverty governance in the United States.

RACE AND NEOLIBERAL PATERNALISM IN THE SUNSHINE STATE

While the neoliberal and paternalist shifts in social welfare policy have been widely discussed, there is scant empirical evidence to demonstrate how their operations affect clients of various backgrounds. Welfare-to-work programs in the United States have adopted a more punitive approach to poverty governance, and have implemented a more decentralized and privatized system for carrying out this disciplinary agenda. Yet little is known about how these two developments intersect with race to influence the "who, where, and when" of penal practice. In what follows, we redress this deficiency by presenting empirical notes on the operation and consequences of the new poverty governance within a single state. To do so, we analyze field observations, interview transcripts, and administrative data regarding the use of sanctions in Florida's version of the Temporary Assistance for Needy Families (TANF) program: Welfare Transition. Like all state TANF programs, Welfare Transition offers poor families time-limited aid that is conditional on adult participants satisfying a variety of behavioral requirements. "Sanctions" are penalties that reduce or eliminate aid when a client fails to comply with such requirements. Sanctions constitute the primary disciplinary action available to TANF case managers as a tool for influencing client behavior and, if deemed necessary, imposing consequences for noncompliant behavior.

Florida makes an ideal case study. Among the American states, Florida has emerged as a leader in administering welfare-to-work for several reasons. First, Florida is a leader in making the punitive turn in poverty management; it relies heavily on sanctions to enforce participation in its welfare-to-work program. Second, it is a leader in relying on the hybridized forms of the "new public management." In particular, it features devolution to regional workforce boards, privatization via for-profit and nonprofit contractors for running the one-stop centers of the workforce system, and the use of performance measurement for ensuring that contractors meet program goals. Florida's innovator status is further cemented by its consistent receipt of federal bonus funds as a "high performance" state under welfare reform. For all these reasons, it has consistently been singled out in legislative deliberations as a model for other state reformers to follow (Austin 2003). Accordingly, we do not treat Florida as a typical case, representative of TANF operations in all states. Rather, we approach it as a "leading edge" case that allows us to view many of the key elements of neoliberal poverty governance in conjunction and in strong form. It serves, not as a microcosm of all TANF programs but rather as an analytically fruitful case for investigating and theorizing the new forms of poverty governance.

In the sections below, we present a number of major findings from our analysis of Welfare Transition administrative data for the years 2000–2005, supplementing where appropriate with findings from our field research in four of Florida's twenty-four workforce regions. Our findings underscore how the enduring factors of race, place, and their interaction are critical to the logic of the emerging forms of new poverty governance.

WELFARE DISCIPLINE: SANCTIONS AND THE NEW POLITICAL ECONOMY

Sanctions have been one of the most widely studied aspects of welfare reform over the past decade (Pavetti, Derr, and Hesketh 2003). This is due to the fact that within the TANF program, clients now confront stricter work requirements, narrower exemption criteria, an expanded menu of behaviors subject to sanction, and stronger penalties for noncompliance (Hasenfeld, Ghose, and Larson 2004). When sanctions are imposed, they can have profound consequences for the well-being of poor families, and in some states, they appear to have been used with enough frequency to play a role in caseload decline (Pavetti et al. 2003). Thus, researchers and policymakers have had good reasons to be concerned about the incidence, distribution, and consequences of sanctions (Goldberg and Schott 2000). The impact of sanctioning can be measured in a number of ways, all of which suggest that sanctioning has had significant effects on both the size and characteristics of the welfare caseload since welfare reform was enacted in 1996.[1]

Several studies have examined the characteristics of sanctioned families, using either surveys of TANF recipients or state administrative data. The findings converge on the conclusion that sanctioned clients tend to exhibit the characteristics of long-term welfare recipients (for a review, see Pavetti et al. 2003). Specifically, these studies find that the probability of being sanctioned is related to a client's race, marital status, age, family size, education level, and job experience (Born, Caudill, and Cordero 1999; Koralek 2000; Westra and Routely 2000; Mancuso and Lindler 2001; Kalil, Seefeldt, and Wang 2002; Keiser, Mueser, and Choi 2004; Hasenfeld et al. 2004; Wu, Cancian, Meyer, and Wallace 2006). Although the samples and research designs have varied across studies, African American clients have consistently been shown to be anywhere from 23 percent (Keiser et al. 2004) to 73 percent (Kalil et al. 2002) more likely to face a sanction than a white client, controlling for other individual-level factors. Explanations for why Blacks are more likely to be sanctioned have included the possibility that racial stereotypes contribute to thinking that Blacks are in need of more coercive and disciplinary approaches which will increase their motivation and change their behavior so that they will be more willing to leave welfare for paid employment (Schram 2006, chap. 4).

Despite this progress in analyzing sanctions, the literature has paid surprisingly little attention to the transformed decentralized implementation processes at the heart of welfare reform. Our case study fills this gap in the literature by examining the use of sanctions in a state that relies on them heavily for implementing welfare reform in the context of a highly decentralized and privatized system that integrates welfare-to-work services into the operations of regional workforce boards. Florida exemplifies how a more punitive approach to poverty management is being rolled out in racially disparate ways through a decentralized system of work enforcement that relies on contract agencies beholden to regional workforce boards.

THE CASE OF FLORIDA: PUNISHMENT PIONEER
IN THE NEW WORLD OF WELFARE-TO-WORK

Florida is a leader among states in creating a decentralized, privatized organizational structure for using the more coercive punitive approach of using sanctions to prod recipients to leave welfare for work (Botsko, Snyder, and Leos-Urbel 2001: 7). While sanctions are an old policy tool in the welfare system, they have received a new level of importance in the implementation of workfare. A sanction is defined as a reduction in benefits for failure to comply with program rules (most often work requirements). All states use sanctions now, some more than others. Florida makes extensive use of sanctions, which are applied to clients at very high rates compared to other states.

Florida is a leader not just in using sanctions but in decentralizing and privatizing welfare reform by integrating its welfare-to-work program into its system of twenty-four regional workforce boards (see Figure 6.1). The workforce boards report to a statewide public-private partnership known as

Workforce Florida, Incorporated, that oversees Florida's implementation of the Workforce Investment Act of 1998.[2] The regional workforce boards rely primarily on for-profit providers to run the local one-stop centers that administer the different jobs programs, including welfare-to-work. Further, Florida uses performance measurement for evaluating contract agencies, which in turn rely heavily on a state-of-the-art management information system to track clients and monitor their participation. Therefore, the Florida system features devolution to regional workforce districts, privatization that relies on for-profit, one-stop agencies for delivering the services, and performance measurement for holding contracted agencies accountable for realizing the goals associated with the various components of the workforce system, including moving recipients off welfare and into paid jobs.

There are additional reasons for suggesting that Florida is an ideal state to study the effects of sanctioning across different communities. Florida is one of the most racially diverse states in the country, with sizable Black and Hispanic populations. The state's welfare population displays even more diversity, as can be seen by an examination of recent caseload data. Between January 2000 and March 2004, 36.2 percent TANF adults were Black; 33.7 percent were white (non-Hispanic)' and 28.5 percent were Hispanic. In addition, Florida is a politically diverse state, a fact that is reflected in recent voting returns

Figure 6.1   Florida's Workforce Regions

in presidential elections. Over the last three presidential elections, the average Democratic share of the two-party vote across Florida's sixty-seven counties has been approximately 44 percent, with a healthy standard deviation of 9.2 percent. The most conservative counties have supported Republicans by a strong majority, with an average Republican vote share as high as 75 percent in some counties (for example, Okaloosa, Santa Rosa, Clay). The most liberal counties have likewise supported Democrats by a significant margin, with Broward and Gadsden counties leading the way (66% and 69% Democratic vote share, respectively). In combination with Florida's heavy emphasis on sanctioning and its decentralized approach to welfare reform, this variation in race and ideology across the state provides an ideal setting for a study of the joint effects of race and ideology on local sanction implementation.

Sanction Rates

After 1996, Florida adopted "some of the strictest time limits and work requirements in the nation" and broadened the pool of clients subject to sanctions by creating "few possibilities for exemptions" (Botsko et al. 2001: 4). The sanctions themselves also fall at the strong end of the continuum, resulting in an immediate, full-family loss of TANF benefits and a reduction of Food Stamp benefits to the fullest extent permitted by federal law (Botsko et al. 2001: 6).

The aggregate trends for sanctioning in Florida in recent years are presented in Figure 6.2. This figure suggests that the number of sanctions issued each month was relatively stable between 2000 and 2004. There are occasional fluctuations around a mean of about 3,200 sanctions per month. To provide some perspective, Figure 6.2 also displays the number of TANF exits that occurred for reasons unrelated to sanctions, or what may be called nonsanction exits. Since 2001, nonsanction exits remained stable at an average of approximately 5,800 exits each month. This therefore implies that from 2000 through early 2004, more than one third of all monthly TANF exits in Florida were due to sanctions.

Although Florida appears to rely heavily on sanctions as a policy tool, this conclusion ultimately rests on a comparison of sanction rates in Florida to sanction rates in other states. This comparison is complicated to carry out because of inconsistencies in the severity of sanction policies across states. That is, in states that impose some form of partial sanction, TANF case managers may be more willing than their counterparts in Florida to issue a sanction because the consequences for TANF clients are less severe. Still, evidence sug-

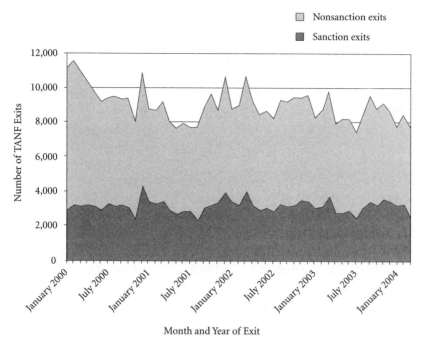

Figure 6.2 Total TANF Sanctions and Nonsanction Exits in Florida, January 2000–March 2004

gests that despite the severity of Florida's sanction policy (it is the strictest allowed by federal law), sanction rates in Florida are quite high in comparison to those in other states. The most commonly reported sanction statistic is the percentage of cases closed due to sanctions. As we noted above, over the period of our study, approximately one third of all case closings in Florida during the study period were due to sanctions. In contrast, comparable data reported by the federal government (for fiscal year 2002) show that only 7 percent of all case closings nationwide were due to sanctions (U.S. Department of Health and Human Services 2004).

Recognizing the fact that such statistics are in part a function of the number of nonsanction exits, Pavetti and associates (2004) recommend a purer measure of sanctioning that is based on the cumulative incidence of sanctioning for a panel of clients over a significant period of time. Using this method, Pavetti and associates (2004) measured the sanction rate in three states (Illinois, New Jersey, and South Carolina) that use immediate, full-family sanctions. For the cohort of adult TANF recipients who entered TANF in November 2001, after eighteen months, 13 percent of the New Jersey cohort and 17 percent of the Illinois cohort were sanctioned. In South Carolina, clients could only be observed for ten months; in this period, 5 percent of clients were ultimately sanctioned. We calculated comparable sanctioning rates in Florida by relying on the same panel method utilized by Pavetti and colleagues (2004). Based on the cohort of Florida's adult TANF recipients who entered TANF in November 2001, our calculations indicate that after ten months, 43 percent of the cohort were sanctioned at least once; after eighteen months, 47 percent were sanctioned. There is thus good reason to believe that Florida is among the leaders in the use of sanctions.

Second-Order Devolution

Florida is also a leader in moving to a highly decentralized system of "second-order devolution" (Gainsborough 2003). In "first-order devolution" the federal government decentralizes significant policy-making authority to states, and in "second-order devolution" states decentralize policy-making authority to substate decision-making bodies, such as counties or regional workforce boards. Florida is one of twenty states that have implemented second-order devolution, and it is one of six states that have implemented second-order devolution by integrating their welfare-to-work program into the array of work programs overseen by their regional workforce boards, which by virtue of their mission increases the focus on moving recipients as quickly as possible from welfare to work. Among these six states, Florida, Michigan, and Texas accord the regional boards substantial authority for deciding how to carry out policy.

Table 6.1 indicates a wide variation in sanctioning across Florida's twenty-four workforce regions. For the period from October 2001 to March 2004, the average monthly sanction rate statewide was 38.18 percent. Yet the twenty-four regions had widely different average monthly sanction rates for this time period. The lowest average monthly sanction rate was 25.47 percent for Region 6, while the highest was 51.97 percent for Region 17. It is possible that these differences are due to clients being more compliant in some regions than others. Yet, there is the distinct possibility that differences in the style of implementation, rooted in political differences across regions, may be a more important cause of the variation. In other words, second-order devolution, by encouraging the exercise of local discretion in implementation, may be creating opportunities for local political preferences to affect the way in which sanctioning policies are being interpreted and applied.

In spite of the focus by most researchers on the individual traits of clients, it may well be a serious oversight to ignore the effects of regional political differences on sanctioning rates. Under decentralization, local areas are given more opportunity to influence how welfare policies, including sanctioning, are administered. Local contract providers are likely to be influenced by local political culture in administering programs. This is especially likely to be the case where second-order devolution allows local governing bodies to have a

Table 6.1 Average Monthly Sanction Rates Across Twenty-Four Workforce Regions in Florida

Region Number	Name	Percentage
6	North Florida Workforce Development Board	25.47
5	Big Bend Jobs and Education Council, Inc.	30.31
12	Workforce Central Florida	32.76
23	Miami-Dade & Monroe County Jobs & Education Partnership	3.82
7	Florida Crown Workforce Development Board	33.83
9	Alachua, Bradford Workforce Development Board	33.95
2	Okaloosa-Walton Jobs & Education Partnership, Inc.	33.95
24	Southwest Florida Workforce Development Board	34.48
20	Workforce Development Board of the Treasure Coast	34.72
11	Workforce Development Board of Flagler and Volusia Counties, Inc.	37.12
21	Palm Beach County Workforce Development Board	37.33
	Statewide Average	38.18
18	Suncoast Workforce Development Board, Inc. 38.28	38.28
15	Hillsborough County Workforce Board	38.58
10	Citrus Levy Marion Workforce Development Board	38.61
3	Chipola Regional Workforce Planning Board	9.09
4	Gulf Coast Workforce Development Board	39.16
19	Heartland Workforce Investment Board, Inc.	41.08
14	Pinellas Workforce Development Board	41.43
8	First Coast Workforce Development, Inc.	41.67
13	Brevard Workforce Development Board, Inc.	43.48
1	Escarosa Regional Workforce Development Board, Inc.	44.40
22	Broward Workforce Development Board	45.09
16	Pasco-Hernando Jobs & Education Partnership Regional Board, Inc.	45.72
17	Polk County Workforce Development Board, Inc.	51.97

NOTE: The sanction rate is the average percentage of the caseload that is sanctioned each month during the period October 2001–March 2004.

role in establishing how policy will be implemented. Under these conditions, conservative regions are more likely to insist on strict compliance with sanctioning policy, and liberal regions might be more willing to allow case managers greater flexibility to grant exemptions for noncompliant clients who offer excuses for rule violations (for an extended discussion, see Fording, Soss, and Schram 2007a). Therefore, while we would still expect individual traits to affect the probability of clients being sanctioned, the impact of local political ideology, as well as other regional characteristics, should be examined as well.

To test for the possibility of regional effects in TANF sanctioning, we utilize data from Florida's TANF program, which not only includes information on the timing of sanctions for the entire TANF caseload but also includes variables measuring individual client characteristics and the characteristics of the locales in which clients reside. Using this data set, we conducted a series of event-history analyses of client records for TANF recipients in Florida who entered TANF from January 2001 through December 2002. These data are provided by the Florida Department of Children and Families. They are supplemented with data on regional/county political and socioeconomic characteristics. The sample consists of all new adult clients entering TANF during the twenty-four-month period from January 2001 through December 2002.[3] Thus, the entire period of analysis extends from January 2001 (when the first cohort enters) through November 2003 (the twelfth month of the spell for the last cohort). The dependent variable is dichotomous, taking on a value of 1 in the month that a client is sanctioned. Each client in each of the twenty-four cohorts is followed for a maximum of twelve consecutive months or until a sanction is imposed (whichever comes first). Clients who exit for reasons other than sanction, or who are not sanctioned by the twelfth month of the spell, are treated as right-censored.

For the purposes of this analysis, attention is restricted to each individual's first TANF spell during this period. A spell is defined as continuous months of TANF receipt. As a result of this definition and the elimination of a small percentage of cases for which data are missing, the total sample includes 60,045 individuals; this results in 169,438 person-month observations. For each of the variables in the model, the estimated hazard ratio is reported. This reflects the proportional change in the risk of sanction given a one-unit increase in the independent variable of interest.[4]

In order to test if the political environment of the local workforce region affected the sanction rate, we constructed a regional conservatism index based on local support for eighteen constitutional amendments that appeared on a statewide ballot over the period 1996–2004.[5] We also present results for a second model that relies on an alternative indicator of local political ideology—the average percentage of the vote that went to Republican candidates during the last three presidential elections within each workforce region.

The findings for the two models are presented in Table 6.2 and are basically identical. For both models, as we would expect, sanctions are significantly related to various client traits. Specifically, TANF sanctions are significantly more likely to be applied to the small number of men in the program, relative to the large majority of adult women in the program. The probability of being sanctioned is associated positively with the ages of the children and two-parent families and negatively associated with client age and human capital (as measured by wage income and education). These results are largely consistent with the findings of past studies (Born et al. 1999; Koralek 2000; Westra and Routely 2000; Mancuso and Lindler 2001; Hasenfeld et al. 2004; Kalil et al. 2002; Keiser et al. 2004; Wu et al. 2006).

Turning to the effects of race and ethnicity, we have a more complicated story. Model diagnostics determined that these effects vary in magnitude across the duration of the TANF spell.[6] Our models accordingly include multiplicative terms, which multiply the race or ethnicity of client and a simple counter variable (1–12) that represents the month of the TANF spell (for example, *Black × Month of Spell, Hispanic × Month of Spell*). Table 6.2 presents results for the third, sixth, and ninth month of spells. These results suggest that in the earliest months of a participation spell, white clients are significantly more likely to be sanctioned than Black or Hispanic clients. However, as the length of the spell grows, Black and Hispanic clients become more likely than their white counterparts to experience a sanction (however, in the case of Hispanic clients, the difference at the sixth and ninth month of the spell is not statistically significant). By the twelfth month of the spell, Black clients are predicted to be sanctioned at a rate that is approximately 31 percent higher than that for whites (depending on model specification). This interaction between race and ethnicity and month of spell is extremely robust and underscores the importance of employing a longitudinal design, such as event-history analysis, to study racial dynamics in TANF sanctioning.[7] This finding is also noteworthy since according to state officials, sanctions in the first month of a spell are often the result of clients dropping out of the program after registering, but not participating. These sanctions are in effect self-imposed.

Sanctions in subsequent months are initiated by caseworkers on clients who have been participating in the program.

Turning to the effects of regional characteristics, we see that consistent with our reasoning, clients in more conservative regions are at a statistically significant greater risk of being sanctioned in any month than clients in more liberal regions. Figure 6.3 enables us to observe the cumulative effect of local political ideology over the course of the entire TANF spell. Figure 6.3 plots cumulative survival rates for a typical TANF client across two contexts (the

Table 6.2 Cox Proportional Hazard Models of Effect of Individual and Community-Level Characteristics on Sanction Initiation

Independent Variables	Model I	Model II
Individual characteristics:		
Gender (male)	1.181**	1.180**
Age	.980**	.980**
Marital status (single parent)	.859**	.859**
Number of children (reference = zero to one):		
Two	.993	.993
Three or more	1.013	1.014
Age of youngest child (reference = 0–2 months):		
3 months–2 years	3.883**	3.884**
3–4 years	3.796**	3.797**
5–12 years	4.112**	4.112**
More than 12 years	4.433**	4.432**
Wage income	.986**	.986**
Education (reference = more than H.S.):		
Less than H.S.	1.448**	1.449**
H.S.	1.127**	1.128**
Race or ethnicity (reference = white, non-Hispanic):		
Black:		
Third month of TANF spell	.964	.964
Sixth month of TANF spell	1.125**	1.125**
Ninth month of TANF spell	1.313**	1.313**
Hispanic:		
Third month of TANF spell	.913**	.913**
Sixth month of TANF spell	1.033	1.033
Ninth month of TANF spell	1.169	1.169

most liberal workforce region, and the most conservative). For the purposes of this illustration, we define a "typical" TANF client as a thirty-one-year-old single white woman with one child (age 3–4 years), with twelve years of education, and an average level of wage income in the quarter preceding the current month. These estimates are based on the results presented in Table 6.2 (Model I). As can be seen in the figure, the survival curves indicate that in a conservative region the client's probability of surviving on welfare through the twelfth month of a TANF spell without a sanction is approximately .20.

Independent Variables	Model I	Model II
Political environment:		
Regional conservatism index	1.003**	---
Regional Republican vote share	---	1.006*
County Black population (%)	.995*	.994*
County Hispanic population (%)	.991**	.991**
Socioeconomic environment:		
Annual wage in food service and drinking places	.971	.962*
County unemployment rate $(t-1)$	1.008	1.012
County poverty rate	1.036**	1.031*
County population (in millions)	1.285**	1.280**
County TANF caseload $(t-1)$	.841**	.834**
Number of subjects	60,045	60,045
Number of failures	23,568	23,568
Time at risk (person-months)	169,438	169,438

NOTE: The sample for this analysis consists of all new clients who entered TANF from January 2001 through December 2002. All clients are observed for a maximum of twelve months (clients who exit without being sanctioned, or who were sanctioned after twelve months, are treated as censored). Cell entries are hazard ratios, and p values are based on robust standard errors (adjusted for error-clustering at the regional level). See first table in Appendix ("Variable Definitions, Sources, and Descriptive Statistics . . .") for detailed information on the variables.

$* p < .05; ** p < .01$

H.S. = high school education; TANF = Temporary Assistance for Needy Families. Variables are described in Fording, Soss, and Schram 2007a.

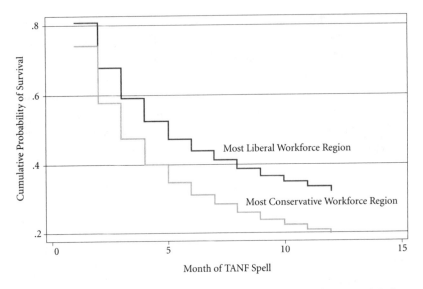

Figure 6.3 Estimated Cumulative Survival Function for a Typical TANF Adult, by Regional Political Ideology

In contrast, the probability that the same (hypothetical) client will survive through the twelfth month without a sanction in the most liberal region is approximately 60 percent larger at approximately .32. Of course, very few clients in Florida experience twelve-month TANF spells, but this simulation does provide additional perspective on the substantive effect of regional political ideology on sanctioning outcomes.

Thus far, our analysis finds that both race and place play an important role in determining local sanctioning rates. However, in addition to these effects, further analysis finds that the race/ethnicity of a TANF client and the local political ideology also interact to affect sanctioning. More specifically, we find that residing in a conservative as opposed to a liberal region increases the probability of being sanctioned much more for Black and Hispanic TANF clients than it does for whites. This interaction is reflected in Figure 6.4, which displays predicted hazard ratios comparing the relative risk of sanction for Black and Hispanic TANF clients (compared to white non-Hispanic clients) across alternative political environments. The vertical distance between the curves presented in each panel of Figure 6.4 reflects the effect of local ideology, and indicates precisely how the odds of being sanctioned are predicted to increase for Black and Hispanic clients as a function of local conservatism throughout the duration of the TANF spell.[8] In the most liberal political environment, both Black and Hispanic clients begin the spell with a significantly lower risk of being sanctioned than white non-Hispanic clients. For Hispanics, this disparity diminishes throughout the spell, and by the twelfth month Hispanic clients and white non-Hispanic clients are predicted to be sanctioned at an equal rate. The predicted hazard ratio increases more quickly for Black clients, and by the twelfth month of the spell Black clients are predicted to be sanctioned at a rate that is 37 percent higher than whites. Thus, in the most liberal environment, with the exception of months 8–12 for Black clients, Black and Hispanic clients are predicted to be sanctioned at a rate that is either less than or roughly equal to the rate for white non-Hispanic clients.

This is not the case in the most conservative political environment. Indeed, at no time during the TANF spell are Black or Hispanic clients in the most conservative environment predicted to be sanctioned at a rate that is lower than that of whites. For Hispanics the hazard ratio reaches a maximum of 1.44 by the twelfth month, and for Black clients the hazard ratio reaches 2.11 by

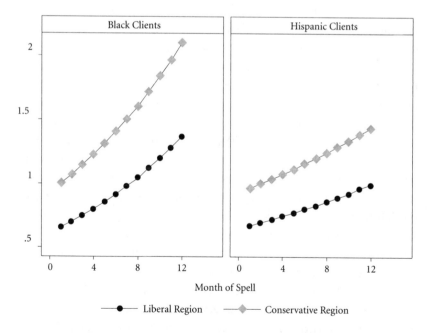

Figure 6.4. Predicted Odds of Being Sanctioned for Black and Hispanic TANF Clients (Compared to White Non-Hispanic Clients) by Political Environment

the twelfth month. This suggests that by the end of our observation window, the risk of being sanctioned for Hispanic and Black clients is predicted to be 44 percent and 110 percent greater than that for whites, respectively.[9] In sum, we find that both race and place matter in determining who gets sanctioned, and that the interaction of race and place matters even more. Blacks are more likely to be sanctioned, and clients in conservative regions are more likely to be sanctioned; but Blacks in conservative regions are by far the most likely to experience sanctioning.

Performance Measurement

We find that these racial disparities in sanctioning are intensified when we add performance measurement to the mix. Gilman (2001: 600–601) warns that performance measurement may create incentives for contract agencies to "resort to 'creaming' off those candidates most likely to succeed or 'churning' off low-skilled candidates by making the process so difficult to navigate that applicants give up." Yet, it might be an oversimplification to suggest that trying to eliminate "hard-to-serve" clients is the explanation for any relationship between sanctioning and performance measurement in a welfare-to-work program. Instead, the effect of performance measurement on sanctioning may be largely a result of trying to motivate clients to participate. The threat of a sanction is one of the few tools case managers have to motivate clients to participate as required. When that fails, the threat inexorably turns into a reality. Once a client is put on notice, a failure to comply has to be addressed. Further, this is more likely to happen in some regions and with some clients than others. Case managers may be more likely to feel obligated to complete the process in conservative regions than in liberal ones, especially with clients they are more likely to see as not cooperating. Nonwhites' lower human capital and higher unemployment rates might make them more likely to fall into the noncooperating category, irrespective of their personal effort. In sum, it is possible that the performance measurement system puts pressure on agencies and their case managers to threaten sanctioning as a way to improve their performance rankings, and that this leads to greater sanctioning in conservative regions in patterns that accentuate racial disparities.

To test this hypothesis we move back to the regional level, utilizing a panel data set that consists of monthly observations for each of Florida's twenty-four Workforce Board regions. This data set spans the period of October 2001 through March 2004 and therefore consists of thirty monthly observations for each region.[10] To estimate the policy response to performance measurement, we constructed a measure of regional performance that is based on the average (monthly) regional ranking (1–24) across the three key performance measures used by the state Workforce Board to monitor regional performance in Florida's welfare-to-work program, namely, the entered employment rate, the welfare return rate, and the entered wage rate. We utilized the regional ranking rather than the actual performance measures because performance incentives are largely based on a region's performance relative to other regions in the state.[11]

The primary dependent variable for our analyses is the regional sanction rate, which we define for each region and month as the percentage of the monthly caseload that received a sanction during that month. In addition to our measure of performance feedback described above, the independent variables for our analyses consist of a variety of characteristics of the adult caseload, including racial/ethnic composition, average age, the work participation rate, family structure, family size, TANF dependency, and the overall size of the monthly adult caseload. Detailed definitions for each of these variables, along with descriptive statistics, are presented in the first table of the Appendix to this chapter. Finally, for each of our analyses we include a full set of regional and monthly fixed effects. The inclusion of regional fixed effects controls for all time-invariant variables that vary across regions, thus providing further control for important differences in regional contexts that may affect client outcomes. The monthly fixed effects control for time-varying variables that do not vary across regions, such as state-level changes in policy that affect all regions.

Based on this model, Figure 6.5 summarizes the main effects of performance measurement rankings on the sanction rates for different groups. Negative performance feedback based on a decrease in regional rankings (and thus an increase in our independent variable measuring regional performance) is associated with significant increases in sanctioning for all regions, but increases in sanctioning are larger in conservative regions. In addition, the effects of performance feedback on sanctioning within conservative regions appear to be disproportionately large for Black clients and clients with less than a high school education. This is not the case among the liberal regions. To summarize, the pressure to compete for better performance rankings leads to higher use of sanctions, especially in conservative regions, and most significantly for Black and less educated clients, which is perhaps due to relatively lower levels of human capital.

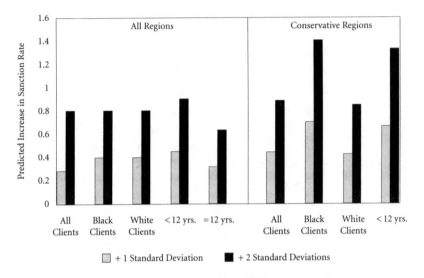

Figure 6.5 Predicted Effects of Performance Feedback on Regional Sanction Rates

NOTE: The bars in the figure represent the predicted increase in the regional sanction rate (the monthly percentage of clients sanctioned) given a one and two standard deviation increase in our measure of (negative) regional performance feedback.

Outcomes

Thus far we have summarized our findings concerning the determinants of sanctioning in the Florida TANF program. It is difficult to judge the implications of these regional and racial effects, however, without understanding the impact of sanctions on the lives of TANF clients. The punitive nature of sanctions in Florida's TANF program (immediate, full-family sanctions) might lead us to expect sanctioning to diminish the well-being of TANF clients and their families. This is especially likely if clients are unable to meet TANF requirements (and thus experience a sanction) because of circumstances that are largely beyond their control. By contrast, if clients are generally sanctioned for reasons that are within their control (lack of strong work ethic, and so on), then we might expect sanctions to teach them a valuable lesson, which in turn may result in greater success in the workforce. If this is the case, then the sanction experience may ultimately lead to an improvement in the well-being of TANF families. In recent years, a number of empirical studies have examined the impact of sanctions on client outcomes. These studies have largely examined sanction effects within a single state and have reached varying conclusions. However, the bulk of the evidence points to the conclusion that sanctioning tends to be applied to clients who are worse off, and ultimately exacerbates their condition (see Meyers, Harper, Klawitter, and Lindhorst [2006] for a review of this literature).

Using our data on TANF clients from Florida, we examine the impact of sanctioning on one important measure of client well-being—client earnings. To determine the impact of sanctions on earnings, we estimate a model of client income where the dependent variable is coded in a dichotomous fashion. Specifically, the dependent variable is coded as 1 for clients whose earnings during the observation quarter were equivalent to what one could earn in Florida by working at least thirty hours per week at minimum wage. The dependent variable is coded as 0 for clients whose earnings fell below this threshold. The sample consists of eight cohorts of (first-time) TANF clients who entered TANF at the beginning of a quarter (January, April, July, or October) and remained on TANF for exactly one quarter (three months) during 2001–2. We estimated the model using binary logit analysis, running separate logit models for the entire eight-cohort sample, for each of seven quarters (three quarters prior to entering TANF, one quarter during which the client received TANF, and three quarters after exiting TANF). The independent variables for each of these seven logit models were identical and included individual characteristics (race, education, marital status, citizenship, age, and gender) as well as selected contextual characteristics (county wage level and poverty rate). Finally, for each model we also included a dichotomous variable indicating whether a client exited TANF because of a sanction.[12]

The logic of the analysis is straightforward. For each of the seven models, the coefficient for the sanction variable indicates the "earnings gap" between sanctioned and nonsanctioned clients. By comparing this coefficient across the seven quarterly regressions, we can determine how this gap changes after the TANF experience. Estimating this model for the entire sample, we find that on exiting TANF, the clients' earnings gap increases, suggesting that clients who exited as a result of sanction were significantly less likely to earn an income level equivalent to full-time, minimum wage employment. This evidence is consistent with research suggesting that sanctioning leads to a decrease in client well-being.

However, much like our findings concerning the determinants of sanctioning, the effect of sanctioning is highly dependent on the region in which a client resides. Indeed, if we estimate our models separately for liberal and conservative regions (using the same measure of local political ideology described earlier), we find that the earnings gap is largest for clients residing in conservative workforce regions while less significant for clients residing in liberal regions. These regional disparities in earnings across sanctioned and nonsanctioned clients are clearly indicated in Figure 6.6. In the first panel, we see that in liberal regions sanctioned clients are no less likely to have reported full-time equivalent earnings prior to or after receiving welfare, compared

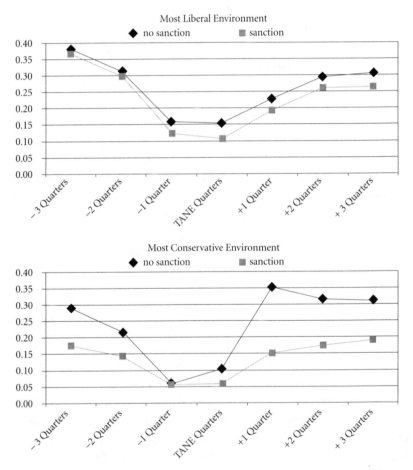

Figure 6.6 Probability of Full-Time Work After Leaving Welfare for Sanctioned and Nonsanctioned Clients, by Local Political Environment

NOTE: Dependent variable = 1 when wages for quarter ≥ $2048 (based on 30 hours per week, $5.25 per hour); = 0 otherwise. Independent variables are sanction status, other individual traits (race, education, marital status, citizenship, age, gender), and selected contextual characteristics (county wage level and poverty percentage). Logit regressions are cross-sectional, with separate regression for each quarter (three quarters prior to TANF quarter through three quarters after TANF quarter, for a total of seven regressions). From these regressions we get predicted probabilities for Y = 1 for sanctioned versus nonsanctioned clients (with other independent variables held at their mode or mean). Predicted probability of earning at least $2048 in a quarter, for typical client, by sanction status.

to nonsanctioned clients. The pattern changes in the second panel, as we see that in more conservative regions sanctioned clients have a significantly lower probability of reporting full-time earnings both prior to and especially after receiving welfare, compared to nonsanctioned clients. Thus, in conservative regions sanctioning is more often applied to the worse-off, and ultimately, sanctioning leaves them even further behind once they return to employment.

NEOLIBERAL-PATERNALIST POVERTY GOVERNANCE

Florida is widely heralded as an innovator in implementing welfare reform. More than most states, it relies heavily on sanctions to enforce participation in its welfare-to-work program. The Florida Welfare Transition program features key dimensions of the new public management: devolution, privatization, and performance measurement. It is a leader in using sanctions to push a more paternalist approach disciplining recipients to practice personal responsibility. Florida provides a leading-edge example for examining the new forms of neoliberal-paternalist poverty governance. By studying Florida, we can see that the welfare state is not being rolled back as much as a new, neoliberal system of poverty governance is being rolled out into communities in ways that facilitate the regimentation of subordinate populations into the emerging low-wage labor markets of a globalizing economy.

For some, neoliberal paternalism is associated with a rollback of the welfare state that then necessarily leads to the imposition of more disciplinary policies to contain the collateral damage associated with those cutbacks (Wacquant 2001). For others, neoliberal paternalism implies not so much that the welfare state is being rolled back as much as it is being rolled out into communities in a more disciplinary form (Peck 2002). The rollout actually extends the state, implicating diverse actors and agencies in new, more disciplinary forms of governance for regimenting subordinate populations into low-wage labor markets (Sassen 2006). It integrates public and private actors and agencies via systems that rely on key facets of the new public management: devolution, privatization, and performance measurement (Lobao 2007). Welfare-to-work provides a good example of a policy area where new forms of governance involve significant innovations in both organizational structures and policy tools (Cho, Kelleher, Wright, and Yackee 2005). Welfare-to-work programs can be provided largely via local, for-profit, contract agencies where performance pressures encourage the use of coercive policy tools such as sanctions that prod clients to move into paid employment as quickly as possible (Morgen 2001; Shaw, Goldrick-Rab, Mazzeo, and Jacobs 2006; Dias and Maynard-

Moody 2007). Florida provides a critical case study for examining how the neoliberal-paternalist regime is being rolled out across communities.

Our findings from Florida, however, go beyond the issues of neoliberal paternalism per se. They provide a much needed empirical foundation for understanding the significance of race in rolling out the new forms of neoliberal poverty governance. The rollout creates opportunities for different communities to treat different clients differently for purposes of enforcing the more disciplinary regime. A key question concerning the new forms of governance associated with welfare-to-work is whether these changes lead to different effects for clients of different racial and ethnic backgrounds. We know there are important historical reasons for thinking that variation in organizational structure and policy tools within a policy area such as social welfare will affect how clients with different racial identities are treated (see Lieberman 1998, 2005). Our analysis provides direct evidence of this effect for the contemporary period. The old effects of race, place, and their interaction are visible in the new neoliberal system of poverty governance.

The empirical findings we have presented highlight how the rollout of the new disciplinary welfare-to-work system creates opportunities for different regions to treat diverse clients in dissimilar ways. We find that race and place matter in affecting the probability of being sanctioned in Florida's transformed system of welfare-to-work. Blacks are more likely to be sanctioned compared to whites, especially in conservative workforce regions. These factors interact, and their effects are intensified by the organizational and managerial features of the new system. Blacks are more likely to be sanctioned compared to whites in conservative regions, but especially when those regions are behind in their performance rankings. The inequities are matched by a perversity in outcomes: sanctions tend to be applied to the financially vulnerable, thus making them ever more vulnerable to poverty. These empirical findings may not be definitive and could be subject to alternative interpretations; however, their consistency across a number of tests raises at a minimum, troubling questions about how the enduring influences of race, place, and their interaction continue to be at work in the new forms of poverty governance.

Whether the persistence of these influences today indicates a more generalized pattern is an important question. There is however reason to think it is part of a more systematic response to changes in the political economy. Our findings reflect a new decentralized system of punishment that disciplines subordinate populations for their failure to integrate into low-wage labor markets. Our findings point to troubling disparities associated with a new neoliberal-paternalist regime that is being rolled out in the current era of globalization. In Florida we find evidence that this system allows local communities to vary sanction practices in ways that have disparate racial effects and varying implications for client well-being. These issues need further attention, especially because our findings are from a "leading" state, which others are now increasingly being expected to emulate.

APPENDIX

Variable Definitions, Sources, and Descriptive Statistics for Analyses Presented in Table 6.2

Independent Variable	Definition	Mean	S.D.	Minimum-Maximum
Individual characteristics:				
Gender	0 = female, 1 = male	.119	.325	0–1
Age	Client age (in years)	30.926	8.706	18–72
Marital status	1 = single parent, 0=otherwise, based on number of adults in family	.811	.391	0–1
Number of children (ref. = 0–1):				
Two	1 = 2 children, 0 = otherwise	.303	.460	0–1
Three or more	1 = 3 or more children, 0 = otherwise	.256	.436	0–1
Age of youngest child (ref. = 0–2 months):				
3 months–2 years	1 = 3 months–2 years, 0 = otherwise	.365	.482	0–1
3–4 years	1 = 3–4 years, 0 = otherwise	.129	.335	0–1
5–12 years	1 = 5–12 years, 0 = otherwise	.276	.447	0–1
More than 12 years	1 = more than 12 years, 0 = otherwise	.126	.332	0–1
Wage income	Wage income, from previous quarter, in 1000s	.552	1.611	0–200
Education (ref. = more than 12 years):				
Less than H.S.	1= more than 12 years, 0 = otherwise	.458	.498	0–1
H.S.	1= 12 years, 0 = otherwise	.348	.476	0–1
Race or ethnicity (ref. = white, non-Hispanic):				
Black	1 = Black, 0 = otherwise	.425	.494	0–1
Hispanic	1 = Hispanic, 0 = otherwise	.176	.381	0–1

Political environment:

County conservatism index	See in this appendix, Construction of Index of County Political Ideology	.465	.220	0–1
County Black population (%)	Percentage of Blacks in county of client in 2000 (County and City Data Books 2003)	15.495	7.351	2.1–57.1
County Hispanic population (%)	Percentage of Hispanics in county of client in 2000 (County and City Data Books 2003)	17.593	18.634	1.5–57.3

Socioeconomic environment:

Annual wage in food service and drinking places	Average annual income in 1997 for employees in NAICS subsector 722, in 1000s (County and City Data Books 2003)	12.556	1.868	7.795–16.674
County unemployment rate ($t-1$)	Unemployment rate in county of client, measured each month (Florida Research and Economic Database)	5.286	1.625	1.7–19.7
County poverty rate	County poverty rate for all persons in 2000 (U.S. Census Bureau, Small Area Income and Poverty Estimates)	12.545	3.289	6.9–24.2
County TANF caseload ($t-1$)	Number of TANF recipients per 100,000 county residents (calculated by authors)	2.092	1.083	.142–6.907
County population (in millions)	Total county population in 2000, in millions (County and City Data Books 2003)	.893	.745	.007–2.253

NOTE: Ref. = reference category; H.S. = high school education; TANF = Temporary Assistance for Needy Families; NAICS = North American Industry Classification System; S.D. = standard deviation.

SOURCE: Data on client characteristics were provided by the Florida Department of Children and Families.

Construction of Index of County Political Ideology

To construct our index of local ideology we collected data on eighteen ideologically relevant constitutional amendments that appeared on a statewide ballot for ratification from 1996 through 2004. We computed the percentage of yes votes for each amendment, for each county, and conducted a factor analysis using all eighteen amendments (thus, 18 variables, $N = 67$ counties). The specific amendments are listed in the table below.

Ballot Title	Election Year	Ballot Number	To Amend
Should Two-Thirds Vote Be Required for New Constitutionally-Imposed State Taxes/Fees?	1996	Constitutional Amendment 1	Art. XI, sec. 7
Fee on Everglades Sugar Production	1996	Constitutional Amendment 4	Art. VII, sec. 9

Responsibility for Paying Costs for Water Pollution Abatement in the Everglades	1996	Constitutional Amendment 5	Art. II, sec. 7
Preservation of the Death Penalty; United States Supreme Court Interpretation of Cruel and Unusual Punishment	1998	Constitutional Amendment 2	Art. I, sec. 17
Additional Homestead Tax Exemption	1998	Constitutional Amendment 3	Art. VII, sec. 6
Public Education of Children	1998	Constitutional Amendment 6	Art. IX, sec. 1
Basic Rights	1998	Constitutional Amendment 9	Art. I, sec. 2
Ballot Access, Public Campaign Financing, and Election Process Revisions	1998	Constitutional Amendment 11	Art. IV, sec. 5a; Art. VI, subsecs. 1,2,5,7; Art. IX, sec. 4a
Firearms Purchases: Local Option for Criminal History Records Check and Waiting Period	1998	Constitutional Amendment 12	Art. VIII, sec. 5
Florida Transportation Initiative for Statewide High Speed Monorail, Fixed Guideway of Magnetic Levitation System	000	Constitutional Amendment 1	Art. X, sec. 19
Protect People from the Health Hazards of Second-Hand Tobacco Smoke by Prohibiting Workplace Smoking	2002	Constitutional Amendment 6	Art. X, sec. 20
Voluntary Universal Pre-Kindergarten Education	2002	Constitutional Amendment 8	Art. IX, sec. 1
Florida's Amendment to Reduce Class Size	2002	Constitutional Amendment 9	Art. IX, sec. 1
Animal Cruelty Amendment: Limiting Cruel and Inhumane Confinement of Pigs During Pregnancy	2002	Constitutional Amendment 10	Art. X, sec. 19
Parental Notification of a Minor's Termination of Pregnancy	2004	Constitutional Amendment 1	Art. X, sec. 22
Florida Minimum Wage Amendment	2004	Constitutional Amendment 5	Art. X
The Medical Liability Claimant's Compensation Amendment	2004	Constitutional Amendment 3	Art. I, sec. 26
Authorizes Miami-Dade and Broward County Voters to Approve Slot Machines in Parimutuel Facilities	2004	Constitutional Amendment 4	Art. X, sec. 19

7 THE CASE OF BEN LAGUER AND THE 2006 MASSACHUSETTS GUBERNATORIAL ELECTION

Joy James

Criminal court cases appear and disappear in the public eye with the ebbs and flows of commercial or entertainment value, political advantage in electoral politics, and civil rights and fair-trial activism. Some may view the Ben LaGuer case as an anomaly or as "exceptional." Yet, contemporary expressions of racial-sexual bias and control through the courts have historical antecedents. From the Scottsboro case in the 1930s to the 1989–2002 Central Park case, charges of interracial rape against, and convictions of, Black and Latino youths and men have proved instrumental in solidifying white racial identity embedded within deep-seated phobias and anti-Black racism and rage. What should be readily apparent in a society and state rooted in white supremacy and patriarchy, however, is often overlooked; and once brought out for our consideration, volatile issues may prove more complex than we imagine. Consider the facts of prisoner Willie Horton's violence against a white couple, and his raping of the woman, during his work furlough release in Massachusetts. That Republican operatives and candidates could capitalize on the assaults to garner a presidential victory in 1988 speaks to the endurance of racist stereotypes and sexual fetish in the mainstream mind. Yet the reality of the rape and violence inflicted by Horton is not contested. When similar operatives and candidates attempted the same racist-sexist strategy in the 2006 Massachusetts gubernatorial race, they went down in electoral defeat; this speaks to some subtle shift in racial consciousness or political practice that we may not yet be able to fully comprehend. Is it because of credible advocates who assert the innocence of Ben LaGuer, or is it because mainstream America has allowed itself a more public acceptance of "worthy Blacks" in service to white America, that Deval Patrick was elected Massachusetts' first Black governor in 2006?

Racial matters and sexual violence are complicated, or at least we are told that they are so. A year before the Willie Horton campaign to elect George H. W. Bush in 1988, the Reverend Al Sharpton propelled his own political career by championing Tawana Brawley, a Black teen who falsely claimed that she had been sexually assaulted by white male officials of New York State. In the year following Bush's election, district attorneys, journalists, and pundits promoted their careers by condemning the Black and Latino youths of the Central Park case. The pretrial (and posttrial) media convictions for a crime these youths did not commit—the brutal assault and rape of an affluent white female "jogger" in 1989—were never fully and publicly retracted. The state exoneration of the youths in 2002 has done little to correct the public record and racial memory in the mainstream mind. Few remember the specific details; few can recall the police malfeasance; few acknowledge that it was the multiracial jury, academics, and authors who rushed to judgment without material evidence, and helped to condone the incarceration of teens criminalized by their Blackness.

Elsewhere I have written about these interracial assault cases, the state that enabled social injustice to thrive, and the gender and ethnic diversity in complicity with the state's punitive mandate (James 1996, 1997, 1999). In this chapter, I recognize the egregious ignorance and racial superstition of our national culture, and focus on one case as a form of witnessing the specific and general injustices we face when confronting racialized sexual violence. In four sections I offer a narrative around the Benjamin LaGuer case. First, I provide the specific details of an interracial rape case with which we should familiarize ourselves. The traumatized victim(s), the disturbing behavior of prosecuting officials, the opportunistic public outrage and voyeurism concerning rape, the imprisonment of a man for nearly three decades, allegedly without credible material evidence—all create a moral mandate and political imperative to witness. Second, I explore how a former advocate against injustice—and counsel or executive for corporations such as Texaco, Coca-Cola, and Ameriquest—became a politician who in order to win election as a "historic first" jettisoned the inconvenient truth that the U.S. criminal justice system is corrupt, undermined by racial, sexual, class, and national biases.[1]

Third, I write of the complicated witnessing of sexual-racial violence through a century of struggle, dating from Ida B. Wells-Barnett, journalist and anti-lynching crusader. In conventional witnessing, the bodies and perspectives of Black women—who are also raped and also lynched—tend to be overlooked, or consumed in the fire of making "greater" political points. Fourth and finally, I try to get out of the way so that the imprisoned may speak for himself through his correspondence with the outside world. But before he does, it will be useful to contextualize the case, itself encased in centuries of racial-sexual mandates that have cordoned off justice.

In "The Ethical Obligations of Prosecutors in Cases Involving Postconviction Claims of Innocence," legal scholars Judith A. Goldberg and David M. Siegel (2002) outline the obstacles facing defendants who claim that they are wrongfully incarcerated. The authors maintain:

> Defendants must litigate these new claims against prosecutors whose primary objective is maintaining the integrity of the convictions, who may themselves have custody or control of both the evidence to be tested and the information concerning the evidence, and who typically have superior resources. The promise of innocence-based post-conviction relief is hollow unless prosecutors adopt new ethical obligations to guide their responses to such claims. We propose that when faced with an innocence-based postconviction claim requesting the application of "new" science to "old" evidence, prosecutors should promptly seek the fullest accounting of the truth, effect the fullest possible disclosure, and use the most accurate science. (389)

Notes in the above article indicate that Siegel, a professor of law at Boston's New England School of Law, was "counsel of record to a Massachusetts inmate who sought post-conviction DNA testing of evidence"; that person was likely Ben LaGuer. The LaGuer case has provoked considerable controversy. His persistent claims of innocence and his ability to attract prominent supporters to his cause have garnered national attention and shaped debates about civil rights and the prosecution of rape and race in the media, courts, civil society, and electoral campaigns. During the 2006 Massachusetts gubernatorial race, one that pitted a white female Republican lieutenant governor against a Black male civil rights attorney, the Ben LaGuer case became both template and touchstone for violence and social justice, and a vehicle for losing or obtaining votes.

FRAME A CASE

Even given the heinousness of the crime, it is difficult to understand why Ben LaGuer is imprisoned today.[2] On February 17, 1984, LaGuer was sentenced to life in prison with the possibility of parole for aggravated rape. Until one factors in race, his more than twenty-seven years' incarceration following a 1984 rape conviction seems unusual. According to the U.S. Department of Justice website, the average sentence for those convicted of rape in the 1990s was 117 months, and the average time served was 65 months. The vast majority of reported sexual assaults are intraracial, according to FBI crime statistics; and most rape cases—with the exception of Willie Horton's interracial sexual assault, which invigorated George H. W. Bush's 1988 presidential campaign—are not sensationalized during an election.

When race makes the crime of rape even more of an atrocity, that is, when it turns the prosecution of rape into the prosecution of interracial rape, hence punishable for the violation not only of sexual mores and rights but also of racial taboos, sensationalism becomes the filter through which most people encounter cases such as the *Commonwealth of Massachusetts v. Benjamin LaGuer*. The complexities surrounding LaGuer's case rarely circulate in media or in academic texts, although LaGuer and his supporters maintain a website devoted to his case, and LaGuer himself became a surrogate Horton in the campaign for the governor's mansion in 2006. (After candidate Deval Patrick issued a statement that "justice had been served" in light of the 2002 DNA test results [discussed later], Patrick's quotes in support of LaGuer were removed from the prisoner's website.)

A Black Puerto Rican in his early twenties, Ben LaGuer was arrested on July 15, 1983, in Leominster, Massachusetts, for aggravated rape against Lenice Plante, a white woman in her late fifties. In "LaGuer Reconsidered," western Massachusetts-based journalist Eric Goldscheider, the most knowledgeable critical writer on this case, raises important details that are inconsistent with a fair trial and just conviction.[3]

State malfeasance in the LaGuer case stems from the now-deceased lead detective, Ronald Carignan, whose unorthodox procedures were later supported by the district attorney, John Conte. With no physical evidence or confession, Carignan decided the guilt of LaGuer, who at the time of the crime was living in his father's apartment next door to the victim. Yet, LaGuer's supporters maintain that another Black Puerto Rican had also lived in and had access to the building, and had associated with the survivor; that he had a history of mental illness and sexual assault yet was never interviewed by police; and that LaGuer shares the same race and ethnicity of this man, is only five years younger, and is very similar in height and build.

The grand jury, according to Goldscheider, indicted LaGuer on Carignan's disinformation. Carignan told the grand jury that the crime had occurred in LaGuer's apartment; it had in fact occurred in the victim's apartment. The detective claimed that the victim was unable to appear at the hearing, although she had already been released from the hospital. He stated that the victim had already identified LaGuer as her assailant to the chief investigator, although she denied this under oath at trial. She would, however, later identify LaGuer in court as her attacker. Carignan testified that he had recovered only one partial fingerprint from the scene of a crime that reputedly took place over eight hours. Yet, in 2001, a report generated the day LaGuer was arrested in 1983 emerged, showing that four full fingerprints were retrieved from the base of a telephone whose cord had been used to bind the victim's wrists. None of the prints belonged to LaGuer. The recovered prints were subsequently lost (or destroyed) by the district attorney's office, preventing a match with any known felon.

Plante—who died in 1999 from causes unrelated to the assault—pointed LaGuer out in the courtroom as her assailant, but the jury was not informed that she had been institutionalized over an extended period of time for mental illness, which allegedly included schizophrenia. Her mental and emotional states were never introduced at trial nor were witnesses, confessions, or credible material evidence. Only Plante's and police testimonies linked LaGuer to the assault for nearly twenty years, that is, until LaGuer's much sought-after DNA testing was permitted by the state.

Goldscheider has described a web of complex relationships surrounding Ben LaGuer.[4] In 1998 (and again in May 2010), LaGuer was eligible for parole but was denied because he would not admit to the crime. Despite lengthy incarceration and vilification, LaGuer nonetheless managed to mobilize influential supporters. James C. Rehnquist, son of the late U.S. Supreme Court chief justice William Rehnquist, was his former attorney. Currently, his new legal team consists of Isaac Borenstein, who spent sixteen years as an associate justice of the Superior Court of Massachusetts, and his former law clerk, Lisa Billowitz.

Over the years, prominent intellectuals and academics such as Elie Wiesel, William Styron, Henry Louis Gates Jr., Noam Chomsky, and John Silber have lent their support for a fair hearing or review for LaGuer. While imprisoned,

LaGuer earned a bachelor's degree with honors from Boston University and a prestigious Pen Award. When U.S. senator Jessie Helms effectively terminated the use of Pell grants for the education and rehabilitation of inmates in 1994, Boston University president John Silber kept the university's prison education program afloat. Although an outspoken conservative Democrat who had opposed progressive intellectuals such as Noam Chomsky and Howard Zinn (years earlier, Silber had tried to fire Zinn, a popular Boston University professor and antiwar activist), Silber joined progressives in supporting LaGuer's right to a fair review. The eloquent prisoner had become a cause célèbre.

For years, LaGuer and his advocates had positioned juror racism as the key factor mandating a new hearing and trial. When the parole board rejected Ben LaGuer's appeals, Silber met with LaGuer in prison. He then contributed substantial funds to the DNA testing. David Siegel subsequently became involved in the case.

A founding member of the New England Innocence Project (created in 1992 by Barry Scheck and Peter Neufeld), Siegel serves on its Case Review Committee and directs the Criminal Justice Project of the New England Law School's Center for Law and Social Responsibility. He had earlier served as public defender in Nashville, Tennessee. According to Goldscheider, Siegel worked on the LaGuer case pro bono and was instrumental in assisting LaGuer's claim of rights to DNA testing. (LaGuer had admitted to having tampered with a saliva sample ordered by the court in order to determine his blood type while in prison—he states because of his distrust of the government; the parole board maintains because of his guilt.) Siegel and former FBI agent, attorney Richard Slowe, found missing trial evidence in the clerk's office in the county courthouse. Although it was noted that the clerk had handed them a box with a broken seal, they went forward with DNA testing despite the possibility of tampered or compromised evidence.

In April 2001, through the Freedom of Information Act, Ben LaGuer was able to see his Leominster police file, which included a fax of the original forensic police department report. On the fax was written "Benji's underwear." Critics allege that without a warrant, Detective Carignan had taken LaGuer's underwear from his family's apartment and mingled it with evidence taken from the crime scene. (Years after the trial, Leominster police presented to the courts evidence that was never officially preserved.) The detective also kept the rape kit in the trunk of his car for a week during the summer before delivering it to the state police laboratory. No physical evidence was introduced at the trial that convicted LaGuer in 1983, but compromised evidence would be used in 2002 as "reliable" samples for DNA testing to cement that conviction.

Two labs were selected for the DNA review. One could not find any male DNA evidence; the other offered a DNA profile report authored by Ed Blake, which was based on a miniscule and, it is argued, contaminated sample. Neither rape kits nor DNA testing are exact sciences. The quality of the evidence and the quality of the examiner determine outcomes used to exonerate or incarcerate. The scientific verdict of LaGuer's guilt proved sufficient to drive away many supporters—including civil rights attorneys and politicians seeking high office.

In 2002, disputed DNA results established the only physical evidence indicating LaGuer's guilt. However, in 2006, forensic consultant Dean Wideman's *Forensic Case Review of Commonwealth of Massachusetts v. Benjamin LaGuer* heavily criticized the 2002 report done by Ed Blake. Conducting his review at the request of Massachusetts state representative Ellen Story, Wideman argued that the samples taken from the nearly twenty-year-old evidence were too miniscule and compromised by contamination for accurate or conclusive results. Wideman's tests would also indicate that no semen or blood were detectable on the vaginal or anal swabs or underwear of the victim following what court transcripts recorded as an eight-hour ordeal of violent rape and sodomy. However, the 2010 parole board asserts that Plante's examination while hospitalized revealed serious injuries and semen recovered from her throat and vagina.

The *Forensic Case Review* was issued months before the 2006 Massachusetts vote to replace conservative Republican governor Mitt Romney. However, the review received little mention on the campaign trail; neither the candidates nor the media expressed much interest in the March 2006 report. Opposition to Democrat Deval Patrick's candidacy singled out his past support for Ben LaGuer's right to an impartial hearing or parole. A decades-old interracial sexual crime and conviction seemed to derail the campaign for Massachusetts' first Black governor as individuals involved in the case began to surface as opponents of Deval Patrick.

WIN AN ELECTION

In the 1988 presidential contest between Republican vice president George H. W. Bush and Democratic Massachusetts governor Michael Dukakis, Republican National Committee strategist Lee Atwater infamously boasted that he would make convicted Black murderer and rapist Willie Horton Dukakis's running mate. While on work furlough in a program sponsored by then Governor Dukakis, Horton had brutalized a white couple, raping the woman. The sexual assault was sensationalized the most in the negative campaign ads. Nearly twenty years later, trailing in the polls, Lt. Governor Healey tried to position Ben LaGuer in the public's mind in a similar shadowy relationship to Deval Patrick. Patrick's past support for parole for LaGuer seemed a perfect opportunity for his opponents to recycle the Horton strategy. On the campaign trail, Patrick was sufficiently able to differentiate himself from LaGuer, although he was less than candid, or his memory was flawed, as the candidate claimed. Initially, Patrick denied supporting LaGuer, failing to remember his past support in letters (excerpted in the *Boston Globe* and other press during the campaign[5]) and by way of financial assistance for DNA testing. For the voters, and as a defense against his critics, Patrick finally, in effect, pronounced Ben LaGuer guilty as charged months before the election.

Racially driven negative advertisements, attributed by some to Atwater mentee Karl Rove, became biofuel for the Republican gubernatorial campaign. However, perhaps having witnessed firsthand their governor's 1988 presidential defeat by smear tactics—which included false rumors that his wife, Kitty Dukakis, had burned an American flag while participating in radical student protests in the 1960s—Massachusetts voters appeared largely unimpressed in 2006 by similar tactics. When Kerry Healey attempted to portray Patrick as a sympathizer of rapists, she would derail her campaign. Still, the animus against Patrick was fed by various private and public personas.

In 1983, a young police officer, Dean Mazzarella, was among the first to arrive at the scene of the crime. Apparently, he was the only police officer who rode with the victim in the ambulance to the hospital. Over twenty years later, in September 2006, Massachusetts media reported that Leominster mayor Dean Mazzarella believed that if Deval Patrick were elected governor, he would grant LaGuer "preferential treatment." In the following weeks, through the media, including incendiary local talk radio, Mayor Mazzarella attacked LaGuer and Patrick's past support for a review of the case. According to journalist Goldscheider, Mazzarella's aired descriptions of the victim's brutalization fed hostilities towards both Black men—prisoner and candidate. During the campaign, when the Leominster mayor demanded a meeting with candidate Patrick, he complied. (Later, Governor Patrick would appoint Mazzarella to a special commission on Massachusetts towns and cities.)

According to Goldscheider, Plante's son-in-law, Robert Barry, echoed Mazzarella's 2006 airwave attacks on Patrick. Barry would repeat gruesome details of the assault while fundraising on air for medical treatment for his (now deceased) wife, Elizabeth Barry, who suffered from Lou Gehrig's disease. When Robert and Elizabeth Barry demanded an official apology from the Democratic candidate, Patrick called to offer his sympathy for the pain caused by the recent publicity. Robert Barry publicly rebuked him for not issuing a stronger disavowal of LaGuer; he then invited television crews into their home. At a later press conference, with Elizabeth Barry wheelchair-bound and suffering from the crippling disease, the Barrys endorsed Kerry Healey.

On television and radio, the Barry family and the Healey campaign denounced Patrick for his past support for LaGuer and heralded Healey as the champion of victims' rights, visually rendered as white lower-middle-class or working-class victims against Black predators. Neither the Republican nor the Democratic campaigns addressed the reality of *Blacks* victimized by a racist criminal justice system. The media recorded no memory of a historical context of racially and sexually driven violence against Black bodies. Given his years of service as an attorney for the National Association for the Advancement of Colored People (NAACP) and in the civil rights division of the Clinton administration, Patrick was very familiar with racial and class bias in the judicial system. Yet when Healey's campaign postured that racial bias in prosecution and sentencing were irrelevant to mainstream or white America, thus distancing the campaign from fair-trial advocacy for LaGuer, Patrick concurred.

Patrick's 1998 letter written on behalf of LaGuer's petition for parole, and resubmitted at a 2000 hearing, did not sway the review board. During the campaign, media and opponents began to widely quote from Patrick's letter(s) to the parole board: "He [LaGuer] appears well prepared to make a positive re-entry and important contribution to the community of responsible citizens." After Patrick denied having made a financial contribution to LaGuer's exoneration or release, the media revealed that Patrick had written a check for five thousand dollars in support of LaGuer's quest for DNA testing.

Patrick's gubernatorial campaign appeared to unravel under the weight of public condemnation. His vulnerabilities included his lack of executive experience and generalities in his policy positions. Those limitations, along with his race, did not alienate substantial numbers of voters dissatisfied with the Republican administration. As a result, Patrick's other vulnerabilities would come to dominate the press and the Healey campaign's press releases, which focused on two examples of moral failing in the view of the opposition: Patrick had helped to fund LaGuer's DNA testing, and he had misinformed the public about this when questioned. Civil rights advocacy and critiques of racial bias in policing and prosecution—witnessing of injustice, demanding redress—became a handicap for the politician; thus they were jettisoned in order to craft a winning strategy.

Understanding political vulnerability, the Republicans began airing info-mercials decrying Patrick's "affinity" for criminals. The Healey campaign un-veiled a television advertisement attacking Patrick, who while working for the NAACP, had successfully represented a (white) Florida man on death row for killing a police officer, reducing his sentence to life in prison. Massachusetts attorneys and the Massachusetts Bar immediately condemned Healey, who is not an attorney, for the "guilt by association" attack; many lawyers serve as public defenders, or do pro bono work on behalf of (or accept fees from) criminal defendants.

Still, radio and television outlets continued to portray Patrick as indif-ferent to rape solely on the basis of his support for Ben LaGuer. Unlike in the smear campaign against the Massachusetts Democratic contender in 1988, Patrick's Blackness forced him into closer proximity with the stereotyped sexual predator than Dukakis ever would have experienced. Dukakis's white-ness gave him distance; that representational distance from the Black convict rapist eluded a Black male candidate. For potential voters who were unclear about racial guilt by association, Healey campaign volunteers organized a pseudo-vigilante group, dressed in prison garb to picket the home of Patrick's campaign manager, the self-proclaimed "Inmates for Deval."

After running an ad that focused on Patrick's misleading statements about his relationship with LaGuer, the Healey campaign pulled ahead of Patrick among white male voters. She continued to trail among white women. Seek-ing to close that gender gap, the Republicans released an advertisement that inadvertently destroyed Healey's campaign and, to some extent, her public reputation. The attack ad—which can no longer be located on the Internet—used Patrick's statements, made years earlier, which echoed the sentiments of Boston University president Silber and others about LaGuer's eloquence and thoughtfulness. Patrick's comments appeared in a television commercial in which a nervous (white) woman walks through a dimly lit parking garage with the voice-over: "Have you ever heard a woman compliment a rapist? Deval Patrick—he should be ashamed, not governor."

The ad was released simultaneously with a *Boston Herald* article suggest-ing that Patrick had helped shield his brother-in-law from registering as a sex offender when he moved to Massachusetts. The marital rape of Patrick's sister had taken place twenty years earlier; the couple had sought counseling and reunited, never informing their children about the domestic violence. After the media went public with the family trauma, Patrick immediately called a press conference to passionately denounce the Healey campaign tactics as "pathetic": "This is the politics of Kerry Healey and it disgusts me and it has to stop." The following week, the majority of polled voters expressed a negative view of the Republican candidate.

Months later, Deval Patrick made history, becoming the second Black governor to be elected since the end of Reconstruction.[6] Patrick also emerged in national politics as cochair of the Barack Obama campaign. Patrick's 2006 ordeal provides insightful instruction into campaign mandates. Both campaigns featured lesser-experienced Black male politicians embattled against seasoned white female politicians. In the case of the 2008 Democratic primaries, the campaign lacked the gravitas of the incarceration of a possibly innocent person, and the psychosexual politics of interracial rape, yet Obama faced a white female opponent (who would later become his secretary of state) whose claims to being "tougher" on crime led him to distance himself from critiques of institutional racism in the policing of Black bodies; that is, to reject witnessing. Patrick and Obama, both Harvard Law School graduates, mirror each other in political trajectories, language, and reform agendas. Patrick's experiences on the campaign trail likely proved useful to his presidential counterpart. Despite whatever "change mandates" Black ivy-educated elites (who are well versed in respect for the law) may represent or advocate, such politicians remain embraceable to majority white voters only as long as they do not offer narratives of antiracist, social justice advocacy. Such silence or speechlessness problematizes past, present, and future analyses of lynching and rape.

WITNESSING AMERICAN VIOLATIONS:
CONTEXTS FOR THE CASE OF BEN LAGUER

To truly witness violence and violation, one must remember, locate, and relate the atrocity. When the very culture that provides context and meaning to individual trauma is itself rooted in violations of whole peoples designated as "minorities" and stereotyped as primitive, such witnessing becomes very complicated. Whatever registers as atrocity in a society dictates immediate action on the part of citizenry and government. Whatever enables such a crisis is, logically, desperately redressed, for a crisis left unaddressed will dis-aggregate the social order. In our society, only some violence against some bodies registers as such. Yet if violence against some bodies is thus considered mundane and commonplace—and the state is presumed to inflict not violence but justice against unworthy (racially fashioned) aggressors—how does one witness from the collective perspective of the criminalized, the racially fashioned, the sexually deviant? That is, how does one witness from the site of Blackness?

Academic interventions, lurid crime tales, fair-trial advocacy, forensic reports—all are forms of testimony and witnessing. However, if done without reference to or claims about the social and historical context of race, sex, and violence that encircles every interracial rape case, the result is a partial narrative leading to false witnessing and fabricated testimony. That which is incomplete is not the truth, the whole truth, and nothing but the truth.

Along with economic wealth, racial and gender dynamics shape the power differentials that alter outcomes in criminal justice, the rule of law, and social presumptions of innocence. Simply put, the power dynamic is this: White life is a positive; Black life, a negative. Whites are to be protected, and Black life is to be contained in order to protect whites and their property (both personal and public or institutional). From cradle to grave, in foster care removals, juvenile detention centers, drug sentencing, police surveillance and harassment, and in executions, disproportionality in confinement is driven by race. The state disproportionately removes Black children from their families, mandating them as wards of the state in foster care, even though Black families are no more violent or dysfunctional than white families, according to legal scholar Dorothy Roberts (2002). The state is seven times more likely to incarcerate Blacks than whites for the same offense, according to the Washington-based Sentencing Project. Those convicted of murdering whites are nearly four times more likely to receive the death penalty, particularly if they are "colored," than those convicted of murdering "nonwhites." Antisocial behavior is criminalized. So too is Blackness, and it is regulated as such in social life in the Americas and in Europe, where whites have historically punished a racial formation they themselves created in opposition to whiteness.

In the American antebellum years, the majority of lynch victims were white. The majority of rape victims were not. Following the dismantling of Reconstruction, the majority of lynch victims were now Black, while rape remained a privatized, undocumented violation, as no crusader (such as Ida B. Wells) would painstakingly, and painfully, gather the data.

The disappearances, mutilations, and deaths of Blacks through the convict prison lease system led to no substantial criminal prosecutions or civil litigations for damages. The emancipated became the racial wards and victims of civil society and the state: Blacks remained captive to sovereign whiteness. Whites terrorized Blacks through lynching; males terrorized females (and other males and children) through rape. Whiteness in men was a shield from prosecution. Whiteness in women permitted a surrogate phallic protection; enforced by white males, this protection usually did not work for white women against the interests of the enforcers. Meanwhile, Black women had no power by proxy.

How then should the victims of sexual and racial violence witness the case of Ben LaGuer?

A century ago, indifference to anti-Black lynching and to rape (except, that is, for interracial sexual assault against white women) seemed the norm for government and "mainstream" society. Apologists for lynching exerted little effort to ascertain facts, to uphold democratic ideals when the atrocity was considered necessary to ensure public (white) safety. When the mob relinquished its role to the state, the sanitized court reenactments of lynch victimizers and victims appeared so mundane as to become nearly invisible to white America.

In the late nineteenth century, Ida B. Wells, while excoriating lynching, created and expanded upon a moral and political template contesting racist violence. As a journalist and newspaper publisher—before being forced by threat of a lynching to flee the South—Wells risked her life to investigate and write about racial murder and sexual obsession. Wells documented atrocities in her 1892 pamphlet *Southern Horrors: Lynch Law in All Its Phases*.[7] She bore witness by organizing editorials, economic boycotts, and Black out-migration, all around a distinct view of racial terror being enacted by sheriffs and judges who mingled with mobs. Half a century later, Black activists sought to bring witness to anti-Black violence as a human rights violation before the international community. William Patterson and the Civil Rights Congress compiled and published *We Charge Genocide* in 1951, presenting this book-length petition, rife with its own forms of sexism and gender repression, to the United Nations. Signed by such radical notables as W.E.B. Du Bois and Paul Robeson, *We Charge Genocide* documented state-sponsored racist violence and state complicity in the destruction of Black political, economic, and cultural life in the United States. The manuscript's most visceral photographs were of tortured Black men in multiple lynchings. Yet despite the "embarrassment" felt by the state and its desire to suppress the publication—which circulated widely through International Publishers' and the Communist Party's extensive Cold War information and propaganda network—the work of lynching apologists continued largely unabated, for legal lynching and racially driven prosecution had replaced mob rule.

Traumatized by *it*—the riot, the racial rage, the sexual psychotic—one remembers and so is forced to some measure or degree to witness. The legal system with its layers of complexity and specialized languages encourages you to forget. Those who have seen images, or heard the stories, of bodies swinging from limbs, dismembered in the char of campfires, soaked and bloated beyond recognition in Mississippi waters, know that they have seen violation and "victim."[8] But they are told to *forget*. Dispersing the mob and enabling the judicial system to render verdicts on Black life and culpability, the state brought order; it dismissed the spectacle, and recognition of violence dissipated.

Even as historical racial victims disappear in discourse, their historical victimizers claim—without the vulnerability of racial stigma—their narratives. National Public Radio's February 1, 2009, coverage of the murder or killing of Oscar Grant, under the title "Court of Public Opinion," offered the following quote from attorney Steve Meister, who represents police accused of misconduct and brutality: "This whole case, the way the DA has proceeded, the way the civic leadership has proceeded, and the way the civic activists and the citizens have proceeded—the whole thing strikes me as a politically correct lynch mob."[9] Meister was defending Johannes Mehserle, a twenty-seven-year-old white Oakland transit police officer who shot and killed Grant, a twenty-two-year-old African American, on January 8, 2009. At the time he was killed, Grant was lying facedown, handcuffed, and subdued by police on a subway platform.[10] Transit passengers witnessed the execution and captured it on their cell phones. The images circulated on the Internet and in the media, and protestors demanded justice. News reports relayed the statements of attorney and former police officer Michael Rains that citizen clashes with police—following the delay of Mehserle's arrest after killing the unarmed Grant—constituted a "legal lynching." (On July 9, 2010, a Los Angeles court tried Mehserle for murder and convicted him of a lesser charge, involuntary manslaughter.)

The aggrieved white (or conservative Black man, such as 1991 Supreme Court justice nominee Clarence Thomas decrying a "high-tech" lynching in the face of allegations of sexual harassment of Anita Hill, a Black woman) asserts him- or herself as violated, using the language forged in antiracist struggles. Sovereign whiteness (and its allies) remains indignant and defensive in the face of its critics. When the role of victim resides with whiteness in interracial conflicts, evidence that does not substantiate the metanarrative of white vindication can be viewed as secondary, if not marginally relevant. If Blackness is presumed to have little innocence, Black rights are easily lost, and defendants' claims to innocence are rarely seen as compelling.

What transpires in witnessing when the contextual meaning determines the value of specific events? For example, whether Emmett Till actually whistled at Carole Bryant in her family store is irrelevant in the restoration of context and meaning in witnessing the specific event within the larger narrative. The fourteen-year-old Black Chicagoan visiting his relatives in 1955 Mississippi was already a lynch victim in waiting. The trigger for the actual assault was the word of any white person who stated that an assault (a whistle on a dare or in flirtation) had or would take place. The trigger exists prior to any utterance or act: the first instigation to punish is the appearance of the Black wherever racial victimization has been analogized as whiteness.

In Leominster, Massachusetts, the analogy of whiteness with purity of vulnerability in the face of a perpetual Black aggressor provided an important context for understanding the conviction of Ben LaGuer, and how this crime (both the assault and the unethical trial) would be witnessed by society and prosecutors. The inability to establish a context that acknowledged a pervasive history of anti-Black anima and violation meant that twenty-three years after LaGuer's conviction, a gubernatorial campaign could use his case to fuel both conservative and liberal agendas.

Violence, such as lengthy incarceration, is considered by some to be the only form of communication that quells the *bête noire*—the stereotypical Black rapist whose desire for white females stimulates and violates her male kin.[11] Fictive kinship encompasses white civil society, multicultural white supremacists, and the state. Such kinship based on repression establishes relationships among those who deny institutional anti-Black violence and seek solidarity against an alleged Black aggression. But that saves no one from sexual aggression, for Black existence and predatory behavior are not synonyms although racism has presented them as such for centuries.

Rape is an underpoliced and underpunished offence in the United States. Sexual violence is pandemic; it is widely experienced in the home, school, workplace, public spaces, and recreational sites such as sports arenas and parks. Yet in major cities, such as Los Angeles, thousands of rape kits have remained unopened and untested for years; this despite federal funds to assist in processing, and the painful, painstaking collecting of evidence from the bodies of victims who assume they are helping to protect themselves and others.[12]

The case of Ben LaGuer is disturbing, not just because of its possible wrongful incarceration and political opportunism but because something happened to Lenice Plante. And whatever happened to her was not important enough to witness with the truth about what was happening to LaGuer. During the prosecutorial phase of the case, which continues, one may pit a Black man against a white woman and celebrate some Pyrrhic victory with whomever (or whose ever memory) prevails. Still, in the absence of witnessing through the construction of a narrative that brings meaning to the implications of these conflicts and traumas, social justice seems a losing proposition.

THE CORRESPONDENCE OF BEN LAGUER

"Breaking" the Ben LaGuer case—proving absolute innocence or guilt—is compelling. Yet the legal process does not actually prove guilt or innocence. Rather, it illuminates a process, overt and covert, by which certain crimes (and social castes) are punished.

The testimonies of police, courts, media, politicians, advocates, and DNA testers are not objective. Nor is the testimony of the convicted and incarcerated. However, a more complete telling of this case requires the witnessing of Ben LaGuer himself. The following correspondence and state documents sent by Ben LaGuer do not provide "evidence" or "proof" of a legal lynching. Nonetheless, in addition to previously shared information, they frame this case as highly problematic. They trouble the reader. They request or demand the burden of social scrutiny and analysis in a criminal case that became a political commodity. This case, like countless others shaped by bias and institutional prejudice, resides in the cold container of past, present, and future violations that we will either witness or ignore as our democracy, and the legal system which enables it, unfolds.

.   .   .

6/24/07

Dear Joy (if I may)

I hope you are enjoying your summer. I got word of your interest
in the case obviously from Eric. My sole purpose in writing
today is purely introductory; for me to say how happy I am that
a person of your spirit and academic curiosity would notice
me from the road you was travelling. These 23 years in prison
have been quite a burden to carry, but not in the sense most
people might think. When you carry the weight of history and
biography the body and spirit start to gain enough muscle to carry
that weight. One can carry as much as one's hope and dreams. I
have witnessed, as well as felt in the deepest places of the heart
how race, gender and affluence destroy some and build others. The
politics of race and class have never been silent in any
discussion pertaining to my guilt or innocence. In 2001, a juror
in my case told a newspaper, "The life sentence showed the judge
agreed with the verdict. We saw an animal, and he saw the same
animal." This juror makes it quite clear that I was no peer
of his. At a deeper level, near the realm of Dred Scott, what
"animal" has rights "which the white man was bound to respect[?]"
I want you to know that I want to help/cooperate in what truths
you are seeking in the journey of your life. I am enclosing a
couple of articles for your own interest. I hope, when it all ends,
you may end liking me as a person too. Write me when you are
ready. Be well.

Peace & Blessings (of course)

Ben

Figure 7.1 LaGuer Letter

6/24/07

Dear Joy (if I may)

I hope you are enjoying your summer. I got word of your interest in the case obviously from Eric. My sole purpose in writing today is purely introductory; for me to say how happy I am that a person of your spirit and academic curiosity would notice me from the road you was travelling. These 23 years in prison have been quite a burden to carry, but not in the sense most people might think. When you carry the weight of history and biography the body and spirit start to gain enough muscle to carry that weight. One can carry as much as one's hope and dreams. I have witnessed, as well as felt in the deepest places of the heart how race, gender and affluence destroy some and build others. The politics of race and class have never been silent in any discussion pertaining to my guilt or innocence. In 2001, a juror in my case told a newspaper, "The life sentence showed the judge agreed with the verdict. We saw an animal, and he saw the same animal." This juror makes it quite clear that I was no peer of his. At a deeper level, near the realm of Dred Scott, what "animal" has rights "which the white man was bound to respect[?]" I want you to know that I want to help/cooperate in what truths you are seeking in the journey of your life. I am enclosing a couple of articles for your interest. I hope, when it all ends, you may end liking me as a person too. Write me when you are ready. Be well.

Peace & Blessings (of course)

Ben

21 January 2008

Dear Professor James

Greetings, good sister. I just wanted to write and share with you the news that the Governor's Advisory Board of Pardons sent the governor their report. The letter I wrote is pretty self explanatory. I think there may still be a chance that a public hearing [will] be afforded. While I did not write this down, I now remember that there was another case to draw a comparison. I was denied a clemency hearing because I have a impending parole hearing. However Gerald Amirault, a white man convicted in the infamous Falls Acres child molestation case, was granted a clemency hearing despite his impending parole. The only difference between us is that Amirault is white and I am not. I hope you are well, good sister. I would like to read your essay on the case whenever you are ready to make it public.

Peace & Blessings
Ben

. . .

The Commonwealth of Massachusetts
Executive Office of Public Safety
Advisory Board of Pardons
January 18, 2008
Benjamin LaGuer, W40280
c/o North Central Correction Institute
P.O. Box 466
500 Colony Road
Gardner, MA 01440

RE: Commutation Petition

Dear Mr. LaGuer:

After reviewing the materials you provided, including the December 13, 2007 supplemental submission, and following careful objective analysis, the unanimous membership of the Advisory Board of Pardons denied your request for a commutation hearing by a vote of (6–0).

In reaching its decision, the Advisory Board of Pardons noted that you have an administrative remedy available through the parole process in June 2008, therefore, you do not meet the threshold requirements set forth in the 2007 Governor's Guidelines.

A copy of the Board's report will be forwarded to His Excellency, the Governor, for review.

Sincerely,
Julie Pease
Advisory Board of Pardons
Executive Clemency Coordinator

. . .

18 January 2008
Governor Deval Patrick
State House
Boston, MA 02133

In Re: *A Response to the Governor's Advisory Board of Pardons Report Of 18 January 2008*

Dear Governor Patrick

Around the time of this past Thanksgiving I filed a petition for executive clemency with your administration based on actual innocence. Despite your pledge on the WBZ radio program, hosted by Dan Rea, that a hearing would be granted to me on that petition, a forum that was expected to expose police and prosecutorial abuses, today the Advisory Board of Pardons voted to deny me the very hearing you pledged.

It does not seem possible that the Advisory Board of Pardons could be capable of confusing the governing criteria for executive clemency based on a claim of actual innocence with a request for a commutation of sentence, which requires merely a petitioner to have . . . "made exceptional strides in self development and self improvement" rather than establishing a clear and convincing case of actual innocence, but that error is plain for you to reverse.

The Board of Pardons denied me a "commutation hearing" but I had specifically requested executive clemency.

How could the Board of Pardons mistake a request for executive clemency under the US Supreme Court ruling of *Herrera* -Vs- *Collins* with a request for commutation of sentence is baffling, since these are separate processes even under the Parole Board guidelines.

A request for executive clemency based on actual innocence, under *Herrera*, envisions that the Board of Pardons will afford petitioner a public hearing to collect evidence of his or her claims to report on their merit to the governor. In the absence of a hearing to collect the facts that tend to either support or negate that claim of actual innocence. How can the Board of Pardons have written a credible report addressing the merit of the specific claim?

The Board of Pardons, in its letter dated 18 January 2008 "noted that you have an administrative remedy available through the parole process in June 2008, therefore, you do not meet the threshold requirements set forth in that

2007 Governor's Guidelines." The letter also states that "the Advisory Board of Pardons denied your request for a commutation hearing by a vote of (6–0)."

But a clemency petition based on actual innocence, if granted under the Herrera definition, would bring about a determination of actual innocence, thus obliterating any need for a parole. Why should the state have a innocent citizen on lifetime parole?

But this is also a catch 22. The Parole Board, which considered this petition as the Advisory Board of Pardons, has denied me parole on three occasions. Each time the Board cited this assertion of actual innocence. When I come up again for parole in June 2008, Governor, will the Parole Board cited again the petitioner's claim of actual innocence? Will the Parole Board chairman say to me, as chairpersons have in the past, "Mr LaGuer, we are not here to retry the facts of your trial." Will the Parole Board forget that I requested a proper and legal process for establishing the evidence of actual innocence, for establishing evidence of police and prosecutorial abuses, but they chose not to grant me "a commutation hearing" which, in a better day, should have been a clemency hearing.

Governor, this is a comedy of errors. I have been fighting for justice for 24 years, despite the fact that I could have accepted a guilty plea and been out 22 years ago. (In the presence of John Strahinich of the Boston Herald, my trial attorney Peter L Ettenberg read from his notes, confirming the deal that I had been offered. Strahinich wrote about this deal in the November 1987 issue of Boston Magazine.)

What the courts and parole board of this state have done against me is simply outrageous. I am more sad than disillusioned that your administration is playing political games with my life and biography. I require no special treatment of favors on account of our personal history. I seek no special favors or treatment from any governmental agency. But a group of prominent forensic experts have publicly stated that County prosecutors provided the wrong samples to the State Police crime lab for DNA analysis, which resulted in the wrong result in March 2002. I have written your public safety chief four letters for him to double check the provenance of the sample which County lawyers provided the state police crime lab.

This report from the Advisory Board of Pardons cannot possible be considered legitimate, since the Board held no hearing to collect any facts. The Advisory Board of Pardons also applied a "Commutation of Sentence" criteria for judging a petition specifically filed under Herrera's analysis for "Executive clemency based on actual innocence."

The Advisory Board of Pardons cannot be said to have discharged its duties to your office, in the absence of a hearing to collect the facts. A hearing will ensure that all parties including the Worcester County District Attorney Joseph D Early, are provided ample opportunity to support or rebute [sic] these claims of actual innocence and prosecutorial abuses.

Whether I am eligible for parole in June 2008 is totally irrelevant to whether I am actually innocent, since I can legally avail myself of a grant of executive clemency based on actual innocence, which would make a parole unnecessary.

Finally, the report from the Advisory Board of pardons should be rejected. This improperly denied petition should be immediately returned to the Advisory Board of Pardons for them to hold a hearing on the merits of a claim of actual innocence, as the US Supreme Court set forth in *Herrera*. If this report is allowed to stand, Governor, history will judge this process as a farse of liberal overcompensation. Too many people in office today are afraid of acting on behalf of the truth out of the perception that defending the innocent may cost too high a price. What the Advisory Board of Pardon did today was a travesty that needs to be corrected by returning the clemency petition to them for a real public hearing.

With peace and blessings,
Sincerely
Ben LaGuer

cc
E Abim Thomas, Deputy Legal Counsel
Office of the Governor's Legal Counsel
Kevin Burke, Secretary of Public Safety
Executive Office of Public Safety

COMMONWEALTH OF MASSACHUSETTS
DEPARTMENT OF CORRECTION
INMATE GRIEVANCE FORM
FORWARD TO INSTITUTIONAL GRIEVANCE COORDINATOR (IGC)

Name LAGUER BENJAMEN	**Grievance#** 33698	**Institution** NCCI GARDNER		
Commit No. W40280	**Housing** THOMPSON-3	**Date Of Incident** 20080501	**Date Of Grievance** 20080501	

Complaint For a number of years I have had the telephone number of attorney James C. Rehnquist, a partner at the Boston Law firm Goodwin, Procter, LLP, installed on the system as my attorney of record. Recently, I began to notice how the telephone system was announcing "This call may be recorded or monitored," a sure sign that our priviledge conversations have been recorded against all legal and regulatory DOC doctrine. Other attorney numbers, when dialed, are repsonded with a "Please hold" comment and the system proceeds to connect the telephone call. This is a serious breach of attorney/client privilege. I recently requested that the telephone number of State Representative Ellen Story be installed, a State House number, and these conversations are also being announced as "recorded or monitored." I have offered proof that both Rehnquist and Story are members of the court. Ms. Story is a member of the Commonwealth of Massachusetts General Court.

Remedy Requested I am requesting that these conversations not be recorded or monitored. I am requesting to ascertain how long have these conversations been recorded in specific terms. I wish to ascertain if any of these conversations are in storage, and whether these conversations have been shared with any governmental agency.

Staff Recipient Winn William F CPO III

Staff Involved

Signature

- -

RECEIPT BY INSTITUTIONAL GRIEVANCE COORDINATOR

Date Received 20080505   **Decision Date**

Signature

Final Decision

Decision

Signature   **Date**

Denied grievances may be appealed to the Superintendent within 10 working days of Institution Grievance Coordinator's decision.

- -

INMATE RECEIPT

Name LAGUER BENJAMEN		**Institution** NCCI GARDNER
Commit No. W40280	**Grievance#** 33698	**Date Received** 20080505

Signature. Winn William F CPO III

Figure 7.2 Grievance Form

Commonwealth of Massachusetts
Department of Correction
Inmate Grievance Form
Forward to Institutional Grievance Coordinator (IGC)
Name LAGUER BENJAMEN
Grievance # 33698
Institution NCCI GARDNER
Commit No. W40280
Housing THOMPSON-3
Date of Incident 20080501
Date of Grievance 20080501

Complaint
For a number of years I have had the telephone number of attorney James C.
Rehnquist, a partner at the Boston Law firm Goodwin, Procter, LLP, installed
on the system as my attorney of record. Recently, I began to notice how the
telephone system was announcing "This call may be recorded or monitored,"
a sure sign that our privilege conversations have been recorded against all
legal and regulatory DOC doctrine. Other attorney numbers, when dialed,
are responded with a "Please hold" comment and the system proceeds to
connect the telephone call. This is a serious breach of attorney/client privilege.
I recently requested that the telephone number of State Representative Ellen
Story be installed, a State House number, and these conversations are also
being announced as "recorded or monitored." I have offered proof that both
Rehnquist and Story are members of the court. Ms. Story is a member of the
Commonwealth of Massachusetts General Court.

Remedy Requested
I am requesting that these conversations not be recorded or monitored. I am
requesting to ascertain how long these conversations been recorded in specific
terms. I wish to ascertain if any of these conversations are in storage, and
whether these conversations have been shared with any governmental agency.

The Commonwealth of Massachusetts
Executive Office of Public Safety
ADVISORY BOARD OF PARDONS
12 Mercer Road
Natick, Massachusetts 01760

Deval L. Patrick
Governor

Timothy P. Murray
Lieutenant Governor

Kevin M. Burke
Secretary

Telephone # (508) 650-4500
Facsimile # (508) 650-4599

Maureen E. Walsh
Chairman

Donald V. Giancioppo
Executive Director

May 1, 2008

Benjamin LaGuer, W40280
c/o North Central Correction Institute
P.O. Box 466
500 Colony Road
Gardner, MA 01440

RE: Commutation Petition

Dear Mr. LaGuer:

As you know, on **January 18, 2008,** the Advisory Board of Pardons recommended to Governor Deval Patrick that he deny your request for executive clemency. Pursuant to Section IV(2) of the Governor's Executive Clemency Guidelines, since the Governor has neither disapproved of nor taken any other action on that recommendation within 90 days, it is presumed that the Governor concurs in that adverse recommendation. Accordingly, your petition has been denied without prejudice.

Please be advised that you may not submit an application for a pardon until **April 18, 2009,** one year from the date the petition was denied.

A copy of this letter has been forwarded to the Office of the Governor's Chief Legal Counsel.

Sincerely,

Julie Pease
Advisory Board of Pardons
Executive Clemency Coordinator

Figure 7.3 Pardons Letter

The Commonwealth of Massachusetts
Executive Office of Public Safety
Advisory Board of Pardons

May 1, 2008

Benjamin LaGuer, W40280
c/o North Central Correction Institute
P.O. Box 466
500 Colony Road
Gardner, MA 01440

RE: Commutation Petition

Dear Mr. LaGuer:

As you know, on **January 18, 2008,** the Advisory Board of Pardons
recommended to Governor Deval Patrick that he deny your request for
executive clemency. Pursuant to Section IV(2) of the Governor's Executive
Clemency Guidelines, since the Governor has neither disapproved of nor
taken any other action on that recommendation within 90 days, it is presumed
that the Governor concurs in that adverse recommendation. Accordingly, your
petition has been denied without prejudice.

Please be advised that you may not submit an application for a pardon until
April 18, 2009, one year from the date the petition was denied.

A copy of this letter has been forwarded to the Office of the Governor's Chief
Legal Counsel.

Sincerely,

Julie Pease
Advisory Board of Pardons
Executive Clemency Coordinator

POSTSCRIPT: THE RELUCTANT WITNESS

The last words were to be Ben LaGuer's, but he is facing his third decade of incarceration. In 2010, the Commonwealth of Massachusetts Executive Office of Public Safety Parole Board again denied LaGuer parole. The board cited his refusal to engage in "significant sex offender treatment," fighting and possession of "pornographic images," and "combative and evasive" rhetoric during questioning as "negative personality traits that would make community supervision of Mr. LaGuer difficult if not impossible."[13] Following this decision, media expressed contempt that LaGuer—a convicted Puerto Rican politicized as Black—had for decades felt "entitled" to justice, education, employment, family, love, liberty. Perhaps this sense of "entitlement" damned him before the parole board and press, and thus became a punishable offense, as it has historically been for even the most apolitical of us. Punishment, though, does not always create passivity.

For several years, Ben LaGuer has written to me, despite my sporadic, brief, and formal responses infused with an academic reluctance to "get involved." Violations familiar to captives who resist only *seem* familiar to the outside witness. Yet, witnessing without the certainty and power to end injustice presents a trigger that once released offers a gift: greater intimacy with violence and the resistance to it, which one is always free to initiate. Even the most reluctant witness can appreciate an intimate: just recall ancestor Lady Day's delicate, devastating rendering of the production of strange fruit.

NEWSPAPER ARTICLES CONSULTED

"*Commonwealth v. Benjamin LaGuer* Timeline." Ben LaGuer Homepage. Retrieved May 28, 2007 (http://benlaguer.com.hosting.domaindirect.com/time_line.html).

"Deval Patrick for Governor." 2006. *Lawyers Weekly*, October 16.

"Errors in the Ben LaGuer DNA Analysis." Ben LaGuer Homepage. Retrieved May 28, 2007 (http://www.BenLaGuer.com).

"Lab Exam: Handling of DNA Evidence Must Be Meticulous, Timely." 2007. *Telegram and Gazette*, Opinion Section, January 19.

Arnold, David. 2002. "DNA Testing Backfires for Convicted Rapist." Florida Division of the International Association for Identification. March. Retrieved April 2, 2008 (http://www.fdiai.org/dna_testing_backfires_for_concic.html).

Atkins, Kimberly. 2006. "Numbers Falling, Hillman Attacks Own Camp's Ads." *Boston Herald*, November 1.

Atkins, Kimberly. 2006. "Rivals Take Law Into Their Hands." *Boston Herald*, October 7.

Bruun, Matthew. 2006. "Case Campaign Fallout Embraced by LaGuer." *Telegram and Gazette*, October 6.

Bruun, Matthew. 2006. "LaGuer Team Fires Back at Prosecution in Appeal." *Telegram and Gazette*, December 13.

Bruun, Matthew. 2007. "SJC Grills Lawyer as LaGuer Appeals: Justice Calls DNA Evidence Important." *Telegram and Gazette*, January 5.

Carr, Howie. 2006. "If You Thought Duke's Commutations Were Bad, Be Warned: Patrick's Could Be So Much Worse." *Boston Herald*, October 6.

Cohen, Laurie P. "Accuracy of New DNA Test Is Called in Question." The Macdonald Case News Archive. Retrieved April 2, 2008 (http://www.themacdonaldcase.org/accuracy.html).

Crimaldi, Laura. 2006. "Victim's Advocates Rip Healey for TV Ad with Rape Message." *Boston Herald*, October 19.

Eagan, Margery. 2006. "Three vs. One Dynamic Dooms Healey." *Boston Herald*, November 6.

Estes, Andrea. 2006. "Patrick Tried Twice to Aid Parole Bid: Candidate Changes Course on Release of Convicted Rapist." *Boston Globe*, City and Region, October 4.

Estes, Andrea. 2006. "Healey, Patrick Duel on Crime: Leniency Plea Targeted in Ad." *Boston Globe*, October 5.

Estes, Andrea. 2006. "Patrick Apologizes for Disclosure Missteps: Cites Research Lack on Link to Convict." *Boston Globe*, October 6.

Feifer, Jason. 2006. "LaGuer Rape Issue Ignored: Healey Appears in Leominster." *Telegram and Gazette*, October 22.

Frank, David E. 2007. "Lawyer Challenges DNA Evidence in Wake of Crime Lab's Mistakes." *Lawyers Weekly*, February 26.

Goldscheider, Eric. 2006. "LaGuer Reconsidered." *Valley Advocate*, August 17. Retrieved February 1, 2009 (http://www.bluemassgroup.com/showDiary.do?diaryId=3254).

Goldscheider, Eric. 2007. "Weak Links: The State Police Laboratory Should Be the Last Bastion of Impartiality. Is It?" *Valley Advocate*, March 22.

LeBlanc, Steve. 2006. "Healey Ad Drawing Fire Among Females: Critics Say New Spot Panders to Women's Fears of Sexual Assault." *Telegram and Gazette*, October 19.

Lehigh, Scot. 2006. "Kerry Healey: Queen of the Ring." *Boston Globe*, October 5.

McFalane, Clive. 2006. "LaGuer Story Still in Limelight." *Telegram and Gazette*, October 11.

Monahan, John J. 2006. "Benjamin LaGuer Factor Flares: Votes at Stake over Long, Convoluted Rape Case." *Telegram and Gazette*, October 5.

Monahan, John J. 2006. "Attack Ads Skew Gubernatorial Campaign." *Telegram and Gazette*, October 15.

Monahan, John J. 2006. "Healey Vows to Tone Down Calls on Rape Case." *Telegram and Gazette*, October 13.

Monahan, John J. 2006. "Patrick, Healey Work LaGuer Angle." *Telegram and Gazette*, October 6.

Monahan, John J. 2006. "Healey Presses LaGuer Attack as Mayor Meets with Patrick." *Telegram and Gazette*, October 11.

Saltzman, Jonathan. 2006. "LaGuer Says He Does Not Feel Betrayed." *Boston Globe*, City and Region, October 7.

Saltzman, Jonathan. 2006. "Convict Will Appeal on Patrick's Day." *Boston Globe*, City and Region, December 30.

Shanahan, Mark. 2007. "Healey Rejected by Theater Board." *Boston Globe*, City and Region, April 4.

Sutner, Shaun. 2006. "Peterson Takes on Murray: Legal Work for Sex Offenders Blasted." *Telegram and Gazette*, October 14.

Taylor, John. 1994. "And the Truth Shall Set Him Free. Or Will It?" *Esquire*, May.

Wedge, Dave. 2006. "Rapist's Ex-Lawyer in Healey Camp." *Boston Herald*, October 27.

Wideman, Dean A. 2006. "Forensic Case Review: *Commonwealth of Massachusetts v. Benjamin LaGuer*." Case No. 83–103391. March 30.

Williamson, Diane. 2006. "Lawyers Have Right to Object: Election Will Be Judge of Healey Scare Tactics." *Telegram and Gazette*, October 17.

TERRITORY AND TERROR

Part 3

8 NOT A CITIZEN, ONLY A SUSPECT
Racialized Immigration Law Enforcement Practices

Mary Romero

After setting into motion two major enforcement operations targeting street gangs and other criminals in 2005, the Department of Homeland Security announced another immigration operation that mobilized local, state, and federal law enforcement agents. Calling the operation, Return to Sender, the Immigration and Customs Enforcement framed the massive immigration raids across the nation as an effort to deport criminal aliens and to crack down on the criminal infrastructure associated with illegal immigration. Across the country, human rights activists and immigration advocates characterized the operation as a campaign of terror and intimidation involving raids of private residence (usually late at night or in the early dawn) without warrants in search of undocumented immigrants. In raids conducted in the workplace, law enforcement agents entered premises with warrants identifying a few individuals and then proceeded to target only Latino workers for citizenship inspection. A few months before announcing Operation Return to Sender, the Department of Homeland Security awarded a $385 million contingency contract to Halliburton's subsidiary KBR to build detention camps. In the meantime, Latino communities and families again find themselves facing anti-immigration legislation and sentiment that fuel popular images of Latinos in the United States as illegal, criminal, inferior, and terrorist.

This chapter examines the practices of racial profiling in immigration law enforcement and the embedded racism in targeting Latinos as potential aliens. I begin with a brief overview of the history of immigration legislation that has targeted persons of Mexican ancestry. Included in this account is a discussion of the racist citizen vigilantism encouraged by the state's rhetoric, which links "immigration" to economic, educational, welfare, and security problems. Using data from a case study on a 1997 immigration raid in Arizona, I analyze policing tactics used in raids conducted in collaboration between local and national law enforcement agents. The data consist of two separate investigation reports, depositions collected in one of the lawsuits filed against the local police department, and newspaper articles. The investigation reports include deportation forms, local police logs of activity, selected radio dispatch transcripts of traffic-spotters, and narratives detailing encounters with law enforcement agents. Since the data documented during the raid are limited to stops resulting in deportations, data on all stops that occurred during this five-day raid are not available. However, witness narratives and depositions do provide a unique source of data on incidents not documented by state officials. Data from the investigation and witness narratives provide significant resources that identify a relationship between racism and the state, reinforced in U.S. immigration policy and law enforcement. Before I turn to the case study, a brief history of racialized immigration policy aimed at Mexicans and Mexican Americans may set the legal narrative for analyzing raids as racial violence.

RACE, MEXICANS, AND IMMIGRATION

Racist characterizations of Mexicans are easily documented as early as the annexation of Texas, which eventually escalated relations between the United States and Mexico into war. The disregard for Mexicans as humans is evident throughout the history of U.S. expansion into northern Mexico, the war, and its aftermath. Carey McWilliams (1990: 101) quotes General Winfield Scott's descriptions of war crimes committed under the American flag as "atrocities to make Heaven weep and every American of Christian morals blush for his country. Murder, robbery and rape of mothers and daughters in the presence of tied-up males of the families have been common all along the Rio Grande." For several decades following the war, whites were rarely if ever prosecuted for killing Mexicans, who were characterized as thieves, murderers, and half-breeds (Acuña 2000). Through legal and illegal strategies, persons of Mexican ancestry were dispossessed of their land, reduced to wage laborers, and recruited to work in mines, on ranches, and as agricultural workers. Women were confined to employment as domestics, cooks, laundresses, and farmworkers. Racialization of labor in the Southwest resulted in the practice of peonage, the use of a "Mexican wage" to assure whites a higher wage, and the regulation of the most dangerous and menial jobs as "Mexican jobs" (Barrera

1979). Both the Texas and Arizona Rangers were notorious for protecting the illegal practices of cattle barons in Texas, and later for assisting in controlling workers in labor disputes in the Arizona mines. Meanwhile, federal and state governments turned a blind eye to the killing and lynching of Mexicans (McWilliams 1990; Acuña 2000; Montejano 1987).

Immediately following the war, the state treated Mexicans as immigrants and noncitizens, with a few exceptions made for the wealthy, such as the class identified as "*los ricos*" in New Mexico—who were frequently referred to as Spanish rather than Mexican (Romero 2007). Although the Treaty of Guadalupe Hidalgo incorporated provisions protecting the rights of Mexicans under occupied territory, including the rights and duties of U.S. citizenship, reference to Mexicans became synonymous with "foreigner." Dubbed as aliens regardless of their citizenship status, Mexicans were perceived as both an economic and a security threat to the United States. Consequently, they were targeted in all anti-immigration legislation and campaigns. For instance, the California legislature aimed the Miners Foreign Tax of 1852 at Chinese miners but applied restrictions to Mexican and Mexican American miners as well (Acuña 2000; Gutiérrez 1995). However, because of the shortage of labor to build the railroads in the West, and a need for miners, both Mexican Americans and Mexican immigrants were recruited (Zamora 1993; Barrera 1979). Vigilantism was frequently a locally sanctioned means of controlling labor and deterring unionization efforts (Davis and Chacon 2006). In the following generations, immigration legislation and law enforcement were commonly used to curtail unionization campaigns (Weber 1994). The most common practices in controlling the movement of labor involved restricting immigration enforcement during harvest time, and scheduling massive raids during economic recessions and union activity (Acuña 2000; Guerin-Gonzales 1994). The most notorious deportation and repatriation campaign against Mexicans occurred during the Great Depression. Only Mexican immigrants were scapegoated for the widespread unemployment (Guerin-Gonzales 1994). An estimated five hundred to six hundred thousand Mexicans and their U.S.-born children were moved to Mexico between 1929 and 1939. The final estimate of the number of Mexicans deported or repatriated is as high as two million (Acuña 2000).

A reversal in immigration policy towards Mexico occurred as the United States entered World War II and began to intern Japanese Americans. With the country facing labor shortages, the most significant labor program in the twentieth century, known as the Bracero Program, was created. The United

States signed bilateral agreements with Mexico to recruit Mexican men to work in agriculture. Over 4.5 million Mexican nationals were legally contracted to work in the fields from 1942 to 1964. Under short-term labor contracts, Mexican nationals were employed by small farmers, large growers, and farm associations throughout the country. Although the program outlined provisions for adequate housing, food, occupational insurance, and transportation back to Mexico, abuses were abundant and resulted in cheap and exploitable labor for agribusiness (Galarza 1964; Gamboa 1990; Calavita 1992). Although the migration program was legally ended in 1964, the state continued to work closely with agribusiness to assure adequate flows of cheap, easily exploitable labor supply during peak harvest seasons. During the twenty-four-year period of the Bracero Program, the use of immigration raids was not entirely abandoned. In 1954, the Immigration and Naturalization Service (INS) began a major immigration campaign aimed at Mexican immigrants. Using the racial slur, the program was named Operation Wetback. Raids and sweeps were conducted throughout Mexican American neighborhoods, making random stops and conducting mandatory citizenship inspections of persons "looking Mexican" (Garcia 1980). An estimated 3.7 million Mexicans, including U.S. citizens, were deported between 1954 and 1957 (Bender 2005). Militarized sweeps of Mexican residents kept families and neighborhoods in "a state of permanent insecurity" as "raids, arrests, and deportation drives" continued throughout the 1950s (Acuña 2000: 306).

The cycle of selective immigration law enforcement has changed little over the following fifty years: controlling the flow and movement of available labor, disciplining labor by obstructing unionization activity with threats of deportation, and removing workers during recessions (Ngai 2004; Calavita 1992; Cockcroft 1986). Scholars have traced the cycles of raids to fulfilling other political agendas, such as increasing INS budgets or pandering to alarmist anti-immigrant public discourse (Nevins 2002; Andreas 2000; Massey, Durand, and Malone 2002; Chavez 2001). The last few decades have seen several insidious and draconian anti-immigration policies and practices that threatened livelihoods and the loss of human lives. Both Operation Blockade (later referred to as Operation Hold the Line) and Operation Gatekeeper drastically changed policing the border into a militarized operation. Immigration and drug enforcement policies became intertwined to further the image of sealing the U.S.-Mexico border for national security (Dunn 1996; Nevins 2002). Increased militarization of the border has increased the number of cases of human rights violations (Johnson 2004; Fernandes 2007). These operations also fueled state anti-immigration policies, resulting in decreased public funding to low-income communities and further racist attacks on affirmative action policies (Chavez 2001; Lee, Ottati, and Hussain 2001). While research has consistently shown that militarizing the border has done little to curb immigration or to restrict U.S. employers' access to vulnerable, cheap labor, the policies have clearly increased the human cost in crossing the border (Cornelius 2001; Eschbach, Hagan, Rodriguez, Hernández-León, and Bailey 1999). Between 1990 and 2005, Arizona experienced a twenty-fold increase of deaths resulting from the "funnel effect" created by militarization operations that forced migrants to cross the desolate and isolated Sonoran desert (Rubio-Goldsmith, McCormick, Martinez, and Duarte 2006).

I now turn to a case study of an immigration raid to examine how the state reinforces racism through immigration law enforcement. Data on immigration law enforcement made publicly available through state records report only the number of persons apprehended, not the number of citizens or legal residents stopped and searched. Therefore, the prevalence of racialized immigration law enforcement and its impact on communities of color remain invisible in legal reporting procedures. Documentary practices consist of standardized modes of monitoring, observing, coordinating, and classifying that are based on a racialized form of rationality, objectivity, or actualities. These institutional practices are "relations of ruling" and unravel the everyday management of social control and domination (Smith 1990, 1999). In rare instances, such as official investigations into allegations of civil rights or human rights violations, data become available to uncover what Daniel Georges-Abeyie (2001: xiv) refers to as the "more covert, hidden forms of discrimination." Investigations resulting from lawsuits or community protests are more likely to disclose immigration enforcement processes that usually remain invisible and concealed from public view.

In identifying more invisible forms of discrimination in the criminal justice system, Dragan Milovanovic and Katheryn Russell (2001) point to the range of covert or informal forms to overt or formal forms. Racial profiling can be an official practice targeting a particular group or an informal practice that police or immigration law enforcement officers incorporate into their everyday work. An overt and formal form of discrimination appears in the 1975 landmark case U.S. v. Brignoni-Ponce, in which the Supreme Court ruled on guidelines for assessing "probable cause" and "reasonableness": "Mexican appearance" could remain on the list as long as it was not the sole factor used to justify stops (Valencia, García, Flore, and Juárez 2004). Covert discriminatory practices can be nonverbal "gestures, mannerisms; omissions; civility not offered," presumption of illegal status, intimidation, and other forms of dehumanization. Informal verbal practices include "putdowns, fighting words, expletives, hate/racist speech, insults; messages/discourses of hate and racial inferiority" (Milovanovic and Russell 2001: xx).

I analyze these case documents to identify racialized patterns of inclusion and exclusion, and to identify the ideological understandings invoked by the state's immigration policies and practices. If racialized factors are the sole purpose of the stop, then law enforcement practices of racial profiling circumscribe illegality and citizenship onto specific bodies. Racial profiling results in micro- and macroaggressions. This type of immigration law enforcement is harmful to Mexicans and other racialized Latinos because the practices "belittle, demean, ridicule or subordinate on the one hand, and on the other, they limit access to equal opportunities and fair dealings before the law" (Henry and Milovanovic 1996: 103). In this case study, I am particularly interested in how an individual's "Mexicanness" is used to establish "reasonable suspicion" or "probable cause," and in the informal or covert discriminatory practices embedded in conducting immigration raids. My analysis is based on an immigration raid that occurred prior to 9/11 and before local police departments were mandated to engage in immigration law enforcement. Therefore, in this case, the basis for a joint operation between a local police department and the INS was an issue under investigation and attributed to the call for an internal investigation.

CASE STUDY OF AN IMMIGRATION RAID

In the summer of 1997, the Chandler, Arizona, Police Department and Border Patrol agents from Casa Grande Station and the Tucson area joined forces to conduct four major immigration raids. Like the previous raids, the fourth raid focused on the most highly populated Latino section of the city. Over five days, 432 suspected undocumented immigrants were arrested. Daily results of immigration law enforcement were summarized by the chief patrol agent as follows:

> Day 1, July 27, 1997: "Within three hours . . . more than 75 arrests out of approximately 100 contacts" were made through "casual contacts . . . along the streets in and around public areas." A total of eighty-three arrests were made that day (eighty-two Mexicans and one Guatemalan).

Day 2, July 28, 1997: The target area was "expanded to one square mile of the downtown Chandler area" and "nearly all contacts occurred outside dwellings," and "the exceptions were the result of specific information or probable cause." On this day, the border patrol arrested 102 Mexicans.

Day 3, July 29, 1997: Working with Chandler police between 4:00 A.M. and 8:00 A.M., they arrested sixty-nine (ethnicity not noted). Bicycle patrols working public areas and trailer parks arrested an additional forty-nine.

Day 4, July 30, 1997: A total of seventy-seven illegal aliens were arrested.

Day 5, July 31, 1997: Fifty-two arrests were made.

Calling attention to law enforcement officers' treatment of persons of Mexican ancestry as "strays," in allusion to the Old West cowboy, the immigration sweep came to be known as the Chandler Roundup. In response to demonstrations, protests, and community meetings with public officials, two investigations into the raids were conducted. The primary focus was on police misconduct and violations of civil rights, and a secondary concern was the role of local police officers who participated in the joint operation with INS. Given the nature of the complaints, public officials were particularly concerned about the reasons behind the raids, the timing of the raids, criteria used by police to assess "probable cause" and "reasonable suspicion," incidents involving entering homes without warrants, and the use of excessive force or inappropriate behavior.

In addition to the controversy over the occurrence of civil rights violations was the debate over the actual goal of the joint operation. City and police officials claimed the raids were an attempt to decrease crime and illegal immigration, while local residents argued that the raids were an act of intimidation and violence against the community in order to remove Mexican Americans, Mexican immigrants, and Mexican businesses from the downtown area, which developers planned to rebuild. For their part, police officials argued that the raids were their contribution to the City of Chandler's 1995 urban renewal project, Operation Restoration. However, residents argued that surveys taken to develop that plan did not identify immigration as a problem but rather indicated a need for better street lighting, cleaner streets, regular garbage service, and maintained alleys.

After an immediate investigation conducted by the office of Attorney General Grant Woods, the report, *Results of the Chandler Survey*, was issued in December 1997. The report was based on information collected from minutes of the community meetings held with public officials, interviews with citizens and legal residents stopped during the five-day operation, minutes of city council meetings with community members, newspaper articles, memoranda between city officials, Chandler police radio dispatch audiotapes, police field notes, and witness testimonies and complaints. In response to the attorney general's report, the City of Chandler paid for an independent study to investigate their findings. The independent investigation was conducted the following summer and issued a three-volume final report, *Report of Independent Investigation into July 1997 Joint Operation Between Border Patrol and Chandler Police Department*. Volume 1 includes a mission statement, narrative, and summaries of interviews conducted with public officials. Volume 2, *Complainants*, is the independent investigators' direct response to the descriptive accounts of civil rights violations formally filed with the Chandler police, the Office of the Attorney General, or the Mexican Consulate's office. Volume 3, *Appendices to Report of Independent Investigation*, includes four maps (the Tucson sector of the Border Patrol, Chandler and vicinity, area of Operation Restoration, and areas covered in the joint operation); excerpts from policy and procedure handbooks; a survey of policies regarding illegal aliens of fourteen cities along border states; a survey of how the media learned of the 1997 joint operation; the Chandler Police Department's community-oriented policing programs; and eighty-nine records of Border Patrol form I-213 (Deportable Alien) produced during the joint operation. Since the City of Chandler's report focused on disputing allegations made by persons who filed complaints or were interviewed by the attorney general's office, legitimations of complaints or incidents of wrongdoing were found accurate only if they were consistent with official public documents, such as arrest records, police notes, and radio transcripts, or were corroborated in interviews with police officers.

Racial Profiling Tactics in Immigration Law Enforcement

Immediate attention to local and federal law enforcement's use of racial profiling appeared in news accounts. The media reported incidents of Mexican Americans and legal residents being stopped, while whites in the same vicinity were not. As one Mexican American resident told a reporter from the *Los Angeles Times*, "They were looking for dark-skinned workers speaking Spanish" (Sahagun 1997: A5). Other citizens reported similar police practices. Celso Vasquez, a Mexican national and a legal U.S. resident, was stopped while driving and was asked for proof of citizenship as well as the car title and registration (Tobar 1999). Juan Gonzales told another reporter that he was required to show proof of citizenship at a gas station while Anglos pumping gas alongside him were not. "A lot of my white friends have been in this country as long as I have. So how come I'm treated differently? . . . How come I have to prove I'm a U.S. citizen? That's just not right" (Amparano 1997: A1). Racial profiling was so blatant that a blond, blue-eyed illegal Irish immigrant, who was employed at a law firm and had never been asked about her immigration status, stated, "I don't have to worry. I blend in well" (Amparano 1997: A1). In his letter to the editor, Jose Antonio Franco summarized the community experiences of the five-day immigration raid: "INS, in collaboration with the Chandler Police Department has been accosting people shopping at Southwest Supermarket, driving down Chandler Boulevard or sitting at home and demanding they produce documents or face deportation."

In analyzing internal documents related to the planning stages of the raid, the attorney general's office found that the four-square-mile downtown redevelopment zone selected for the raid was not linked to any "articulated criminal activity." In reviewing police radio dispatch tapes, they found that "Mexican appearance" was the primary, and many times the only, stated criteria to determine "reasonable suspicion" or "probable cause." A summary of Day 3 of the raid illustrates a pattern used during the five-day operation:

> a total of forty-three (43) vehicles were specifically singled out in a two hour period of time from 4:00–6:00 a.m. The officers identified seven (7) vehicles because of known violations of the law warranting a stop. However, of the remaining thirty-six (36) vehicles called in, seven (7) calls describing vehicles were made despite the officers stating that there was no probable cause to believe that violations had occurred. The other twenty-nine (29) vehicles were singled out without articulation of what, if any, violation of law may have been observed by the reporting officer.

The consistent practice of using "Mexican appearance" as the basis for determining "reasonable suspicion" or "probable cause" was further documented in the computer-printed *Record of Deportable Alien* forms used by the INS. In preparation for the raid, the forms had several categories *already* filled out: "Mexico and/or Mexican" filled in for "Country of Origin"; "Laborer" for "Occupation"; "Black" for "Hair"; "Brown" for "Eyes"; and "Med" for "Complexion." Identifying race and national origin prior to any arrest points to the use of racial profiling as an overt or formal discriminatory practice sanctioned by local and federal law enforcement agents. Both the police summary of policing activities and the prepared deportation forms reveal the institutional practices of monitoring, observing, and classifying Mexicans to be foreigners, illegals, and criminals.

An analysis of the data from complaints filed indicates that policing practices targeted working-class persons perceived to be Mexican. On the surface, a review of the numbers and ethnicity noted does not suggest class distinction: a total of seventy-one complaints were filed, which involved ninety-one separate incidents of persons stopped by officers. The information given in the *Report of Independent Investigation* is incomplete, but certain patterns are still suggested from these data. Although the citizenship status of the twenty-nine complainants (involving forty-one stops) is not included in the report, eleven were identified as U.S. citizens of Mexican ancestry; fifteen were identified as Latino and legal residents; and one complainant, identified as Latino, was a permanent resident. Complainants' activity at the time of the stop was recorded. Of the legal residents who were stopped, twenty-three were walking, twenty-five were driving, ten were shopping, two were at work, two were riding a bike, two were using public telephones, and sixteen involved police officers entering the complainant's home and requesting proof of citizenship status. On closer consideration, many of these activities do suggest class-based behavior. Given the extreme heat of Arizona summers, walking or biking during the day are avoided unless a person does not have a motor vehicle. Common ownership of cell phones makes the use of public telephones a class marker. All the persons stopped while driving were driving in the four-mile radius that included residents of the working-class and poor Latino population and Mexican-owned businesses.

In the analysis of complaints in the *Report of Independent Investigation*, I found both overt and covert forms of discriminatory practice. Complainants' descriptions of encounters with law enforcement do not implicate them with criminal behavior or actions that can be identified as "reasonable suspicion," but they do strongly suggest the overt use of racial profiling, as well as the use of discretionary enforcement of minor violations. Forms of covert discriminatory practices are evident in the presumption that Mexicans residing and shopping in this neighborhood do not have legal status in the United States; in the entering of homes without warrants; and in the use of excessive force. Race appears to serve as a proxy for "dangerous," thus requiring law enforcement officers to summarily enter private residences in order to apprehend suspected criminals, that is, illegal aliens. All of these acts perpetuate stereotypes about

Mexican and immigrant status in the United States. Holding these individuals in the extreme heat of day for several hours and using handcuffs further serve to engender fear and to dehumanize persons of Mexican ancestry.

While police and INS documents reveal overt and formal discriminatory practices against persons on the basis of their physical appearance, testimonies given at the city council meeting and witness accounts given to the attorney general's office illustrate cultural characteristics embedded in racial profiling practices. Both verbal and nonverbal covert discrimination practices were used in policing low-income Latino neighborhoods. One nonverbal covert discriminatory practice present in all witness accounts is the officers' presumption that illegal or criminal status can be determined by racial appearance. In addition to being stopped on the basis of appearance rather than behavior, witnesses describe a range of gestures, postures, and mannerisms used by law enforcement agents that were disrespectful, intimidating, and belittling. The range of discretion used by officers is apparent in the wide range of identification documents persons were expected to be carrying, the length of time persons were detained, the amount of intimidation and force used, and the overall treatment of individuals. A more detailed presentation of witness accounts illustrates the level of pain, humiliation, fear, violation, embarrassment, and mortification persons experienced during the raids. I have selected five narratives to exemplify the types of microaggressions that occur in immigration raids.

Witness Accounts of Microaggressions

Identified as "F" in the attorney general's report, this young mother described herself as having family roots in the United States since the Mexican-American War. She was stopped in the grocery store parking lot in the presence of white shoppers who were not being stopped or questioned by the police. As she left the store, she was speaking in Spanish to her three young children. "F" expressed humiliation from being targeted for citizenship inspection as she walked to her car. Unwilling to accept her driver's license as proof of citizenship, the police detained her in the parking lot until she was able to produce another form of identification. The following quote from the account summarized in the Attorney General's Office reveals her intense feelings of mortification from this affront of being racially profiled:

> She feels that she has to watch what she wears and that she cannot look unkempt. The officer made her feel stereotyped on the basis of what she was wearing. She felt that she did not belong. A number of people were going in and out of the

store and one couple looked at her. F did not see anyone else stopped. The only time she has gone back to Chandler has been for the meeting at the church. She has not gone back to the store because she does not feel welcome; she feels violated. This has also affected her plans to have her children spend some time with relatives in Mexico. She canceled their trip because she does not want to risk her children picking up an accent.

Treated as a criminal in front of her children and strangers made "F" aware of her "otherness" in a nation that allows skin color to serve as a proxy for "reasonable suspicion" and that defines citizenship by whiteness. The experience of being racialized as a foreigner and illegal immigrant points to the way that law enforcement officers perceived her—a person of "dark complexion" and bilingual abilities—as inferior to monolingual white citizens also shopping in the vicinity. The possibility of looking unkempt or of speaking with a Spanish accent, along with her dark skin, made her susceptible to being publicly humiliated by the police. In order to protect her children from being placed at risk before the law, "F" concludes that she must fully integrate them into white middle-class society and cut all ties with her Mexican community, including her family in Mexico. Her account points to the assumptions she has about citizenship privileges and how she plans to protect herself and her children from being treated as inferior by stripping their lives of any traces of "Mexicanness."

Another U.S. citizen reported an incident that occurred as her two daughters walked home from elementary school. In the attorney general's report, the mother is referred to as "Q."

On July 30, 1997, Q was running [a] little late picking up her daughters, age 7 and 10, from Fry School in Chandler so the girls started walking home. When Q caught up with them, half a block from school, the girls were crying. Q asked why they were in tears and they told Q, "It is your fault," and asked, "What is a birth certificate?" The girls pointed down the street and said that the officers told us to keep our birth certificates with us or they will send us back to Mexico. Both girls kept saying, "Mom, we don't know Mexico." In order to verify who had stopped her daughters, Q put the girls in her vehicle and began to drive in the direction the girls said the officers had gone. Q saw three Chandler Police officers on bicycles not far from the school. No INS/Border Patrol agents were in sight. Now, when someone is at the door, the girls hide, bundle up with each other, and ask their mother not to open the door because "maybe it is the police." Before this incident both girls were always eager to go with her on errands; now, they cry so she will let them stay at home. Both girls insist on having their birth certificates pinned to their clothes or around their necks and no longer want to walk home from school or play outdoors.

"Q"'s witness account illustrates the level of intimidation and the loss of security and well-being that her children experience from police officers' threat to deport them. Unlike their white classmates, these girls become marked as "illegal" on the basis of their appearance. Being instructed by a representative of the state that a birth certificate is necessary to assure their safety, they no longer trust their mother's ability to protect them. These children cannot expect to be treated as citizens, because they are stereotyped as noncitizens. Seen by the police as belonging to Mexico, a country that is unfamiliar to the children, they come to understand Mexico as a reference to punishment. The daughters' fear of the police as state representatives is not based on engaging in bad behavior but rather on their being. Thus, they conclude that they must restrict all of their movement outside their home.

The witness identified as "E" is a grandmother who gives an account of being stopped by police as she walked with her grandchild to the drugstore. Her account illustrates the impact of the discretion used by immigration law enforcement to intimidate family members.

E is a grandmother who immigrated from Mexico ten years ago. She is a widow of a United States citizen. In July 1997, she was walking to the pharmacy to pick up medication for her diabetes and was accompanied by her seven year old granddaughter. Half a block from Arizona Avenue, they were approached by a Chandler police officer on a bicycle who motioned for them to stop. When E stopped, the officer approached them and began questioning her in English, asking if she had papers. E asked if the officer wanted to see her papers and he said yes; he then took her papers and residency card and scrutinized the card front and back. Next he asked if the girl had papers and what her name was. The girl looked very serious and wide-eyed. E told the officer that her granddaughter had been born in Nogales, Arizona. The officer then told E that she should carry her granddaughter's birth certificate wherever she went and that she should further get a letter from the girl's mother verifying that E was the grandmother. He then said that she should teach her granddaughter to say, "I'm an American citizen." The officer did not tell E why he stopped her and he took no notes. The officer asked the granddaughter if she was in school and she told him she was in the first grade. He then said good-bye and drove straight ahead as he left.

"E"'s account does not identify any action that she or her grandchild were engaged in that might be construed as illegal behavior or as "probable cause" or "reasonable suspicion" that they were illegally residing in the United States. Physical appearance was the sole criterion used by the police officer in making the stop. The officer's statement that the grandmother must carry official documentation proving that the child is a U.S. citizen and that she is her grandchild is further evidence that citizenship is assumed to be inscribed on the body. Having seen her residency card and passing her immigration inspection, the police officer tried to intimidate "E" by informing her of the need to carry documented proof of her relationship to the child. Embedded in this statement is the implied threat that the police may remove her grandchild from her care. Grandmothers are generally not required by law to possess written parental consent when caring for their grandchildren. This action taken by a state official informs "E"'s grandchild of the risk she is in when she is under the care of her grandmother without documentation.

The following witness account illustrates the range of microaggressions embedded in everyday policing tactics involving youth of color in low-income areas. A sixteen-year-old Latino male, identified as "I," was immediately treated as a "suspect" on the basis of his appearance, not his action. As the account reveals, there was no criminal behavior or circumstances that could possibly be construed as "probable cause."

In late July, "I" was stopped near Erie Street and Arizona Avenue. He and a friend had gone to buy a pizza at Little Caesar's. While they were in Little Caesar's, he and his friend were approached by two bicycle officers, one a Chandler Police officer and the other an immigration officer. The Chandler Police officer addressed him and the INS/Border Patrol officer spoke with his friend. Both spoke English. The police officer asked "I" for his social security number and asked if he was legal. He stated he could not remember the social security number and told the officer he was a legal resident. Both men were then asked to come out of the store and the police officer directed Little Caesar's staff to return their money to them. The Chandler Police officer then radioed for a car. Outside the restaurant the police officer asked "I" for his wallet and "I" explained that he did not have his wallet with him and he was only 16. The officer said he should always have his wallet with him. He then repeatedly asked for the social security which "I" could not remember. He was allowed to call his mother after asking the officers twice. He was also told to get into a Chandler Police vehicle, where he waited for about 30 minutes. His mother eventually came and verified his Social Security Number. His friend was taken away in the Chandler police vehicle and was deported.

This incident highlights the level of discretion that law enforcement officers use in their encounters with persons stereotyped as the "other" and thus not entitled to the same treatment as white middle-class youth. Since purchasing pizza is not a criminal act, and the officers acknowledged that the young men had already paid for the pizza, there was no evidence that a crime was in process or being planned. "I" and his friend's physical appearance was the only reason the officers entered Little Caesar's and demanded identification from these two customers. No other customers or employees in the restaurant were asked to show proof of citizenship or required to show their Social Security cards. Interrupting a legitimate commercial transaction and calling the restaurant staff and customers' attention to the youths being detained reinforces the stereotype of criminality in Latino male youth. Using the discretion given by the state, these officers did not immediately allow "I" to contact his mother. Being detained in the police car until his mother arrived with the required identification increased the period of public humiliation and further served to dehumanize the youth. Creating a public spectacle of policing activity legitimates stereotypes of Mexican youth as criminal and dangerous.

In the fifth witness account, the police entered a private residence without a warrant and proceeded to interrogate both children and adults in the household. Verbal and nonverbal discriminatory practices were described by one of the adult males, identified as "B." This incident occurred after 11:00 P.M., when everyone in the household had gone to bed.

The family was awakened by a loud banging on the front door and bright lights shining through the windows. When B looked around, he saw two Chandler police officers, with an INS/Border Patrol agent behind them. All officers were bicycle officers. The officers demanded to be allowed into the trailer and when B asked if they had the right to come in, he was told, "We can do whatever we want, we are the Chandler Police Department. You have people who are here illegally." Although B denied that there were any undocumented aliens there, the officers insisted on entering the trailer, rousing everyone from bed. The family members were all in their sleep clothes, but the officers refused to allow them to dress. None of the officers indicated that they had warrants authorizing them to enter the dwelling. Two of the children were United States citizens, and except for the brother-in-law, all the rest were legal aliens; the brother-in-law had entered the country legally but his visa had expired and [he] was in the process of getting it renewed. When the officers discovered that the brother-in-law did not have proper papers, they called the Chandler Police Department back up vehicle and took him away in a patrol car. B attempted to give his brother-in-law street clothes when the officers were taking him away, but the officers would not allow this and took him away in his sleep clothes. He was later readmitted to the United States with the renewed visa he had been awaiting. The others were detained in the trailer for approximately ninety minutes; they were not searched but they were questioned even after they showed the papers demonstrating that they were legally in the United States. The police told B that they had spoken with the park manager and that he had given them permission to search the trailers, had given them a map, and had marked on the map where Hispanic residents lived. The four children involved in this incident are still fearful when someone knocks at the door of the trailer, and continue to be nervous when they see police officers on the street.

The police action taken against a family identified as "Hispanic" does not read like a description of policing in a democratic society but rather of a police state. Law enforcement agents' request to the manager of a housing project to identify households on the basis of race legitimates and reinforces racist beliefs about Mexicans as foreign, criminal, and unauthorized to be in the United States. Planning night raids on personal property without warrants maintains the image that Latino families living in the area are a threat to the local community. All of the family members, regardless of their citizenship or immigration status, were subjected to the discretion of the officers, who proceeded to demand identification from all adults and children. Treated as inferior and lacking any rights, the family continued to be questioned and detained by the officers even after proof of citizenship or immigration status had been established. Family members were shown no respect, and officers made no attempt to offer civility. The power of the state is evident in both verbal and nonverbal discriminatory practices. Announcing that "we can do whatever we want, we are the Chandler Police Department" informed the family of their subordinate status in society. The state official's use of terror, fear, and excessive force is a frequently invisible dimension of the racism embedded in immigration law enforcement when it is conducted in private residences or other places outside the view of the general public and media.

These five witness accounts exemplify the forms of microaggression that women, men, and children endure when the state formally and informally uses racist characteristics to profile "illegal" immigrants. As a consequence of their treatment as criminal and inferior to whites in the United States, these persons were subjected to various degrees of intimidation and humiliation. Racial affronts by state officials exacerbate the Latino community's distrust towards public officials and law enforcement. The use of discriminatory practices in law enforcement serves to deter political participation and cooperation with policing activities. Unlike other citizens and legal residents, persons who appear to be Mexican, regardless of age or citizenship status, were instructed by state officials that they were required to carry various forms of identification. While immigration law enforcement permitted Latino immigrants throughout the Phoenix metropolitan area to enter middle- and upper-class neighborhoods to work as gardeners, maids, and nannies, their freedom to engage in shopping, driving, walking, and other activities near their homes was restricted. Mexican Americans and Mexican immigrants who were stopped during the raid were presumed to be inferior, and their right to belong was challenged. These U.S. citizens and legal residents felt betrayed by the city and federal government that denied their legitimate status to drive, walk, work, attend school, and occupy homes like white citizens and legal residents of European descent.

Following the protests, residents impacted by the raids confronted the Chandler City Council at its August 14 meeting, just two weeks after the fourth raid. The council allowed twelve residents to offer public testimonies about the raids. Summaries of three of these testimonies were included in the attorney general's report. To illustrate the link that both whites and Mexican Americans made between racism and the state, I turn to the analysis of testimonies. Unlike the summary witness accounts documented by the office of attorney Woods, testimonies included additional information about the impact the raid had on the community. And as the following testimonies reveal, the state's racist policies and practices impact the larger community.

Testimonies of Microaggression

The first testimony presented was given by Catalina Veloz, who is a U.S. citizen raised in Arizona. She described two incidents of law enforcement officers who requested proof of citizenship. Both incidents occurred on the same day. In the first, the INS Border Patrol agent spoke to her in Spanish and asked her, "Where were you born?" and "In what hospital?" She was asked to show her driver's license, car registration, or proof of car insurance. At the end of their conversation in Spanish, the officer yelled to a nearby Border Patrol officer, "This one's a go!" Recognizing that the officer assumed she was unable to speak English, and thus was not a citizen, she quickly spoke in English and cursed the officer in English and Spanish. She felt angry and humiliated. On hearing her speak English, the officer said, "Oh, so you speak English?" and allowed her to drive away.

> Later that same day, Veloz was approached by another joint operation team as she drove into the parking lot of a Circle K to get a 12-pack of soda and a pack of cigarettes. Veloz stated that she was playing Mexican music, which she loves. A bicycle patrol officer parked his bicycle beside her and asked her for papers. Veloz testified that the questions she was asked the second time were the same as the first. . . . Again, Veloz was not cited nor given an explanation for why she was approached.

Veloz's five-year-old son was with her when both stops occurred. He now cries every time he sees a Chandler police officer and says, "Mom, here comes the *migra* to pick you up." He is so frightened that he might lose his mother that he has asked her to hide. She also reported that during the raids, several neighbors who are legal residents requested her to grocery-shop or fill prescriptions for them because they feared to leave their homes. Veloz experienced the stops and identification as a criminal on the basis of the "color of her skin" as painful and humiliating. She ended her testimony with a question to the city council members: "What's next? Are they going to expect us to carry our birth certificates or papers around with us or tattoo numbers on our arms?"

In the following two testimonies, residents point to the racism spurred by the state's racist action. In his testimony, Jim Ryan, a white U.S. citizen, stressed that the joint operation impacted not only the Latino neighborhoods but the larger Chandler community.

> He [Ryan] said that he came to testify because he thought it was important that the City Council hear from someone who was not Hispanic to emphasize that this was not just a Hispanic issue, but one that is of concern to everyone in the community. He also stated that although he is an attorney, he cared more about the policy issue of conducting joint operations with the INS/Border Patrol than about the legal issues involved. He further told the City Council that it seems obvious there will be negative reaction when a police operation is defined by an ethnic characteristic. Ryan also expressed his belief that all people, regardless of legal status, should feel comfortable approaching the authorities to provide information about a crime without fear that the inquiry would be turned against them.

Ryan points to racial tension created throughout the city when law enforcement officers use racial profiling. He recognizes that this type of policing creates fear and distrust towards the police, and as a consequence, immigrants will be less likely to call for help, report a crime, or cooperate in criminal investigations. Ryan notes that in the end, the entire community suffers and is less safe.

James Peña, a legal resident married to a U.S. citizen and residing in Chandler for the last forty-five years, recounted an episode involving several bicycle patrol officers circling him as he walked to his parked car as he exited a supermarket. While they never asked him to stop or show identification, they continued to circle him in an escort fashion to his car. He pointed to police behavior during the action as proof of their lack of training in immigration law enforcement. The officers acted as if they had the right to violate his civil rights because he is of Mexican ancestry and an immigrant. Peña described the police action as intimidating and expressed resentment towards city officials for allowing residents to feel uncomfortable and unsafe. He felt betrayed that the city council approved and supported the joint operation without taking measures to protect the rights of all citizens in Chandler, regardless of race or income level. As a result of the raids, he pointed to deterioration of race relations in the larger community.

> Peña stated that the joint operation has affected his daughter's relationships with her friends at Chandler High School, where students of all different races used to get along with each other. Since the operation took place, his daughter has told him that she does not understand why she can no longer get along with her "White" friends.

Peña noted an increasing racial tension as more affluent whites move into the area and as Latinos are treated as if they no longer belong. He argued that raids were part of urban renewal and that the best strategy for addressing the changing demographics in the city was to teach tolerance and respect. Residents of Mexican ancestry were subjected to insults, were belittled, and felt the "unofficial" message that they no longer belonged in the city.

Although many of the residents attended the city council meeting in hopes of receiving an apology and recognition of their mistreatment, the city attorney referred to the policy as legal and the city manager maintained that the local police only acted in a "support capacity" to immigration officers. In response to the testimonies given at the meeting, Police Chief Harris told local reporters that police tactics used during the five-day raid were no different than the everyday experiences of all U.S. citizens crossing the border. "Every time you go to San Diego, they stop you and ask you if you're a U.S. citizen. Is it a violation to ask a person if they're a U.S. citizen? I don't think so" (Walsh 1997: B1). Comparing INS Border Patrol stops at U.S. borders to racially selected police stops in an urban area 120 miles away from the U.S.-Mexico border minimizes the harm inflicted by discriminatory practices that Mexican Americans and immigrants endured during the Chandler Roundup. Arguing that the operation was legal and that police only provided backup to the INS further legitimated the treatment of residents of Mexican ancestry as second-class citizens, as inferior, and as criminal. Unwilling to express an apology or even regret for the consequences of the raid not only officially condoned discriminatory police practices but sent a message that racism against anyone perceived to be an immigrant was tolerated.

Each of these testimonies conveys recognition by residents that the local government, along with federal agents, approved a series of raids that permitted law enforcement agents to use discriminatory practices. Racial profiling identifies persons as suspects, as well as limits their movement in and out of areas defined as ghettos or barrios. Mexican Americans were treated as second-class citizens, and their civil rights were never considered. By targeting specific neighborhoods and businesses, the operation was planned to protect the civil rights of whites, who were not intimidated or humiliated. Cultural aspects of "Mexicanness," such as language and music, were used as a proxy for race in racial profiling. Legal status was assumed to be prescribed on bodies; thus persons of Mexican ancestry were treated as noncitizens because police were acting on the assumption that only whites are U.S. citizens. The emphasis on race and culture in immigration law enforcement is no different from the policing procedures used by racist dictatorships that the United States has denounced in the past. In the selection of specific areas for carrying out immigration raids, the state legitimated the accepted view of racial segregation as "natural." Divining persons for citizenship inspection on the basis of race and culture at the state level has serious consequences, which shape and influence everyday race relations. Law enforcement officers acted on racial stereotypes about citizenship in racially profiling a group. This type of action by state officials reinforces stereotypes about people of color and legitimates racist behavior.

CONCLUSION

The U.S. government has a long history of racist immigration policy and law enforcement practices. National, state, and local governments have been more than willing to use state violence to control labor or move unwanted residents to less desirable locations. The army was used in the Mexican-American War; the state police throughout the Southwest were used to deport Mexican immigrants and their U.S. born children in the 1950s; and local police have been used to curtail union and citizenship activity. Racialized state violence has also provided the social, political, and legal environment for vigilante organizations to function alongside other everyday practices of racism towards Mexicans. Agribusinesses have frequently used vigilante activity to intimidate workers on strike and have relied on the enforcement of immigration laws to gain access to cheap and vulnerable labor during harvest then to eliminate the presence of farm labor when it is no longer needed. The state has maintained the use of racist immigration policies and law enforcement practices into the twenty-first century. By the end of the last century, the United States had militarized the border area and incorporated the weapons of war into immigration law enforcement. Immigration enforcement is embedded in racism and frequently lends itself to violence. As Renato Rosaldo (1997: 21) pointed out, "The U.S.-Mexico border has become theater, and border theater has become social violence. Actual violence has become inseparable from symbolic ritual on the border—crossings, invasions, lines of defense, high-tech surveillance, and more."

Immigration raids take this violence beyond the border. Mexicans, particularly working class and the poor, carry what Robert Chang (1999) refers to as a bodily "figurative border." Racial profiling used in immigration law enforcement assumes a physical presence of citizenship that is inscribed on the body. Assumed to be a suspect rather than a citizen in immigration raids, Mexicans find themselves at risk before the law as a consequence of discretionary stops, use of intimidation, and limited access to fair and impartial treatment before the law. Catalina Veloz was not off the mark when she asked if numbers would soon be tattooed on the arms of brown people to signify their status as citizens.

Since 9/11, federal legislation has blurred distinctions between "alien immigrant" and "criminal." As Teresa Miller (2005: 113) notes, "[c]riminal aliens (deportable for their post-entry criminal conduct), illegal aliens (deportable for their surreptitious crossing of the U.S. border), and terrorists (deportable for the grave risk they pose to national security) are all deemed dangerous foreigners for whom criminally punitive treatment and removal are uniformly appropriate and urgently necessary." Broadening the definition of "aggravated felony" to include less serious convictions drastically increases the number of noncitizens facing detention, deportation, and barred reentry. Recent draconian policies subject immigrants to compulsory deportation for almost any criminal misdemeanor. At the state and local levels, a broad range of measures threatening the livelihood of immigrants and their families has been proposed and passed. Among these ordinances are denying driver's licenses, fines and prosecution against landlords and employers, imposing citizenship prerequisites on certain state job requirements, and refusing to allow immigrant students and the children of immigrants access to higher education (Johnson 2004; Johnson and Trujillo 2007; Fernandes 2007; Romero 2008). Like immigration law enforcement in the past, citizenship inspection continues to place racialized Latinos at risk before the law and designate them as second-class citizens with inferior rights (Romero 2006).

Local, state, and national governments' participation in alarmist immigration rhetoric and in laws embracing "alien immigrant," "criminal," and "terrorist" as one and the same lend legitimacy to a range of anti-immigration activities conducted by civilians. The state's reference to immigrants as threats to national security has strengthened the position of anti-immigrant border vigilantes like the Minuteman Civil Defense Corps (MCDC). As the state shifts immigration policy to terrorism, MCDC, Mothers Against Illegal Aliens (MAIA), and other vigilante groups are provided a shield of patriotism to conceal their nativist and racist attacks against Latinos in the United States (Romero 2008). Anti-immigrant vigilante groups continue to operate without much state interference and are sometimes encouraged or celebrated by public officials (Chacón and Davis 2006). Research on the rise of nativist movements has pointed to the ways that "immigration" has become the new code word for "race" (Balibar and Wallerstein 1985). Fear is generated by claiming that Spanish is becoming the dominant language of the country or that a "majority non-white" population threatens our national culture and way of life (Chavez 2001). Using metaphors such as "immigrants swarming," "hordes of immigrants," "flood gates are open," or "reconquest of the Southwest" serves to dehumanize and further enhance the image of the immigrant, terrorist, and criminal as synonymous (Santa Ana 2002).

9 THE LANGUAGE OF TERROR

Panic, Peril, Racism

Junaid Rana

"Sand nigger," I'm called,
and the name fits: I am
the light-skinned nigger
with black eyes and the look
difficult to figure—a look
of indifference, a look to kill.

—**Lawrence Joseph (1988: 29)**

OUTSIDE THE LAW

Recently, a number of scholars have used the concept of moral panic to analyze the growth of anti-Muslim racism and Islamophobia (Ewing 2008; Maira
2007; Razack 2008; Werbner 2005). The events of September 11, 2001, and the
ensuing rapid escalation of racial violence and terror (Ahmad 2002, 2004),
made evident the presence of moral panics and the construction of enemies
to enforce a racial order through state policies, media, and popular culture. In
this chapter I offer a theoretical explanation that connects moral panics to the
concept of Islamic peril and the formation of a global racial system (Mullings
2005; Winant 2001, 2004). From evidence surrounding two events—one an
instance of moral panic, the other of peril—it is argued that racial constructions of potential terrorists are instrumental to anti-immigrant narratives
that rely on ideas of illegality and criminality. Through this logic and language of terror, the construction of transnational migrants in the U.S. public sphere locates Muslims as both religious and racial subjects. Terror, fear,
panic, and peril are the rhetorical terms that organize these religious subjects

as racial subjects. In this case, multiple diasporas are overlapped in meaning and time by which migrants are collapsed with the illegal and criminalized activities of terrorism. Muslims, with their patterns of multiple migrations, become an object of fear and panic to the state. The articulation of this fear through a homogeneous racial discourse then allows the state to comprehend the Muslim subject as a threat with the potentiality of terror.

The racial violence that followed 9/11 most resembled a moral panic that surged in waves through the U.S. population.[1] In this sense this moral panic was clearly a kind of racial panic, and is often compared to fear in the United States after the attack on Pearl Harbor that led to the internment of Japanese Americans in World War II.[2] The role of racial panics in American history is intimately related to sex panics, red scares, and other forms of social, cultural, and political difference that enacts modes of moral reform and regulation (Duggan 1995; Rubin 1984). Violence and persecution often follow these moments, as demonization and scapegoating become part of an exclusionary logic of purging problems and threats. Deviance then becomes the measure to restate the dominance of a heteronormative social structure and the upward accumulation by dispossession of resources and rights (Duggan 2003). The role of such moral reform is to maintain forms of inequality present in society and to sanction racial, sexual, and gendered regulation, particularly through the control of migration (Luibheid 2002). The concept of the moral panic, then, receives its specificity through the contextual practices of national fear at the local, everyday level, practices that are then modified through the creation of specific demonized figures. The role of the racial panic is to intensify the categories of racialization within the racial formation. The aftermath of the 9/11 moral panic resulted in the tragic violent assaults upon Arab, Muslim, and South Asian communities across the United States. Muslims were not the sole target in these racial attacks; indeed the racial profiling of those who appeared to be Muslims included members of other faiths such as Sikhs, Hindus, and Christians. It also included a wide variety of national and ethnic groups such as Latinos and others with brown skin and other purported "Muslim-like" features.

For the fields of U.S. ethnic and racial studies these racial techniques force the geographic reconsideration of Muslims from West Asia to South Asia to Southeast Asia as part of their political project. Indeed, the example of "yellow" peril in Asian American history informs the construction of a Muslim or Islamic peril within the bounds of the United States (Karim 2000). Simultaneously, Muslim Americans must be considered from a comparative framework given that Arab Americans and other Muslim groups are part of ambiguous racial categories in the United States and also often categorized as Asian American, African American, and white (Gualtieri 2001, 2009; Naber 2000). This challenge to the study of race and racism raises important historical questions in terms of racial techniques of the state but also of the constitution of U.S. ethnic and racial studies. Beyond these domestic fields of study, the racialization of the Muslim is now clearly transnational and must be considered on the basis of its global effects. Indeed, such a process of panics and perils must be examined not only through the state's role in a system that enacts biopolitical difference in terms of race, gender, religion, civilization, and so on but also through its relationship to violence and terror, which proceeds at a global level.

Terror has become a keyword of the twenty-first century, even as some argue that its antecedents go as far back as the first century of the Common Era.[3] Terror in its simplest sense is about manufacturing fear. Thus the current "War on Terror" in an important sense is about the management of fear.[4] Specifically, in this analysis I examine the role that racial techniques of the state have played in constructing terror subjects and subjects of terror and in placing them within the U.S. racial formation. As I argue, the rhetoric of terror in the domestic and global War on Terror is instrumental to constructions of racialized Muslims within both the U.S. racial formation and a much broader global racial system. This is not to say that the state has a single rationale when it comes to the constructions of terror threats; rather, the mobilization and practice of particular kinds of tactics, strategies, and ideologies have the effect of reinforcing popular discourses of racialization. As I argue, the rhetoric of terror in the domestic and global War on Terror is instrumental to constructions of racialized Muslims within the U.S. racial formation and a much broader global racial system. Terror enables the fiction of an enemy that goes beyond an action and continues to have its effect through waves of meaning (Zulaika and Douglass 1996). It is in this way that the use of panics and perils as techniques of racial formation is a fictionalizing process of risk, fear, and potential but also serves the purpose of fictionalizing the racialized nation. As a grammar this process develops a vocabulary in the post–9/11 landscape to describe the terrorist, the criminal, and the immigrant in the racial figure of the Muslim.

The state as arbiter of racial violence proliferates its exertions of power through widespread racial panics that resonate not only in the law but through the generation of news, popular culture, and social ideologies. In the midst of these examples of racial profiling, illegalization, and criminalization of Muslims is a logic and history of a population considered to be a threat. Moral panics as a symptom of social control are also an expression of manufactured fear and racial formation. The anxiety over assumed threats is the result of a racist common sense that couples racial profiling with racial violence. These moments of racial violence and subsequent moments of terror threats are as much a moral panic over terrorism and the racial figure of the Muslim as they are the emergence of a newly configured peril. By exploring the creation of racial panics and the constitution of an Islamic peril through the language of terrorism, I map the shifting terrain of race and racism in which the equation of antiterror with anti-immigrant has led to the transparency of a racialized Muslim. Further, I explore how these techniques of fiction-making maintain their effects through the biopolitics of racism. To describe this racial reasoning in the post–9/11 era, I recount the racial techniques of the state in its use of the rhetoric of terror through panics and perils, and through newspaper accounts, reports, and insights from ethnographic fieldwork. These examples lay bare how the state's logic of antiterror becomes a form of anti-immigrant racism through moral regulation, policing, and immigration control.

TERROR EVENT 1: PANIC

On December 29, 2002, the Federal Bureau of Investigation, in collaboration with the Homeland Security Agencies, released an alert that identified five individuals thought to have entered the United States illegally, presenting a potential and immediate terrorist threat. Through the rapidity of telecommunications technology, news media outlets distributed this information across the United States and globally as a high-level terror alert, warning of a terrorist plot designed to disrupt the New Year's holiday. Pictures of the men along with their names and possible dates of birth were copied from the original FBI press release and prominently displayed in the electronic and print media. The FBI press release dated December 29, 2002, stated the following:

> The Federal Bureau of Investigation is seeking the public's assistance in determining the whereabouts of the following individuals:
>
> ABID NORAIZ ALI, DOB AUGUST 15, 1977
>
> IFTIKHAR KHOZMAI ALI, DOB SEPTEMBER 20, 1981
>
> MUSTAFA KHAN OWASI, DOB DECEMBER 11, 1969

ADIL PERVEZ, DOB DECEMBER 27, 1983

AKBAR JAMAL, DOB NOVEMBER 1, 1974

The above identified individuals, whose names and dates of birth may be fictitious, are believed to have entered the United States illegally on or about December 24, 2002. Although the FBI has no specific information that these individuals are connected to any potential terrorist activities, based upon information developed in the course of on-going investigations, the FBI would like to locate and question these persons.

The FBI has been working with Homeland Security Agencies (U.S. Customs, INS, TSA) to locate these individuals. The above information has also been disseminated to the appropriate law enforcement agencies around the United States and throughout the world.

Anyone with any information pertaining to these individuals is asked to contact their nearest FBI office. Photographs of the [sic] these individuals can be found on the FBI's web site at www.FBI.gov.[5]

Admitting that the "names and dates of birth may be fictitious" did not give any pause as to the reliability of the information in the original press release; rather, it served to heighten the risk of danger and impending terror. On the basis of this press release and the information provided in a press conference, the *New York Times* reported that "an administration official said it was unclear if the men were simply illegal immigrants or if they were involved in something connected to terrorist activities" (Lewis 2002). Instead of questioning the lack of specific information in the original FBI alert and the plausibility of any potential terrorism, the news media propelled this alert into a heightened security threat and a call for vigilance. The pivot of the alert relied on the identities of the persons of interest—their names, their faces, their social and cultural background. The rush to invoke a threat to security, and the gathering panic that ensued, depended on the connection of illegal immigration to terrorism. The article continued by describing the precautionary measures taken as a result of the serious nature of this threat: "In New York City, the police increased their counterterrorist efforts as a result of the warning. . . . The names of the five men listed in the alert have been sent to all police department commands." Hence, the original FBI press release seemingly unmasked a number of uncertainties of the security and intelligence community that would translate a call for questioning into a national security panic.

In this example, the ambiguity of the original FBI alert contained a system of signs and symbols that were readily interpreted into a racialized figure that recalled illegal border crossing and terrorist radicalism. Such profiling is often interpreted as a cautionary measure that requires the definition of threats and dangers to national security. In other words, the deterrence of terror requires the outlining of target profiles. In the caption describing the pictures and names of the five men, the FBI report states that the men were of Middle Eastern descent and that they entered the United States around the Christmas holiday. Here the naming of these individuals is a practice of racializing such names as threats by using "Middle Eastern" as the obvious stand-in for Arab and Muslim; and second, of marking the correspondence with the Christian holiday season to amplify the stereotypical notion of Islamic radicals disrupting the major shopping season in a clash with capitalism that would have widespread effects. It was with this implied meaning and assumptions that an imminent terrorist threat existed. This was enough for the U.S. media to spread this alert of a possible terrorist attack, creating a heightened situation with the characteristics of a racial panic. Because of the incoherence of the information, fear and anxiety spread rapidly. The faulty syllogistic logic unraveled in which the words "illegal immigrants *may have* terrorist intentions" changed to an imagined "Middle Eastern illegal immigrants *have* terrorist intentions."

Four days later, on January 2, 2003, the national panic over the terror alert slightly subsided. Nothing had happened, despite the widespread warnings. The *New York Times* ran a follow-up piece explaining the situation. It turned out that this was a case of mistaken identity, or rather, stolen identity. One of the five terror suspects, the individual identified as Mustafa Khan Owasi, was in fact a jeweler living in Lahore, Pakistan, by the name of Muhammad Ashgar. Ashgar claimed he had never stepped foot in the United States but had attempted to travel to Britain two months earlier on forged documents, when he was stopped at the airport in Dubai, in the United Arab Emirates. There his false documents were detected, and he was immediately deported back to Pakistan. The article ended by stating that

> FBI agents investigating falsified identity papers are expanding their dragnet for a growing list of foreign-born men they believe may have entered the United States illegally from Canada. Officials caution they have no specific evidence the men are involved in any terrorism plot, but said they may have connections to a fake-ID and smuggling ring that involves people with terrorist connections.[6]

After its earlier vagueness the FBI now drew a closer connection to those involved in illegal migration, underground smuggling networks, and terrorist activity, a connection based on suppositions and assumptions without any clear claims and evidentiary linkages. The misinformation that these were Middle Eastern men was replaced by the fact that the picture of Mustafa Khan Owasi, at least, was in reality of Muhammad Ashgar, originally from Pakistan.

The substitution of nationality with an entire region articulated how the terms of race, religion, and geography solidified in this panic. The circulation of the alert unwittingly revealed a system predicated on the social construction of threats to match and identify terrorist profiles, the targets of which are not ambiguous but for the purposes of public consumption may be presented as such. The claims in this example serve to racially homogenize the Islamic world and Muslims as a single group in order to fit the needs of the U.S. security apparatus. Embodied in the religious practice of Islam, Muslims are figured as ideologically in opposition to America. Such a representation serves to translate religious difference not only into cultural difference but also into an innate and essential difference between America and Islam. Going against the logic of the U.S. racial formation that generally assigns race according to phenotypic characteristics, the War on Terror broadly defines racial phenotype in terms of Islam as a religion that is naturalized and biologized onto Muslim bodies in a version of cultural racism. That is, culture is racialized through phenotypic difference in a logic that homogenizes Islam with the vague signifier of the Middle East, and terror through a politics of fear. This alternative geography defines terror as emanating from the Middle East, and Islamic countries as regions riddled with terrorists. Pakistan, generally considered to be in South Asia, is part of this flawed geographic continuum that constructs terrorist threats out of global Islamic trouble spots, equating Muslim men with Arabic-sounding names; and that purports the Middle East to have a greater propensity for terrorist activity.

In this racial panic, the attribute of illegality connects migration to terrorism through the object relations of fungibility and dissimulation. Illegality is itself constructed as a global system that conflates the criminality of smuggling and trafficking with terrorism. The final statement by the *New York Times* confirms this by connecting immigration to terrorism in a logic that defines illegality as a set of practices and networks brought together through a causal link. Illegal immigration, terrorism, and trafficking go together in this schema of interchangeable objects that ultimately work to control and regulate immigration through the rhetoric of antiterrorism. In other words, uncontrolled border crossing brings not only dangerous people but dangerous objects, ideas, and practices. In this sense, undocumented migrants are threats that represent the potential actions of terrorist activity, and as carriers of such potential through ideological and physiological means. The body is itself racialized as a container of dangerous ideas and uses. Thus, in the range of post–9/11 regulatory policing, illegal immigrants represent at most the potential of terrorist violence, and at the least the manipulation and systems of migration and the violation of legal sovereignty. A second anxiety that appears in this construction of illegality is the apparent duplicity of the immigrants themselves. Using fake, stolen, and mistaken identities confounds systems of surveillance that cannot clearly differentiate bodies that might bear a close resemblance. As a frame of visual dissimulation such interchangeable identities point to the threat of concealment that relies on the discernment of racialized biological difference.

Almost a week after the initial incident, and on the other side of the globe, the Pakistani press began to report the details of this increasingly absurd case. In an article dated January 8, 2003, *The News* reported that the FBI had been given fabricated evidence from a smuggler named Michael John Hamdani, arrested in Canada on October 31, 2002, on human trafficking charges. His smuggling racket brought people from Pakistan to the United States via Canada and Britain. Hamdani, a Pakistan-born Canadian, voluntarily submitted himself for extradition to the United States, where he named the five men the FBI originally thought might pose a terrorist threat. Muhammad Ashgar, when interviewed, admitted he knew Hamdani, but also stated the possibility that his picture and false identity had been used by another smuggler.[7] By January 12, 2003, another article appeared in *The News* that was based on an extensive interview with Muhammad Ashgar. Mr. Ashgar, in thinking through the reliability of the media, realized his own need to address this fiasco. He states in *The News* interview, "initially, I tried to dismiss it as a mistake our newspapers make daily but when I went home in the evening, every television channel was broadcasting the photograph with ominous warnings by American authorities . . . I was horrified" (Alam 2003). The mistakes of the FBI were compounded by the panic that surrounded this assumed threat.

Muhammad Ashgar worked in the lower-middle-class neighborhood of Krishan Nagar, in Lahore, as a jeweler and goldsmith. Developed as a colonial neighborhood in the early 1920s, Krishan Nagar had been a bustling suburb prominent for its Hindu jewelers and gold traders (Glover 2008: 149). After partition most of the Hindu residents fled to India, and the neighborhood transitioned mainly to a residential area while continuing its reputation for jewelry making. Still popularly called Krishan Nagar by most residents, the area has been redubbed Islampura and is close to important commercial areas of Lahore's old city, such as the Anarkali bazaar. As an older neighborhood, it is removed from many of the newer commercial areas in outlying suburbs, such as the Defense Housing Authority, Gulberg, and more recent developments outside of the city, where many of the lucrative jewelry shops are located. Because of this urban transition and location within the city, jewelry shops in Krishan Nagar are limited by the ever-changing consumption practices of the lower-middle-class residents from within the neighborhood, a dwindling customer base, and the uncertain long-term opportunity for expansion of their businesses. Because of this, many of the goldsmiths in Krishan Nagar continue to service the main jewelry shops that open in the latest commercial developments. A highly elaborated tier system is thus created spatially and in terms of wages, with jewelry-makers remaining in one neighborhood while shop owners and jewelry-sellers operate in elite upscale markets.

It was in this context that Ashgar worked as a jewelry-maker and dreamt of owning his own shop. Married with three children, he wanted more economic security and a better life for his family. To obtain this future, he planned to accumulate enough capital by travelling abroad to work odd jobs, and by taking positions selling jewelry overseas whenever the opportunity arose. Through his social networks he travelled to Dubai several times building his contacts and hoping to establish a history of business travel that he hoped would eventually allow him to travel to destinations with greater opportunities.[8] Eventually, Ashgar went to Hong Kong where at times he sold costume jewelry and counterfeit merchandise. By his own admission he hoped to obtain a business visa to the United States or United Kingdom by generating a history of travel for commercial purposes. It was in Hong Kong that he came into contact with a broker, or agent, named Michael John Hamdani, who promised travel to the United States. Hamdani sold Ashgar false documents and provided a PC, or photochange passport, and visa, material that Hamdani would later use to negotiate with U.S. authorities. A few days before the pictures surfaced in the FBI terrorist alert, Ashgar was deported by authorities in the United Arab Emirates and released to the

Federal Investigation Agency in Pakistan.[9] For seven days he was held and interrogated by officials in Islamabad, who questioned him on his fake identity documentation, work abroad, and the social networks that had aided him in obtaining these. Ashgar was terrified by the intensity of his extended experience under interrogation and incarceration. A probable hypothesis for this experience is that he was being investigated for a connection to illegal smuggling and to Hamdani, who was already on the radar of international intelligence agencies.[10]

The tragedy of this incident is that it relied on a system of racial formation that makes migrants who seek greater opportunity into villains. An example of structural inequality, migrants in these circumstances are easy targets for manufactured racial panics and for the reinforcement of moral reform, regulation, and social control. This racial panic solidified the connection between illegality, terrorism, and migration but also constructed an enemy profile of dangerous Muslims that expanded the notion of "Middle Eastern" to Arabic-sounding names, a geography ranging from Arab countries to Pakistan, and the supposed dangers posed by illegal border-crossers. In creating this profile, a map is drawn of Pakistani migrants going to the Middle East on their way to Britain or Canada with the hope of making it to the United States. The barriers to this migration are now compounded through state controls that work not only to physically bar such movement but to create an ideological terrain in which migration of certain groups of people, namely Muslims, is tied to larger threats and the potential of terrorist activity.

The recent characterization of Muslims in post–9/11 racial events displays some of the themes and representations central to the logic of contemporary racism. The process of conjuring Muslims as a racial composite is eminently about how culture translates into race to manage and configure fear, risk, and the possibility of terror (Bayoumi 2006). As such, the racial containment of Muslims within the U.S. racial formation is centrally about the potentiality of a terrorist threat. This logic has a long history in the modern Euro-American conception of Islam and more recently in the geopolitical relationship of the United States to the Middle East and Muslim countries that relies on colonial conceptions of diplomacy, military intervention, and rule (Little 2002; McAlister 2005). The archaeology of the racial discourse of the figure of the Muslim and the terrorist is expressed in moral panics that continue to sway public opinion and awareness throughout the United States and Europe since 9/11.

TERROR EVENT 2: PERIL

Incidents of false alarm are symptomatic of the national security panics that take place in the United States. In the aftermath of September 11, 2001, it appeared as if the U.S. racial formation changed in a fundamental way. Arguments circulated widely that Muslim Americans were the new suspect racial category, on the basis of contemporary events but also on older forms of antireligious racism and the historical connection of Islam to the race-concept (Rana 2007). Rather than the completely new inclusion of a Muslim-looking race, I argue that the process of racialization incorporated new forms of racial demonization and policing. In this moment the category of the Muslim emerged as a category of race that was policed through narratives of migration, diaspora, criminality, and terror. Arabs from Saudi Arabia and Yemen were suddenly linked to people from Pakistan and Afghanistan through a broadly defined notion of the Middle East. These same people were tied to Filipinos and Indonesians encompassing the larger Muslim world. And all of them were centrally linked to Palestinians and their struggle for liberation. In the fiasco of the 2002 New Year's terrorist threat the connection of terrorism to illegal migration reveals some of the new logic on race. To begin with, terror must be associated with illegal activity, an idea that presupposes that anything linked to terrorism, or its possibility, must be illegal. Illegal immigrants, because of their ties to the underworld of forged documents and smuggling, might also be connected with the underworld of terrorist activity. The possibility of terror is the new language of preemption, social control, and racial boundary-making.

The place that Muslims as a category are filling in the U.S. racial formation is historically associated with the discourse on immigration, Islamic fundamentalism and radicalism, and terrorism. What is more, the racial discourse on Muslims in the United States is increasingly transnational, linked to a geography of Muslim diaspora. For example, in a mapping of the terror threats facing the United States and Europe, the *New York Times* charted what it called a "Terror Diaspora," in which a map detailed "A World of Cells and Plots" by al-Qaeda operatives that have targeted American and European interests in recent attempts of terrorism. The map of this diaspora surmised that

> it is a frustratingly uncertain business, hunting terrorism. The impulse is to want to connect the dots, so that a recognizable picture of the enemy will emerge. But the very nature of the quarry—secretive, multi-headed, loosely structured and passionate about staying so—keeps the picture blurry and incomplete.[11]

The so-called Terror Diaspora demonstrates a shift in the perceived enemy for U.S. foreign policy, a shift that not only is linked to 9/11 but goes back to the end of the Cold War. This period saw the transition from enmities largely between nation-states, that is, the Communist Enemy against the Democratic State, to the isolation of rogue "terrorist" states (reconfigured as the "Axis of Evil") and of drug cartels, arms traffickers, and the illegal underworlds of transnational criminal activity. For the intelligence industry such a mapping is centrally about a clash of civilizations in which the impulse is to connect the dots to a uniform threat, that is, in one way or another to the notion of Islamic peril. This kind of rationalism is informed by a racist logic that will defy causal links, and for that matter guilt or innocence, to find the "enemy."[12] In this logic, moral panics are necessary to the production of a larger peril that constructs a racial object of vilification. As a technology of terror prevention, racial panic manufactures an enemy for the state to mobilize against in the name of security.

This language of diaspora connecting Islam and terror was in early use by op-ed writers such as Thomas Friedman of the *New York Times*, who panders to assimilationist and culturalist arguments to explain terrorism and its appeal to Muslim immigrants. Rather than explore how racism has historically operated in collusion with power to dominate, Friedman prefers to argue that Muslim diasporas must change their culture.[13] He contends that Muslim societies are invested in a culture of terror that is somehow an inherent trait, and that somehow explains the violent history in the Muslim world. Culture in this sense is of the reified kind that can be exchanged through civilizational growth and the adoption of market capitalism. This appeal to neoliberal economic strategy thinly hides a cultural racism that places blame on Muslims through a frozen idea of culture which lacks an understanding of how power operates. The thrust of arguments like Friedman's, which channel the rationales of doyens of a clash of civilizations, such as Samuel Huntington and Bernard Lewis, is that it is up to Muslim moderates to change their society. In other words, following the neoliberal idea of self-care and market reform, Muslims after 9/11 must become compliant subjects of the U.S./global North economic hegemony.[14] As this form of thought homogenizes the problems of Muslims throughout the world, it arbitrarily places blame on an abstraction called the culture of terror. Terror is a much messier business, particularly in view of the culpability of the U.S. government in foreign policy objectives that have included training, producing, and controlling forces of counterinsurgency and terror.[15]

What is remarkable about the language of such arguments is that they fail to see their connection to the botched racial profiling, panics, and perils associated with the mistaken FBI report discussed above. These constructions of Muslims as a racial group are drawn from a historical genealogy that comprehends Islam as the antithesis of Western modernity. Further, Islam is perceived as a threat to modernity, democracy, and the freedoms that they bring. These are not new ideas but are in fact representative of the historic confrontation of the Islamic world and the Western world. Both in Europe and the United States this construction of a new racism has led to the rise of moral panics that place Islam as an enemy and a threat. Moral panics in this instance serve to consolidate fear with racial conceptions of criminality. Here, criminality shifts from petty crime to terror and crimes against humanity. This thinking fits into the streams of anti-immigrant sentiment that have fed racist backlashes on both sides of the Atlantic.

The idea of peril manufactured through these moral panics is exemplary in the capture of Khalid Shaikh Mohammed in March 2003, popularly referred to as KSM in security and intelligence circles and who was known as "the engineer." According to his profile in the *9/11 Commission Report*, he is one of the paradigmatic terrorist entrepreneurs, a profile that is widely cited on the Internet.[16] In the outline of his personal traits in association with the 9/11 attacks on the World Trade Center and Pentagon he is described thus:

> Highly educated and equally comfortable in a government office or a terrorist safehouse, KSM applied his imagination, technical aptitude, and managerial skills to hatching and planning an extraordinary array of terrorist schemes. These ideas included conventional car bombing, political assassination, aircraft bombing, hijacking, reservoir poisoning, and, ultimately, the use of aircraft as missiles guided by suicide operatives.[17]

Captured in Rawalpindi, outside Islamabad, the Pakistani capital, Mohammed is pictured in the photograph released in the media in a fairy-tale representation of the ogre: slouched, stuporous, stripped down to his undershirt. Arrested by the elite police forces of Pakistan in collaboration with the FBI, and considered al-Qaeda's Number 3 after Osama bin Laden and Ayman al-Zawahiri, he admitted under U.S. interrogation to plotting the 9/11 attacks in addition to the bombings of U.S. embassies in Tanzania and Kenya, and the murder of Daniel Pearl—a total of some thirty-one plots.[18] Ramzi Youssef, another high-profile capture in Pakistan found guilty in the 1992 bombing of the World Trade Center, is a cousin of Mohammed through marriage. Following the initial arrest of Mohammed, a number of stories appeared in the print media that followed the makings of a terrorist mind, a narrative that reappeared after Mohammed admitted his involvement in al-Qaeda and the planning and execution of terrorist plots, albeit under the duress of torture. Indeed, this piecing together of such stories saw a remarkable growth after 9/11, frequently in the vein of "Why do they hate us?" but also as a tacit warning of the dangers of potential terror.

Distinctly, these stories were more often than not migration narratives, as well as stories that pondered the role of race and ethnicity in terror. For example, the narrative life stories of John Walker Lindh, Jose Padilla, Richard Reid, and other numerous Britons who joined the Taliban were reconstructed with the intent of determining what created the pathology of terrorism and the draw of radical Islam and what has come to be called *jihadi* culture. This kind of reasoning is rampant in the U.S. military, where a cross section of Muslim Americans—from South Asian to Arab to Southeast Asian, and those who converted—joined the Armed Forces in a show of patriotism. The most controversial case of suspected espionage tied to religious belief and racism is that of the Muslim chaplain in the U.S. military, Joseph Yee, who was charged with colluding with detainees considered enemy combatants. Yee was called the Chinese Taliban and was persecuted for serving the Muslim detainees of Guantánamo Bay. As the evidence and the suspicions were clearly based on hearsay and innuendo, he was later brought up on charges of adultery, which were eventually dropped (Yee and Molloy 2005).

The visual representation of Khalid Shaikh Mohammed is part of the depiction of a model terrorist that is mutable and can shift in comportment. At home in Arab dress or Western codes of professional attire, the lasting and overrepresented image is that of the captured Mohammed who is disheveled and disoriented—a crafted image, no doubt, that relays the message of a terrorist organization on its heels in the War on Terror. This multiplicity of images coincides with the other hallmarks of terrorists, who are trained not only to act like chameleons in their sleeper environments but to maintain multiple aliases in addition to forged documents and carefully planned trails to confuse law enforcement.[19] As a so-called terrorist mastermind, Mohammed, one can argue, has used the protocols of international migration to his advantage; but his profile is also undoubtedly paradigmatic of a narrative that the ideological War on Terror has used to police transnational migrants.

Khalid Shaikh Mohammed was born in Kuwait to Pakistani immigrants from the province of Baluchistan who had come to Kuwait in the 1950s. Kuwait's fairly stringent citizenship laws make it nearly impossible for foreign nationals to become citizens. Noncitizen labor migrants make up over a million of the Kuwaiti inhabitants, about a third to a half of the current estimated population of three to four million. Mohammed traces his lineage as an ethnic Baluchi of Pakistan, an area that borders Iran. His father, Ali Mohammed al-Jazmi, arrived in Kuwait in the 1950s as a merchant and eventually found work in the oilfields. Enigmatically, little is known about his mother, Halema, who is thought to have worked cleaning women's bodies for burial. Khalid was born in 1965 in the town of Ahmadi in Kuwait, an immigrant town where there are a large number of foreign workers. As reported in the *New York Times*, many of these workers are Egyptian, Palestinian, or Pakistani, among others—a context that imagines the discontent of Muslim youth as connected to the alienation created out of living in a foreign land and in a working-class locality, but one that also suggests an imagined geographic sensibility connecting Muslim workers from the Middle East to those of South Asia (Santora 2003).

Eventually Mohammed made it out of Kuwait to study in North Carolina, first at Chowan College and then on to North Carolina State A&T University in engineering in the early 1980s.[20] After this time Mohammed became a key target of capture for U.S. officials but kept eluding them in a global chase. Mohammed's radicalization took place when he went to Afghanistan to fight against the Soviet Union, and after his later inclusion within the Taliban. This of course was the heyday of the CIA's involvement and training of the Taliban (Rashid 2001). As a Pakistani national fluent in Arabic and English, he played an important role as a mediator not only for Arabs, Pakistanis, and Afghans but with the CIA. Ironically, his linguistic capabilities and diasporic life story have led some reporters to mistakenly call him an Afghan Arab, a term used to describe the many Arabs who stayed in Afghanistan and Pakistan after they were recruited to fight for the Taliban.

The case of Khalid Shaikh Mohammed is emblematic of an overwhelming trend to understand terrorism and the rationalization of it through the terms of Islam, migration, and alienation. Through the so-called KSM and stories such as his, the peril is not only one of terror but of migration. This idea of real and imagined terror is encompassed in the notion of Islamic peril that envisions a network of sleeper cells connected by illicit transactions of money, goods, and people across borders. In this imagined peril Muslims in countries such as Australia and in European countries like Germany, France, the Netherlands, Spain, and the United Kingdom align with the security interests of the United States. Much like the logic of panics, this kind of peril is nothing new. The perils represented by Asian America center on ideas of immigration and a cultural contestation of white supremacy. Here, in a modified form, the threat of Islam is a threat to a larger global order. This is the case not only because of the potentiality of terror but because of the expanding notion of the U.S. racial formation brought on by the need for the racial categorization of the Muslim for state security purposes. The intelligence apparatus of the state, alongside media and popular culture, maps such a threat formation onto a racialized geography of the world.

CONCLUSION: BIOPOLITICS, MUSLIMS, AND THE GLOBAL RACIAL SYSTEM

In the above examples of racial event and the manufacture of an Islamic peril, the biopolitical grammar of racism challenges notions of kinship, sexuality, and the body. Understanding heteronormative modes of kinship is central to assigning the logic of terrorist cell structure to notions of migrant patterns of kinship and gender. That the profile of a suspected terrorist is overwhelmingly male goes without saying, but this male subject is feminized in a heterosexual framework in which figures of the immigrant, the terrorist, and the Muslim are deemed to have abnormal sexualities, deviant gendered relationships, and a failed domestic life. Labor migrants as vulnerable subjects of exploitation are rendered in ways that queer them through notions of impossibility and invisibility. As Chandan Reddy (2005) has argued in the context of framing the "gay Pakistani immigrant" in the struggle over immigrant rights in the United States, notions of family and enforced heterosexuality within U.S. immigration law regulate a policed boundary that excludes queer subjects through assumptions about masculinity, heterosexuality, race, and terror.[21] This exclusion of migrants through sexuality makes the visibility of certain figures within the South Asian diaspora impossible (Gopinath 2005; Puar 2007), not unlike the invisibility of the everyday life of the Pakistani transnational migrant in the case under discussion.

The framing of Muslim bodies through race, gender, and sexuality has naturalized the idea of the male body as a terrorist, and indeed as a migrant. The process of exclusion has made apparent the immediate elimination of women and families from this narrative in favor of notions of cell structures as the language of kinship and family structure—thus eclipsing the notion of the transnational family structure. With the idea of clandestine sleeper agents ready to awake out of terror cells, migrant workers are similarly framed through the invisibility and concealment of an underclass. Further, queer immigrants who do not fit the narrative of the heteronormative immigrant are in yet another bind through regulations that use the language of family to restrict sexuality-based rights.

The broader argument in relationship to migrants is that there is a logic of race and gender that depends on notions of kinship and on cultural ideas of how social relationships are arranged for the racialized Muslim migrant. This logic depends on a racial and sexual economy to define the ideological values associated with migration, which is then overlapped on a logic about the War on Terror. Suspects of terror plots in the current global War on Terror are more often than not immigrant men, who in the view of the media are read outside the context of family or social relationships. When they *are* read in terms of kinship, it is through male relationships, most prominently the patrilineal and consanguineous terms of father and son, and the metaphors associated with that relationship. The imagination of the familial linkages of these relationships works to further imagine the *biological* and social terms of the relationship. This can be seen as a rudimentary analysis of the most basic relationships of terror plots in which the father-son relationship becomes a metaphoric one through the notion of fictive kin. Leaders of terror cells become like fathers, as do veteran immigrants to novice migrants who become like sons when they enter into paternalistic relationships with the benefactors of their transnational social networks. The reliance on modes of kinship to analyze terrorism and migration serves to analogize these two issues in the formation of narratives of race and racialization.

In the two events discussed here, the racial formation of a Muslim subject is made apparent in the use of the discourse of terror and racial panic. Narratives of migration, illegality, and criminality are central to the explanatory frameworks that attempt to comprehend terrorism and thus police transnational migration. The complex global racial system based on the race concept, labor migration, and neoliberalism, as well as on imperial, colonial, and capitalist systems of exploitation, are masked in this process of representing terror, race, and migration. The terms that connect terror to migration are based on the establishment of the figure of the Muslim as a racialized subject both in the U.S. racial formation and in a broader global racial system. This system of making racial categories depends on a history of colonial labor migration that established state control of this movement. In the postcolonial era race-making depends on the apparatus of state security and the functions of a global economy that work through the strategies of neoliberalism, empire, and capitalism.

10 UNMASKING THE STATE
Racial/Gender Terror and Hate Crimes

Andrea Smith

As part of my organizing activities in graduate school, I helped coordinate a forum on indigenous women in prisons. As part of the outreach for that forum, I sent out a series of e-mail notifications of the event to people at school. In response to the event notifications I sent, I received an e-mail from a white student threatening me with bodily harm. Concerned by this correspondence, I forwarded his e-mail to the campus Women of Color and Native listservs. Almost as soon as I sent out the e-mail, I was deluged with responses from people I did not know, offering their support to have this student disciplined for hate speech. What was interesting about this outpouring is that in the previous year I had sent an e-mail to the same lists alerting people to the fact that the dean of the university said he would not support Native American studies as he considered it a "squandering of resources." However, there was virtually no response or outcry to *this* e-mail. Why were people so quick to mobilize around a student who ultimately had relatively little power to impact their lives but reluctant to organize against an administration that had the power to dismantle Native studies completely?

This incident is symptomatic of the politics of hate crime organizing within the United States as a whole. A strategy taken by organizers against racialized and gendered terror is to articulate this terror as "hate crime." The publicizing of a hate crime can often quickly mobilize even relatively complacent citizens to "fight the hate." From James Byrd to Matthew Shepherd to Vincent Chin, we see even conservative sectors of the U.S. public responding to cries to "teach tolerance." In this chapter, I assess some of the political effects of hate crime organizing. When organizing against racial and/or gender terror adopts the strategy of making this terror a crime, it actually serves to reproduce patriarchy and white supremacy by masking the sexism and the racism of capitalism and the nation-state. This chapter examines how the articulation of racial and gender violence as "hate crime" becomes an apology for the racial and gender violence of the state. This articulation is inherent in the phrase "hate crime" itself. I will explore both parts of the phrase—"crime" and "hate"—to assess the (re)productive power of this rhetorical strategy.

CRIME

Valerie Jenness and Ryken Grattet trace the development of the hate crimes movement as a confluence of identity-based racial and other social justice movements with the crime victim's movement. Racial and gender justice groups focused on violence as one aspect of racial and gender oppression. Meanwhile, the crime victim's movement, which in many respects actually supported a repressive anticrime agenda at odds with racial justice organizing, articulated crime victims as an oppressed group with "rights." The confluence of these movements then served to highlight victims of racial or gender bias or hate crimes as people deserving particular legal rights (Jenness and Grattet 2001). To add to Jenness and Grattet's analysis, it would also seem that as more radical racial and social justice organizations were either crushed or co-opted by the U.S. government during the 1970s, these movements shifted from a focus on radically restructuring the political and economic system to one articulating identity-based claims that did not necessarily challenge the prevailing power structure (Brown 1995; Incite 2007; Maracle 1988). If groups were not going to directly challenge the state, they could then call on the state to recognize their claims to equality and redress harms perpetrated by other social actors. According to James Jacobs and Kimberly Potter, the term "hate crime" emerged in 1985 with a bill, the Hate Crime Statistics Act, sponsored by the House of Representatives (Jacobs and Potter 1998: 4), and it became officially recognized by the state. Thus, there is a convergence, but not a complete overlap, between the evocation of "hate crimes" within popular discourse and particular crimes defined as hate crimes under state and federal law. Different constituencies also debate as to which types of crimes should be defined as hate crimes, particularly hate crimes based on sexual orientation.

Ironically, then, the same U.S. government that codified slavery, segregation, anti-immigrant racism, and the genocide of indigenous peoples now becomes the body that will protect people of color from racial terror. In fact the Southern Poverty Law Center announced that it had begun a cooperative relationship with the state by collaborating with the Federal Law Enforcement Training Center to train law enforcement officers to recognize and respond to hate crimes. Defining race hate as a crime appears to mirror the strategy adopted by the antiviolence movement to define violence against women as a crime. Thus, race and gender hatred is supposed to be "against the law," thereby permitting the state to intervene and protect women and people of color against those who would perpetrate race and gender hate crimes. The question, however, then arises: What are we to do with the fact that, as Native scholar Luana Ross notes, genocide has never been against the law in the United States? (Ross 1998: 15). On the contrary, Native genocide has been expressly sanctioned *as* the law. Examples would include the Indian Removal Act, which displaced Native tribes from the east to the west of the Mississippi River, leading to the death of one third of Cherokee and other tribal populations. Similarly, the prison-industrial complex, an institution that oppresses communities of color (Davis 2003; Rodriguez 2005), is not currently against the law; rather, it is intrinsic to the very enforcement of the law.

As Beth Richie notes, the co-optation of the antiviolence movement can be traced in part to when that movement chose to argue that domestic violence is a crime. The state, rather than being recognized for its complicity in gender violence, became the institution promising to protect women from domestic and sexual violence by providing a provisional "sanctuary" of sorts from the now criminally defined "other" (Richie 2000). As I have argued in my other works, the state is largely responsible for introducing gender violence into indigenous communities as part of a colonial strategy that follows a logic of sexual violence. Gender violence becomes the mechanism by which U.S. colonialism is effectively and pervasively exerted on Native nations. Colonizers did not just kill off indigenous peoples in this land, but Native massacres were always accompanied by sexual mutilation and rape. As I have argued elsewhere, the goal of colonialism is not just to kill colonized peoples but to destroy their sense of being people. It is through sexual violence that a colonizing group attempts to render a colonized people as inherently rapable, their lands as inherently invadable, and their resources as inherently extractable (Smith 2005). The complicity of the state in perpetrating gender violence in other communities of color through slavery, prisons, and border patrol is also well documented (Bhattacharjee 2001; Davis 1981; Incite 2006; James 1996; Smith 2005).

Rather than target the state then as a perpetrator of gender violence, activists in the rape crisis and domestic violence movements have for many years promoted strengthening the criminal justice system as the primary means to reduce sexual and domestic violence. Particularly since the passage of the Violence Against Women Act of 1994 (VAWA), antiviolence centers have been able to receive a considerable amount of funding from the state to the point where most agencies have become dependent on the state for their continued existence. Consequently, their strategies tend to be state-friendly: hire more police, give longer sentences to rapists, pass mandatory arrests laws, and so on. However, as mentioned previously, the state is largely responsible for the epidemic rates of gender violence in many communities. For instance, it is through the forced removal of Native children into boarding schools, where they were routinely sexually, emotionally, and physically abused, that we see such significant rates of gender violence in Native communities, where it was relatively rare prior to colonization (Smith 2005). There is a bit of contradiction then in thinking that the state is now going to be the solution to the problem it has created in the first place. The antiviolence movement has always contested the notion of home as a safe place, because the majority of violence that women suffer happens at home. Furthermore, the notion that violence happens "out there," inflicted by the stranger in the dark alley, prevents us from recognizing that the home is in fact the place of greatest danger for women. However, the strategies the domestic violence movement employs to address violence are actually premised on the danger coming from "out there" rather than from home. Reliance on the criminal justice system to address gender violence would make sense if the threat were a few crazed men whom we can lock up. But the prison system is not equipped to address a violent culture in which 25–50 percent (or more) of women can expect to be battered in their lifetime, unless we are prepared to imprison millions of people (MacKinnon 1987; National Resource Center on Domestic Violence 2002).

Criminalization has not actually led to a decrease in violence against women. As a number of studies have demonstrated, more prisons and more police do not lead to lower crime rates (Currie 1998; Donziger 1996; Walker 1998). For instance, the Rand Corporation found that California's three-strikes legislation, which requires life sentences for three-time convicted felons, did not reduce the rate of "murders, rapes, and robberies that many people believe to be the law's principal targets" (Walker 1998: 139). Criminologist Elliott Currie similarly finds that "the *best* face put on the impact of massive prison increases, in a study routinely used by prison supporters to prove that 'prison works,' shows that prison growth seems not to have 'worked' at all for homicide or assault, barely if at all for rape" (Currie 1998: 59). Antiviolence activists and scholars have also widely critiqued the supposed efficacy of criminalization (Incite 2006; Sokoloff 2005; Strang and Braithwaite 2002; White 2004). These contradictions are noted by scholars who argue that while violence against women is a "crime," it should not be constituted as a "hate crime" because of "the pervasiveness of violent crimes against women" (Jenness and Grattet 2001: 67). But if it does not make sense to demarcate crimes against women as hate crimes because they so pervasive, then why would we demarcate some crimes against people of color as hate crimes if we also understand race hatred to be pervasive? One problem with this argument is that the whole notion of hate crime then has to be predicated on the idea that racial hate is relatively rare by contrast to gender hate, thus obscuring the pervasiveness of racism. So if we understand racial hatred *and* gender hatred to be pervasive rather than rare, criminalization is not an approach equipped to address them.

Unfortunately, the "remedies" that have been pursued by the mainstream antiviolence movement have often strengthened rather than undercut state violence. While the anti–sexual violence and anti–domestic violence movements have been vital in breaking the silence around violence against women and in providing critically needed services to survivors of sexual and domestic violence, these movements have also become increasingly professionalized in providing services; consequently, there is often reluctance to address sexual and domestic violence within the larger context of institutionalized violence. In addition, those who go to prison for domestic violence are disproportionately people of color. Julie Ostrowski reports that of the men who go to domestic violence courts in New York, only 12 percent are white. Half of them are unemployed, and the average income of those who are employed is $12,655 (Ostrowski 2004). The issue is not primarily that antiviolence advocates are supporting the prison-industrial complex by sending batterers and rapists to jail, for many antiviolence advocates say, "If people are guilty of violence, should they not be in jail regardless of their racial background?" The co-optation of the antiviolence movement by the criminal justice system has far-reaching effects besides those on the immediate victims of domestic violence. The Right has been very successful in using antiviolence rhetoric to mobilize support for a repressive anticrime agenda that includes three-strikes legislation and antidrug bills. These anticrime measures make abused women more likely to find themselves in prison if they are coerced by partners to engage in illegal activity. When men of color are disproportionately incarcerated because of these laws, which have been passed in part through the co-optation of antiviolence rhetoric, the entire community, particularly women, who are often the community caretakers, is negatively impacted. Who is left to care for the children when men are taken from their communities? The Violence Against Women Act was attached to the repressive Violent Crime Control and Law Enforcement Act, which increased the use of the death penalty, added over fifty federal offenses—many of which criminalized youth of color—eliminated Pell Grants for prisoners, and expanded the prison-industrial complex by 9.7 billion dollars. It was then heralded by antiviolence advocates as "feminist" legislation.

Furthermore, as Kimberle Crenshaw notes, this racialization of criminalization serves not just to criminalize men of color but to codify the rapability of women of color (Crenshaw 1996: 358). That is, what determines criminality is not just the race of the perpetrator but the race of the victim (Ogletree and Sarat 2006). Perpetrators of gender crimes are more likely to be acquitted or receive a lighter sentence if their victims are not white (Crenshaw 1996). So those who commit violent acts against women of color are least likely to be criminalized. The perpetrators of sexual violence against Native women on reservations in particular are almost never arrested, much less tried and convicted (Amnesty International 2007; Smith 2005). This rapability of women of color under the law is continuous with the rapability of Black women under slavery and Native women in colonial massacres of indigenous peoples (Smith 2005).

Essentially, then, the adoption of hate crimes as a strategy for addressing racial/gender justice has shifted our analysis from articulating the state as partially constituted by heteropatriarchy and white supremacy to uncritically upholding the liberal multicultural state as that institution that *recognizes* and legitimizes legal and political claims based on gender and race. As Elizabeth Povinelli has so aptly demonstrated, the liberal state depends on a politics of multicultural recognition that includes "social difference without social consequence" (Povinelli 2002: 16). As she further states, "These state, public, and capital multicultural discourses, apparatuses, and imaginaries defuse struggles for liberation waged against the modern liberal state and recuperate these struggles as moments in which the future of the nation and its core institutions and values are ensured rather than shaken" (29).

Thus, the state, rather than being understood as defined through gender and racial differentiation and subordination becomes positioned as the body to recognize and protect racial and gender difference. Because these differences are recognized within the liberal multicultural nation-state, the differences that can be recognized as subject to protection are those that are least threatening to the state. Sociopolitical economies that have a recognizable capitalist component operate intrinsically, though discretely, through gender subordination and commodification. It is the process of commodification that enables capitalism to function, and therefore acts of criminalization or even decriminalization fundamentally fail to alter the capitalist economy of subordination, which places a hierarchy of value on labor. At heart, those occupying the social margins continue to reside simply under differently sanctioned labels that are variously related to criminal identity (state-sanctioned labels of identity) as opposed to self- or community-derived identity. Thus, when "women" are protected by domestic violence, these women are not generally sex workers, women who are addicted or otherwise criminalized, poor women, and so on.

Furthermore, because the state actually has no interest in gender or racial justice, laws passed supposedly to protect survivors of gender violence are then often used against the people they supposedly protect. For instance, the *New York Times* recently reported that the effect of the strengthened anti–domestic violence legislation is that battered women kill their abusive partners less frequently; however, batterers do *not* kill their partners less frequently, this being more the case in Black than in white communities (Butterfield 2000). Ironically, laws passed to protect battered women are actually protecting their batterers! At a hate crimes training session I attended in 1991 with the Chicago Police Department, the trainer reported that almost half of the people the Chicago police arrest for hate crimes are people of color accused of committing hate crimes against white people. The Uniform Crime Reports from 1991 to 1998 show a lesser but still significant 23 percent of all reported racial hate crimes as crimes committed against white people (Jenness and Grattet 2001: 46). One of the stated intents of supporting hate crimes legislation was that, as John Conyers (D-MI) (one of the original cosponsors of the first federal hate crimes bill) argued, "hate crimes . . . are intended to not just harm the victim, but to send a message of intimidation to an entire community of people" (3). This statement implicitly holds that the political effects of crime differ when perpetrated by people coming from communities which have different power statuses in society. This justification for hate crimes legislation is thus under-mined when hate crimes are framed in liberal law's terms of simple equality under the law, where rights can then be adjudicated by the state. Thus anyone can be protected by hate crimes laws, including white people, who do not be-long to communities that are under attack *as* white communities.

In the name of racial and gender justice, then, the hate crimes approach serves to reproduce the white supremacy and the patriarchy of the liberal multicultural state. Unfortunately, even radical thinkers tend not to challenge the foundations of the liberal multicultural state. For instance, in Judith But-ler's analysis of hate speech she notes that those who propose hate speech pros-ecution obfuscate "the interpretive violence by nation-states" (Butler 1997: 48). That is, the very means by which states narrate certain people as subject to "premature death" (Gilmore 2002: 261) under the law through racialized applications of the death penalty and so on is hidden when private individuals only are targeted as purveyors of hate speech. Rather, citizen-subjects become refigured as having the power of the state to deprive other citizen-subjects of rights. She asks, "Is the violence perpetrated by courts unwittingly back-grounded in favor of a politics that presumes the fairness and efficacy of the courts in adjudicating matters of hate speech?" (Butler 1997: 48). However, rather than following the logical conclusions of this analysis with a more radi-cal critique of the state itself, she concludes with, "It will be necessary to dis-tinguish between those kinds of violence that are the necessary conditions of the binding character of legal language, and those kinds which exploit that very necessity in order to redouble that injury in the service of injustice" (62). Thus Butler seems to distinguish the enactments of law from enactments of injustice. This analysis dovetails with her claims that after 9/11 George W. Bush's evocation of sovereignty prompted theorists to reduce sovereignty to "as providing legitimacy of the rule of law and offering a guarantor for the pre-sentational claims of state power" (Butler 2004: 52). According to Butler, the resurgence of sovereignty happens in a context of "suspension of law" (2004: 55), whereby the nation can in the name of sovereignty act against "existing legal frameworks, civil, military, and international. . . . Under this mantle of sovereignty, the state proceeds to extend its own power to imprison indefi-nitely a group of people without trial" (57). Butler may be arguing that after 9/11 the rule of law through sovereignty (seemingly displaced in Foucault's analysis during the rise of capitalism) has made a comeback as a legitimizing notion that works in tandem with governmentality to extend state power. But this argument, as the work of Joy James and Rey Chow demonstrates, fails to consider how governmentality has *always* operated through sovereign power exacted through racial violence (Chow 2002; Jacobs 2000; James 1996). Thus the argument that we are currently under a resurgence of sovereignty, itself normalizes the history of U.S. sovereign power exacted against the bodies of indigenous peoples and peoples of color. In addition, as legal scholar Sora Han points out, none of these post–9/11 practices are actually extraconstitutional or extralegal. In fact the U.S. Constitution confers the right of the state to maintain itself over and above the rights of its citizenry (Han 2006). There can thus be a tendency among even radical thinkers to unwittingly look to the U.S. Constitution from an Edenic perspective—the basis of guaranteed rights from which we have deviated. Butler's analysis is predicated on what David Kazanjian refers to as the "colonizing trick"—the liberal myth of the United States as founded on democratic principles that have been eroded through post–9/11 policies, rather than as a state built on the pillars of capitalism, colonialism, and white supremacy (Kazanjian 2003).

Lisa Lowe further explains how white supremacy is integral to the logics of capital and the state in her analysis of the contradiction between capital and nation-state imperatives. Capital, she argues, is often understood to be unconcerned with the identities of its labor force, because it simply requires its labor force to be exploitable. And yet the history of capitalism suggests that those most exploited are racialized and gendered. This contradiction she explains through the logic of the nation-state, which desires a unified culture that participates in the public sphere and seeks to maintain a citizenry bound by race, culture, and language. This contradiction is resolved when, through race and gender stratification and legal exclusions, certain sectors of the population, such as Asian immigrants, are both excluded from the citizenry and relegated to the lowest-paying and most-exploited jobs (Lowe 1996: 13). She states that citizenship is thus "simultaneously a 'technology' of racialization and gendering" (11). Timothy Kaufman-Osborn, in his analysis of the connections between lynching and the death penalty, further explores how the death penalty both continues and supersedes lynching in that it allows the state to reproduce white supremacy while disavowing this reproduction by allowing racism to be perpetrated under the cover of law and bureaucracy: "The practices constitutive of due process . . . are a 'pretense' not in the sense that they render capital punishment and lynching identical but, rather, in the more subtle sense that they mask the continued articulation of the racial contract within a polity that no longer openly espouses the rhetoric of white supremacy" (Kaufman-Osborn 2006: 48–49).

He mirrors Philip Deloria's analysis of institutionalization of anti-Indian racism within U.S. polity in the 1900s. Deloria argues that while the state's investment in Native colonialism did not end, the state did seek to ensure that the sole executor of colonialism would be the state. Consequently, it began to condemn the massacres conducted by settlers acting independently of the purview of the state in order to ensure the omnipresence of the "law" (Deloria 2004). Thus, in both cases we see that as Foucault notes, genocide and white supremacy become routinized through the law, while at the same time the regime of the law is perfected over white people as well (Foucault 1977). That is, while white supremacy is to be maintained by the state, it is equally important to ensure that it is maintained *through* the state rather than through whites acting outside the law. Even white people are not to exist outside the regime of law. Thus, by extending Kaufman-Osborn's and Deloria's analyses, we could look at hate crimes as the strategy by which the state reserves the right to perpetrate hate crimes to itself.

As Ruth Frankenburg further argues, "notions of race are closely linked to ideas about legitimate ownership of the nation, with 'whiteness' and 'Americanness' linked tightly together" (Frankenburg 1993: 6). Borrowing from Charles Mills's *The Racial Contract*, which contends that the United States is a system fundamentally based on white supremacy, Kaufman-Osborn contend that racism represents not a "deviation from the (fictive) norm but adherence to the actual norm" (2006: 48). Thus the nation-state, particularly the United States, is not a bastion of freedom, some of the ideals of which were being eroded under the Bush regime; rather, the Bush regime was in fact the *fulfillment* of the ideals of U.S. democracy. The logic of the U.S. state is white supremacy and patriarchy—it is not going to protect us from racial or gender terror.

HATE

While one tends to think of individuals who "hate," one does not often think of institutions or the state as something that hates. When one's analysis focuses on institutionalized white supremacy, such as the prison-industrial complex and the continued occupation of indigenous lands, one sees not so much hatred but a normalized set of relations that maintain a racialized and gendered economic and political system benefiting the few at the expense of the many. This quotidian racism then becomes contrasted to race hate. That is, racial hate seems to be a more extreme version of the everyday racism and sexism we live under. As in the story at the beginning of the chapter, it is the hate speech of the student that makes the speech of the academic dean seem insignificant. In fact, institutions that benefit from white supremacy can now be called upon to stop hate crimes. While I do not wish to minimize the trauma of hate crimes, it is certainly the case that if, for example, we look to Ruthie Gilmore's definition of racism as "state-sanctioned and/or extralegal production and exploitation of group-differentiated vulnerability to premature death" (2002: 261), then the daily practices embedded in institutions of white supremacy cause much more premature death than do individual hate crimes. George W. Bush's attack on Iraq is generally not articulated as a hate crime. In fact, Bush partially contrasted the two when he began advocating for the aggressive prosecution of hate crimes against Arab Americans while simultaneously launching his War on Terror against Arab countries. "While our brave soldiers are fighting aggression overseas, a few hate mongers here at home are perpetrating their own brand of cowardly aggression. These hate crimes have no place in a free society and we are not going to stand for them" (Jenness and Grattet 2001: 2). The former (acts of violence against individual Arab Americans) qualifies as hate crimes, while the latter (killing thousands of Arab people through military invasion) is normalized as foreign policy.

To illustrate further, a magazine ran a photo-essay on the Ku Klux Klan. One of its captions noted that there are no "hate groups" in South Dakota (KKK: The Next Generation 2005). This fact will be of considerable interest to the indigenous nations in South Dakota, who have seen no shortage of hate directed at them by the state and its white residents. For example, townsperson Mike Whelan made the following statement at a 1990 zoning hearing, where he called for the denial of a permit for an Indian battered women's shelter in South Dakota:

> Indian Culture as I view it, is presently so mongrelized as to be a mix of dependency on the Federal Government and a primitive society wholly on the outside of the mainstream of western civilization and thought. The Native American Culture as we know it now, not as it formerly existed, is a culture of hopelessness, godlessness, of joblessness, and lawlessness. . . . Alcoholism, social disease, child abuse, and poverty are the hallmarks of this so called culture that you seek to promote, and I would suggest to you that the brave men of the ghost dance would hang their heads in shame at what you now pass off as that

culture. . . . I think that the Indian way of life as you call it, to me means cigarette burns in arms of children, double checking the locks on my cars, keeping a loaded shotgun by my door, and car bodies and beer cans on the front lawn. . . . This is not a matter of race, it is a matter of keeping our community and neighborhood away from that evil that you and your ideas promote. (Native American Women's Health Education Resource Center 1990: 2–3)

This testimony along with others became the basis of the state's denying the Native American Women's Health Education Resource Center a zoning permit. In this case, racial hate became adopted by the state as such. But this "hate" codified by the state itself becomes invisible when racial terror is focused on hate groups or hate crimes. Or could we instead understand South Dakota as itself a hate group?

Of course, as Alison Bailey states, it is possible to address hate crimes in a context of institutionalized racism as a whole. Bailey focuses on taking community responsibility for hate crimes by "addressing the social and systemic dimensions of violence that permit hate crimes to flourish" (Bailey 2001: 219). I would add by contrast, however, that it is the social production of hate crimes that allows social and systemic dimensions of violence to flourish. In line with Foucault's analysis of the social production of homosexuality, it is the production of the hate crime that rather than simply naming a phenomena, actually (re)produces the patriarchy and the white supremacy of the state, and the everyday practices within it, by rendering them invisible.

THE HETEROPATRIARCHAL RACIAL STATE

The question then becomes how we address racial and gender terror if we simultaneously recognize that the state also hates us and has no interest in protecting us from hate. If we recognize that genocide has in fact been the law of the land, then instead of arguing that gender/race crimes should be "against the law," should not our organizing be against the law? Certainly, Native American studies should provide a critical intervention in this discourse because the United States could not exist without the genocide of Native peoples: genocide is not a mistake or aberration of U.S. democracy; it is foundational to it. As Sandy Grande states:

The United States is a nation defined by its original sin: the genocide of American Indians. . . . American Indian tribes are viewed as an inherent threat to the nation, poised to expose the great lies of U.S. democracy: that we are a nation of laws and not random power; that we are guided by reason and not faith; that we are governed by representation and not executive order; and finally, that we stand as a self-determined citizenry and not a kingdom of blood or aristocracy.... From the perspective of American Indians, "democracy" has been wielded with impunity as the first and most virulent weapon of mass destruction. (Grande 2004: 31–32)

Native feminist analyses question the idea that what we need is basically a "kinder, gentler" United States. By extension, they question the idea that nation-states in general are either necessary or beneficial forms of governance. Such a political project is particularly important for colonized peoples seeking national liberation because it allows us to differentiate "nation" from "nation-state." Helpful in this project of imagination is the work of Native women activists who have begun articulating notions of nation and sovereignty that are separate from those of nation-states. Whereas nation-states are governed through domination and coercion, indigenous sovereignty and nationhood are predicated on interrelatedness and responsibility. As I have argued elsewhere, indigenous feminists and feminists of color have challenged how we conceptualize indigenous sovereignty—it is not an add-on to the heteropatriarchal nation-state (Smith 2008). Implicit in this analysis is the understanding that heteropatriarchy is essential for the building of U.S. empire. That is, patriarchy is the logic that naturalizes social hierarchy. Just as men are supposed to naturally dominate women on the basis of biology, so too should the social elites of a society naturally rule everyone else through a nation-state form of governance that is constructed through domination, violence, and control. Patriarchy in turn presumes a heteronormative gender binary system.

This understanding of indigenous nationhood also requires a different relationship to the land. As Mishuana Goeman and Patricia Monture-Angus argue, indigenous nationhood is not based on control of territory or land but on relationship with and responsibility for land.

Although Aboriginal Peoples maintain a close relationship with the land ... it is not about control of the land.... Earth is mother and she nurtures us all ... it is the human race that is dependent on the earth and not vice versa....

Sovereignty, when defined as my right to be responsible ... requires a relationship with territory (and not a relationship based on control of that territory).... What must be understood then is that Aboriginal request to have our sovereignty respected is really a request to be responsible. I do not know of anywhere else in history where a group of people have had to fight so hard just to be responsible. (Monture-Angus 1999: 125, 36)

It is within the realm of recognition in legal and cultural battles that Native peoples are forced to argue for their right to control and to be recognized by the settler colonial state. But while such short-term strategies may be necessary at times, it would be a mistake to presume that this is the most beneficial long-term political goal for Native peoples. The battle for recognition can make even Native peoples forget that they have alternative genealogies for their relationship to the land, a relationship based on respect for land rather than control over territory, and genealogies that fundamentally question nation-state forms of governance which are premised on control, exclusivity, domination, and violence. As Glen Coulthard (2007) argues,

> [the] key problem with the politics of recognition when applied to the colonial context . . . [is that it] rests on the problematic assumption that the flourishing of Indigenous Peoples as distinct and self-determining agents is somehow dependent on their being granted recognition and institutional accommodation from the surrounding settler-state and society. . . . Not only will the terms of recognition tend to remain the property of those in power to grant to their inferiors in ways that they deem appropriate, but also under these conditions, the Indigenous population will often come to see their limited and structurally constrained terms of recognition granted to them as *their own*. In effect, the colonized come to *identify* with "white liberty and white justice."

Indigenous women and feminists of color are organizing against violence through the construction of alternative governance systems that do not rely on the colonial nation-state (Smith 2005). While an in-depth analysis of these interventions is a topic for another occasion, they do point to the need to think outside the state for racial and gender justice. When we say, "Our human rights should be protected," or "Hate crimes should be punished," we must finish the sentence with "by whom?" In our analysis of hate crimes, we have to unmask the role of the state as foundational to gender and racial violence rather than allow it be the invisible arbiter of racial and gender claims.

11 THE BLACK DIASPORA AS GENOCIDE

Brazil and the United States—
A Supranational Geography of Death and Its Alternatives

João H. Costa Vargas

There's an urgency imperative to this chapter. To approach the vexing problem of the Black Diaspora is not just an academic exercise divorced of political ramifications (if such an exercise could ever be). In the midst of a U.S.-centric wave of undefined yet effectively galvanizing hope, fueled in no small measure by the ascension of Barack Obama to the top executive post of a recognizable empire, I despair that the lives of those deemed less than human, made invisible and prone to the historical and contemporary disproportionate negative effects of state policies and societal neglect, will be made further irrelevant in the hegemonic calculus of what constitutes the good and worthy nation—and indeed, from the standpoint of empire, the good and worthy international community. I am talking about the endangered and prematurely terminated lives of those caught in the U.S.-renewed war efforts abroad; and in what concerns more directly the focus of this chapter, I am referring to the ongoing endangered and prematurely terminated lives of Black people, mostly U.S. citizens, due to a constellation of policies, practices, and beliefs that affect the ways in which the criminal justice system, health care, and work, among other institutions, are managed and experienced. To attempt to add to the definition of the Black Diaspora, therefore, means to draw on the urgency that emerges out of the likely—if not already emplaced—ostracism of dissonant voices, voices claiming not only that the U.S. empire, its representatives, members, and ideological justifications are always suspect, but that they, We, are always excluding, and often murderous, in our choices of ignorance and silence. At the very least, the empire that We participate in, willingly or not, makes the claims of inclusive multiracialism and multiculturalism the political farce—under imperialism and colonialism more generally, and under Black genocide more pointedly—that continues to manifest its ugly heads (for example, Sexton 2010).

As it suggests a notion of the Black Diaspora as marked by a multiplicity of anti-Black genocidal processes, this chapter aims at the following: First, to decenter the United States, to dislocate its/our seldom-conscious imperial gaze and self-understanding, by recentering it in the Black Diaspora in order to show how anti-Black processes, more easily associated with so-called third world locations, are not only prevalent but foundational in this imperial nation-state. It may seem counterintuitive that at a time when a Black president sits in the White House, anti-Black state- and society-sanctioned marginalizations not only prevail but indeed define the scope and nature of the U.S. polity—as they indeed define the Black Diaspora. The notions of Diaspora available in the United States, Canada, and the Anglophone Caribbean, while at times conscious of their epistemic and nationalist limitations, hardly attempt to engage with, and thus effectively relativize, their Anglocentric (even if unwilling) nationalisms (Yelvington, 2001; Walcott, 2005). By bringing together living experiences from Brazil and the United States, this chapter draws lines of continuity rather than disjuncture; I suggest that anti-Black genocidal practices that characterize a bona fide Lusophone so-called third world country, rather than constituting exceptions, are in fact part of a continuum that marks nations of the Black Diaspora, the Anglophone United States squarely included.

Second, this chapter proposes a complementary concept of Diaspora that while attentive to its shifting, experiential, performative, and ultimately political facets, focuses on racial terror (for example, Gilroy 1993) and more specifically on Black genocide as its foundational characteristic. Members of Black communities in the Diaspora are never meant to survive fully as citizens and human beings—the fact of genocide constitutes the fulcrum, the basis on which varied manifestations of Blackness that define the Diaspora take place. Inspired in writings of Audre Lorde (1984), Cedric Robinson (2000), Faye Harrison (2002), and Howard Winant (2001) in the United States, and Abdias do Nascimento (1989) and Jurema Werneck (2007) in Brazil, this chapter suggests a concept of the Black Diaspora that locates the common experiences of state racial subjugation (more obviously, but not only restricted to police brutality), disproportionate unemployment and massive incarceration, premature death, and preventable disease, among other widely shared social facts among Blacks, as the basis on which the Diaspora exists, struggles, and perishes. As a process and as a condition (Patterson and Kelley 2000), the Black Diaspora necessarily draws on, challenges, and survives such transnational social phenomena. To exemplify the materiality of the Black Diaspora as genocide, I analyze available data on the criminal justice system, health care, and work in Brazil and the United States.

Third, as it recognizes the urgency of survival, which necessarily implies the related requirement of political struggle, the perspective offered in this chapter centers on the immanent liberatory imperative of the Black Diaspora. If some of the conditions of possibility of nation-states such as Brazil and the United States rest on the impossibility of the Black condition—the impossibility of full citizenship, the impossibility of a fully recognized and lived humanity, the impossibility of *not* being magnets for bullets (Wilderson 2005)—then what are the political options open to members of the Black Diaspora? What theoretical and practical political alternatives have members of Black Diaspora communities, under permanent siege, elaborated against the varied state and societal assaults launched against them? All of which is to say that to define and locate the Black Diaspora as genocide is to recognize its permanent state of resistance and rebellion. In the face of genocide, and in the absence of resistance and rebellion, there would be no vibrant Black Diaspora as we know it. By focusing on specific analyses and strategies of resistance devised by Black activists working collectively across nation-state borders, I will show how the Black Diaspora is not only a geography of death but also, necessarily, a set of shared ontological and political knowledge that is immanently insurgent.

The analytical perspective I propose aims to complement current views on the Black Diaspora. I choose to emphasize Black as opposed to African, not to diminish the horizontal, mutually constitutive role that the African continent has on multidirectional currents of experiences and processes related to the Diaspora (Yelvington 2001), but rather to call attention to a set of seldom-articulated yet necessarily linked facts that, I argue, constitute genocide outside of the African continent. To put it bluntly, it is seemingly more acceptable to conceptualize genocide in the African continent (albeit persistently difficult to juridically define and enforce punishment against it) than it is to recognize the traits of genocide in non-African nations of the Black Diaspora. Specifically, Black Diaspora nations in the Americas, including the United States, although at times recognized as engendering varied challenges to its

Black members, are very rarely criticized as constitutively creating and maintaining conditions under which the sheer survival of Black community members is constantly challenged. My emphasis here on the Black Diaspora aims at putting genocidal processes and conditions at the center and front of what constitutes bases from which Black identities and politics are experienced throughout the Diaspora, especially in the Americas. African and American nations have in common the survival challenges their Black communities face as constitutive of their experience. As such, their membership in the Black Diaspora has less to do with geographical location or with matters of origin than with a shared transnational experience of and fight against genocide.[1]

Whereas important scholarly contributions have offered insight on the Black Diaspora as a set of more or less shifting cultural, experiential, historical, and otherwise political processes, I want to add to such contributions by focusing on an apparently disparate, underlying set of political economic circumstances. When analytically connected, such deceivingly disparate circumstances become meaningful as a supranational (albeit not devoid of national inflections) social and factual constellation that disproportionately affects Black communities in the Diaspora. If the work of colonialism and imperialism is to be located and neutralized, then we must put back together that which has been rendered separate and discontinuous:

> [W]e will destabilize that which hegemony has rendered coherent or fixed; reassemble that which appears to be disparate, scattered, or otherwise idiosyncratic; foreground that which is latent and therefore powerful in its apparent absence; and analyze that which is apparently self-evident, which hegemony casts as commonsensical and natural, but which we shall read as gestures of power that deploy violence to normalize and discipline. (Alexander, 2006: 192)

The tasks of ethnographically documenting and understanding the Black Diaspora, and seriously taking into account what members of such seemingly disparate realities make of the permanent assaults on their well-being (Gordon and Anderson 1999), require engaging with the theorizations and political strategies elaborated in limit conditions—conditions that are supranational, historically persistent, and that produce quantifiable negative and disproportionate effects on Black peoples yet are seldom named and challenged for what they are: genocide.

The modern coinage of the term *genocide* is attributed to Polish jurist Raphael Lemkin, who fled Poland in 1939 for the United States. At a time when the horrors of the Jewish Holocaust, as well as other mass atrocities committed by powerful states since the turn of the twentieth century, lacked a concept by which they could be described and prosecuted, Lemkin's 1944 definition of genocide, which appeared in his *Axis Rule in Occupied Europe*, encompassed a multifaceted perspective. It included attacks on political, cultural, and economic institutions. Genocide did not necessitate killings. Actions that infringed on the liberty, dignity, and safety of members of a group were enough to qualify them as genocide. The United Nations' initial definition of genocide, which appears in its 1946 General Assembly, followed Lemkin's broad conceptual reach.

The more restricted concept of genocide that stands today is the result of a series of political battles waged at the United Nations by powerful nation-states that obviously were not interested in a definition of genocide which could criminalize their actions. Representatives of the United Kingdom, the Soviet Union, the United States, and France, for example, were concerned about the implications of the U.N. resolution vis-à-vis their own internal and international colonial endeavors. Such were the stakes that the United States, for example, only ratified the already watered-down 1948 definition forty years later, and even then with two "reservations" and five "understandings."[2]

The definition of genocide that serves as a reference in this chapter is the Convention on the Prevention and Punishment of the Crime of Genocide, approved by the United Nations General Assembly Resolution 260 A (III) of December 9, 1948, which became effective on January 12, 1951. According to Article II of the convention, genocide is "any of the following acts committed with intent to destroy, in whole or in part, a national, ethnic, racial, or religious group as such:

(a)   Killing members of the group;

(b)   Causing serious bodily or mental harm to members of the group;

(c)   Deliberately inflicting on the group conditions of life calculated to bring about its physical destruction in whole or in part;

(d)   Imposing measures intended to prevent births within the group;

(e)   Forcibly transferring children of the group to another group."

To present and analyze the perspectives Black Diaspora activists have developed in times of genocide, and in the process have contributed to a broadening of our understanding of what the Black Diaspora is and could be, I present below the following. First, I describe the conditions under which the encounter between Black Brazilian and U.S. activists took place in 1993. In spite of the fact that I am a Brazilian national, I came into contact with the Rio de Janeiro activists through former Los Angeles Black Panthers and their comrades. I collaborated with the Coalition Against Police Abuse, located in South Central Los Angeles, between 1996 and 2006. In 2000, persons working there called my attention to progressive activists in the Jacarezinho community and urged me to find institutional ways to support their projects. Following this initial collaboration (Vargas 2003), I have been involved mostly in solidarity work with organizations of Rio since 2001, the details of which I will explain below.[3] Second, on the basis of these activist and solidarity work experiences, I draw on concepts of genocide developed by the Civil Rights Congress in the early 1950s, and by contemporary activist intellectuals in the United States and Brazil. I then explore the applicability and the theoretical and practical importance of the concept of genocide for ongoing Black struggles. Finally, I reflect on the possibilities for liberation and explain why given the ubiquity and persistence of Black genocide, liberation is a necessity we cannot afford not to fight for. The Black Diaspora as genocide creates the imperative of radical transformation and leaves us with no choice but to destroy the social conditions that generate it. The Black Diaspora as a geography of death produced by anti-Black necropolitics (Mbembe 2003) is therefore, and necessarily, also a living network of biopolitics that is an affirmation of survival, persistence, and creativity. Such biopolitics, as it projects a Black Diaspora that is the antithesis of genocide, automatically makes claims against the anti-Black, hierarchical, and imperial natures of our cognition and polities.[4]

BRAZIL, OR A LUSOPHONE SIDE
OF THE BLACK DIASPORA IN THE AMERICAS

The current political moment in Brazil, from a Black Diaspora perspective, is one of contradictions: as the Brazilian Black movements become relatively successful in pressing for and sometimes implementing affirmative action public policies, longstanding institutional and ideological practices further the imposed marginalization of Black communities. Militarized police abuse, residential segregation, unemployment, and early death, as I will specify further below, continue to disproportionately affect Afro-descended persons at the same time two interrelated, mutually constitutive and contradictory processes show their faces.[5] One of them is a relatively new public recognition of the corrupt and discriminating nature of Brazilian police and of the criminal justice system in general.[6] The other is a multifaceted anti–affirmative action campaign that draws its momentum from television programs, newspaper and magazine articles, and newly published books. Race does not exist and should not serve as a basis for public policies: this is the logic informing the campaign that recycles the racial democracy ideology and as such makes a misleadingly appealing case for the resistance, refusal, and renegotiation of the few but important affirmative action gains Brazil has witnessed in the last few years.[7]

The economic policies adopted by the Lula government provide a further context in which this moment of contradictions unfolds. Among the very poor majority in Brazil, which is disproportionately Black,[8] Lula's reelection in 2006 marked the plebiscitarian support for such policies. An improved macroeconomic context associated with a lowering of historically high interest rates has generated, especially for the poorest parcel of the Brazilian population, unprecedented access to consumer credit and, what is more important, basic necessities such as food, clothing, and personal hygiene products.

Although by international standards Brazil's annual growth rate during the final three years of Lula's first mandate, that is, between 2004 and 2006, is an unimpressive estimated 3.4 percent, it more than doubles the 1.3 percent growth rate of the previous three-year period, which included the Fernando Henrique Cardoso administration's last three years and Lula's first year. Combined with a lowering of inflation to a record 4 percent in 2006 and an appreciation of the currency by more than 25 percent relative to the U.S. dollar since 2004, these macroeconomic features frame the expansion of consumer credit, especially to low-income and first-time borrowers.[9]

Further contributing to the incorporation of the poor population into the consumer market, Lula's administration increased the minimum wage so that its purchasing power augmented by a substantial 23 percent between 2003 and 2006. Combined with income transfer programs and social safety initiatives aimed at reducing poverty—for example, the Bolsa Família, or Family Stipend, provides R$15 monthly (roughly the equivalent of 7 dollars) per child attending school to a maximum of three children—these social policies have effectively reduced absolute poverty. Brazilians living under the poverty line have declined from 28 percent in 2003 to 23 percent in 2005. By some estimates, absolute poverty declined in the first three years of Lula's presidency by approximately 15 percent.[10] One of the results of these policies is that between 2005 and 2006 the poorer 50 percent's share of the national total income augmented from 14.3 percent to 15.1 percent. Taken together, these data suggest a significant increase in income redistribution benefiting those most affected by poverty.

In spite of these macroeconomic programs, however, the Lula government falls short of achieving structural change. Notwithstanding the marked improvement in earnings for those in the lower-income brackets, per capita government social spending has decreased vis-à-vis the Cardoso administration, with the highest cuts registered in housing and urban infrastructure. The Lula government has not been able to avert a structural and historical tendency: cuts in the government social budget amount to R$19.3 billion in the period 2001–3 (Pochmann 2005: 2). Expanding favelas in Brazil's urban landscapes are a symptom of the collapse of the home loan system. It is estimated that only 20 percent of families in need of home loans have access to them. There is a linear correlation between the increase in number and size of favelas and the unavailability of credit: in the city of Rio de Janeiro, each 10 percent increase in the favelas corresponds to a 2.3 percent decrease in home loan access (Oliveira 2004).

Inasmuch as the structural and historical social inequalities are not addressed frontally, the racialized systems of hierarchies—that feed from and inflect social inequalities—remain as the logic determining life chances. An example of this logic serves as introduction to the multifaceted manifestations of Black genocide I will expand on below. Consider that in the city of Rio, where Blacks are 40.2 percent of the population, they are 66.5 percent of the inmate population. If criminal justice policies are part of a web of racialized historical understandings of the lifeworld, then the overrepresentation of Afro-Brazilians in cages is an index to analogous discrimination in the education, work, housing, and health care systems.

This moment of programmatic changes (for example, the Family Stipend) within racialized structural permanence (cuts in federal home loans for those in poverty, which disproportionately affects Black people living in favelas) is also marked by the predictable reaction orchestrated by those who have always benefited materially and symbolically the most from the racial paradise mythology. Black U.S. and Brazilian activists know that at play is more than just formal recognition of rights and access to resources. As pressing as the here and now pragmatic battle is, the larger war to be fought is about Black people's fully recognized and guaranteed humanity—indeed, it is a war of survival. What are the diagnoses Black Brazilian and U.S. activists elaborate about their polities? What real and imagined communities are they crafting? What notions of Black Diaspora emerge out of such collaborations?

THE CHANGING SAME, OR LOS ANGELES AND RIO DE JANEIRO

Michael Zinzun, cofounder of the Coalition Against Police Abuse (CAPA) in Los Angeles and the main idealizer of the transnational activist alliances I focus on in this chapter, passed in July 2006. Yet the interchanges he initiated over a decade ago, and the Black radical tradition (Robinson 2000) that animates the need to conceptualize and carry through liberation, are alive. The battles have been carried forward and engaged on varied fronts. There are now collaborations between U.S.-based activists and persons and organizations in Rio that are the direct product of that first dialogue. An example is the course Theory and Politics of the African Diaspora, organized by Criola, a Black women's organization based in Rio; Proafro, a center at the State University of Rio de Janeiro; and the Center for African and African American Studies at the University of Texas at Austin. Course planning extended over three years, and the course finally happened in June 2007. Most of the participants were Black Brazilian women activists.

This alliance started in 1993, when a group of fifteen Black residents of South Central Los Angeles, members of two local grassroots organizations, CAPA and the Community in Support of the Gang Truce (CSGT), traveled to Rio de Janeiro to exchange knowledge about their political struggles. CAPA and CSGT were built on their older members' participation in the Black Panther Party, whose programs for community empowerment and transnational perspectives oriented much of the U.S. activists' approach to the Brazilian political connections. The Black U.S. militants interacted with several nongovernmental organizations (among which is one of the first Black NGOs in Brazil, the Instituto de Pesquisa das Culturas Negras) but mostly with inhabitants of one of the poorest, most violent, stigmatized, and dilapidated neighborhoods in Rio, the Jacarezinho favela, where more than 150,000 people live under the despotism of drug dealers and state-sanctioned brutality exercised by the police, as well as under state neglect, which is apparent in the decrepit schooling, health care, transportation, and sanitation infrastructure in the area.

In Jacarezinho, as in many of the larger and more politicized favelas in Rio, groups of courageous women and men began in the early 1990s to challenge the control that corrupt police officers and drug dealers had over the favela's everyday life and politics. Whereas the repressive presence of the police in the favelas is as enduring as the favelas themselves, the dominance of drug dealers is a relatively recent phenomenon. Since the mid-1980s, drug dealers have exerted life-and-death powers over the favelas' dwellers and their neighborhood associations (Associação de Moradores). CAPA and CSGT members met some of those women and men who were organizing in Jacarezinho under new premises of full citizenship, autonomy, and racial pride. The African Americans not only became interested in the reform and programs Jacarezinho organizers were discussing in the community but offered their support in the form of strategies and limited but much-valued financial resources. Brazilians and U.S. Blacks shared the experiences of police brutality, poverty, unemployment, and the effects of the drug trade, and while the ensuing alliance between these two groups recognized the specificities of each context, it nevertheless emphasized the possibility of common strategies and the necessity of addressing local problems through a transnational prism. Above all, the implicit but powerful notion of the Black Diaspora that energized this political alliance recognized a set of shared circumstances that, unless effective local initiatives were put in place, threatened the very viability of vibrant Black communities. The Black Diaspora and its attendant experiences of Blackness made sense insofar as they recognized the dire pragmatic commonalities and the imperatives of sound analysis and forceful, collective, transnational action.

Zinzun frequently remarked on the depressingly similar conditions Blacks experienced in U.S. ghettos and Brazilian favelas. Imminent death at the hands of drug dealers and police officers was only the most obvious condition. He often stated that "you are me, and I am you" when communicating with fellow Brazilian activists. There was a mutual understanding of what it meant to be Black in nation-states that by different means and discourses managed to marginalize and kill Black people while presenting themselves as democratic and inclusive. U.S. color-blind, post–affirmative action ideology, and Brazilian persistent racial democracy mythology produced similar genocidal outcomes in spite of their historical, political, cultural, and geographical specificities.

Denouncing police brutality, formulating analyses that stressed differences but above all commonalities between the United States and Brazil, and proposing police reform not surprisingly featured prominently in the dialogues. Since that first meeting, Brazilian community organizers have stayed in Los Angeles and other U.S. cities for periods ranging from a week to several months, and members of CAPA and CSGT have reciprocated. During these interchanges, Brazilians and U.S. African Americans participate in workshops and seminars on the theory and praxis of community organizing. They also visit different cities, thus becoming further familiarized with each other's realities and political programs. The Internet has provided an additional channel through which information is communicated instantaneously and frequently.[11]

BLACK GENOCIDE, OR REPETITION IN DIFFERENCE

The awareness of Black genocide that consolidates itself in the transnational collaborations between activists in Rio and Los Angeles is rooted in a history of imposed marginalization and in efforts Blacks have undertaken to conceptualize and counter their dehumanization. This awareness often comes explicitly in analyses made by activists, as when they remark on the accumulated effects of police operations in the poor and mostly Black areas in Rio, and call these effects genocide. At other times, the awareness of genocide is more diffuse and is expressed by reference to disparate phenomena such as early death from preventable disease, murders in Black communities perpetrated by residents, persistent high unemployment, and high incidence of HIV/AIDS. The concept of genocide may not be used in these instances, yet what becomes apparent is the understanding that Black Diaspora communities are preferential victims of multiple and related structural social processes that result from active (as in the case of police brutality) or passive public policy (of which inadequate health care is an example). The broadly shared cultural stereotypes both fuel and become further energized by such public policies.

In this section I want to show that the awareness and perception of genocide is the product of present and past activist initiatives. The writings of activist-intellectuals, reflecting theory and pragmatic action employed by political actors, are sources of systematic perspectives on genocide. These writings help us to understand and contextualize the contemporary theorizations conducted by activists when they engage with genocide. Contemporary activist initiatives that combat Black genocide have a political genealogy going back in historical time as well as revealing theoretical rhizomes traversing nation-states.

From the U.S. standpoint, William Patterson, Manning Marable, and Joy James, among others, can be considered examples of diasporic activist-intellectuals who have theorized Black genocide and linked it to political practice. Not surprisingly, given the global nature of Black genocide, such a body of work intersects with that of Black Brazilian activist, elected representative, screenwriter, actor, and painter Abdias do Nascimento. Below I delineate key aspects of the ways genocide was conceived of by such activist-intellectuals, beginning with the Civil Rights Congress definition of genocide developed in the early 1950s. I then discuss the applicability of the concept to our times and to diasporic Black communities. I close this section with specific data on the contemporary manifestations of Black genocide in the United States and Brazil.

On December 17, 1951, William Patterson led a delegation before the United Nations secretary-general charging the United States government with the genocide of Black Americans. The delegation's arguments were meticulously compiled in a landmark publication edited by Patterson (1951), then national executive secretary of the Civil Rights Congress, entitled *We Charge Genocide: The Historic Petition to the United Nations for Relief from a Crime of the United States Government Against the Negro People*. The point of the present analysis is to utilize the theoretical tools as well as the political commitment embodied in *We Charge Genocide* as strategies to make sense of and begin to combat the multiple forms of Black genocide that are taking place before our eyes. For Patterson and his collaborators, the persistence of lynchings and of Jim Crow policies was—in those postwar times when the United States invested heavily in its self-image as the guardian of world democracy and foe of communist totalitarianism—the main object of the campaign (Horne 1988; Tyson 1999). Yet *We Charge Genocide* is far more complex than a compilation of systematic, institutionalized, and everyday atrocities committed by white people against Black people in all parts of the United States (not just the South) between 1945 and 1951.

·　·　·

In Patterson's volume, genocide, besides referring to the killing of Black individuals, implied domestic and international fascism, often leading to genocidal war against racialized nations: "White supremacy at home makes for colored massacres abroad."[12] It related to the economic and political oppression of Black communities, justified and furthered by public statements and policies, "not plotted in the dark but incited over the radio into the ears of millions, urged in the glare of public forums by Senators and Governors" (5). And it was carried out by a widely shared yet seldom expressed racial knowledge, "a part of the mores of the ruling class often concealed by euphemisms, but always directed to oppressing the Negro people" (6), translating into low wages, continued residential segregation, and political disenfranchisement.

Genocide of Blacks in the United States resulted in deep psychological and physical terror, perpetrated by the Ku Klux Klan and sanctioned by public figures such as Governors J. Strom Thurmond of South Carolina, Fielding M. Wright of Mississippi, and Frank M. Dixon of Alabama—all of whom incited violence against Blacks to prevent them from voting (16–19). The various facets of Black genocide squarely questioned the nature, scope, and alleged universality of democracy in the United States.

These multidimensional manifestations of genocide suggest that at the core of Black genocidal processes in the United States lies a set of dominant values and representations that dehumanize Blacks, restrict their access to rights and resources, exclude them from full citizenship, and justify their continued disrespect, suffering, and death. A crucial aspect of Black genocide is that it brings considerable advantages to the perpetrators: intimidation and death of Blacks were clearly linked to political power (preventing Blacks from voting), and economic power (preventing Blacks from competing with whites in job and housing markets).

What Patterson and his collaborators knew then about the ideological justifications and the multiple manifestations of genocide can be *theoretically* utilized today to make sense of countless representations, actions, and public policies whose result is the unmistakable dehumanization, exclusion, and death of Black people. Here I emphasize theory both to preserve the specificity of time and space of the United States in the 1950s, and to call attention to Patterson's analytical perspective, which becomes a powerful tool for uncovering the contemporary facets of Black genocide. *We Charge Genocide* is a unique document and political act in that it utilized international legal grammar to denounce the benefits that U.S. whites accrued from systematically discriminating against Blacks—a complex dynamic of overt genocidal violence and no-less-effective tacit race knowledge that George Lipsitz (2006) has described as the possessive investment in whiteness.[13]

THE GENOCIDAL CONTINUUM, OR BLACK SUFFERING WITHIN AND ACROSS NATIONAL BORDERS

What is to be gained from an analytical and political perspective stressing the genocide against Black people in the Diaspora? How can we transpose the theoretical importance and the vitality of the political will contained in *We Charge Genocide* to our times and to varied geographies of the Black Diaspora, while being aware of the historical and spatial/national specificity within which Patterson and his collaborators elaborated the document? By stressing the connections between imperial policies applied abroad (including military campaigns) and domestic Black genocidal processes, *We Charge Genocide* suggested a notion of the Black Diaspora that necessarily decentered the United States by contextualizing it in transnational, mutually affected and affecting, and thus integrated fields of political forces. Put another way, the focus on Black genocide within national borders required the recognition of a supranational Black Diaspora marked by analogous experiences of forced marginalization (among Blacks and nonwhite communities).

There cannot be an effective political strategy to combat anti-Black racisms without a deep and broad—indeed global—perspective on the multiple facets of genocidal discrimination, nor can there be a sound and ethical research agenda without on-the-ground engagement with real problems as they are experienced by real people and real community organizations.[14] This is to say, rather than adopting the sadly commonsensical, self-proclaimed, detached social-scientific gaze, I argue for an analytical approach that gains insight and depth precisely because it is informed by grassroots efforts, past and present, to analyze and intervene in racist genocidal processes.

Manning Marable's insights can be taken as examples of the contemporary applicability of the concept of genocide to make sense of the Black Diaspora—as it concerns the United States more obviously but, as I will show, as equally germane to other nation-states. Writing on the U.S. economic and social policies of the 1980s, Marable (2000 [1983]: 252, 253) states:

> What is qualitatively *new* about the current period is that the racist/capitalist state under Reagan has proceeded down a public policy road which would inevitably involve the complete obliteration of the entire Black reserve army of labor and sections of the Black working class. The decision to save capitalism at all costs, to provide adequate capital for the restructuring of the private sector, fundamentally conflicts with the survival of millions of people who are now permanently outside the workplace. Reaganomics must, if it intends to succeed, place the onerous burden of unemployment on the shoulders of the poor (Blacks, Latinos and even whites) so securely that middle to upper income Americans will not protest the vicious suppression of this stratum. Unlike classical fascism, Reaganism must pursue its policies without publicly attacking Blacks or Puerto Ricans by obvious racial slurs. . . . But the final results of these socioeconomic policies, carried to their logical conclusions, would be the total

destruction of all-Black institutions, the political separation of the Black elite and intelligentsia from the working class, and the benign but deadly elimination of the "parasitic" ghetto class that has ceased to be a necessary or productive element within modern capitalism. . . . The genocidal logic of the situation could demand, in the not too distant future, the rejection of the ghetto's right to survival in the new capitalist order. Without gas chambers or pogroms, the dark ghetto's economic and social institutions might be destroyed, and *many of its residents would simply cease to exist.*

Marable's formulation can be read as pointing to the contemporary symbiosis between the self-proclaimed color-blind polices that characterized and have been recycled since the Reagan era, and the unmistakable racialized character of those policies' social effects. A necessary aspect of this logic is its anti-Black (and indeed anti-nonstraight U.S. white male) animus. It is this animus that allows us to talk about a genocidal continuum. The continuum includes the punitive policies that have transcended the times of Reagan, the negative effects—isolated and compounded—that they produce, and the cultural understandings about those most negatively affected by them. The continuum explains why the obliteration of Black communities is acceptable.

The genocidal continuum was recently elaborated by anthropologist Nancy Sheper-Hughes (2002: 373): "it is socially incremental and often experienced by perpetrators, collaborators, bystanders—and even by the victims themselves—as expected, routine, even justified." This is analogous to what William Patterson and his collaborators conceptualized as they described the everyday forms of psychological, physical, political, and economic oppression Blacks experienced for being Black in a white supremacist polity. While lynchings, segregation, and police brutality were structural occurrences, they necessitated a shared cognitive matrix in which Black lives were systematically and unproblematically devalued. The notion of the genocidal continuum allows us to link these variedly scaled genocidal phenomena into a permanent, totalizing, and ubiquitous event—much in the same way that Omi and Winant (1994) interpret the significance of race in the United States—and to trace the resulting mass killing of Black people to quotidian acts and representations of discrimination, dehumanization, and ultimate exclusion. Reaganomics and its contemporary manifestations, in the United States and elsewhere, was possible and successful because it drew from such quotidian acts and shared representations.

Everyday acts of hostility can be equated to symbolic violence, which is central to the microphysics of capitalist heteronormative white supremacist hegemonic practices, and which also energizes institutions such as schools, hospitals, workplaces, news media, and of course the criminal justice system (see, for example, Bourdieu 1977). Symbolic violence offers the conceptual and factual link between what happens in a myriad of seemingly disparate events and the systemic actual physical violence often leading to massive incarceration, dehumanization, and premature death. While genocide cannot be subsumed into symbolic violence, symbolic violence can be seen as integral to the process of genocide. The concept of symbolic violence indeed provides a tool with which we can see the connections between the representational and the factual, the local event and the general trends, everyday violence and genocide, history and present reality.

Symbolic violence and the multifaceted aspect of anti-Black discrimination suggest an angle that sees genocide as culturally rooted and having a conceptual kinship to racism. Joy James (1996: 46) remarked on the ways in which "[t]he moral import of racism is virtually meaningless after it has been severed from genocide." This insight requires that we reconnect that which the dominant discourses have severed: the everyday acts of hostility toward non-whites, women, the nonheteronormative, the nonpropertied; the structural marginalization and persisting dehumanization of such groups; the concrete manifestations of these political and ideological processes—the suffering and premature, preventable deaths of excluded social groups, among which are a disproportionate number of Blacks. If we reconnect these processes, the cognitive map provides meaning to apparently disparate phenomena, in time, space, quality, and number.

It is by now apparent that the genocidal continuum is also about temporal and spatial connectedness. The various nation-state geographies of Black suffering and death that characterize the Diaspora suggest locally inflected social phenomena that are necessarily linked by common experiences of anti-Black discrimination. As well, the Black Diaspora as genocide recycles, often amplifies, the logic of Black death upon which the social institutions and mores of slavery depended. That these days the logic of slavery presents itself as just its opposite—at times as multicultural or multiracial heaven, at times as a racial-democracy paradise—is evidence of its historical continuity and contemporary vitality (for example, James 2005, introduction). If the political and cognitive material that connects such seemingly disparate temporal and spatial coordinates has unmistakable anti-Black coding, generating the negative aspects of the Diaspora, then it must also create the very political and cognitive basis of insurgency and transformation. The imperatives of such insurgency and transformation should be as difficult to grasp as the need to guarantee the conditions necessary for one's full and uncontested humanity.

As Black activists and artists in Los Angeles and Rio de Janeiro detect and reassemble the various pieces of the genocidal processes that mark their lives, that destabilize their objectification, and that analyze and interrogate their naturalized subordination, they also forge powerful critiques of our ingrained vertical modes of classifying the social world. In the process, a notion of the Black Diaspora emerges that points to both the conditions making genocide possible and, more important, the imperatives of suppressing genocide.

In the following sections, I explore some of the quantified and ideological contemporary manifestations of Black genocide in the United States and in Brazil. This will show that anti-Black discrimination occurs not only through systematic official policies but also through less perceptible but nevertheless equally effective shared representations of nonwhites—especially Blacks—which dehumanize them and justify their continued imposed massive marginalization and early death. It is in relation to the genocidal effects of institutionalized, everyday, and cultural anti-Black racism that transnational practices become vital for the survival of Afro-diasporic communities and as projects of social organization that suggest alternatives to a dehumanizing, hierarchical, and ultimately unjust lifeworld. It bears repeating that such genocidal effects are themselves multifaceted and affect the existence of Black peoples in a variety of ways: the genocidal killing is of the body, mind, and spirit. The urgency energizing Afro-logical worldviews is a testament to how vital it is that these killings be addressed and prevented. Genocide creates theoretical and practical imperatives for radical transformation.

MULTIPLE FACETS OF THE CONTEMPORARY
BLACK GENOCIDE CONTINUUM IN THE UNITED STATES

Dimensions of Black genocide in the contemporary United States include mass imprisonment, police brutality, high infant mortality, early death (of children, men, women, and the elderly), deficient medical treatment, lack of competitive education and economic opportunities, everyday violence in the inner cities, and chronic depression.

As Mike Davis (1992) wrote in his now classic *City of Quartz*, the future can be excavated in the City of Angels. Consider, for example, that in 2001 the murder rate in Los Angeles augmented by 10 percent. Police Chief William Bratton urged, predictably, for a new antigang campaign. State interventions such as this leave untouched the conditions that lead to high murder rates, some of which should be obvious: substandard education, physically deteriorated neighborhoods, and the negative impact of mass incarceration on the lives of young men and women. Young Black men are four times more likely to be murdered than young Latinos, and *eighteen* times more likely than young Anglos. Blacks are 40 percent of murder victims, even though they are about 11 percent of the total population (Levoy 2003). Break such numbers down by gender and age, and the disproportions will be even more glaring: young Black men are the overwhelming objects of violence and the preferred victims of death by violence.

The available data on the criminal justice system and the prison-industrial complex are unequivocal. Whereas one in three young African American males are under the supervision of the criminal justice system today, by 2020, if the trends recorded between 1980 and 1993 continue, two in three young Blacks will be either incarcerated, on probation, or on parole (Donziger 1996). At this point, there is almost no doubt that if you are a Black man you will be arrested at least once in your lifetime. In Washington, D.C., conservative data reveal that the probability is greater than 75 percent (Braman 2002: 117).

Almost 70 percent of the two million people currently incarcerated in the United States are Black or Brown, the great majority being nonviolent offenders. Men aren't the only targets; African American women are the fastest-growing prison population (Davis 2003). While in the 1990s the male prison population increased 77 percent, the number of women in prison more than doubled—an increase of 110 percent (Chesney-Lind 2002: 81). What these numbers suggest is that the continuing war on drugs is significantly a war on women, especially Black women (Kurshan 1996). Dismantle welfare and lock them up, but not before attempting to sterilize as many African American women as possible (Roberts 1997). This is the order of the day, whose consequence is to transform "welfare mothers" into the newest unpaid labor army, producing office furniture, license plates, and clothing, or making airline and hotel reservations via telephone from prison. The logic behind the concept and expansion of the prison-industrial complex dates back at the very least to Nixon's rise to power (Gilmore 1998–99). As Angela Davis (for example,

2003) frequently remarks, the prison of the plantation, characteristic of slavery and the convict lease system instituted shortly thereafter, has become the contemporary plantation of the prison, in which inmates make a fraction of a dollar per hour of work.

If this weren't enough, another little-talked-about process has been furthering the genocide of Blacks in the United States as well as in the Americas overall and in Africa. In 1990, adult Blacks were disproportionately represented in the numbers of persons with HIV/AIDS in the United States, composing roughly one third of all cases. Data from the Centers for Disease Control and Prevention from 1988 suggest that Blacks account for 57 percent of all new HIV infections; Black children under thirteen represent 58 percent (Cohen 1999: 20–23). Whereas official 1998 data revealed that among women Blacks represent 56 percent of all new cases, 2003 data show that Black women were 67 percent of those diagnosed with HIV during that year.[15] AIDS is increasingly a disease disproportionately affecting communities of color, especially Latinas/os and Blacks.

Creating or tolerating such conditions is genocidal. We do not have to dwell upon the intent of policies, everyday practices, or symbolic forms of violence—or the intent behind the absence of redressive policies and practices—to comprehend that what really matters are the *results* of such (in)actions, results that are unquestionably racialized and gendered and that produce massive harm and death. In this regard, the debate about intentionality surrounding the definition and prevention of genocide becomes irrelevant, as a number of authors have proposed: there is enough evidence of suffering and killings of substantial numbers of people to define the event as genocide regardless of whether these facts conform to core intentions (Charny 1994).[16] Wallimann and Dobkowski (1987), furthermore, remind us of how in highly bureaucratized and anonymous social organizations it becomes almost impossible to locate intentionality structuring institutions and policies.

Rather than looking for intentions, therefore, we should recognize that in a context defined by racial hierarchies—by white supremacy—apparently neutral policies necessarily become molded by the hegemonic social order. The concepts of symbolic violence and genocidal continuum allow for the understanding of genocide as part of a constellation of phenomena ranging from everyday forms of individualized discrimination to structural marginalization (residential segregation, unemployment, barred access to credit), historically persistent killing of those deemed less than human, and globally connected state policies and cultural knowledge (Winant 2004). If we were to divert our attention to the search for intentions, or if we did not adopt a systemic and incremental perspective on genocide, such phenomena would appear disparate in space, time, and nature, and there would be no genocide to account for.

The Federal Bureau of Investigation's Counter-Intelligence Programs, which explicitly targeted Black and Indian organizers for elimination (Churchill and Vander Wall 1990), and the government's complicity in the "crack epidemic" (Webb 1999) among other well-documented facts, are only some of the most visible faces of a system that works by devaluing the lives of nonwhites and perceiving their autonomous and legitimate organizations as threats. There is no room for detachment in these matters. The inescapable fact is that Blacks are dying, suffering, being incarcerated, and being monitored in unprecedented numbers. Most of these processes take place in segregated communities, invisible and sealed off to the great majority of whites.

A comparison of premature deaths of whites and African Americans gives us a well-defined image of the dimension of Black genocide. In the last thirty years, extra premature deaths among Blacks—due to disease, homicide, accident, suicide, pregnancy, and birth—are estimated to number 2,368,530. Consider that had whites experienced the same death rate as Blacks for the same causes, in the same period there would have been 19,427,250 extra premature deaths of whites (Johnson and Leighton 1995).

Why the silence about the conditions Black people experience? Would such silence exist if whites endured what Blacks experience? Would there be such indifference if young whites were being killed at the rate young Blacks are? Would there be so many crime bills—and so much support for them— and so many new prisons if whites were the main objects of such policies and corporate ventures? Why are we so unwilling to put the facts together and recognize that premature deaths, combined with massive incarceration and its collateral consequences—broken families, chronic unemployment, neighborhood deterioration, and generalized lack of perspective—especially for more disadvantaged Blacks, is leading to the physical and spiritual destruction of this racialized group? Would there be such inertia if whites were the ones undergoing such processes?

BLACK GENOCIDE IN BRAZIL: A SYNOPSIS

Abdias do Nascimento (1989) utilized the concept of genocide in his *Brazil: Mixture or Massacre: Essays in the Genocide of a Black People.* In this book, as in his plays, paintings, and public pronouncements, Nascimento denounced, on the one hand, the farce of Brazilian racial democracy and, on the other, the material and psychological effects of anti-Black racism as it translates into unemployment, low-quality education and earnings, low self-esteem, and premature death—all determined by race as becomes evident when compared to how whites fare.

Indeed, Brazil is one of the most unequal countries in the world, and its inequality is profoundly marked by race. Median annual income for the richest 20 percent is US$21,134, roughly equivalent to that of France and twenty-six times greater than the median income of the poorest 20 percent, which is $828, roughly the same as that of the Congo. That is, the richest 20 percent have 64 percent of the total national income, while the poorest 20 percent have only 3 percent (INSPIR/DIEESE/AFL-CIO 1999). The parallels with a mostly white country and with a mostly Black nation are not accidental: they illustrate how deep economic inequalities are racialized.

At this time, when Lula's presidency is completing its second term, a paradox is evident. While the myth of racial democracy is as challenged as ever, the ideological and material facets of Black genocide are intensifying to unparalleled dimensions. Never has Brazil had so many Black nongovernmental organizations focusing on health, violence, media, culture, and electoral politics. Never has Brazil had such a number and quality of Black music and dance groups engaging with, openly criticizing, and proposing alternatives to endemic Brazilian racism—Olodum and Ilê-Aiyê in Salvador, Cidade Negra and Afroreggae in Rio being examples of a vital movement that does not shy away from the national public sphere while being immersed in local grassroots antiracist efforts. Never has Brazil had such vigorous debate on affirmative action, reparations, and historical forms of racialized discrimination. Never has Brazil had so many self-defined Afro-Brazilian elected representatives at local, state, and national levels. Never has Brazil had so many weekly magazines run by and targeted to Blacks. And, it sadly seems, never has Brazil had such levels of police brutality, death, and other forms of violence perpetrated against Blacks, especially in large cities such as São Paulo, Rio de Janeiro, Belo Horizonte, Salvador, and Recife. Blacks are still, and increasingly, the main and disproportionate victims of preventable diseases, malnutrition, jobless-ness, HIV infection, and clinical depression.

Consistent with the theoretical framework Patterson and his collaborators elaborated in *We Charge Genocide*, Black genocide in Brazil is multifaceted and is part of a continuum. The various dimensions of Black genocide can be schematized into two dimensions—material and ideological—both of which are perpetrated and (at least tacitly) supported by the wider society.

The ideological dimension of Black genocide in Brazil is at first difficult to distinguish. As I have argued elsewhere, Brazilian social relations—their practices and their representations—are marked by a hyperconsciousness of race. However, such hyperconsciousness, while symptomatic of how Brazil-ians classify and position themselves in the lifeworld, is manifested by the often vehement negation of the importance of race. This negation forcefully suggests that race is not an analytical and morally valid tool, nor does it play a central role in determining Brazilian social relations, hierarchies, and distri-bution of power and resources. Try talking to Brazilians of varied racial back-grounds, places of residence, occupation, age, gender, sexuality, and levels of formal instruction about the matter, and most often you will find yourself accused of racism (for insisting on a theme that has no relevance in that coun-try) or the conversation will swiftly be redirected away from race (D'Adesky 2001; Degler 1986 [1971]; Gilliam 1992; Twine 1998).

The focus on the dynamic of hyperconsciousness and negation of race opens a window into hegemonic racial common sense.[17] The ideological di-mensions of Black genocide in Brazil include whitening ideals, according to which Afro-Brazilians are encouraged to identify as white, to dissociate themselves from Blacks, and to seek lighter-skinned friends, partners, and self-images. It is common in nonwhite families to hear from elders that "we need to purify our blood," a purification that is well understood as getting rid of as many Black traits in one's appearance and behavior as possible. The resistance against identifying as Black, which is often accompanied by anti-Black sentiments and statements, takes place even among nonwhite persons who are otherwise progressive.

The relevance of race, however, is not restricted to the realm of mythology and everyday talk of color. Analyses of political economy confirm and give a concrete, appalling dimension to the white/nonwhite binary informing Brazil-ian social structure: greater differences in life chances and outcomes (employ-ment, education, infant mortality, susceptibility to police abuse, for example) exist between nonwhites and whites than among nonwhites (Kahn 2002; Human Rights Watch/Americas 1997; Mitchell and Wood 1998; Telles 1999).

The 1996 Pesquisa Nacional por Amostra de Domicílios (National Household Sample Survey) observed that whereas in the richest Southeast region—comprising the states of São Paulo, Rio de Janeiro, Minas Gerais, and Espírito Santo—infant mortality for whites stood at 25.1 per thousand infants born alive, for Blacks the rate was 43.1 percent. In the country as a whole, whereas barely 50 percent of Black households are connected to a sewage system, the rate is 73.6 percent for white households. When we apply the United Nations' Index of Human Development, utilized as a measure of life quality on a scale of 0 to 1, we see that whereas it stands at 0.796 for the Brazilian population as a whole, it is 0.573 for Afro-Brazilians. Black infant mortality in the Southeast reflects such inequalities (IGBE 1996).

Salary disparities confirm the white-Black gap. In São Paulo's metropolitan region, Blacks make an average of R$2.94 per day; whites make R$5.50 (INSPIR/DIEESE/AFL-CIO 1999: 39). All socioeconomic data reveal that "non-whites are subject to a 'process of cumulative disadvantages' in their social trajectories," which blocks their social mobility (Hasenbalg and Silva 1999: 218). Whites, on the other hand, are markedly more successful in attaining upward social mobility. This process, by which Blacks and whites have distinct life-trajectory paths, is similar to what happens in the United States, as evidenced by Oliver and Shapiro (1995).

Police brutality, as it disproportionately affects Blacks in Brazil, is another sad parallel that can be made with the United States. The reality for Afro-Brazilians, however, is far worse than it is for African Americans. In Rio de Janeiro, for example, the police killed nine hundred people between January and August 2003, almost 75 percent of which occurred in the favelas, predominantly Black communities (Jeter 2003). Paul Amar (2003: 37–42) reminds us that "this trend, if continued, would have pushed the tally of police executions above 1,500 in 2003 in Rio state alone, approaching parity with Baghdad, beyond the realm of media metaphors, as the Iraqi capital suffered around 1,700 civilian fatalities during this year's war [of occupation]." In a month, Rio police kill more than 2.5 times people than the New York Police Department kills in a whole year (Human Rights Watch/Americas 1997). The ubiquitous cases of police misconduct (for example, Cano 1997; Paixão 1995) are part of an emblematic, persistent pattern of the widespread anti-Black racism that pervades Brazilian society (Mitchell and Wood 1998).

GENOCIDE OR LIBERATION:
THE IMPERATIVE OF REVOLT IN THE BLACK DIASPORA

White supremacy and anti-Black racism are genocidal. Complementing their most obvious, final manifestations, white supremacy and anti-Black racism also work through silence, inaction, and ignorance. White supremacy and anti-Black racism happen because of what we and others do as well as what we and others don't do. Consequently, silence, inaction, and ignorance are as genocidal as the most overt racist acts and thoughts.

What is to be done? A crucial step in the organized struggle against anti-Black racism in Brazil is to denounce the historical and ongoing genocide against people of African descent. This is not only the genocide that is taking place through hegemonic whitening ideals, whereby Black people are encouraged to look like and seek lighter-skinned partners (Nascimento 1989; Wade 1993) but also the more direct genocide that causes the physical, spiritual, and civil death of members of the Black Diaspora in the Americas through multiple forms of marginalization.

In times of a recrudescing public sentiment and political campaigns against affirmative action in both the United States and Brazil, in times of increased institutionalization of "mixed-race" classifications (whose results are the obvious dilution of the already fragile political clout of the Black population), there is a need for committed research and political agendas. Such commitment is well incarnated in the ongoing political alliances between Blacks in the United States, members of local grassroots organizations in Los Angeles, and Afro-Brazilian activists in Rio de Janeiro. The fight against police brutality, drug commerce violence, and a gamut of health problems affecting Blacks of the Diaspora, especially women, constitute the agenda around which courageous and vibrant transnational efforts are opposing and building alternatives to the genocidal continuum.

The developments of the alliance established in 1993 serve as templates for struggles and as reminders that such transnational initiatives can have effective and long-lasting impact. Let me briefly comment on a few of the outcomes of such alliances.

The founding of the Zinzun Center in the Jacarezinho neighborhood in 2001, as short-lived and embattled as it was, put into practice a series of strategies that go beyond that particular experience. First, and perhaps most important, the Zinzun Center was a clear indication of the fact that Jacarezinho's militants were not alone in their fight against police brutality and for greater social justice. Second, the Zinzun Center was to adopt many of CAPA's tactics to document cases of police abuse, providing juridical assistance to the victims of police misconduct and, as importantly, transforming such cases into catalysts for popular mobilization. As was the case in Los Angeles since at least 1975, when CAPA was founded, the various cases of police misconduct in Jacarezinho were to serve as starting points for organizing people against unjust law enforcement and against the various social and economic problems afflicting the favela.[18] The third strategy informing the inauguration of the Zinzun Center was to call media attention to the new neighborhood administration in Jacarezinho. The tactic is contradictory because even though public exposure may raise the stakes for those contemplating the assassination of activists, it also can generate further resentment and resolve from those who are threatened by the activists' agenda. Still, the dialogues with U.S. organizers who have embraced the mass communications networks as a necessary arena of struggle, as well as previous experiences in Rio, have convinced Jacarezinho's activists to seek out the media. Thus, when activists announced the inauguration of the Zinzun Center, the event was reported in most of the major local newspapers and television channels, and even made it into São Paulo's main daily, *Folha de S.Paulo*.[19]

All of this indicates how international alliances constitute a fundamental aspect of the favela struggle in providing an expanded ideological and practical horizon of possibilities. The favela movement's adversaries are powerful and deadly. The symbolic and practical effects that alliances with former Black Panthers and Los Angeles gang members working to maintain the truce have on the local police, politicians, and drug dealers should not be underestimated. Because of their well-known history of confrontational politics against law enforcement in particular and oppressive institutions in general, CAPA and CSGT militants provide Brazilians with a tactical edge insofar as they embody a tradition that has proven to be effective in fighting institutionalized forms of power.

As importantly, the alliances with progressive Black U.S. activists work to diffuse the common accusations of involvement with drug commerce that are waged against favela representatives. These accusations have become a pattern since the end of the dictatorship. Whereas during the military repression, politicized communities and their leaders were tagged as communists (and thus, from the state apparatus' perspective, justifiably harassed, imprisoned, and killed), beginning in the 1980s representatives of the favelas who did not automatically subscribe to official party guidelines and discourses were frequently dismissed as spokespersons for drug dealers. The irony is that even leftist parties such as the Partido dos Trabalhadores (Worker's Party) were, through some of their members in Rio, quick to condemn the efforts by Jacarezinho's neighborhood association to curb police brutality, in these same terms. Because the women and men working in the favela have dialogued with Los Angeles gang members who established the gang truce in 1992, they are able to deflect accusations of drug trade involvement by stressing their commitment to constructing peace between the different drug commerce factions.

The Zinzun Center was short-lived. A combination of events—the harassment of activists by local civil and military police, negative press coverage, and competing interests in the community[20]—contributed to the end of the experiment. Yet the center can be seen as the materialization of a radical vision, of a revolutionary utopia. Although the practical goals of the initiative are not to be ignored, if we are to continue the struggle in ways that search for the yet-to-be-known, in ways that accept *failure* as pregnant with lessons and inspiration, then we must balance our undisputable need for pragmatic, concrete objectives and results with a commitment to the experimental, to the need to continue with efforts against Black genocide that recognize our vulnerability and yet make that condition the creative ground from which liberation and transformation can germinate.

The battles, however, are not only against hegemonic, white-dominated institutions exercising their historical dominance. Just as urgent, conflicts between distinct Black social groups also define the nature and effectiveness with which genocide happens or is opposed. In other words, the strategies of individual survival and the political programs defended by progressive Black community organizations are as much a reflection of the internal divisions among Blacks in the Diaspora as they are against institutionalized and everyday forms of racism originating in the wider polity. This is to say that we are also responsible for our genocide, be it because we passively watch as it unfolds, because we agree with the rationalizations for the wretchedness and death of our people, or because, after all, we have been so thoroughly colonized that we are as hierarchy dependent, nationalistic, oppressive, and therefore as indifferent as our worst oppressors. The responsible and liberation-oriented persons and organizations whose lives we need to learn about are challenging all facets of the genocide—they have no choice but to resist and imagine and work for a better world.

To imagine this better world, we need first to destroy our present institutional and cultural architectures. If Black genocide is at the core of our society's self-understanding, if it is at the core of our purported ethical standards, and indeed is the foundation of modern polities in the Americas, especially those with a past in slavery economies dependent on the ultimate exploitation and dehumanization of African laborers, then it is the very power relations and cognitive apparatuses that sustain our polities that need deconstruction. As Black genocide is at the core of our society's foundations, Black genocide is at the core of our cognition—we make sense of and seek the good society, often unknowingly, according to the often silent expectations that Blacks are not fully human and therefore not worthy of full inclusion in it. We will overcome these expectations only when and if our society, our collectivities, and our subjectivities are radically transformed, stripped of the premises that require and perpetuate Black genocide yet desensitize us to its manifestations. Such radical transformation is revolution.

As ubiquitous and persistent as Black genocide is, it is only a manifestation of our learned dependence on social classifications that are immanently hierarchical and thus excluding. In the same way that we are hierarchical beings, we are complicit in Black genocide; in the same way that Black genocide requires exclusion and desensitization to the origins and consequences of such exclusion, so too do hegemonic notions of belonging that depend on nation, social class, gender, sexuality, age, and place of residence, to name just a few. Recognizing and combating Black genocide means recognizing and combating the various forms of foundational oppression on which our societies are based; recognizing and combating Black genocide locates the impossibility of the Black existence as the condition of possibility of our present subjectivities and polities. If, to quote Audre Lorde, Blacks were never meant to survive,[21] then we must destroy the conditions under which this statement continues to be true, and invent alternative realities so that Blacks will survive.

Supranational alliances in the Black Diaspora provide counternarratives—critical knowledge, pragmatic political strategies, extended geographies of recognition, and utopian musings—that are as crucial to liberation movements as they are to the survival of communities under permanent siege. They generate, at the very least, a sense of diasporic security, a groundedness and confidence that cannot be achieved otherwise. Putting the idea of the Black Diaspora to work, these alliances address genocide and attempt to overcome it; they also embody, in the very theory and practice of insurgency, a perspective on our humanity that is not dependent on hierarchies nor on exclusions. Whether this U.S.-decentered perspective on the Black Diaspora can be shared and become foundational is not just a matter of political struggle: it lies at the very core of the social beings we must become and lifeworld we must construct that oppose the current geographies of death.

REFERENCE MATTER

NOTES

Introduction

This chapter is an abbreviated and revised version of my article "White Supremacist Constitution of the U.S. Empire-State: A Short Conceptual Look at the Long First Century," *Political Power and Social Theory* 20 (2009), copyright Emerald Group Publishing Limited. I thank Tyrone Forman, Tom Guglielmo, J. Kēhaulani Kauanui, Amanda Lewis, George Lipsitz, Anna Marshall, Erin Murphy, Dave Roediger, Robert Warrior, Robert A. Williams, and Caroline Yang, who were prematurely subjected to the longer piece, more or less voluntarily, and gave valuable comments.

1. My aim is not to privilege constitutional law at the expense of other institutions of the state or nonstate actors. It is rather to furnish a measure of coherence and concision to the discussion.

2. Legal scholars, historians, cultural critics, and others substantially outpace sociologists in recognizing the full spatial and temporal scope of the U.S. colonial empire.

3. The quotes are attributed to General Philip Sheridan, in 1869, and Captain Richard Pratt, in 1892. The former, however, is the popular rendering of what Sheridan might actually have said: "The only good Indians I ever saw were dead" (Hutton 1999: 180).

4. Other exceptions include American Samoa, Northern Mariana Islands, Panama Canal Zone, and Virgin Islands.

5. For an example related to the law, see Perea (2001).

6. Similar dynamics prevailed for the territories of New Mexico and Oklahoma (Levinson and Sparrow 2005).

7. White supremacy was not, however, a sufficient condition for a short and smooth path to statehood. Utah, with its Mormon population, had a particularly long and rough ride.

8. Section 2 of Article I excludes "Indians not taxed" from enumeration for apportioning seats in the House of Representatives and "direct Taxes," which was later

reproduced in the Fourteenth Amendment. In the same article, section 8 empowers Congress to "regulate Commerce with foreign Nations, and among the several States, and with the Indian Tribes."

9. *Johnson v. M'Intosh*, 21 U.S. (8 Wheat.) 543 (1823) at 573–74.

10. Ibid. at 587. For recent discussions of the discovery doctrine, see Miller (2008), Newcomb (2008), and Robertson (2005).

11. *Cherokee Nation v. Georgia*, 30 U.S. (5 Pet.) 1 (1831) at 16–17; emphasis added.

12. *Worcester v. Georgia*, 31 U.S. (6 Pet.) 551 (1832) at 559.

13. Ibid. at 561.

14. 118 U.S. 375 (1886).

15. Perhaps the most devastating was the General Allotment Act of 1887, which privatized reservation lands and distributed parcels to individual Indians. After such allotment, the remaining lands, often the choicest, were sold by the government to whites, the proceeds from which went toward programs for assimilating Indians. In this way, nearly two-thirds of Indian-held lands were taken between 1887 and 1934 (Frantz 1999; O'Brien 1989).

16. 187 U.S. 553 (1903) at 565–67.

17. The oft quoted passage from *Dred Scott v. Sandford* that Quey paraphrased is, "They [Blacks] had for more than a century before been regarded as beings of an inferior order, and altogether unfit to associate with the white race either in social or political relations, and so far inferior that they had no rights which the white man was bound to respect, and that the negro might justly and lawfully be reduced to slavery for his benefit" (60 U.S. [19 How.] 393 [1857] at 407).

18. Of those mentioned, the colonial status of Mexicans would be the most questionable, as a vast majority of Mexican-origin people in the United States today are migrants or descendants of migrants, not descendants of those who had once lived under Mexican sovereignty in what is now the U.S. Southwest.

19. With regard to Native Americans, Vine Deloria Jr. and David Wilkins (1999: 55) write, "Incisive and tedious review of Supreme Court decisions would show that this tendency to write law without reference to any doctrines or precedents is more the rule than the exception."

20. *Dred Scott v. Sandford*, 60 U.S. (19 How.) 393 (1857) at 418, 420.

21. Ibid. at 403–4.

22. 45 U.S. (4 How.) 567 (1846) at 571–72. For an in-depth discussion, see Wilkins (1997: 38–51).

23. *Dred Scott v. Sandford*, 60 U.S. (19 How.) 393 (1857) at 419.

24. Ibid. at 578. As Rogers Smith (1997) suggests, Curtis's concession was rash and ultimately undermined his own argument.

25. *Dred Scott v. Sandford*, 60 U.S. (19 How.) 393 (1857) at 586. Curtis cited three

treaties: "Treaties with the Choctaws, of September 27, 1830, art. 14; with the Cherokees, of May 23, 1836, art. 12; Treaty of Guadalupe Hidalgo, February 2, 1848, art. 8."

26. Ibid. at 533.

27. Ibid. at 419.

28. Ibid. at 418–19; emphasis added. There is no acknowledgment here that he had noted earlier in the opinion that "the white race claimed the ultimate right of *dominion*" (ibid. at 403–4; emphasis added).

29. Ibid. at 417; emphasis added.

30. Ibid. at 413–14, 416.

31. Although two earlier rulings, including *Marbury v. Madison* (5 U.S. [1 Cranch] 137 [1803]), established the doctrine of judicial review, "*Dred Scott* was the only case in the eighty years of pre-Civil-War constitutional history in which the Supreme Court limited congressional power in any significant way" (Newman and Gass 2004: 8).

32. *Dred Scott v. Sandford*, 60 U.S. (19 How.) 393 (1857) at 432. With the last phrase "from a foreign Government," Taney rhetorically skirted around the thorny fact that two states, North Carolina and Georgia, had not yet ceded their trans-Appalachian lands when the Constitution was adopted. But since the cessions had been anticipated at the time, he could not plausibly argue that the framers had not intended the Territorial Clause to be operative there.

33. Ibid. at 446, 449.

34. Ibid. at 451.

35. *Downes v. Bidwell*, 182 U.S. 244 at 384–85.

36. Ibid. at 360.

37. Ibid. at 274.

38. Ibid. at 291–93.

39. *Downes v. Bidwell*, 182 U.S. 244 at 341–42.

40. As Burnett and Marshall (2001a: 11) note, the Constitution has never applied in full in any territory.

41. *Dorr v. United States*, 195 U.S. 138 (1904) at 142.

42. *Downes v. Bidwell*, 182 U.S. 244 at 279.

43. Ibid. at 287.

44. Ibid. at 280–81, 283.

45. Ibid. at 306.

46. Ibid. at 279.

47. Ibid. at 286.

48. Also known as the *Chinese Exclusion Case*, 130 U.S. 581 (1889).

49. 187 U.S. 553 (1903) at 566.

50. 169 U.S. 649 (1898) at 693. Exemplifying once again the interconnectedness of noncolonial and colonial racial rule, this case dealing with the Chinese also addressed

the U.S. citizenship status of American Indians through a discussion of *Elk v. Wilkins* (1884). Further, both of these cases cited *Dred Scott.*

51. For example, to this day, residents of Puerto Rico cannot elect representatives or senators to Congress or cast a vote for the presidency. They receive fewer and lower social welfare benefits. Puerto Rico's self-governance does not undermine but is enabled, and can be overridden, by congressional plenary power. Constitutional rights, including those enumerated in the Bill of Rights, do not apply in Puerto Rico of their own force but were extended there by Congress (Aleinikoff 2002). Legislatively granted by Congress, birthright citizenship itself of those born in Puerto Rico is "not equal, permanent, irrevocable citizenship protected by the Fourteenth Amendment" (H.R. Report No. 105–131, pt. 1, 1997, p. 19, as quoted in Román 1998: 3).

52. Stephen J. Field on *Plessy* was replaced by Joseph McKenna before the two later cases. Though on the court at the time, David J. Brewer did not participate in *Plessy*, nor did McKenna in *Wong Kim Ark.*

53. *Plessy v. Ferguson,* 163 U.S. 537 (1896) at 559–60.

54. Ibid. at 559.

55. Ibid. at 561. Though not discussed here, the well-known majority opinion in *Plessy* also referred to the Chinese (ibid. at 542, 550).

56. How Harlan determined that "by the statute in question, a Chinaman can ride in the same passenger coach with white citizens of the United States" is unclear. The majority opinion's two references to the Chinese did not concern their treatment under the Louisiana statute. Among the briefs filed in the case, I found only one buried reference to the Chinese, which hardly necessitated and did not likely trigger Harlan's disquisition ("Brief for Plaintiff in Error," as reprinted in Kurland and Casper 1975: 78).

57. *Plessy v. Ferguson,* 163 U.S. 537 (1896) at 553.

Chapter 1

1. However, there are dissenters: see, for example, Isaac (2004).

2. This is the mainstream, non-Hobbesian contract of Locke and Kant, the version that is central to liberalism. For Hobbes, there is no morality in the state of nature, so his starting point is not the moral equality of human beings.

3. The standard English translation is: the struggle to come to terms with the past.

4. Rodney C. Roberts (2002: 1) has argued that there is a longstanding pattern in Western philosophy of paying "relatively little attention to questions of injustice and its rectification," thereby favoring the perspective of the privileged, since "the concerns of victims of injustice . . . have little place in our deliberations about justice."

Chapter 2

The author is grateful to the editors of this collection for their patience, energy, and political-intellectual commitment to a collective project of which this book is a small but significant part.

1. In addition to smaller state and local archives distributed across the South, the National Archives has recently completed a project in which it compiled and micro-filmed Freedmen's Bureau headquarters records, assistant commissioner and education official reports, and field office records. This chapter relies primarily on the congressional records and testimonials.

Chapter 3

This chapter is a slightly revised and shortened version of a speech that Eduardo Bonilla-Silva gave at Wayne State University in 2007 on the larger subject of race and citizenship. We have left the document with some of the character and drama of a speech, hoping to inspire readers' passions (whichever direction they go). We have added footnotes and citations for this chapter.

1. Incidents like this happen to men of color all the time. And the reaction from whites is all too often to doubt the nature of the event ("Are you sure this was about race? Aren't you being too sensitive here?") or to "blame the victim" ("As a professional, you should have worked to deescalate this situation!"). Note the recent case of Harvard professor Henry Louis Gates, who was profiled in his own house—he was asked to provide *two* forms of identification to an officer to demonstrate that the house belonged to him—and after he exercised his rights as a citizen (asking for the officer's identification and telling him that he believed he was being profiled), he was arrested on his front porch for engaging in "tumultuous behavior."

2. Thomas Hobbes, through his patron, was involved in the affairs of the Virginia Company.

3. Montesquieu, in his famous *The Spirit of the Laws*, justified slavery, as Susan Buck-Morss argues, on pragmatic, climatic, and blatantly racist grounds, describing Blacks as having "flat noses," being "black from head to foot," and lacking in "common sense." Thus, not surprisingly, he concluded, "Weak minds exaggerate too much the injustice done to Africans" by colonial slavery (Buck-Morss 2003: 828).

4. John Locke was against slavery. Slavery for him, however, was a metaphor for legal tyranny, as he had shareholder standing in the Royal African Company, which was involved in the colonial policy of the Carolinas.

5. Liberty meant protection of private property; thus, enslaved Africans were not subjects of history but chattel.

6. Before we move on to our next task, we must give a caveat. These enlightened men were "men of their times" and, as such, not "monsters." But this should not be used

as an excuse against exposing their racism, sexism, and class elitism. When we realize "the dark side of the Enlightenment" (Sala-Molins 2006) and when we understand that these men did not shine their lights on us, we will be able to appreciate what happened in the ensuing four hundred years.

7. States included requirements for foreigners to attain the right of citizenship, such as an "oath of allegiance" and "assurances of fidelity," and a few states included a "belief in the Christian religion" (Kettner 1978).

8. Vermont was the first state to ban slavery when in 1777 they declared in their constitution that "All men are born equally free and independent" (Klinker and Smith 1999: 20). Of course, then and today, Vermont was a white state (97 percent white in 2005); their enlightened stand was thus practically meaningless.

9. A stereotypical child abduction is "perpetuated by a stranger or slight acquaintance and involving a child who was transported 50 or more miles, detained overnight, held for ransom or with the intent to keep the child permanently, or killed" (Finkelhor, Hammer, and Sedlak 2002).

10. These strategies include citizen councils in the South and neighborhood associations in the North (on Detroit, see Thomas Sugrue's 1996 *The Origins of the Urban Crisis: Race and Inequality in Post-War Detroit*), banks and realtors, housing covenants, and the federal government's role in creating "vanilla suburbs and chocolate cities" through the construction of a highway system for white suburbanites.

11. Analysts like Massey and Denton, in their 1993 book *American Apartheid*, argue that residential segregation is the linchpin of America's racial problem.

12. More systematic and larger studies carried out in 2001 and 2004 found that discrimination against Blacks and Latinos in eastern Massachusetts (Lowell) ranged from 52 percent to a high of 67 percent.

13. Despite the trickery, housing discrimination complaints to state, federal, and nonprofit agencies have been increasing. They climbed to 27,319 in 2004 from 25,148 in 2003, an 8.6 percent increase.

14. Latinos were also more likely to pay higher rates, but for Latinos the biggest issue is rental discrimination (exclusion and higher rates).

15. Why does the banking industry continue its discriminatory practices despite lawsuits and the loss of prestige from the negative public relations these cases create? Because they are all in bed with subprime lenders (loan shark industry) and make a killing by targeting desperate minority folks—some of them at high income levels. Also, white bankers, as all whites, generally see Blacks as lesser citizens. This explains why white bankers target Blacks for discrimination and give poor whites a break.

16. Of course, police officers state again that they do this, not on the basis of race but—as was the case in Charlottesville—on whether the person "fits the description and is acting suspiciously" (Williams 2004).

17. "Blair Shelton of Ann Arbor, Mich., gave a DNA sample in 1995 after police

investigating a series of rapes visited him at work and threatened to get a court order to compel him to give a sample. Shelton's compliance was technically voluntary, but he thought he 'had little choice in the matter.' The rapist was later caught fleeing from a crime scene by a cab driver—and not through the dragnet. Shelton sued in state court and had his DNA sample returned. He is the only dragnet participant who has sued and retrieved his DNA, says the ACLU's Steinhardt" (Willing 2003).

18. This racist logic is also present in the 1999 National Research Council study on school shootings, which concluded that the shootings in white schools are substantially different from those in minority schools, thus discounting the concerns of unequal treatment among minority folks.

19. In the 2000 election, "spoiled ballots" amounted to two million; about one million of them were cast by Black voters (in Florida, this amounted to ninety thousand votes).

20. Some states even created checkpoints for license registration on election day. Florida's own attorney general later said this was unnecessary and that it should never happen again.

21. In Cook County, Illinois, they asked for identification and told Blacks that if they were convicted felons they could not vote.

22. The exceptions are for group-based claims that are exercised in the private sphere, such as freedom of religion.

23. The most progressive scholars of citizenship write about "multicultural" and "international" citizenship, and we think this is a nice gesture. However, we caution that new iterations of the citizenship category will be limited unless they are part of a global process of restructuring. The struggles by people all over the world for their rights and humanity will be what will ultimately produce universality, and not the other way around.

Chapter 4

1. For example, in 1999 the American Civil Liberties Union filed a lawsuit on behalf of students in a Southern California school, noting the significant differential in the availability of advanced placement courses to students in predominantly minority schools in the state. See Dupuis 1999.

2. For a related discussion of the role of race in mental health diagnoses over time see Metzl 2010.

Chapter 6

1. The most reliable studies of the impact of sanctions have utilized panel designs to study TANF clients over time, and have found that anywhere from 5 percent (South Carolina) to 60 percent (Delaware) of the sample experienced some type of sanction, depending on the period (12–18 months) and state examined (Fein and Lee 1999; Pavetti et al. 2004). Given these estimates, it is not surprising that state-level studies of caseload

reduction conclude that states with the strictest sanctioning policies have experienced as much as a 25 percent greater caseload reduction than have states with the least stringent policies (Mead 2005; Rector and Youseff 1999). For an initial discussion, see Fording, Schram, and Soss (2006a).

2. The Workforce Investment Act of 1998 was passed by Congress one year after welfare reform was implemented and serves displaced and unemployed workers.

3. We define "new" TANF clients as those clients who have spent at least twelve continuous months without TANF benefits (see Fording, Schram, and Soss 2006b).

4. Our analysis uses the Cox proportional hazards model, which allows for flexible, nonparametric estimation of the baseline hazard, i.e., the effect of spell duration on the probability of sanction (Box-Steffensmeier and Jones 2004). The findings are replicated using other estimation methods, including parametric methods (Weibull) and a discrete-time (logit) model. Given the multilevel character of our data, the p-values reported in Table 6.2 are based on standard errors that are adjusted for error correlation within regions.

5. The eighteen constitutional amendments span a wide range of ideologically relevant issues, including abortion, the death penalty, taxation, legalized gambling, gun control, and the minimum wage. For more detail on how the regional political ideology index was calculated, see Fording, Soss, and Schram (2007a).

6. Specifically, we examined the interaction of client race or ethnicity with alternative measures of the duration of the TANF spell (linear and nonlinear time trends and dummy variable versions). All analyses found a statistically significant interaction between race or ethnicity of client and the month of the TANF spell. For the sake of parsimony, the results in Table 6.2 report an interaction between race or ethnicity of client and a linear version of the month of the TANF spell.

7. The effect of the local political climate on the probability of being sanctioned also holds if clients from the Miami-Dade region (the largest, most liberal, and most racially diverse region) are removed from the analysis.

8. The predicted hazard ratios presented in Figure 6.4 are based on an extension of the analyses reported in Table 6.2. Specifically, we introduced multiplicative terms for race/ethnicity of client and local conservatism (*Black × Regional conservatism index; Hispanic × Regional conservatism index*). Each of these interaction terms was found to be statistically significant, while the effects of the other independent variables listed in Table 6.2 remained virtually unchanged. The specific values of *Regional conservatism index* used in all of these illustrations reflect the minimum and maximum values across the estimation sample. For more detailed analyses, see Fording, Soss, and Schram (2007b).

9. Each of these values is statistically distinguishable from 0.

10. This time period reflects the maximum amount of time for which we are able to obtain data for regional performance rankings, regional sanction rates, and the characteristics of TANF clients.

11. Details on how the performance-ranking measure is calculated are provided in Fording, Schram, and Soss (2006c).

12. For more details concerning this analysis, see Fording, Schram, and Soss (2007).

Chapter 7

This chapter benefited from the support of the Community Engagement Center at the University of Texas, Austin; the Carter G. Woodson Institute for African and African American Studies at the University of Virginia; and the editorial insights of Eric Goldscheider, Maddy Dwertman, and Sam Seidel.

1. For a comparative analysis of the new Black politician in service to mainstream voting America, see the discussion of Barack Obama and Deval Patrick in Joy James's "Campaigns Against 'Blackness': Criminality, Incivility, and Election to Executive Office." In 2010, Isaac Borenstein, newly appointed to Ben LaGuer's legal defense, began filing a motion for a new trial as Governor Deval Patrick began his reelection campaign. Journalist Eric Goldscheider has a forthcoming book on the LaGuer case, tentatively titled *Faith in the System*.

2. This and the following section are based on newspaper articles listed at the end of this chapter.

3. See Goldscheider (2006) in the list of articles consulted for this chapter, located at the end of chapter.

4. Author's phone interview with Eric Goldscheider, April 1, 2008.

5. See Estes (2006) in the list of articles consulted for this chapter, located at the end of chapter.

6. Deval Patrick is one of three Black governors, all Democrats, all male, to serve since Reconstruction: Virginia governor Douglas Wilder was elected in 1990; Lieutenant Governor David Patterson became governor of New York in 2008 after Eliot Spitzer resigned in scandal.

7. http://www.gutenberg.org/etext/14975, accessed February 1, 2009.

8. http://www.withoutsanctuary.org/, accessed February 1, 2009.

9. http://www.npr.org/templates/story/story.php?storyId=99905334, accessed February 1, 2009.

10. http://www.youtube.com/watch?v=bmJukcFzEX4, accessed February 1, 2009.

11. The "myth of the black rapist," of which Angela Y. Davis (1981) wrote in *Women, Race, and Class*, is not that Black men do not assault. Males from all categories have enacted sexual violence. The argument is rather that the mythological beast need not create a victim—the traumatized body of a girl or woman, or boy or man, or infant—for the mythic beast is none other than the victim displaying an unforgivable Blackness and bestialized sexuality. Hence, the actual rapist need not be punished in the aftermath of a rape; a surrogate can take his place. More importantly, a rape need not even occur for

punishment to ensue, if the accused is Black and the accuser—or her spokesmen—are white. This is what Wells mocked, and Davis analyzed: The violent sexual objectification of Blacks creates permanent categories of victim/victimizer by inverting the order of de facto social and political violence (Davis 1981).

12. For Los Angeles City government documents on this matter, see http://www .lacity.org/ctr/audits/DNA_FinalReport_102008.pdf, accessed February 1, 2009.

13. The Commonwealth of Massachusetts Executive Office of Public Safety Parole Board, "Record of Decision in the Matter of BENJAMIN LAGUER W-40280," May 20, 2010.

Chapter 9

1. Cohen first described moral panics in terms of fears and anxieties surrounding youth culture:

> Societies appear to be subject, every now and then, to periods of moral panic. A condition, episode, person or group of persons emerges to become defined as a threat to societal values and interests; its nature is presented in a stylised and stereotypical fashion by the mass media; the moral barricades are manned by editors, bishops, politicians and other right-thinking people; socially accredited experts pronounce their diagnoses and solutions; ways of coping are evolved or (more often) resorted to; the condition then disappears, submerges or deteriorates and becomes more visible. Sometimes the panic is passed over and forgotten, but at other times it has more serious and long-term repercussions and it might produce changes in legal and social policy or even in the way in which the societies conceive themselves. (Cohen 1972: 9)

Moral panics involve a process whereby social anxieties and fears are organized in a fashion that they come to be seen as rational and logical. As Cohen describes, moral panics are part of the rationality that becomes the explanation of events.

2. Following Cohen's insights, in the late 1970s sociologist Stuart Hall and his colleagues at the Birmingham Center for Contemporary Cultural Studies argued that moral panics arise under conditions of economic and political crisis in which moral panics of Black criminality are alleviated by the state intervention of police action and the creation of an ideological superstructure to justify authoritarian measures (Hall et al. 1978). Central to the configuration of Black criminality is the concept of a law-and-order society (CCCS 1982). This is to say that in moments of crisis the upholding of the rule of law is the means of legitimizing the practices of the state apparatus through the arm of the police.

3. Walter Laqueur places the origins of the use of terror to the first century C.E., see Laqueur (2001: 7). For an important analysis of the Schmittian idea of friend and foe as it relates to framings of terror, see Anidjar (2004).

4. In 1998, Eqbal Ahmad, in a lecture entitled "Terrorism: Theirs and Ours," eloquently defined terrorism in terms of "the use of violence that is used illegally, extraconstitutionally, to coerce" (Ahmad 2001: 17). This definition for Ahmad derives from

Webster's Collegiate Dictionary, which defines "terror as an intense, overpowering fear" and terrorism as "the use of terrorizing methods to govern or resist a government." He then goes on to give a precise and coherent schematization of what constitutes terrorism. This definition emphasizes two important aspects; first, the place of the state, and second, the place of the law.

5. See http://www.fbi.gov/pressrel/pressrel02/122902press.htm, accessed July 9, 2010.

6. "Pakistani Says FBI Mug Shot Is a Case of Stolen Identity," *New York Times*, January 2, 2003, p. 9.

7. "FBI Admits Tip on Illegal Immigrants in Terror Probe Was False," *The News International [Pakistan]*, January 8, 2003.

8. Often migrants travel abroad through travel agents who are unofficial brokers for overseas laborers. These brokers possess access to networks of social affiliation that can provide jobs for clients who lack official work visas. As Ashgar makes clear, he was in contact with a number of brokers and agents throughout his travels.

9. The Federal Investigation Agency (FIA) in Pakistan is the equivalent of the FBI in the United States.

10. Interview, Badar Alam, February 2006.

11. "Terror Diaspora," *New York Times*, March 3, 2002, p. Wk 5.

12. The use of the term "enemy combatant" is telling in relation to this because it represents figures who are outside the law, both the rule of law of nation-states (in this example the United States) and the rule of international law.

13. As an example, see Friedman (2002).

14. For a trenchant reading of neoliberalism and its cultivation of notions of self-care and a pandering to identity politics at the cost of democratic expansion, see Duggan (2003).

15. See Gill (2004) for an ethnography on the role of the U.S. Army in counter-insurgency training in the Americas.

16. For example, http://www.globalsecurity.org/military/world/para/ksm.htm, accessed July 9, 2010.

17. National Commission on Terrorist Attacks upon the United States (2004: 145).

18. The CIA, long reported to use the illegal torture technique of waterboarding, has now admitted using this technique on three detainees, including Khalid Shaikh Mohammed, in offshore detention prisons referred to as "black sites." See Mayer (2007).

19. Mohammed is thought to have over fifty aliases, including: Ashraf Refaat Nabith Henin, Khalid Adbul Wadood, Salem Ali, Fahd Bin Adballah Bin Khalid, Abdulrahman A.A. Alghamdi, Mukhtar the Baluchi, Hashim Abdulrahman, Hashim Ahmed, and Khalid al-Shaykh al-Ballushi. In intelligence briefings, several transliterations of Mohammed's name also have been used: Khalid Sheikh Mohammed, Khalid Shaikh Muhammed, Khalid Shaykh Mohammad, Khaled Shaikh Mohammad, and Khalid

Shaykh Muhammed. For example, see http://www.globalsecurity.org/security/profiles/ khalid_shaikh_mohammed.htm, accessed July 9, 2010.

20. See, for example, James Risen (2003).

21. See also the Audre Lorde Project Report, *Community at a Crossroads* (Bennett and Reddy 2004), on the targeting of queer immigrants of color.

Chapter 11

Many thanks to Jaime Alves, with whom I have discussed many of these concepts and authored a recent article on São Paulo's geography of death.

1. Brazilian President Luiz Inácio Lula da Silva's recent declaration that the world economic crisis is caused by "blond, blue-eyed people" and that it is not fair that "black and indigenous populations" bear the brunt of such mistakes may be contextualized by this notion of the Black Diaspora. In it, Blacks and nonwhite communities are unmistakably disadvantaged, while white national, regional, and personal privileges are the parameters according to which state policies and cultural understandings are elaborated.

2. "Lemkin's breakthrough enabled the International Military Tribunal convened at Nuremberg in 1946 to advance an appropriate description of the charges against the major nazi defendants" (Churchill 1997: 408). Churchill's book offers a meticulous analysis of the political struggles around the U.N. genocide convention; it also shows how much of the United Nations' definitional hesitation and legal timidity has to do with U.S. influence in the formulation of the final document on genocide.

3. By solidarity work I mean a form of activist scholarship that, while in dialogue with and support of political projects of liberation, is aware of the many privileges that I have vis-à-vis the activists on the ground. My green card, my relatively secure middle-class position and job in the United States, my gender and light skin complexion are some of the many advantages I hold that the activists in Jacarezinho and South Central L.A. have no way of accessing. The clearest indication of the gulf that separates me from these activists is that whereas they have no choice but to live the often deadly militarization of their everyday lives, I always leave for the spaces of middle-class security. Writing about Rio and L.A. from Tejas, in the air-conditioned room and on the worldwide-web-connected computer provided by my employers at the heavily segregated and policed campus of the University of Texas, brings the point home exemplarily.

4. On the immanent, anti-Black cognition, see Goff et al. (2008).

5. I have written on residential segregation in Rio. See, for example, Vargas (2006).

6. A high point of Rio police demoralization took place on July 19, 2001, when on prime-time national television, during the *Jornal Nacional*, the massively watched evening news, a videotape was shown of a group of police officers receiving money from drug dealers in the favela Morro da Providência. "In times of war the corrupt police officers would have been executed," said the military police general-commander, Wilton

Ribeiro. His words, printed in the largest letters, were on the first page of *O Dia* the following day, next to photographs of the officers receiving money from dealers.

7. Examples of this campaign abound. In its June 6, 2007, edition, the weekly *Veja* published a front-page article stating, "Race does not exist." The subheading read, "Identical twins, Alex and Alan, were considered by the quota system as Black and white [respectively]. It's one more proof that race does not exist." Relatively recent publications make the argument for the fluidity of identity, and therefore point to the danger of adopting strict categories of race as a basis for public policy and social analysis. See, for example, Maggie and Rezende (2002). In 2002, the State University of Rio de Janeiro (UERJ) became the first university in Brazil to institute a quota system in its admission exam: it reserved 50 percent of its admittance to students of the public system, and 40 percent to those who self-declared as Black or Brown (*negro* or *pardo*). Today, many state and federal universities as well as public and private colleges adopt variations on these policies. For example: Universidade Federal da Bahia (Ufba), Universidade Federal de Alagoas (Ufal), Universidade Federal do Rio Grande do Norte (UFRN), Universidade Federal do Pará (Ufpa), Universidade Federal do Paraná (UFPR), Universidade Federal de São Paulo (Unifesp), Universidade de Brasília (UnB), Universidade Federal de Juiz de Fora (UFJF), Universidade Estadual da Bahia (Uneb), Universidade do Estado da Bahia (Ueba), Universidade Estadual de Minas Gerais (Uemg), Universidade Estadual Norte Fluminense (UENF), Universidade Estadual de Londrina (UEL), Universidade Estadual do Mato-Grosso do Sul (UEMS), Universidade do Estado de Mato Grosso (Unemat), Universidade Estadual do Rio Grande do Norte (Uern), Universidade Estadual do Amazonas (Uea), Universidade Estadual de Goiás (Ueg), Universidade de Campinas (Unicamp), Universidade Estadual de Montes Claros (Unimontes), Universidade de Pernambuco (Upe), Universidade Estadual do Oeste do Paraná (UNIOESTE), and Universidade Estadual do Rio Grande do Sul (UERGS).

8. Whereas according to the official 2000 Brazilian census, nonwhites (Blacks and Browns) compose 47.3 percent of the population, they are 52 percent among the lowest-earning 40 percent, that is, among those earning less than the equivalent of US$200 per month. Only 29 percent of whites are included in this group. The highest income bracket ($2,000 or more), in contrast, comprises 7.5 percent of the white population but only 1.5 percent of nonwhites. See Telles (2004: 110).

9. For an analysis of the Brazilian macroeconomy's recent performance, see the volume organized by Carneiro (2006).

10. See, for example, data in Hunter and Power (2007).

11. For a further description and analysis of that collaboration, see Vargas (2003).

12. W. Patterson et al. (1951: 7). Subsequent pages numbers appear in the main text.

13. Carol Anderson (2003: 189–209) documents Patterson's difficulties in presenting the genocide petition to the United Nations, pressured by both the National Association for the Advancement of Colored People and the State Department. Paul Robeson and W.E.B. Du Bois, who planned to support the petition and Patterson's efforts in

Paris, ended up not being able to make the trip: the State Department, suspecting that Robeson had written *We Charge Genocide*, denied him a passport; and Du Bois, having just won a long and tiring legal battle against the Justice Department, was energetically advised by his physician, his attorney, and his wife not to travel. Patterson, alone in Paris and harassed by the State Department and the U.S. embassy, which attempted to confiscate his passport, found himself having to flee to Eastern Europe to avoid the confiscation. He later returned to Paris when new incidents of racist violence in the United States made the claims in *We Charge Genocide* all the more urgent. More recently, in 1996, the National Black United Front (NBUF) launched a national petition drive charging the U.S. government with the same accusation. The NBUF's main focus was the scale and scope of crack cocaine affecting Black urban communities. NBUF based its charge on analyses of the "crack epidemic" that linked the import and sale of the drug to complicity by the Central Intelligence Agency. On the latter, see Webb (1999).

14. "The study of the relationship between globalization and racism must, I believe, start with the recognition of global trends in racism, but must primarily focus on the ways in which the specific national histories of race and current racial structures intersect with the new dynamics of globalization" (Barlow 2003: 22). See also Harrison (2002).

15. *Washington Post*, February 6, 2005 (http://www.washingtonpost.com/wp-dyn/articles/A3318–2005Feb6_3.html).

16. A debate about intentionality, drawing from the United Nations' definition, which appears earlier in this chapter, has dominated much of the debate on genocide. See, for example, Fein (1993); Kuper (1994).

17. On common sense and ethnographic practice, see, for example, Gordon (1998); Twine (1998).

18. It is intriguing that although 76 percent of people polled in Rio and São Paulo believe that policemen are active in death squads (Human Rights Watch/Americas 1997), there is little if any support outside the favelas for organizations and events that protest police brutality. A possible conclusion that can be drawn from this context is that while there is recognition of the brutality of the police, there is also an awareness that this very brutality is a necessary, vital support of social and racial hierarchies.

19. A popular Rio newspaper devoted a full page in a Sunday edition to the work of Jacarezinho's neighborhood association. Aside from focusing on Rumba's attempt to curb police brutality by defending the installation of gates and cameras in some of Jacarezinho's access streets, the article emphasized the ongoing collaboration between ex-Black Panther Party members and Jacarezinho's community organizers (Braga 2001: 4). The state of São Paulo's main newspaper also gave a full page to Rumba's work; see Petry (2001).

20. See Vargas (2003, 2006), where I detail the events that led to the formation and fall of the Zinzun Center.

21. "A Litany for Survival," originally published in *The Black Unicorn* (1978), was republished in *The Collected Poems of Audre Lorde* (Lorde 1997: 255–56).

REFERENCES

Ackerley, Brooke, Simone Chambers, Iris Marion Young, Russell Muirhead, Nancy L. Rosenblum, Michael W. Doyle, and Peter Berkowitz. 2006. "Symposium: John Rawls and the Study of Justice: Legacies of Inquiry." *Perspectives on Politics 4*: 1 (March): 75–133.

Acuña, Rodolfo. 2000. *Occupied America*. New York: Longman.

Agamben, Giorgio. 1998. *Homo Sacer: Sovereign Power and Bare Life* (trans. Daniel Heller Roazen). Stanford, CA: Stanford University Press.

———. 2005. *State of Exception*. Chicago: University of Chicago Press.

Agoncillo, Teodoro A. 1990. *History of the Filipino People* (8th ed.). Quezon City, Philippines: Garotech.

Ahmad, Eqbal. 2001. *Terrorism: Theirs and Ours*. New York: Seven Stories Press.

Ahmad, Muneer. 2002. "Homeland Insecurities: Racial Violence the Day After September 11." *Social Text 20* (3): 101–15.

———. 2004. "A Rage Shared by Law: Post-September 11 Racial Violence as Crimes of Passion." *California Law Review 92*(5): 1259–1330.

Ainsworth-Darnell, James, and Douglas B. Downey. 1998. "Assessing the Oppositional Culture Explanation for Racial/Ethnic Differences in School Performance." *American Sociological Review 63*: 536–53.

Alam, Muhammad Badar. 2003. "Fallible Bureau of Investigation." *The News International [Pakistan]*, January 12.

Aleinikoff, T. Alexander. 2002. *Semblances of Sovereignty: The Constitution, the State, and American Citizenship*. Cambridge, MA: Harvard University Press.

Alexander, M. Jacqui. 2006. *Pedagogies of Crossing: Meditations on Feminism, Sexual Politics, Memory, and the Sacred*. Durham, NC: Duke University Press.

Allen, Walter R., Marguerite Bonous-Hammarth, and Robert Ternishi. 2002. *Stony the*

Road We Trod . . . The Black Struggle for Higher Education in California. San Francisco: James Irvine Foundation.

Amar, Paul. 2003. "Reform in Rio: Reconsidering the Myths of Crime and Violence." *NACLA Report on the Americas 37*(2): 37–42.

Amnesty International. 2007. *Maze of Injustice.* New York: Amnesty International.

Amparano, Julie. 1997. "Brown Skin: No Civil Rights? July Sweep of Chandler Draws Fire," *Arizona Republic,* August 27, p. A1.

Anderson, Benedict. 1991. *Imagined Communities.* New York: Verso.

Anderson, Carol. 2003. *Eyes Off the Prize: The United Nations and the African American Struggle for Human Rights.* Cambridge, UK: Cambridge University Press.

Anderson, James D. 1988. *The Education of Blacks in the South, 1860–1935.* Chapel Hill, NC: University of North Carolina Press.

Anderson, Warwick. 2006. *Colonial Pathologies: American Tropical Medicine, Race, and Hygiene in the Philippines.* Durham, NC: Duke University Press.

Andreas, Peter. 2000. *Border Games: Policing the U.S.-Mexico Divide.* Ithaca, NY: Cornell University Press.

Anidjar, Gil. 2004. "Terror Right." *New Centennial Review 3* (3): 35–69.

Ann Arbor Police Department Online History Exhibit. 2007. "The 1990's, Serial Rapist Strikes Ann Arbor." Retrieved December 27, 2007 (http://www.aadl.org/aadp/true crimes/10).

Ansalone, George. 2003. "Poverty, Tracking, and the Social Construction of Failure: International Perspectives on Tracking." *Journal of Children and Poverty 9*(1): 3–20.

———. 2006. "Receptions of Ability and Equity in the US and Japan: Understanding the Pervasiveness of Tracking." *Radical Pedagogy 8*(1). Retrieved January 28, 2009 (http://radicalpedagogy.icaap.org/content/issue8_1/ansalone.html).

Apple, Michael. 1988. "Redefining Equality: Authoritarian Populism and the Conservative Restoration." *Teachers College Record 90*: 167–84.

Au, Kathryn. 1980. "Participation Structures in a Reading Lesson with Hawaiian Children: Analysis of a Culturally Appropriate Instructional Event." *Anthropology and Education Quarterly 11*(2): 91–115.

Au, Kathryn, and Cathie Jordan. 1981. "Teaching Reading to Hawaiian Children: Finding a Culturally Appropriate Solution." Pp. 139–52 in *Culture and the Bilingual Classroom,* ed. H. Trueba, and K. Au. Rawley, MA: Newbury House.

Austin, Curtis. 2003. Testimony of Curtis C. Austin President of Workforce Florida, Inc. Workforce Investment Act Reauthorization Hearing, Senate Committee on Health, Education, Labor and Pensions Subcommittee on Employment, Safety and Training, June 18 (www.workforceflorida.com/wages/wfi/news/news_releases/testimony _austin.htm).

Avery, James M., and Mark Peffley. 2005. "Voter Registration Requirements, Voter Turnout, and Welfare Eligibility Policy: Class Bias Matters." *State Politics and Policy Quarterly* 5(1): 47–67.

Ayers, William, Bernardine Dohrn, and Rick Ayers. 2001. *Zero Tolerance: Resisting the Drive for Punishment in Our Schools. A Handbook for Parents, Students, Educators, and Citizens.* New York: New Press.

Bahr, Michael W., and Douglas Fuchs. 1991. "Are Teachers' Perceptions of Difficult-to-Teach Students Racially Biased?" *School Psychology Review 20*: 599–609.

Bailey, Alison. 2001. "Taking Responsibility for Community Violence." Pp. 219–34 in *Feminists Doing Ethics,* ed. Peggy DesAutels and Joanne Waugh. Lanham, MD: Rowman & Littlefield.

Balibar, Etienne, and Immanuel Wallerstein. 1985. *Race, Nation, Class: Ambiguous Identities* (trans. Chris Turner). New York: Verso, 1991.

Barlow, Andrew. 2003. *Between Fear and Hope: Globalization and Race in the United States.* Lanham, MD: Rowman & Littlefield.

Barrera, Mario. 1979. *Race and Class in the Southwest: A Theory of Racial Inequality.* Notre Dame, IN: University of Notre Dame Press.

Barsh, Russel Lawrence. 1982. "Indian Land Claims Policy in the United States." *North Dakota Law Review 58*: 7–52.

Bayoumi, Moustafa. 2006. "Racing Religion." *New Centennial Review* 6(2): 267–93.

Beede, Benjamin R. 1994. "Pacification." Pp. 395–96 in *The War of 1898 and U.S. Interventions, 1898–1934: An Encyclopedia,* ed. Benjamin R. Beede. New York: Garland, 1994.

Bell, Derrick. 2002. "Bell, J., dissenting." Pp. 185–200 in *What "Brown v. Board of Education" Should Have Said,* ed. Jack M. Balkin. New York: NYU Press.

Bell, Roger John. 1984. *Last Among Equals: Hawaiian Statehood and American Politics.* Honolulu: University of Hawai'i Press.

Bender, Steve. 2005. *Greasers and Gringos.* New York: NYU Press.

Bennett, Natalie D.A., and Chandan Reddy. 2004. *Community at a Crossroads: US Right Wing Policies and Lesbian, Gay, Bisexual, Two Spirit and Transgender Immigrants of Color in New York City.* New York: Audre Lorde Project Report.

Bernasconi, Robert. 2001. "Who Invented the Concept of Race? Kant's Role in the Enlightenment Construction of Race." Pp. 11–36 in *Race,* ed. Robert Bernasconi. Malden, MA: Blackwell.

Bernasconi, Robert, and Anika Maaza Mann. 2005. "The Contradictions of Racism: Locke, Slavery, and the Two Treatises." In *Race and Racism in Modern Philosophy,* ed. Andrew Valls. Ithaca, NY: Cornell University Press.

Beveridge, Albert J. 1900. 56th Congress, Session 1, *Congressional Record 33*: 704–9.

Bevir, Mark, ed. 2007. *The Encyclopedia of Governance* (2 vols.). London: Sage.

Bhattacharjee, Anannya. 2001. *In Whose Safety? Women of Color and the Violence of Law Enforcement.* Philadelphia: American Friends Service Committee.

Biddle, Bruce J., and David C. Berliner. 2003. "What Research Says About Unequal

Funding for Schools in America." *Policy Perspectives.* Retrieved January 15, 2009 (http://www.wested.org/online_pubs/pp-03-01.pdf).

Biolsi, Thomas. 2005. "Imagined Geographies: Sovereignty, Indigenous Space, and American Indian Struggle." *American Ethnologist 32*(2): 239–59.

Blauner, Robert. 1972. *Racial Oppression in America.* New York: Harper & Row.

Blumer, Herbert. 1958. "Race Prejudice as a Sense of Group Position." *Pacific Sociological Review 1*(1)(Spring).

Boaler, Jo. 1997. "Setting, Social Class and the Survival of the Quickest." *British Educational Research Journal 23*(5): 575–95.

Bobbio, Norberto. 2005. *Liberalism and Democracy* (trans. Martin Ryle and Kate Soper). London: Verso.

Bobo, Lawrence, James R. Kluegel, and Ryan A. Smith. 1997. "Laissez Faire Racism: The Crystallization of a 'Kinder, Gentler' Anti-Black Ideology." Pp. 15–42 in *Racial Attitudes in the 1990s: Continuity and Change,* ed. S. Tuch and J. Martin. Westport, CT: Praeger.

Bocian, Debbie Gruenstein, Keith S. Ernst, and Wei Li. 2006. *Unfair Lending: The Effects of Race and Ethnicity on the Price of Subprime Mortgages.* Durham, NC: Center on Responsible Lending. Retrieved December 26, 2007 (http://www.responsiblelending.org/pdfs/rr011-Unfair_Lending-0506.pdf).

Bonilla-Silva, Eduardo. 2001. *White Supremacy and Racism in the Post-Civil Rights Era.* Boulder, CO: Lynne Reinner.

———. 2006. *Racism Without Racists: Color-Blind Racism and the Persistence of Racial Inequality in the United States.* New York: Rowman & Littlefield.

Bonilla-Silva, Eduardo, and Amanda Lewis. 1999. "The New Racism: Racial Structure in the United States, 1960s–1990s." Pp. 55–101 in *Race, Ethnicity, and Nationality in the United States,* ed. P. Wong. Boulder, CO: Westview Press.

Born, Catherine, Pamela Caudill, and Melinda Cordero. 1999. "Life After Welfare: A Look at Sanctioned Families." School of Social Work, University of Maryland, Baltimore.

Borstelmann, Thomas. 2001. *The Cold War and the Color Line: American Race Relations in the Global Arena.* Cambridge, MA: Harvard University Press.

Botsko, Christopher, Kathleen Snyder, and Jacob Leos-Urbel. 2001. *Recent Changes in Florida Welfare and Work, Child Care, and Child Welfare Systems.* Washington, DC: Urban Institute.

Boucher, David, and Paul Kelly, eds. 1994. *The Social Contract from Hobbes to Rawls.* New York: Routledge.

Bourdieu, Pierre. 1977. *Outline of a Theory of Practice* (trans. Richard Nice). Cambridge, UK: Cambridge University Press.

———. 1990. *The Logic of Practice.* Stanford, CA: Stanford University Press.

Box-Steffensmeier, Janet, and Bradford Jones. 2004. *Event History Modeling: A Guide for Social Scientists.* Cambridge, UK: Cambridge University Press.

Braga, Élcio. 2001. "Favela Trancada a Cadeado." *O Dia,* July 8, p. 4.

Braman, Donald. 2002. "Families and Incarceration." Pp. 117–35 in *Invisible Punishment: The Collateral Consequences of Mass Imprisonment,* ed. Marc Mauer and Meda Chesney-Lind. New York: New Press.

Breyer, Stephen. 2007. "Dissenting, 551 U.S.," 2007 Supreme Court of the United States, Nos. 05–908 and 05–915, *Parents Involved in Community Schools v. Seattle School District No.1 et al.*

Brown, Michael K. 1999. *Race, Money, and the American Welfare State.* Ithaca, NY: Cornell University Press.

Brown, Wendy. 1995. *States of Injury.* Princeton, NJ: Princeton University Press.

———. 2003. "Neo-Liberalism and the End of Liberal Democracy." *Theory and Event* 7(1). Retrieved May 23, 2007 (http://muse.jhu.edu/journals/theory_and_event/v007/7.1brown.html).

Bruyneel, Kevin. 2004. "Challenging American Boundaries: Indigenous People and the 'Gift' of U.S. Citizenship." *Studies in American Political Development* 18(1): 30–43.

Bryant, Meredith Lee. 2001. "Combating School Resegregation Through Housing: A Need for a Reconceptualization of American Democracy and the Rights It Protects." Pp. 49–88 in *In Pursuit of a Dream Deferred,* ed. john a. powell, Gavin Kearney, and Vina Kay. New York: Peter Lang.

Buck-Morss, Susan. 2003. "Hegel and Haiti." *Critical Inquiry* 26: 821–65.

Burnett, Christina Duffy. 2005. "The Constitution and Deconstitution of the United States." Pp. 181–208 in *The Louisiana Purchase and American Expansion, 1803–1898,* ed. Sanford Levinson and Bartholomew H. Sparrow. Lanham, MD: Rowman & Littlefield.

Burnett, Christina Duffy, and Burke Marshall. 2001a. "Between the Foreign and the Domestic: The Doctrine of Territorial Incorporation, Invented and Reinvented." Pp. 1–36 in *Foreign in a Domestic Sense: Puerto Rico, American Expansion, and the Constitution,* ed. Christina Duffy Burnett and Burke Marshall. Durham, NC: Duke University Press.

———, eds. 2001b. *Foreign in a Domestic Sense: Puerto Rico, American Expansion, and the Constitution,* ed. Christina Duffy Burnett and Burke Marshall. Durham, NC: Duke University Press.

Butler, Judith. 1997. *Excitable Speech.* New York: Routledge.

———. 2004. *Precarious Life.* London: Verso.

Butterfield, Fox. 2000. "Study Shows a Racial Divide in Domestic Violence Cases." *New York Times,* p. A16.

Calavita, Kitty. 1992. *Inside the State: The Bracero Program, Immigration, and the I.N.S.* New York: Routledge.

Campbell, Ronald F., Luvern L. Cunningham, Raphael O. Nystrand, and Michael D. Usdan. 1990. *The Organization and Control of American Schools*. Columbus, OH: Merrill.

Cano, Ignácio. 1997. *Letalidade da ação policial no Rio de Janeiro*. Rio de Janeiro: ISER.

Card, David, and Alan B. Krueger. 1996. "School Resources and Student Outcomes: An Overview of the Literature and New Evidence from North and South Carolina." *Journal of Economic Perspectives 10*: 31–50.

Carneiro, Ricardo. 2006. *A Supremacia dos Mercados e a Política Econômica do Governo Lula*. São Paulo: Editora Unesp.

Carter, Prudence. 2005. *Keepin' It Real: School Success Beyond Black and White*. New York: Oxford University Press.

Carter, Robert L. 1993. "Thirty-five Years Later: New Perspectives on Brown." Pp. 83–96 in *Race in America: The Struggle for Equality*, ed. Herbert Hill and James E. Jones Jr. Madison: University of Wisconsin Press.

Castles, Stephen, and Alastair Davidson. 2000. *Citizenship and Migration: Globalization and the Politics of Belonging*. New York: Routledge.

Cazden, Courtney B. 1988. *Classroom Discourse: The Language of Teaching and Learning*. Portsmouth, NH: Heinemann Educational Books.

Cazden, Courtney B., Vera P. John, and Dell Hymes. 1972. *Functions of Language in the Classroom*. Prospect Heights, IL: Waveland Press.

CCCS, ed. 1982. *The Empire Strikes Back: Race and Racism in 70s Britain*. London: Hutchinson.

Center for the Future of Teaching and Learning (Santa Cruz, CA). 2008. "California's Teaching Force 2003: Key Issues and Trends." Retrieved March 1, 2009 (www.cftl.org).

Chacón, Justin Akers, and Mike Davis. 2006. *No One Is Illegal: Fighting Racism and State Violence on the U.S.-Mexico Border*. Chicago: Haymarket Books.

Chang, Robert S. 1999. *Disoriented: Asian Americans, Law, and the Nation-State*. New York: NYU Press.

Charny, Israel. 1994. "Toward a Generic Definition of Genocide." Pp. 64–94 in *Genocide: Conceptual and Historical Dimensions*, ed. George Andreopoulos. Philadelphia: University of Pennsylvania Press.

Chasnoff, Brian. 2006. "Shooting by Cop Is Called Racist." *San Antonio Express*, December 3. Retrieved February 20, 2009 (http://www.mysanantonio.com/news/MYSA120306_01B_shooting_folo_30fc8f7_html8618.html).

Chatterjee, Partha. 1993. *The Nation and Its Fragments*. Princeton, NJ: Princeton University Press.

Chavez, Leo R. 2001. *Covering Immigration, Popular Images and the Politics of the Nation*. Berkeley: University of California Press.

Chesler, Mark, Amanda Lewis, and Jim Crowfoot. 2004. *Challenging Racism and Promoting Multiculturalism in Higher Education*. Lanham, MD: Rowman & Littlefield.

Chesney-Lind, Meda. 2002. "Imprisoning Women: The Unintended Victims of Mass Imprisonment." Pp. 79–94 in *Invisible Punishment: The Collateral Consequences of Mass Imprisonment*, ed. Marc Mauer and Meda Chesney-Lind. New York: New Press.

Chin, Gabriel. 1996. "The Plessy Myth: Justice Harlan and the Chinese Cases." *Iowa Law Review 82*: 151–82.

Cho, Chung-Lae, Christine A. Kelleher, Deil S. Wright, and Susan Webb Yackee. 2003. "Second Order Devolution and the Implementation of Welfare Reform Objectives." Paper presented at the Annual Conference of the Midwest Political Science Association, Chicago, April 3–6.

———. 2005. "Translating National Policy Objectives into Local Achievements Across Planes of Governance and Among Multiple Actors: Second-Order Devolution and Welfare Reform Implementation." *Journal of Public Administration Research and Theory 15*(1): 31–54.

Chow, Rey. 2002. *The Protestant Ethnic and the Spirit of Capitalism*. New York: Columbia University Press.

Churchill, Ward. 1997. *A Little Matter of Genocide: Holocaust and Denial in the Americas—1492 to the present*. San Francisco: City Lights Books.

Churchill, Ward, and Jim Vander Wall. 1990. *Agents of Repression: The FBI's Secret Wars Against the Black Panther Party and the American Indian Movement*. Boston: South End Press.

Cimbala, Paul A., and Randall M. Miller. 1999. "Preface." Pp. ix–xii in *The Freedmen's Bureau and Reconstruction: Reconsiderations*, ed. Paul A. Cimbala and Randall M. Miller. New York: Fordham University Press.

Clotfelter, Charles. 2004. *After Brown: The Rise and Retreat of School Desegregation*. Princeton, NJ: Princeton University Press.

Clotfelter, Charles T. 2005. "Who Teaches Whom? Race and the Distribution of Novice Teachers." *Economics of Education Review 24*: 377–92.

———. 2006. "Teacher-Student Matching and the Assessment of Teacher Effectiveness." *Journal of Human Resources 41*(4): 778–820.

Clotfelter, Charles T., Helen F. Ladd, and Jacob L. Vigdor. 2004. "Teacher Sorting, Teacher Shopping, and the Assessment of Teacher Effectiveness." Working paper, Sanford Institute of Public Policy, Duke University.

Clotfelter, Charles, Helen F. Ladd, Jacob L. Vigdor, and Roger Aliaga Diaz. 2004. "Do School Accountability Systems Make It More Difficult for Low-Performing Schools to Attract and Retain High-Quality Teachers?" *Journal of Policy Analysis and Management 23*(3): 251–71.

Cockcroft, James D. 1986. *Outlaws in the Promised Land: Mexican Immigrant Workers and America's Future*. New York: Grove Press.

Cohen, Cathy. 1999. *The Boundaries of Blackness: AIDS and the Breakdown of Black Politics*. Chicago: University of Chicago Press.

Cohen, Stanley. 1972. *Folk Devils and Moral Panics: Creation of Mods and Rockers.* London: MacGibbon and Kee.

Coleman, James S., Ernest Q. Campbell, Carol F. Hobson, James M. McPartland, Alexander M. Mood, Frederic D. Weinfeld, and Robert L. York. 1966. *Equality of Educational Opportunity.* Washington, DC: U.S. Government Printing Office.

Collins, Patricia Hill. 1991. *Black Feminist Thought.* New York: Routledge.

———. 1998. *Fighting Words: Black Women and the Search for Justice.* Minneapolis: University of Minnesota Press.

Conchas, Gilberto. 2006. *The Color of Success: Race and High-Achieving Urban Youth.* New York: Teachers College Press.

Condron, Dennis J. 2007. "Stratification and Educational Sorting: Explaining Ascriptive Inequalities in Early Childhood Reading Group Placement." *Social Problems 54*: 139–60.

———. 2008. "An Early Start: Skill Grouping and Unequal Reading Gains in the Elementary Years." *Sociological Quarterly 49*: 363–94.

Conley, Dalton. 1999. *Being Black, Living in the Red: Race, Wealth, and Social Policy in America.* Berkeley: University of California Press.

Constantino, Renato. 1970. "The Mis-education of the Filipino." *Journal of Contemporary Asia 1*(1)(Autumn): 20–36.

Constantino, Renato, with the collaboration of Letizia R. Constantino. 1975. *A History of the Philippines: From the Spanish Colonization to the Second World War.* New York: Monthly Review Press.

Cooper, Frederick. 2005. *Colonialism in Question: Theory, Knowledge, History.* Berkeley: University of California Press.

Cornelius, Wayne A. 2001. "Death at the Border: Efficacy and Unintended Consequences of US Immigration Control Policy." *Population and Development Review 27*(4): 661–85.

Coulthard, Glen. 2007. "Indigenous Peoples and the 'Politics of Recognition' in Colonial Contexts." Paper presented at the Cultural Studies Now Conference, University of East London, London, July 22, 2007.

Crenshaw, Kimberlé. 1996. "Mapping the Margins: Intersectionality, Identity Politics, and Violence Against Women of Color." Pp. 357–83 in *Critical Race Theory*, ed. Kimberlé Crenshaw, Neil Gotanda, Gary Peller, and Kendall Thomas. New York: New Press.

Currie, Elliott. 1998. *Crime and Punishment in America.* New York: Metropolitan Books.

D'Adesky, Jacques. 2001. *Pluralismo étnico e multiculturalismo: Racismos e anti-racismos no Brasil.* Rio de Janeiro: Pallas.

Darling-Hammond, Linda. 2001. "Apartheid in American Education: How Opportunity Is Rationed to Children of Color in the United States." Pp. 39–44 in *Racial Profiling and Punishment in U.S. Public Schools*, ed. Tammy Johnson, Jennifer Emiko Boyden, and William J. Pittz. Oakland, CA: Applied Research Center.

———. 2003. "Colorblind Education: Will It Help Us Leave No Child Behind?" Presentation at conference, Colorblind Racism: The Politics of Controlling Racial and Ethnic Data, Stanford University, Palo Alto, CA, October 3.

Davis, Angela. 1981. *Women, Race and Class.* New York: Vintage.

———. 2003. *Are Prisons Obsolete?* New York: Seven Stories Press.

Davis, Mike. 1992. *City of Quartz: Excavating the Future in Los Angeles.* New York: Vintage.

Davis, Mike, and Justin Ackers Chacón. 2006. *No One Is Illegal: Fighting Racism and State Violence on the U.S.-Mexico Border.* Chicago: Haymarket Books.

Days, Drew, III. 2001. "The Current State of School Desegregation Law: Why Isn't Anybody Laughing?" Pp. 159–82 in *In Pursuit of a Dream Deferred,* ed. john a. powell, Gavin Kearney, and Vina Kay. New York: Peter Lang.

Dean, Mitchell. 1999. *Governmentality: Power and Rule in Modern Society.* Thousand Oaks, CA: Sage.

Degler, Carl. 1986 [1971]. *Neither Black nor White: Slavery and Race Relations in Brazil and the United States.* Madison: University of Wisconsin Press.

Deloria, Philip. 2004. *Indians in Unexpected Places.* Lawrence: University of Kansas Press.

Deloria, Vine, Jr., and David E. Wilkins. 1999. *Tribes, Treaties, and Constitutional Tribulations.* Austin: University of Texas Press.

Delpit, Lisa. 1995. *Other People's Children: Cultural Conflict in the Classroom.* New York: New Press.

Denton, Nancy. 1995–96. "The Persistence of Segregation: Links Between Residential Segregation and School Segregation." *Minnesota Law Review 80:* 795–824.

Diamond, John B., Antonia Randolph, and James P. Spillane. 2004. "Teachers' Expectations and Sense of Responsibility for Student Learning: The Importance of Race, Class, and Organizational Habitus." *Anthropology and Education Quarterly 35:* 75–98.

Dias, Janice Johnson, and Steven Maynard-Moody. 2007. "For-Profit Welfare: Contracts, Conflicts, and the Performance Paradox." *Journal of Public Administration Research and Theory 17*(2): 189–211.

Donziger, Steven. 1996. *The Real War on Crime.* New York: HarperCollins.

Douglass, Frederick. 1850–75. "At Home Again." Pp. 125–27 in *The Life and Writings of Frederick Douglass,* Vol. 2, ed. Philip S. Foner (5 vols.). New York: International.

Du Bois, W.E.B. 1901. "The Freedmen's Bureau." *Atlantic Monthly* (87): 354–65.

———. 1965 [1903]. *The Souls of Black Folk.* Pp. 207–389 in *Three Negro Classics.* New York: Avon Books.

———. 1999. *Black Reconstruction in America 1860–1880.* New York: Free Press.

Duggan, Lisa. 1995. "Sex Panics." In *Sex Wars: Sexual Dissent and Political Culture,* ed. L. Duggan and N. D. Hunter. New York: Routledge.

———. 2003. *The Twilight of Equality? Neoliberalism, Cultural Politics, and the Attack on Democracy.* Boston: Beacon Press.

Dunn, Timothy J. 1996. *The Militarization of the U.S.-Mexico Border.* Austin: CMAS Books, University of Texas.

Dupuis, Joanna. 1999. "California Lawsuit Notes Unequal Access to AP Courses." *Rethinking Schools 14*(1).

Eschbach, Karl, Jacqueline Hagan, Nestor Rodriquez, Rúben Hernández-León, and Stanley Bailey. 1999. "Death at the Border." *International Migration Review 33*(2): 430–54.

Ewing, Katherine Pratt. 2008. *Stolen Honor: Stigmatizing Muslim Men in Berlin.* Stanford, CA: Stanford University Press.

Fair Housing Center of Greater Boston. 2006. "You Don't Know What You're Missing: Realtors Disadvantage African American, Latino Homebuyers." Retrieved December 26, 2007 (http://www.bostonfairhousing.org/DontKnow.pdf).

Fanon, Frantz. 1967. *Black Skin, White Masks* (trans. Charles Lam Markmann). New York: Grove Press.

———. 1968 [1961]. *The Wretched of the Earth* (trans. Constance Farrington). New York: Grove Press.

Farkas, George. 2003. "Racial Disparities and Discrimination in Education: What Do We Know, How Do We Know It, and What Do We Need to Know?" *Teachers College Record 105*(6): 1119.

Feagin, Joe. 2000. *Racist America: Roots, Current Realities and Future Reparations.* New York: Routledge.

———. 2006. *Systemic Racism: A Theory of Oppression.* New York: Routledge.

Fein, David J., and Wang S. Lee. 1999. "The ABC Evaluation: Carrying and Using the Stick: Financial Sanctions in Delaware's A Better Chance Program." Cambridge, MA: Abt Associates.

Fein, Helen. 1993. *Genocide: A Sociological Perspective.* London: Sage.

Feldman, Megan. 2006. "Splitsville: No Border Fences Make for Mad Neighbors in Farmers Branch." *Dallas Observer*, November 2. Retrieved December 26, 2007 (http://www.dallasobserver.com/2006-11-02/news/splitsville/vull).

Ferguson, Ann A. 2000. *Bad Boys: Public Schools in the Making of Black Masculinity.* Ann Arbor: University of Michigan Press.

Ferguson, Ronald F. 1998a. "Can Schools Narrow the Black-White Test Score Gap?" Pp. 318–74 in *The Black-White Test Score Gap*, ed. C. Jencks and M. Phillips. Washington, DC: Brookings Institution Press.

———. 1998b. "Teachers' Perceptions and Expectations and the Black-White Test Score Gap." Pp. 273–317 in *The Black-White Test Score Gap*, ed. C. Jencks and M. Phillips. Washington, DC: Brookings Institution Press.

Fernandes, Deepa. 2007. *Targeted: Homeland Security and the Business of Immigration.* New York: Seven Stories Press.

Fierros, Edward G., and James W. Conroy. 2002. *Double Jeopardy: An Exploration of Re-*

strictiveness and Race in Special Education. Cambridge, MA: Harvard Education Publishing Group.

Finkelhor, David, Heather Hammer, and Andrea J. Sedlak. 2002. "Nonfamily Abducted Children: Estimates and Characteristics." *NISMART Bulletin* (October). Retrieved March 26, 2009 (http://www.ncjrs.gov/html/ojjdp/nismart/03/ns1.html).

Florida Governor's Select Task Force on Election Procedures, Standards, and Technology. 2001. "Revitalizing Democracy in Florida." Retrieved December 27, 2007 (http://www.collinscenter.org/usr%5Fdoc/Election%20Report.pdf).

Foner, Eric. 1988. *Reconstruction: America's Unfinished Revolution, 1863–1877.* New York: Harper & Row.

Fordham, Signithia. 1996. "Racelessness as a Factor in Black Students' School Success: Pragmatic Strategy or Pyrrhic Victory?" Pp. 209–44 in *Facing Racism in Education* (2nd ed.), ed. T. Beauboeuf-Lafontant and D. S. Augustine. Cambridge, MA: Harvard Education Review Reprint Series, No. 28.

Fordham, Signithia, and John Ogbu. 1986. "Black Students' School Success: Coping with the 'Burden of Acting White.'" *Urban Review 18*: 176–206.

Fording, Richard C., Sanford F. Schram, and Joe Soss. 2006a. "Devolution, Discretion, and Local Variation in TANF Sanctioning." *Insights on Southern Poverty 4*(1). (http://www.ukcpr.org/Publications/Newsletter-Vol4_1.pdf).

———. 2006b. "Devolution, Discretion, and Local Variation in TANF Sanctioning." Lexington: University of Kentucky Center for Poverty Research, DP2006–04. (http://www.ukcpr.org/Publications/DP2006-04.pdf).

———. 2006c. "The Bottom Line, the Business Model, and the Bogey: Performance Management, Sanctions, and the Brave New World of Welfare-to-Work in Florida." Lexington: University of Kentucky Center for Poverty Research DP2006–10. (http://www.ukcpr.org/Publications/DP2006-10/pdf).

———. 2007. "Making Worse Things Worse: Sanctions, Earnings, and Welfare-to-Work." Unpublished paper.

Fording, Richard C., Joe Soss, and Sanford F. Schram. 2007a. "Devolution, Discretion, and the Effect of Local Political Values on TANF Sanctioning." *Social Service Review 81*(2): 285–316.

———. 2007b. "Distributing Discipline: Race, Politics and Punishment at the Frontlines of Welfare Reform." Lexington: University of Kentucky Center for Poverty Research DP2007–04 (http://www.ukcpr.org/Publications/DP2007-04.pdf).

Forman, Tyrone. 2004. "Color-Blind Racism and Racial Indifference: The Role of Racial Apathy in Facilitating Enduring Inequalities." Pp. 43–66 in *Changing Terrain of Race and Ethnicity*, ed. Marian Krysan and Amanda Lewis. New York: Russell Sage Foundation.

Forman, Tyrone, and Amanda E. Lewis. 2006. "Racial Apathy and Hurricane Katrina:

The Social Anatomy of Prejudice in the Post-Civil Rights Era." *Du Bois Review* 3(1): 175–202.

Forsyth, Murray. 1994. "Hobbes's Contractarianism." In *The Social Contract from Hobbes to Rawls*, ed. David Boucher and Paul Kelly. New York: Routledge.

Foster, Michele. 1997. *Black Teachers on Teaching*. New York: New Press.

Foucault, Michel. 1970. *The Order of Things: An Archeology of the Human Sciences*. New York: Vintage.

———. 1977. *Discipline and Punish*. New York: Vintage Books.

Fox-Piven, France. 2006. *Challenging Authority: How Ordinary People Change America*. Lanham, MD: Rowman & Littlefield.

Francisco, Luzviminda. 1973. "The First Vietnam: The U.S.-Philippine War of 1899." *Bulletin of Concerned Asian Scholars* (1973): 2–16.

Frankenberg, Ruth. 1993. *White Women, Race Matters: The Social Construction of Whiteness*. Minneapolis: University of Minnesota Press.

Franklin, John Hope. 2000. *From Slavery to Freedom: A History of African Americans* (8th ed.). New York: Knopf.

Frantz, Klaus. 1999. *Indian Reservations in the United States: Territory, Sovereignty, and Socioeconomic Change*. Chicago: University of Chicago Press.

Fredrickson, George. 1981. *White Supremacy: A Comparative Study in American and South African History*. New York: Oxford University Press.

Freehling, William W. 2005. "The Louisiana Purchase and the Coming of the Civil War." Pp. 69–82 in *The Louisiana Purchase and American Expansion, 1803–1898*, ed. Sanford Levinson and Bartholomew H. Sparrow. Lanham, MD: Rowman & Littlefield.

Freeman, Samuel, ed. 2003. *The Cambridge Companion to Rawls*. New York: Cambridge University Press.

———. 2007. *Rawls*. New York: Routledge.

Friedman, Thomas. 2002. "The 2 Domes of Belgium." *New York Times*, January 27.

Füredi, Frank. 1998. *The Silent War: Imperialism and the Changing Perception of Race*. New Brunswick, NJ: Rutgers University Press.

Gainsborough, Juliet F. 2003. "To Devolve or Not to Devolve? Welfare Reform in the States." *Policy Studies Journal* 31(4): 603–23.

Galarza, Ernesto. 1964. *Merchants of Labor: The Mexican Bracero Story*. Santa Barbara, CA: McNully and Lofton.

Gamboa, Erasmo. 1990. *Mexican Labor and World War II: Braceros in the Pacific Northwest 1942–1947*. Austin: University of Texas Press.

Garcia, Juan Ramon. 1980. *Operation Wetback: The Mass Deportation of Mexican Undocumented Workers in 1954*. Westport, CT: Greenwood Press.

Garland, David. 2002. *The Culture of Control: Crime and Social Order in Contemporary Society*. Chicago: University of Chicago Press.

Georges-Abeyie, Daniel E. 2001. "Foreword." Pp. ix–xiv in *Petit Apartheid in the U.S.*

Criminal Justice System: The Dark Figure of Racism, ed. Dragan Milovanovic and Katheryn Russell. Durham, NC: Carolina Academic Press.

Gill, Lesley. 2004. *The School of the Americas: Military Training and Political Violence in the Americas, American Encounters/Global Interactions*. Durham, NC: Duke University Press.

Gilens, Martin. 1999. *Why Americans Hate Welfare: Race, Media, and the Politics of Antipoverty Policy*. Chicago: University of Chicago Press.

Gilliam, Angela. 1992. "From Roxbury to Rio—And Back in a Hurry." In *African-American Reflections on Brazil's Racial Paradise*, ed. D. Helwig. Philadelphia: Temple University Press.

Gilman, Michelle. 2001. "Legal Accountability in an Era of Privatized Welfare." *California Law Review 89*(3): 569–642.

Gilmore, Ruth W. 1998–99. "Globalisation and U.S. Prison Growth: From Military Keynesianism to Post-Keynesian Militarism." *Race and Class 40*(2/3): 171–88.

———. 2002. "Race and Globalization." Pp. 261–74 in *Geographies of Global Change* (2nd ed.), ed. R. J. Johnstone et al. Oxford, UK: Blackwell.

Gilroy, Paul. 1993. *The Black Atlantic: Modernity and Double Consciousness*. Cambridge, MA: Harvard University Press.

Ginsburg, Ruth Bader. 1995. "J. dissenting," *Missouri v. Jenkins*, U.S. (1995), *Missouri et al., Petitioners v. Kalima Jenkins et al.*, Certiorari to the United States Court of Appeals for the Eighth Circuit No. 93–1821.

Glassner, Barry. 2000. *The Culture of Fear. Why Americans Are Afraid of the Wrong Things*. New York: Basic Books.

Glenn, Evelyn Nakano. 2002. *Unequal Freedom: How Race and Gender Shaped American Citizenship and Labor*. Cambridge, MA: Harvard University Press.

Glover, William J. 2008. *Making Lahore Modern: Constructing and Imagining a Colonial City*. Minneapolis: University of Minnesota Press.

Go, Julian. 2007. "Waves of Empire: U.S. Hegemony and Imperialistic Activity from the Shores of Tripoli to Iraq, 1787–2003." *International Sociology 22*(1): 5–40.

———. 2008. "Global Fields and Imperial Forms: Field Theory and the British and American Empires." *Sociological Theory 26*(3): 201–29.

Goff, Phillip, J. Eberhard, M. Williams, and M. C. Jackson. 2008. "Not Yet Human: Implicit Knowledge, Historical Dehumanization, and Contemporary Consequences." *Journal of Personality and Social Psychology 94*(2): 292–306.

Gois, Chico de. 2009. "Lula diz que crise é causada por 'gente branca de olhos azuis.'" *O Globo*, March 26. (http://oglobo.globo.com/economia/mat/2009/03/26/lula-diz -que-crise-causada-por-gente-branca-de-olhos-azuis-755003398.asp).

Goldberg, David Theo. 2002. *The Racial State*. Malden, MA: Blackwell.

Goldberg, Heidi, and Liz Schott. 2000. *A Compliance Oriented Approach to Sanctions in*

State and County TANF Programs. Washington, DC: Center on Budget and Policy Priorities.

Goldberg, Judith A., and David M. Siegel. 2002. "The Ethical Obligations of Prosecutors in Cases Involving Postconviction Claims of Innocence." *California Western Law Review* 38: 391–412.Goodin, Robert E., Philip Pettit, and Thomas Pogge, eds. 2007. *A Companion to Contemporary Political Philosophy* (2nd ed., 2 vols.). Malden, MA: Blackwell.

Gopinath, Gayatri. 2005. *Impossible Desires: Queer Diasporas and South Asian Public Cultures, Perverse Modernities*. Durham, NC: Duke University Press.

Gordon, Avery F. 2008. *Ghostly Matters: Haunting and the Sociological Imagination*. Minneapolis: University of Minnesota Press.

Gordon, Edmund. 1998. *Disparate Diasporas: Identity and Politics in an African-Nicaraguan Community*. Austin: University of Texas Press.

Gordon, Edmund T., and Mark Anderson. 1999. "The African Diaspora: Toward an Ethnography of Diasporic Identification." *Journal of American Folklore* 112(445): 282–96.

Gottlieb, Jay, Mark Alter, Barbara W. Gottlieb, and Jerry Wishner. 1994. "Special Education in America: It's Not Justifiable for Many." *Journal of Special Education* 27: 453–65.

Gottlieb, Jay, Barbara W. Gottlieb, and Sharon Trongone. 1991. "Parent and Teacher Referrals for Psychoeducational Evaluation." *Journal of Special Education* 25: 155–67.

Gough, J. W. 1978. *The Social Contract: A Critical Study of Its Development* (2nd ed.). Westport, CT: Greenwood Press.

Gould, Mark. 1999. "Race and Theory: Culture, Poverty, and Adaptation to Discrimination in Wilson and Ogbu." *Sociological Theory* 17: 171–200.

Gramsci, Antonio. 1971. *Selections from the Prison Notebooks* (trans. Quintin Hoare and Geoffrey Nowell Smith). New York: International.

Grande, Sandy. 2004. *Red Pedagogy*. Lanham, MD: Rowman & Littlefield.

Grogger, Jeffrey T., and Lynn A. Karoly. 2005. *Welfare Reform: Effects of a Decade of Change*. Cambridge, MA: Harvard University Press.

Gualtieri, Sarah. 2001. "Becoming 'White': Race, Religion and the Foundations of Syrian/Lebanese Ethnicity in the United States." *Journal of American Ethnic History* 20(4): 29–58.

———. 2009. *Between Arab and White: Race and Ethnicity in the Early Syrian American Diaspora*. Berkeley: University of California Press.

Guerin-Gonzales, Camille. 1994. *Mexican Workers and American Dreams: Immigration Repatriation, and California Farm Labor, 1900–1939*. New Brunswick, NJ: Rutgers University Press.

Guglielmo, Thomas. 2003. *White on Arrival: Italians, Race, Color, and Power in Chicago, 1890–1945*. New York: Oxford University Press.

Guinier, Lani, and Gerald Torres. 2002. *The Miner's Canary*. Cambridge, MA: Harvard University Press.

Gutiérrez, David G. 1995. *Walls and Mirrors: Mexican Americans, Mexican Immigrants, and the Politics of Ethnicity.* Berkeley: University of California Press.

Habermas, Jürgen. 1992. *Moral Consciousness and Communicative Action* (trans. Christian Lenhardt and Shierry Weber Nicholsen). Boston: MIT Press.

Hacker, Jacob S. 2004. "After Welfare." *New Republic,* October 11. (http://www.tnr.com/doc.mhtml?i=20041011&s=hacker101104).

Hadderman, Margaret. 1999. "Equity and Adequacy in Educational Finance." *ERIC Digest* 129. Retrieved July 19, 2009 (http://www.eric.ed.gov/PDFS/ED454566.pdf).

Hall, Stuart. 1980. "Race, Articulation and Societies Structured in Dominance." Pp. 305–45 in *Sociological Theories: Race and Colonialism,* ed. UNESCO. Paris: UNESCO.

Hall, Stuart, C. Critchner, T. Jefferson, J. Clarke, and B. Roberts, eds. 1978. *Policing the Crisis: 'Mugging,' the State, and Law and Order.* London: Macmillan.

Hamill, Sean. 2006. "Altoona, With No Immigrant Problem Decides to Solve It." *New York Times,* December 7. Retrieved December 26, 2007 (http://www.nytimes.com/2006/12/07/us/07altona.html?_r=1&oref=slogin).

Han, Sora. 2006. "Bonds of Representation: Vision, Race and Law in Post-Civil Rights America." Doctoral dissertation, University of California, Santa Cruz.

Hancock, Ange-Marie. 2004. *The Politics of Disgust: The Public Identity of the Welfare Queen.* New York: New York University Press.

Handler, Joel, and Yeheskel Hasenfeld. 2006. *Blame Welfare, Ignore Poverty and Inequality.* New York: Cambridge University Press.

Hanushek, Eric. 1994. "Money Might Matter Somewhere: A Response to Hedges, Laine, and Greenwald." *Educational Researcher 23:* 5–8.

Hanushek, Eric A., John F. Kain, and Steven G. Rivkin. 2004. "Why Public Schools Lose Teachers." *Journal of Human Resources 39:* 326–54.

Hanushek, Eric A., and Ludger Wößmann. 2006. "Does Educational Tracking Affect Performance and Inequality? Differences-in-Differences Evidence Across Countries." *Economic Journal 116:* C63–C76.

Harris, Angel L. 2006. "I (Don't) Hate School: Revisiting 'Oppositional Culture' Theory of Blacks' Resistance to Schooling." *Social Forces 85:* 797–834.

Harris, Angel L., and Keith Robinson. 2007. "Schooling Behaviors or Prior Skills?: A Cautionary Tale of Omitted Variable Bias Within the Oppositional Culture Theory." *Sociology of Education 80:* 139–57.

Harris, Cheryl I. 1993. "Whiteness as Property." *Harvard Law Review 106*(8): 1709–95.

Harris, David, and Nancy McArdle. 2003. "More than Money: The Spatial Mismatch Between Where Homeowners of Color in Metro Boston Can Afford to Live and Where They Actually Reside." Report. Cambridge, MA: Civil Rights Project of Harvard University and the Fair Housing Center of Greater Boston.

Harrison, Faye V. 2002. "Global Apartheid, Foreign Policy, and Human Rights." *Souls* 4(3): 48–68.

Harry, Beth, and Janette Klinger. 2006. *Why Are So Many Minority Students in Special Education? Understanding Race and Disability in Schools.* New York: Teachers College Press.

Hartman, Saidiya V. 1997. *Scenes of Subjection: Terror, Slavery, and Self-Making in Nineteenth-Century America.* Oxford, UK: Oxford University Press.

Hasenbalg, Carlos, and Nélson do Valle e Silva. 1999. "Educação e diferenças raciais na mobilidade ocupacional no Brasil." In *Cor e estratificação social,* ed. C. Hasenbalg, N. V. Silva, and M. Lima. Rio de Janeiro: Contracapa.

Hasenfeld, Yeheskel, and Lisa Evens Powell. 2004. "The Role of Non-Profit Agencies in the Provision of Welfare-to-Work Services." *Administration in Social Work 28*(3/4): 91–110.

Hasenfeld, Yeheskel, Toorjo Ghose, and Kadyce Larson. 2004. "The Logic of Sanctioning Welfare Recipients: An Empirical Assessment." *Social Service Review 78*(2): 304–19.

Henry, Stuart, and Dragan Milovanovic. 1996. *Constitutive Criminology.* London: Sage.

Herrnstein, Richard J., and Charles Murray. 1994. *The Bell Curve: Intelligence and Class Structure in American Life.* New York: Free Press.

Horne, Gerald. 1988. *Communist Front? The Civil Rights Congress, 1946–1956.* Rutherford, NJ: Associated University Presses.

Horsman, Reginald. 1981. *Race and Manifest Destiny: The Origins of American Racial Anglo-Saxonism.* Cambridge, MA: Harvard University Press.

Horvat, Erin, and Carla O'Connor. 2006. *Beyond Acting White: Reframing the Debate on Black Student Achievement.* Lanham, MD: Rowman & Littlefield.

Human Rights Watch/Americas. 1997. *Police Brutality in Urban Brazil.* New York: Human Rights Watch.

Hunter, Wendy, and Timothy J. Power. 2007. "Rewarding Lula: Executive Power, Social Policy, and the Brazilian Elections of 2006." *Latin American Politics and Society 49*(1): 1–30.

Hutton, Paul Andrew. 1999. *Phil Sheridan and His Army.* Tulsa: University of Oklahoma Press.

IBGE, 1996. *Pesquias Nacional por Amostra de Domicílios.* Rio de Janeiro: Instituto Brasileiro de Geografia e Estatística IBGE.

Incite, ed. 2006. *The Color of Violence: Violence Against Women of Color.* Cambridge, MA: South End Press.

———, ed. 2007. *The Revolution Will Not Be Funded: Beyond the Non-Profit Industrial Complex.* Cambridge, MA: South End Press.

INSPIR/DIEESE/AFL-CIO. 1999. *Mapa da população negra no mercado de trabalho.* São Paulo: Instituto Sindical Interamericano pela Igualdade Racial.

Institute for Democracy, Education and Access. 2004. "Separate and Unequal 50 Years After Brown: California's Racial 'Opportunity Gap.'" Graduate School of Education and Information Studies, UCLA.

Institute on Race and Poverty. 2009. "Communities in Crisis: Race and Mortgage Lending in the Twin Cities." Retrieved March 27, 2009 (http://minnesota.publicradio.org /features/2009/02/12_housing/IRP_mortgage_study.pdf).

Irons, Peter. 2004. *Jim Crow's Children*. New York: Penguin Books.

Isaac, Benjamin. 2004. *The Invention of Racism in Classical Antiquity*. Princeton, NJ: Princeton University Press.

Jackson, Kenneth. 1985. *Crabgrass Frontier*. New York: Oxford University Press.

Jacob, Brian A. 2007. "The Challenges of Staffing Urban Schools with Effective Teachers." *Future of Children 17*: 129–53.

Jacobs, Adrian. 2000. "Drumming, Dancing, Chanting and Other Christian Things." *Mission Frontiers 22*: 16–18.

Jacobs, James B., and Kimberly Potter. 1998. *Hate Crimes: Criminal Law and Identity Politics*. Oxford, UK: Oxford University Press.

Jacobson, Matthew Frye. 1998. *Barbarian Virtues: The United States Encounters Foreign Peoples at Home and Abroad, 1876–1917*. New York: Hill and Wang.

James, Joy. 1996. *Resisting State Violence: Radicalism, Gender, and Race in U.S. Culture*. Minneapolis: University of Minnesota Press.

———. 1997. *Transcending the Talented Tenth*. New York: Routledge.

———. 1999. *Shadowboxing: Representations of Black Feminist Politics*. New York: St. Martin's Press.

———, ed. 2005. *The New Abolitionists: (neo) Slave Narratives and Contemporary Prison Writings*. Albany: State University of New York Press.

Jefferson, Thomas. 1982. *The Life and Selected Writings of Thomas Jefferson*, ed. Adrienne Koch and William Peden. Franklin Center, PA: Franklin Library.

Jenness, Valerie, and Ryken Grattet. 2001. *Making Hate a Crime: From Social Movement to Law Enforcement*. New York: Russell Sage Foundation.

Jensen, Joan M. 1988. *Passage from India: Asian Indian Immigrants in North America*. New Haven, CT: Yale University Press.

Jessop, Robert. 1994. "Toward a Schumpeterian Welfare State: Preliminary Remarks on Post-Fordist Political Economy." *Studies in Political Economy 40*: 7–39.

Jeter, Jon. 2003. "Death Squads Feed Terror in Rio Slums." *Seattle Times*, October 27.

Johnson, Heather Beth. 2006. *The American Dream and the Power of Wealth: Choosing Schools and Inheriting Inequality in the Land of Opportunity*. New York: Routledge.

Johnson, Kevin R. 2004. *The "Huddled Masses" Myth: Immigration and Civil Rights*. Philadelphia: Temple University Press.

Johnson, Kevin R., and Bernard Trujillo. 2007. "Immigration Reform, National Security After September 11, and the Future of North American Integration." *Minnesota Law Review 91*(5): 1369–1406.

Johnson, Robert, and Paul Leighton. 1995. "Black Genocide? Preliminary Thoughts on the Plight of America's Poor Black Men." *Journal of African Men 1*(2): 3–21.

Johnson, Tammy, Jennifer Emiko Boyden, and William Pittz. 2001. "Racial Profiling and Punishment in U.S. Public Schools: How Zero Tolerance Policies and High Stakes Testing Subvert Academic Excellence and Racial Equity." Applied Research Center, Oakland, CA.

Joseph, Lawrence. 1988. "Sand Nigger." Pp. 27–29 in *Curriculum Vitae*. Pittsburgh, PA: University of Pittsburgh Press.

Jung, Moon-Kie. 2006. *Reworking Race: The Making of Hawaii's Interracial Labor Movement*. New York: Columbia University Press.

Kahlenberg, Richard. 2001. "Learning from James Coleman." *Public Interest 144*: 54–72.

Kahn, Tulio. 2002. *Velha e nova polícia: Polícia e políticas de segurança pública no Brasil atual*. São Paulo: Editora Sicurezza.

Kalil, Ariel, Kristin S. Seefeldt, and Hui-chen Wang. 2002. "Sanctions and Material Hardship under TANF." *Social Service Review 76*(4): 643–62.

Kane, Eugene. 2006. "Violence Has No Color or Zip Code." *Milwaukee Journal Sentinel*, October 2. Retrieved December 26, 2007 (http://www.jsonline.com/story/index.aspx?id=507345).

Kant, Immanuel. 1960. *Observations on the Feeling of the Beautiful and the Sublime* (trans. John T. Goldthwaith). Berkeley: University of California Press.

———. 2000. "The Different Races of Mankind." Pp. 8–22 in *The Idea of Race*, ed. Tommy Lott and Robert Bernasconi. Indianapolis, IN: Hackett.

Kaplan, Amy. 2002. *The Anarchy of Empire in the Making of U.S. Culture*. Cambridge, MA: Harvard University Press.

Kaplan, Amy, and Donald E. Pease, eds. 1993. *Cultures of United States Imperialism*. Durham, NC: Duke University Press.

Karim, Karim H. 2000. *Islamic Peril: Media and Global Violence*. Montreal: Black Rose Books.

Karp, Stan. 2003. "Money, Schools, and Justice: State by State Battle for Funding Gets Mixed Results." *Rethinking Schools Online 18*: 1. Retrieved January 15, 2009 (http://www.rethinkingschools.org/archive/18_01/just181.shtml).

Katznelson, Ira. 2005. *When Affirmative Action Was White: An Untold History of Racial Inequality in Twentieth-Century America*. New York and London: Norton.

Kaufman-Osborn, Timothy V. 2006. "Capital Punishment as Legal Lynching?" Pp. 21–54 in *From Lynching Mobs to the Killing State*, ed. Charles Ogletree Jr. and Austin Sarat. New York: NYU Press.

Kazanjian, David. 2003. *The Colonizing Trick*. Minneapolis: University of Minnesota Press.

Keiser, Lael R., Peter Meuser, and Seung-Whan Choi. 2004. "Race, Bureaucratic Discretion, and the Implementation of Welfare Reform." *American Journal of Political Science 48*(2): 314–27.

Kelly, Paul. 2005. *Liberalism*. Malden, MA: Polity Press.

Kettl, Donald F. 2002. *The Transformation of Governance: Public Administration for Twenty-First Century America*. Baltimore: Johns Hopkins University Press.

———. 2005. *The Global Public Management Revolution: A Report on the Transformation of Governance*. Washington, DC: Brookings Institution Press.

Kettner, James H. 1978. *The Development of American Citizenship, 1608–1870*. Chapel Hill: University of North Carolina Press.

King, Joyce Elaine. 2005. *Black Education: A Transformative Research and Action Agenda for the New Century*. Mahwah, NJ: Lawrence Erlbaum.

KKK: The Next Generation. 2005. *Shock 1*: 46–51.

Klinker, Philip A., and Rogers M. Smith. 1999. *The Unsteady March: The Rise and Decline of Racial Equality in America*. Chicago: University of Chicago Press.

Kochman, Thomas. 1981. *Black and White: Styles in Conflict*. Chicago: University of Chicago Press.

Koralek, Robin. 2000. "South Carolina Family Independence Program Process Evaluation." Report to the South Carolina Department of Social Services. Urban Institute, Washington, DC.

Kousser, J. Morgan. 1999. *Colorblind Injustice: Minority Voting Rights and the Undoing of the Second Reconstruction*. Chapel Hill: University of North Carolina Press.

Kozol, Jonathan. 1991. *Savage Inequalities*. New York: HarperPerennial.

Kramer, Paul A. 2006. *The Blood of Government: Race, Empire, the United States, and the Philippines*. Chapel Hill: University of North Carolina Press.

Kuper, Leo. 1994. "Theoretical Issues Relating to Genocide: Uses and Abuses." Pp. 31–46 in *Genocide: Conceptual and Historical Dimensions*, ed. G. Andreopoulos. Philadelphia: University of Pennsylvania Press.

Kurland, Philip B., and Gerhard Casper, eds. 1975. *Landmark Briefs and Arguments of the Supreme Court of the United States: Constitutional Law*, Vol. 13. Arlington, VA: University Publications of America.

Kurshan, N. 1996. "Behind the Walls: The History and Current Reality of Women's Imprisonment." Pp. 136–64 in *Criminal Injustice*, ed. E. Rosenblatt. Boston: South End Press.

Kymlicka, Will. 1990. *Contemporary Political Philosophy: An Introduction*. Oxford, UK: Clarendon Press.

Ladson-Billings, Gloria. 1994. *The Dreamkeepers: Successful Teachers of African American Children*. San Francisco: Jossey-Bass.

Lake, Marilyn, and Henry Reynolds. 2008. *Drawing the Global Colour Line: White Men's Countries and the International Challenge of Racial Equality*. New York: Cambridge University Press.

Lakoff, George, and Mark Johnson. 1980. *Metaphors We Live By*. Chicago: University of Chicago Press.

Laqueur, Walter. 2001. *A History of Terrorism*. New Brunswick, NJ: Transaction.

Lareau, Annette, and Erin McNamara Horvat. 1999. "Moments of Social Inclusion and Exclusion: Race, Class, and Cultural Capital in Family-School Relationships." *Sociology of Education 72*: 37–53.

Lawrence, Charles, III, and Mari J. Matsuda. 1997. *We Won't Go Back: Making the Case for Affirmative Action.* New York: Houghton Mifflin.

Lee, Jaekyung. 2002. "Racial and Ethnic Achievement Gap Trends: Reversing the Progress Toward Equity?" *Educational Researcher 31*: 3–12.

Lee, Robert G. 1999. *Orientals: Asian Americans in Popular Culture.* Philadelphia: Temple University Press.

Lee, Yueh-Ting, Victor Ottati, and Imtiaz Hussain. 2001. "Attitudes Towards Illegal Immigration into the United States: California Proposition 187." *Hispanic Journal of Behavioral Sciences 23*(4): 430–43.

Leong, Russell C., and Don T. Nakanishi, eds. 2002. *Asian Americans on War and Peace.* Los Angeles: UCLA Asian American Studies Center Press.

Lessnoff, Michael. 1986. *Social Contract.* Atlantic Highlands, NJ: Humanities Press.

Levinson, Sanford. 2001. "Between the Foreign and the Domestic: The Doctrine of Territorial Incorporation, Invented and Reinvented." Pp. 121–39 in *Foreign in a Domestic Sense: Puerto Rico, American Expansion, and the Constitution,* ed. Christina Duffy Burnett and Burke Marshall. Durham, NC: Duke University Press.

Levinson, Sanford, and Bartholomew H. Sparrow, eds. 2005. *The Louisiana Purchase and American Expansion, 1803–1898.* Lanham, MD: Rowman & Littlefield.

Levoy, Jill. 2003. "The Untold Agony of Black-on-Black Murder." *Los Angeles Times,* January 26.

Lewis, Amanda E. 2003. *Race in the Schoolyard: Negotiating the Color Line in Classrooms and Communities.* New Brunswick, NJ: Rutgers University Press.

Lewis, Amanda E., Maria Krysan, Sharon M. Collins, Korie Edwards, and Geoff Ward. 2004. "Institutional Patterns and Transformations: Race and Ethnicity in Housing, Education, Labor Markets, Religion and Criminal Justice." Pp. 67–119 in *Changing Terrain of Race and Ethnicity,* ed. Marian Krysan and Amanda Lewis. New York: Russell Sage Foundation.

Lewis, Neil A. 2002. "FBI Issues Alert for 5 Illegal Immigrants Uncovered in Terrorist Investigation." *New York Times,* December 30.

Lieberman, Robert. 1998. *Shifting the Color Line: Race and the American Welfare State.* Cambridge, MA: Harvard University Press.

———. 2005. *Shaping Race Policy: The United States in Comparative Perspective.* Princeton, NJ: Princeton University Press.

Linchevski, Liora, and Bilha Kutscher. 1998. "Tell Me with Whom You're Learning, and I'll Tell You How Much You've Learned: Mixed-Ability Versus Same-Ability Grouping in Mathematics." *Journal for Research in Mathematics Education 29*(5): 533–54.

Lipsitz, George. 2006. *The Possessive Investment in Whiteness: How White People Profit from Identity Politics.* Philadelphia: Temple University Press.

Little, Douglas. 2002. *American Orientalism: The United States and the Middle East Since 1945.* Chapel Hill: University of North Carolina Press.

Litwack, Leon. 1979. *Been in the Storm so Long: The Aftermath of Slavery.* New York: Knopf.

———. 1998. *Trouble in Mind: Black Southerners in the Age of Jim Crow.* New York: Vintage Books.

Liu, Goodwin. 2006. "Interstate Inequality in Educational Opportunity." *New York University Law Review 81*: 2044–128.

Lobao, Linda. 2007. "The Local State, Decentralization, and Neoliberal Roll-Out: A Comparative, Subnational Analysis of Growth and Redistribution Responses." *Research in Political Sociology 16*: 85–118.

Locke, John. 1988. *Two Treatises of Government,* ed. Peter Laslett. New York: Cambridge University Press.

Lorde, Audre. 1984. *Sister Outsider: Essays and Speeches.* Berkeley, CA: Crossing Press.

———. 1997. "A Litany for Survival." Pp. 255–56 in *The Collected Poems of Audre Lorde.* New York: Norton. (originally published 1978 in *The Black Unicorn*)

Losen, Daniel, and Gary Orfield. 2002. *Racial Inequality in Special Education.* Cambridge, MA: Harvard Education Publishing Group.

Lowe, Lisa. 1991. *Critical Terrains: French and British Orientalisms.* Ithaca, NY: Cornell University Press.

———. 1996. *Immigrant Acts.* Durham, NC: Duke University Press.

Lowell, Abbott Lawrence. 1899a. "The Colonial Expansion of the United States." *Atlantic Monthly 83*(496): 145–54.

———. 1899b. "The Status of Our New Possessions: A Third View." *Harvard Law Review 13*(3): 155–76.

Lucas, Samuel R. 1999. *Tracking Inequality: Stratification and Mobility in American High Schools.* New York: Teachers College Press.

Lucas, Samuel R., and Mark Berends. 2007. "Race and Track Location in U.S. Public Schools." *Research in Social Stratification and Mobility 25*: 169–87.

Luibheid, Eithne. 2002. *Entry Denied: Controlling Sexuality at the Border.* Minneapolis: University of Minnesota Press.

MacKinnon, Catherine. 1987. *Feminism Unmodified.* Cambridge, MA: Harvard University Press.

———. 2002. "MacKinnon J Concurring with the Judgment." Pp. 143–57 in *What "Brown v. Board" Should Have Said,* ed. Jack Balkin. New York: NYU Press.

MacMillan, Donald L., Frank M. Gresham, Maria F. Lopez, and Kathleen M. Bocian. 1996. "Comparison of Students Nominated for Prereferral Interventions by Ethnicity and Gender." *Journal of Special Education 30*: 133–51.

Maggie, Yvonne, and Cláudia Barcellos Rezende, eds. 2002. *Raça como retórica: a construção da diferença*. Rio de Janeiro: Civilização Brasileira.

Maira, Sunaina. 2007. "Deporting Radicals, Deporting La Migra: The Hayat Case in Lodi." *Cultural Dynamics* 19(1): 39–66.

Majul, Cesar Adib. 1985. *The Contemporary Muslim Movement in the Philippines*. Berkeley, CA: Mizan Press.

Mancuso, David, and Vanessa L. Lindler. 2001. "Examining the Circumstances of Welfare Leavers and Sanctioned Families in Sonoma County [CA], Final Report." Burlingame, CA: SPHERE Institute.

Marable, Manning. 2000 [1983]. *How Capitalism Underdeveloped Black America*. Cambridge, MA: South End Press.

Maracle, Lee. 1988. *I Am Woman*. North Vancouver, BC: Write-On Press.

Marx, Anthony. 2003. *Making Race and Nation: A Comparison of the United States, South Africa, and Brazil*. Cambridge, UK: Cambridge University Press.

Massey, Douglas S., and Nancy A. Denton. 1993. *American Apartheid: Segregation and the Making of the Underclass*. Cambridge, MA: Harvard University Press.

Massey, Douglas S., Jorge Durand, and Nolan J. Malone. 2002. *Beyond Smoke and Mirrors: Mexican Immigration in an Era of Economic Integration*. New York: Russell Sage Foundation.

Mayer, Jane. 2007. "The Black Sites: A Rare Look Inside the C.I.A.'s Secret Interrogation Program." *New Yorker*, August 13 (http://www.newyorker.com/reporting/2007/08/13/070813fa_fact_mayer).

Mbembe, Achille. 2003. "Necropolitics." *Public Culture* 15(1): 11–40.

McAlister, Melani. 2005. *Epic Encounters: Culture, Media, and U.S. Interests in the Middle East Since 1945* (updated ed.). Berkeley: University of California Press.

McBride, Jessica. 2000. "Using Newspaper Deviance Frameworks to Predict Homicide Newsworthiness in Television News." Master's thesis. Department of Mass Communications, University of Wisconsin, Madison.

McCarthy, Thomas. 2002. "*Vergangenheitsbewältigung* in the USA: On the Politics of the Memory of Slavery," Part 1. *Political Theory* 30(5)(October): 623–48.

———. 2004. "Coming to Terms with Our Past: On the Morality and Politics of Reparations for Slavery," Part 2. *Political Theory* 32(6)(December): 750–72.

McKinney, Karyn D., and Joe R. Feagin. 2003. "Diverse Perspectives on Doing Antiracism: The Younger Generation." Pp. 233–53 in *Whiteout: The Continuing Significance of Racism*, ed. Ashley W. Doane and Eduardo Bonilla-Silva. New York: Routledge.

McWilliams, Carey. 1990. *North from Mexico: The Spanish Speaking People of the United States*. New York: Greenwood Press.

Mead, Lawrence M. 1997. *The New Paternalism: Supervisory Approaches to Poverty*. Washington, DC: Brookings Institution Press.

————. 2005. *Government Matters: Welfare Reform in Wisconsin*. Princeton, NJ: Princeton University Press.

Meier, Kenneth J., Joseph Stewart Jr., and Robert E. England. 1989. *Race, Class and Education: The Politics of Second Generation Discrimination*. Madison: University of Wisconsin Press.

Meinig, D. W. 1993. *The Shaping of America: A Geographical Perspective on 500 Years of History*, Vol. 2. New Haven, CT: Yale University Press.

Mendelberg, Tali. 2001. *The Race Card: Campaign Strategy, Implicit Messages, and the Norm of Equality*. Princeton, NJ: Princeton University Press.

Menifield, Charles, Anita K. Brewer, Winfield Rose, and John Homa. 2001. "The Media's Portrayal of Urban and Rural School Violence: A Preliminary Analysis." *Deviant Behavior 22*: 447–64.

Merry, Sally Engle. 2000. *Colonizing Hawai'i: The Cultural Power of Law*. Princeton, NJ: Princeton University Press.

Metzl, Jonathan. 2010. *The Protest Psychosis: How Schizophrenia Became a Black Disease*. Boston: Beacon Press.

Meyers, Marcia, Shannon Harper, Marieka Klawitter, and Taryn Lindhorst. 2006. "Review of Research on TANF Sanctions: Report to Washington State WorkFirst SubCabinet." West Coast Poverty Center, University of Washington.

Mickelson, Roslyn Arlin. 1990. "The Attitude-Achievement Paradox Among Black Adolescents." *Sociology of Education 63*: 44–61.

————. 2001. "Subverting Swann: First and Second-Generation Segregation in the Charlotte-Mecklenburg Schools." *American Educational Research Journal 38*: 215–52.

————. 2003. "When Are Racial Disparities in Education the Result of Racial Discrimination? A Social Science Perspective." *Teachers College Record 105*(6): 1052–86.

Miller, Randall M. 1999. "Introduction." Pp. xiii-xxxii in *The Freedmen's Bureau and Reconstruction: Reconsiderations*, ed. Paul A. Cimbala and Randall M. Miller. New York: Fordham University Press.

Miller, Robert J. 2008. *Native America, Discovered and Conquered: Thomas Jefferson, Lewis and Clark, and Manifest Destiny*. Lincoln: University of Nebraska Press.

Miller, Stuart Creighton. 1982. *"Benevolent Assimilation": The American Conquest of the Philippines, 1899–1903*. New Haven, CT: Yale University Press, 1982.

Miller, Teresa. 2005. "Immigration Law and Human Rights: Legal Line Drawing Post-September 11: Symposium Article: Blurring the Boundaries Between Immigration and Crime Control After September 11th." *Boston Third World Law Journal*, pp. 81–123.

Mills, Charles. 1997. *The Racial Contract*. Ithaca, NY: Cornell University Press.

————. 2005. "Kant's Untermenschen." Pp. 169–93 in *Race and Racism in Modern Philosophy*, ed. Andrew Valls. Ithaca, NY: Cornell University Press.

Milovanovic, Dragan, and Katheryn Russell, eds. 2001. *Petit Apartheid in the U.S. Criminal Justice System: The Dark Figure of Racism.* Durham, NC: Carolina Academic Press.

Milward, H. Brinton, and Keith G. Provan. 2003. "Managing the Hollow State: Collaboration and Contracting." *Public Management Review* 5(1): 1–18.

Mitchell, Michael, and Charles Wood. 1998. "Ironies of Citizenship: Skin Color, Police Brutality, and the Challenge to Democracy in Brazil." *Social Forces* 77(3): 1001–1020.

Montejano, David. 1987. *Anglos and Mexicans in the Making of Texas, 1836–1986.* Austin: University of Texas Press.

Montesquieu, Chales de Secondat. 1989. *The Spirit of the Laws* (trans. Anne M. Choler, Basia Carolyn Miller, and Harold Samuel Stone). New York: Cambridge University Press.

Monture-Angus, Patricia. 1999. *Journeying Forward.* Halifax, NS: Fernwood.

Moore, Kathleen M. 1995. *Al-Mughtaribun: American Law and the Transformation of Muslim Life in the United States.* Albany, NY: SUNY Press.

Moore, Mark H. 2003. "Deadly Lessons: Understanding Lethal School Violence." Washington, DC: National Academic Press.

Morantz, Alison. 1996. "Money and Choice in Kansas City: Major Investments with Modest Returns." Pp. 241–64 in *Dismantling Desegregation,* ed. Gary Orfield, Susan E. Eaton, and the Harvard Project on School Desegregation. New York: New Press.

Morgen, Sandra. 2001. "The Agency of Welfare Workers: Negotiating Devolution, Privatization, and the Meaning of Self-Sufficiency." *American Anthropologist* 103(3): 747–61.

Morris, Edward. 2005. *An Unexpected Minority: White Students in an Urban School.* New Brunswick, NJ: Rutgers University Press.

Mullings, Leith. 2005. "Interrogating Racism: Toward an Antiracist Anthropology." *Annual Review of Anthropology* 34: 667–93.

Murnane, Richard T., and Jennifer Steele. 2007. "What Is the Problem? The Challenge of Providing Effective Teachers for All Children." *Future of Children* 17: 15–43.

Murphy, Erin. 2009. "Women's Anti-Imperialism, 'The White Man's Burden,' and the Philippine-American War: Theorizing Masculinist Ambivalence in Protest." *Gender and Society* 23(2): 244–70.

Muthu, Sankar. 2003. *Enlightenment Against Empire.* Princeton, NJ: Princeton University Press.

Myrdal, Gunnar. 2003 [1944]. *An American Dilemma: The Negro Problem and Modern Democracy* (2 vols.). New Brunswick, NJ: Transaction.

Naber, Nadine C. 2000. "Ambiguous Insiders: An Investigation of Arab American Invisibility." *Ethnic and Racial Studies* 23(1): 37–61.

Nascimento, Abdias do. 1989. *Brazil: Mixture or Massacre?* Dover, MA: Majority Press.

National Commission on Terrorist Attacks upon the United States. 2004. *The 9/11 Commission Report: Final Report of the National Commission on Terrorist Attacks upon the United States.* New York: Norton.

National Network for Election Reform. 2007. "Deceptive Practices and Voter Intimida-tion." Retrieved February 20, 2009 (http://www.nationalcampaignforfairelections.org/page-/Deceptive%20Practices%20Network%20Issue%20Paper.pdf).

National Resource Center on Domestic Violence. 2002. "General Domestic Violence Statistics Packet." Harrisburg, PA: National Resource Center on Domestic Violence.

Native American Women's Health Education Resource Center. 1990. "Discrimination and the Double Whammy." Lake Andes, SD.

Nettles, Michael T., and L. W. Perna. 1997. *The African American Education Data Book.* Fairfax, VA: Frederick D. Patterson Research Institute.

Nevins, Joseph. 2002. *Operation Gatekeeper: The Rise of the "Illegal Alien" and the Making of the U.S.-Mexico Boundary.* New York: Routledge.

Newcomb, Steven T. 2008. *Pagans in the Promised Land: Decoding the Doctrine of Christian Discovery.* Golden, CO: Fulcrum.

Newman, Nathan, and J. J. Gass. 2004. *A New Birth of Freedom: The Forgotten History of the 13th, 14th, and 15th Amendments.* New York: Brennan Center for Justice, NYU School of Law.

Ngai, Mae M. 2004. *Impossible Subjects: Illegal Aliens and the Making of Modern America.* Princeton, NJ: Princeton University Press.

Nieto, Sonia. 2001. *Language, Culture, and Teaching: Critical Perspectives for a New Century.* Lawrence Erlbaum.

Nobles, Gregory H. 1997. *American Frontiers: Cultural Encounters and Continental Conquest.* New York: Hill and Wang.

Noguera, Pedro A., and Jean Yonemura Wing. 2006. *Unfinished Business: Closing the Racial Achievement Gap in Our Schools.* San Francisco: Jossey-Bass.

Oakes, Jeannie. 2003. Presentation at conference, Colorblind Racism: The Politics of Controlling Racial and Ethnic Data, Stanford University, Palo Alto, CA, October 3.

———. 2005. *Keeping Track: How Schools Structure Inequality* (2nd ed.). New Haven, CT: Yale University Press.

Oakes, Jeannie, and Gretchen Guiton. 1995. "Matchmaking: The Dynamics of High School Tracking Decisions." *American Educational Research Journal 32*(1): 3–33.

O'Brien, Sharon. 1989. *American Indian Tribal Governments.* Norman: University of Oklahoma Press.

O'Connor, Carla. 2001. "Making Sense of the Complexity of Social Identity in Relation to Achievement: A Sociological Challenge in the New Millennium." *Sociology of Education 74*(Extra Issue): 159–68.

O'Connor, Carla, Amanda E. Lewis, and J. Mueller. (2007). "Researching African-American's Educational Experiences: Theoretical and Practical Considerations." *Educational Researcher 36*: 541–52.

Ogbu, John. 1978. *Minority Education and Caste: The American System in Cross-Cultural Perspective.* New York: Academic Press.

———. 2003. *Black Americans Students in an Affluent Suburb: A Study of Academic Disengagement.* Mahwah, NJ: Lawrence Erlbaum.

Ogle, Robin S. 1999. "Prison Privatization: An Environmental Catch-22." *Justice Quarterly 16*(3): 579–600.

Ogletree, Charles. 2004. *All Deliberate Speed: Reflections on the First Half Century of Brown v. Board of Education.* New York and London: Norton.

Ogletree, Charles, and Austin Sarat, eds. 2006. *From Lynching Mobs to the Killing State.* New York: NYU Press.

Oliveira, Flávia. 2004. "Desigualdade Morro Acima." *O Globo,* May 10. (http://oglobo .globo.com/online/default.asp).

Oliver, Melvin, and Thomas Shapiro. 1995. *Black Wealth/White Wealth: A New Perspective on Racial Inequality.* New York: Routledge.

Olson, Joel. 2004. The Abolition of White Supremacy. Minneapolis: University of Minnesota Press.

Omi, Michael, and Howard Winant. 1986. *Racial Formation in the United States: From the 1960s to the 1980s* (1st ed.). New York: Routledge.

———. 1994. *Racial Formation in the United States: From the 1960s to the 1990s* (2nd ed.). New York: Routledge.

Orfield, Gary. 1993. "School Desegregation After Two Generations: Race, Schools, and Opportunity in Urban Society." Pp. 234–62 in *Race in America: The Struggle for Equality,* ed. Herbert Hill and James E. Jones Jr. Madison: University of Wisconsin Press.

———. 1996a. "Unexpected Costs and Uncertain Gains of Dismantling Desegregation." Pp. 73–114 in *Dismantling Desegregation,* ed. Gary Orfield, Susan E. Eaton, and the Harvard Project on School Desegregation. New York: New Press.

———. 1996b. "Segregated Housing and School Resegregation." Pp. 291–330 in *Dismantling Desegregation,* ed. Gary Orfield, Susan E, Eaton, and the Harvard Project on School Desegregation. New York: New Press.

Orfield, Gary, and Susan Eaton. 1997. *Dismantling Desegregation: The Quiet Reversal of Brown v. Board of Education.* New York: New Press.

Orfield, Gary, and Nora Gordon. 2001. *Schools More Separate: Consequences of a Decade of Resegregation.* Cambridge, MA: Civil Rights Project, Harvard University.

Orfield, Gary, and Chungmei Lee. 2005. *Why Segregation Matters: Poverty and Educational Inequality.* Cambridge, MA: Civil Rights Project, Harvard University.

Orfield, Gary, and John T Yun. 1999. *Resegregation in American Schools.* Cambridge, MA: Civil Rights Project, Harvard University.

Osorio, Jon Kamakawiwoʻole. 2002. *Dismembering Lāhui: A History of the Hawaiian Nation to 1887.* Honolulu: University of Hawaiʻi Press.

Ostrowski, Julie. 2004. "Race Versus Gender in the Court Room." *Africana.com, May 4.* (http://www.africana.com/articles/daily/bw20040504domestic.asp).

Paixão, Luiz Antonio. 1995. "O Problema da Polícia." In *Violência e Participação Política no Rio de Janeiro*. Rio de Janeiro: IUPERJ, Série Estudos No. 91.

Pateman, Carole. 1988. *The Sexual Contract*. Stanford, CA: Stanford University Press.

Pateman, Carole, and Charles W. Mills. 2007. *Contract and Domination*. Malden, MA: Polity Press.

Patterson, James T. 2001. *Brown v. Board of Education: A Civil Rights Milestone and Its Troubled Legacy*. New York: Oxford University Press.

Patterson, Tiffany Ruby, and Robin D.G. Kelley. 2000. "Unfinished Migrations: Reflections on the African Diaspora and the Making of the Modern World." *African Studies Review 43*(1): 11–45.

Patterson, William, et. al. 1951. *We Charge Genocide: The Historic Petition to the United Nations for Relief from a Crime of the United States Government Against the Negro People*. New York: Civil Rights Congress.

Pavetti, LaDonna, Michelle K. Derr, and Heather Hesketh. 2003. "Review of Sanction Policies and Research Studies: Final Literature Review." Report prepared for Office of the Assistant Secretary for Planning and Evaluation, Mathematica Policy Research, Washington, DC.

Pavetti, LaDonna, Kathleen A. Maloy, Peter Shin, Julie Darnell, and Lea Scarpulla-Nolan. 1998. "A Description and Assessment of State Approaches to Diversion Programs and Activities Under Welfare Reform." Report prepared for Office of the Assistant Secretary for Planning and Evaluation, Mathematica Policy Research, Washington, DC.

Pavetti, LaDonna A., Michelle K. Derr, Gretchen Kirby, Robert G. Wood, and Melissa A. Clark. 2004. "The Use of TANF Work-Oriented Sanctions in Illinois, New Jersey, and South Carolina: Final Report." Report to the U.S. Department of Health and Human Services, Office of the Assistant Secretary for Planning and Evaluation (contract no. 100-01-0011). Mathematica Policy Research, Washington, DC.

Peck, Jamie. 2002. "Political Economies of Scale: Fast Policy, Interscalar Relations, and Neoliberal Workfare." *Economic Geography 78*(3): 331–60.

Peirce, Paul Skeels. 1970 [1904]. *The Freedmen's Bureau: A Chapter in the History of Reconstruction*. Iowa City: University of Iowa.

Perea, Juan F. 2001. "Fulfilling Manifest Destiny: Conquest, Race, and the Insular Cases." Pp. 140–66 in *Foreign in a Domestic Sense: Puerto Rico, American Expansion, and the Constitution*, ed. Christina Duffy Burnett and Burke Marshall. Durham, NC: Duke University Press.

Perez, Becky, Russell J. Skiba, and Choong-Geun Chung. 2008. "Latino Students and Disproportionality in Special Education." *Education Policy Brief 6*: 1–8.

Perry, Teresa, Claude Steele, and Asa Hilliard III. 2004. *Young, Gifted and Black: Promoting High Achievement Among African-American Students*. Boston: Beacon Press.

Petry, Sabrina. 2001. "Morro Carioca cria condomínio-favela." *Folha de S.Paulo*, July 25, p. C1.

Pettit, Philip. 2007. "Analytical Philosophy." Pp. 7–38 in *A Companion to Contemporary Political Philosophy*, Vol. 1 (2nd ed.), ed. Robert E. Goodin, Philip Pettit, and Thomas Pogge. Malden, MA: Blackwell.

Philips, Susan U. 1972. "Participant Structures and Communicative Competence: Warm Springs Children in Community and Classroom." Pp. 370–94 in *Functions of Language in the Classroom*, ed. C. Cazden, V. John, and D. Hymes. Prospect Heights, IL: Waveland Press.

Pitts, Jennifer. 2005. *A Turn to Empire: The Rise of Imperial Liberalism in Britain and France*. Princeton, NJ: Princeton University Press.

Piven, Frances Fox. 1981. "Deviant Behavior and the Remaking of the World." *Social Problems* 28(5): 489–508.

———. 2003. "Why Welfare Is Racist." Pp. 323–36 in *Race and the Politics of Welfare Reform*, ed. Sanford F. Schram, Joe Soss, and Richard C. Fording. Ann Arbor: University of Michigan Press.

Piven, Frances Fox, and Richard A. Cloward. 1993. *Regulating the Poor: The Functions of Public Welfare* (updated ed.). New York: Vintage.

———. 1998. *The Breaking of the American Social Compact*. New York: New Press.

Pochmann, Marcio. 2005. "Gasto Social e distribuição de renda no Brasil." *Jornal da Unicamp* (May): 2.

Pomeroy, William. 1967. "'Pacification' in the Philippines, 1898–1913." *France-Asie/Asia* (1967): 427–46.

Povinelli, Elizabeth. 2002. *The Cunning of Recognition*. Durham, NC: Duke University Press.

Przybyszewky, Linda. 1999. *The Republic According to John Marshall Harlan*. Chapel Hill: University of North Carolina Press.

Puar, Jasbir K. 2007. *Terrorist Assemblages: Homonationalism in Queer Times*. Durham, NC: Duke University Press.

Quadagno, Jill. 1994. *The Color of Welfare: How Racism Undermined the War on Poverty*. New York: Oxford University Press.

Ramos, Efrén Rivera. 2001. "Deconstructing Colonialism: The 'Unincorporated Territory' as a Category of Domination." Pp. 104–17 in *Foreign in a Domestic Sense: Puerto Rico, American Expansion, and the Constitution*, ed. Christina Duffy Burnett and Burke Marshall. Durham, NC: Duke University Press.

———. 2005. "Puerto Rico's Political Status: The Long-Term Effects of American Expansionist Discourse." Pp. 165–80 in *The Louisiana Purchase and American Expansion, 1803–1898*, ed. Sanford Levinson and Bartholomew H. Sparrow. Lanham, MD: Rowman & Littlefield.

Rana, Junaid. 2007. "The Story of Islamophobia." *Souls: A Critical Journal of Black Politics, Culture, and Society* 9(2): 148–61.

Rashid, Ahmed. 2001. *Taliban: Militant Islam, Oil, and Fundamentalism in Central Asia.* New Haven, CT: Yale University Press.

Raskin, Jamin B. 2003. *Overruling Democracy: The Supreme Court vs. The American People.* New York and London: Routledge.

Rawls, John. 1971. *A Theory of Justice.* Cambridge, MA: Harvard University Press.

Razack, Sherene. 2007. *Casting Out: The Eviction of Muslims from Western Law and Politics.* Toronto: University of Toronto Press.

Rector, Robert E., and Sarah E. Youssef. 1999. "The Determinants of Welfare Caseload Decline." Report no. 99-04. Washington, DC: Heritage Foundation.

Reddy, Chandan. 2005. "Asian Diasporas, Neoliberalism, and Family: Reviewing the Case for Homosexual Asylum in the Context of Family Rights." *Social Text 84–85*(3–4): 101–19.

Reid, Stephanie, and Anna Varela. 2006. "Principal Threatens Deportation: Educator Steps Down After Singling Out Latino Students." *Atlanta Journal Constitution,* November 11. Retrieved February 20, 2009 (http://www.freerepublic.com/focus/f-news/1736818/posts).

Revised Laws of Louisiana. Containing the Revised Statutes of the State (Official Edition, 1870) as Amended by Acts of the Legislature, from the Session of 1870 to that of 1896 Inclusive, and All Other Acts of a General Nature for the Same Period (compiled and annotated by Solomon Wolff). 1897. New Orleans, LA: F.F. Hansell.

Reyes, Augustina H. 2006. *Discipline, Achievement, and Race: Is Zero Tolerance the Answer?* Lanham, MD: Rowman & Littlefield Education.

Richie, Beth. 2000. "Plenary presentation." P. 124 in *The Color of Violence: Violence Against Women of Color.* Incite! Women of Color Against Violence, University of California, Santa Cruz.

Risen, James. 2003. "The Suspect: Tied to Many Plots, an Elusive Figure Who Came to US Attention Late." *New York Times,* March 2, p. 10.

Rist, Ray C. 1970. "Student Social Class and Teacher Expectations: The Self-Fulfilling Prophecy in Ghetto Education." *Harvard Educational Review 40:* 72–73.

Roberts, Dorothy. 1997. *Killing the Black Body: Race, Reproduction, and the Meaning of Liberty.* New York: Vintage.

———. 2002. *Shattered Bonds: The Color of Child Welfare.* New York: Basic Books.

Roberts, John. 2007. "Opinion of Roberts, C.J. 551, U.S.," 2007 Supreme Court of the United States, Nos. 05–908 and 05–915, *Parents Involved in Community Schools v. Seattle School District No.1 et al.*

Roberts, Rodney C. 2002. "Introduction." In *Injustice and Rectification,* ed. Rodney C. Roberts. New York: Peter Lang.

Robertson, Lindsay G. 2005. *Conquest by Law: How the Discovery of America Dispossessed Indigenous Peoples of Their Lands.* New York: Oxford University Press.

Robinson, Cedric J. 2000 [1983]. *Black Marxism: The Making of the Black Radical Tradition.* Chapel Hill: University of North Carolina Press.

Rodríguez, Dylan. 2006. *Forced Passages: Imprisoned Radical Intellectuals and the U.S. Prison Regime.* Minneapolis: University of Minnesota Press.

Roediger, David R. 1994. *Toward the Abolition of Whiteness.* New York: Verso.

Román, Ediberto. 1998. "The Alien-Citizen Paradox and Other Consequences of U.S. Colonialism." *Florida State University Law Review 26*(1): 1–47.

Romero, Mary. 2006. "Racial Profiling and Immigration Law Enforcement: Rounding Up of Usual Suspects in the Latino Community." *Critical Sociology 32*(2–3): 449–75.

———. 2007. "Class Struggle and Resistance Against the Transformation of Land Ownership and Usage in Northern New Mexico: The Case of Las Gorras Blancas." *La Raza and the UCLA Chicano/Latino Law Review 26*: 87–110.

———. 2008. "'Go After the Women': Mothers Against Illegal Aliens' (MAIA) Campaign Against Mexican Immigrant Women and Their Children." Symposium Latinos and Latinas at the Epicenter of Contemporary Legal Discourses. *Indiana Law Journal 83*(4): 1355–89.

Rosaldo, Renato. 1997. "Cultural Citizenship, Inequality, and Multiculturalism." Pp. 27–38 in *Latino Cultural Citizenship: Claiming Identify, Space, and Rights,* ed. William V. Flores and Rina Benmayor. Boston: Beacon Press.

Roscigno, Vincent J., and James W. Ainsworth-Darnell. 1999. "Race, Cultural Capital, and Educational Resources: Persistent Inequalities and Achievement Returns." *Sociology of Education 72*: 158–78.

Ross, Luana. 1998. *Inventing the Savage: The Social Construction of Native American Criminality.* Austin: University of Texas Press.

Rothstein, Richard. 2001. "How the U.S. Tax Code Worsens the Education Gap." *New York Times,* April 25, p. A17.

Rousseau, Jean-Jacques. 1968. *The Social Contract* (trans. Maurice Cranston). New York: Penguin Books.

———. 1997. *The "Discourses" and Other Early Political Writings,* ed. and trans. Victor Gourevitch. New York: Cambridge University Press.

Rubin, Gayle. 1984. "Thinking Sex: Notes for a Radical Theory of the Politics of Sexuality." Pp. 267–319 in *Pleasure and Danger: Exploring Female Sexuality,* ed. C. S. Vance. Boston: Routledge & K. Paul.

Rubio-Goldsmith, Raquel, M. Melissa McCormick, Daniel Martinez, and Inez Magdalena Duarte. 2006. "The 'Funnel Effect' and Recovered Bodies of Unauthorized Migrants Processed by the Pima County Office of the Medical Examiner, 1990–2005." Binational Migration Institute, Mexican American Studies & Research Center, University of Arizona.

Russell, Katheryn K. 1997. *The Color of Crime: Racial Hoaxes, White Fear, Black Protectionism, Police Harassment and Other Macroaggressions.* New York: NYU Press.

Sahagun, Louis. 1997. "Civil Rights, Immigration Sweep Stirs Cloud of Controversy; Residents Sue Arizona Town, Saying Crackdown on Illegal Worker Led to Harassment of U.S. Citizens." *Los Angeles Times*, September 1, p. A5.

Said, Edward W. 1978. *Orientalism*. New York: Vintage.

———. 1993. *Culture and Imperialism*. New York: Vintage.

Sala-Molins, Louis. 2006. *Dark Side of the Light: Slavery and the French Enlightenment* (trans. John Conteh-Morgan). Minneapolis: University of Minnesota Press.

Salamon, Lester M. 2002. *The Tools of Government: A Guide to the New Governance*. New York: Oxford University Press.

Santa Ana, Otto. 2002. *Brown Tide Rising: Metaphors of Latinos in Contemporary American Public Discourse*. Austin: University of Texas Press.

Santora, Marc. 2003. "A Boyhood on the Mean Streets of a Wealthy Emirate." *New York Times*, March 3.

Saporito, Salvatore, and Annette Lareau. 1999. "School Selection as a Process: The Multiple Dimensions of Race in Framing Educational Choice." *Social Problems* 46(3): 418–39.

Sartre, Jean-Paul. 1968 [1961]. "Preface." Pp. 7–31 in Frantz Fanon, *The Wretched of the Earth* (trans. Constance Farrington). New York: Grove Weidenfeld.

Sassen, Saskia. 2006. *Territory, Authority, Rights: From Medieval to Global Assemblages*. Princeton, NJ: Princeton University Press.

Schirmer, Daniel. 1972. *Republic or Empire*. Cambridge, MA: Schenkman Books.

Schram, Sanford F. 2006. *Welfare Discipline: Discourse, Governance, and Globalization*. Philadelphia: Temple University Press.

Schueller, Malini Johar. 1998. *U.S. Orientalisms: Race, Nation, and Gender in Literature, 1790–1890*. Ann Arbor: University of Michigan Press.

Schuman, Howard, Charlotte Steeh, Lawrence Bobo, and Maria Krysan. 1997. *Racial Attitudes in America: Trends and Interpretations*. Cambridge, MA: Harvard University Press.

Scott, James C. 1998. *Seeing Like a State: How Certain Schemes to Improve the Human Condition Have Failed*. New Haven, CT: Yale University Press.

Sexton, Jared. 2010. "'The Curtain of the Sky': An Introduction." *Critical Sociology* 36(1): 1–14.

Shaban, Fuad. 1991. *Islam and Arabs in Early American Thought: Roots of Orientalism in America*. Durham, NC: Acorn Press.

Shapiro, Thomas M. 2004. *The Hidden Cost of Being African American: How Wealth Perpetuates Inequality*. New York: Oxford University Press.

Shaw, Angel, and Luis Francia, eds. 2002. *Vestiges of War*. New York: NYU Press.

Shaw, Kathleen, Sara Goldrick-Rab, Christopher Mazzeo, and Jerry A. Jacobs. 2006. *Putting Poor People to Work: How the Work-First Idea Eroded College Access for the Poor*. New York: Russell Sage Foundation.

Shaw, Theodore M. 2001. "Equality and Educational Excellence: Legal Challenges in the

1990s." Pp. 257–68 in *Pursuit of a Dream Deferred: Linking Housing and Education Policy*, ed. john a. powell, Gavin Kearney, and Vina Kay. New York: Peter Lang.

Sheper-Hughes, Nancy. 2002. "Coming to Our Senses: Anthropology and Genocide." Pp. 348–81 in *Annihilating Difference: The Anthropology of Genocide*, ed. A. L. Hinton. Berkeley: University of California Press.

Skiba, Russell J., and Peter E. Leone. 2002. "Profiled and Punished: How San Diego Schools Undermine Latino and African American Student Achievement." Oakland, CA: ERASE Initiative.

Skiba, Russell J., Robert S. Michael, Abra Carroll Nardo, and Reece L. Peterson. 2002. "The Color of Discipline: Sources of Racial and Gender Disproportionality in School Punishment." *Urban Review 34*: 317–42.

Skiba, Russell J., Ada B. Simmons, Shana Ritter, Ashley C. Gibb, M. Karega Rausch, Jason Cuadrado, and Choong-Geun Chung. 2008. "Achieving Equity in Special Education: History, Status, and Current Challenges." *Exceptional Children 74*: 264–88.

Slavin, Robert. 1990. "Ability Grouping in Secondary Schools: A Best-Evidence Synthesis." *Review of Educational Research 60*: 471–99.

Smith, Andrea. 2005. *Conquest: Sexual Violence and American Indian Genocide*. Cambridge, MA: South End Press.

———. 2008. *Native Americans and the Christian Right: The Gendered Politics of Unlikely Alliances*. Durham, NC: Duke University Press.

Smith, Dorothy E. 1990. *Texts, Facts, and Femininity: Exploring the Relations of Ruling*. New York: Routledge.

———. 1999. *Writing the Social: Critique, Theory, and Investigations*. Toronto: University of Toronto Press.

Smith, Robert C. 1995. *Racism in the Post-Civil Rights Era: Now You See It, Now You Don't*. Albany, NY: SUNY Press.

Smith, Rogers M. 1997. *Civic Ideals: Conflicting Visions of Citizenship in U.S. History*. New Haven, CT: Yale University Press.

———. 2001. "The Bitter Roots of Puerto Rican Citizenship." Pp. 373–88 in *Foreign in a Domestic Sense: Puerto Rico, American Expansion, and the Constitution*, ed. Christina Duffy Burnett and Burke Marshall. Durham, NC: Duke University Press.

Smith, Steven Rathgeb. 2002. "Privatization, Devolution and the Welfare State: Rethinking the Prevailing Wisdom." Pp. 78–101 in *Contemporary Challenges of Modern Welfare States: Political Institutions and Policy Change*, ed. B. Rothstein and S. Steinmo. New York: Palgrave MacMillan.

Smith, William A., Walter R. Allen, and Lynette Danley. 2007. "'Assume the Position . . . You Fit the Description': Psychosocial Experiences and Racial Battle Fatigue Among African American Male College Students." *American Behavioral Scientist 51*(4): 551–78.

Sokoloff, Natalie, ed. 2005. *Domestic Violence at the Margins*. New Brunswick, NJ: Rutgers University Press.

Somers, Margaret, and Fred Block. 2005. "From Poverty to Perversity: Ideas, Markets, and Institutions over 200 Years of Welfare Debate." *American Sociological Review* 70(2): 260–87.

Sorenson, Aage B., and Maureen Hallinan. 1986. "Effects of Ability Grouping on Growth in Academic Achievement." *American Educational Research Journal* 23(4): 519–42.

Soss, Joe, Richard C. Fording, and Sanford F. Schram. 2008. "The Color of Devolution: Race, Federalism, and the Politics of Social Control. *American Journal of Political Science* 52(3): 536–53.

Soss, Joe, and Sanford F. Schram. 2007. "A Public Transformed? Welfare Reform as Policy Feedback." *American Political Science Review* 101(1): 111–27.

Soss, Joe, Sanford F. Schram, Thomas Vartanian, and Erin O'Brien. 2001. "Setting the Terms of Relief: Explaining State Policy Choices in the Devolution Revolution." *American Journal of Political Science* 45(2): 378–95.

Souter, David. 1995. "J. dissenting," *Missouri v. Jenkins*, U.S. (1995), *Missouri et al., Petitioners v. Kalima Jenkins et al.*, Certiorari to the United States Court of Appeals for the Eighth Circuit No. 93–1821.

Sparrow, Bartholomew H. 2006. *The Insular Cases and the Emergence of American Empire.* Lawrence: University Press of Kansas.

St. John, Craig, and Nancy A. Bates. 1990. "Racial Composition and Neighborhood Evaluation," *Social Science Research 19(1): 47–61.*

Steele, Claude. 1997. "A Threat in the Air: How Stereotypes Shape Intellectual Identity and Performance." *American Psychologist 53*: 680–81.

Steele, Claude, and Joshua Aronson. 1998. "Stereotype Threat and the Test Performance of Academically Successful African Americans." Pp. 401–30 in *Black-White Test Score Gap*, ed. C. Jencks and M. Phillips. Washington, DC: Brookings Institution Press

Steinmetz, George. 2005. "Return to Empire: The New U.S. Imperialism in Comparative Historical Perspective." *Sociological Theory* 23(4): 339–67.

———. 2006. "Imperialism or Colonialism? From Windhoek to Washington, by Way of Basra." Pp. 135–56 in *Lessons of Empire: Imperial Histories and American Power*, ed. Craig Calhoun, Frederick Cooper, and Kevin W. Moore. New York: New Press.

———. 2008. "The Colonial State as a Social Field: Ethnographic Capital and Native Policy in the German Overseas Empire Before 1914." *American Sociological Review* 73(4): 589–612.

Stoler, Ann Laura. 2006. "On Degrees of Imperial Sovereignty." *Public Culture* 18(1): 125–46.

Strang, Heather, and John Braithwaite, eds. 2002. *Restorative Justice and Family Violence.* Cambridge, UK: Cambridge University Press.

Street, Paul. 2005. "Separate, Unequal: Race, Place, Policy, and the State of African American Chicago." Retrieved March 27, 2009 (http://www.blackcommentator.com /144/144_street_chicago.html).

Sugrue, Thomas. 1996. *The Origins of the Urban Crisis: Race and Inequality in Post-War Detroit.* Princeton, NJ: Princeton University Press.

Sullivan, Roger J. 1989. *Immanuel Kant's Moral Theory.* New York: Cambridge University Press.

Sykes, Leonard. 2002. "'Alexis' Family Gets National Notice at Black Journalists' Convention." *Milwaukee Journal Sentinel,* August 22. Retrieved December 28, 2007 (http://www.highbeam.com/doc/1P2-6115313.html).

Takaki, Ronald T. 1989. *Strangers from a Different Shore: A History of Asian Americans.* Boston: Little, Brown.

Taub, R. D., D. G. Taylor, and J. A. Dunham. 1984. *Paths of Neighborhood Change: Race and Crime in Urban America.* Chicago: University of Chicago Press.

Tchen, John Kuo Wei. 1999. *New York Before Chinatown: Orientalism and the Shaping of American Culture, 1776–1882.* Baltimore: John Hopkins University Press.

Telles, Edward. 1999. "Ethnic Boundaries and Political Mobilization Among African Brazilians: Comparisons with the U.S. Case." Pp. 82–99 in *Racial Politics in Contemporary Brazil,* ed. M. Hanchard. Durham, NC: Duke University Press.

———. 2004. *Race in Another America: The Significance of Skin Color in Brazil.* Princeton, NJ: Princeton University Press.

Tenenbaum, Harriet R., and Martin D. Ruck. 2007. "Are Teachers' Expectations Different for Racial Minority than for European American Students? A Meta-Analysis." *Journal of Educational Psychology* 99: 253–73.

Thomas, Brook. 2001. "A Constitution Led by the Flag: The Insular Cases and the Metaphor of Incorporation." Pp. 82–103 in *Foreign in a Domestic Sense: Puerto Rico, American Expansion, and the Constitution,* ed. Christina Duffy Burnett and Burke Marshall. Durham, NC: Duke University Press.

Thomas, Clarence. 2007. "J. Concurring, 551 U.S.," 2007 Supreme Court of the United States, Nos. 05–908 and 05–915, *Parents Involved in Community Schools v. Seattle School District No.1 et al.*

Thomas, Piri. 1997. *Down These Mean Streets.* New York: Vintage.

Tilly, Charles. 1992. *Coercion, Capital, and European States, AD 990–1992.* Cambridge, MA: Blackwell.

Tobar, Hector. 1999. "Illegal Immigrant Raid Consumes Arizona City; Chandler Still Dealing with '97 'Roundup.'" *Milwaukee Journal Sentinel,* January 10, p. 6.

Tomlins, Christopher. 2001. "Legal Cartography of Colonization, the Legal Polyphony of Settlement: English Intrusions on the American Mainland in the Seventeenth Century." *Law and Social Inquiry* 26(2): 315–72.

Tribe, Laurence H. 1978. *American Constitutional Law.* Mineola, NY: Foundation Press. (quoted in: Richard Thompson Ford. 2001. "The Boundaries of Race: Political Geography in Legal Analysis." P. 244 in *In Pursuit of a Dream Deferred: Linking Hous-*

ing and Education Policy, ed. john a. powell, Gavin Kearney, and Vina Kay. New York: Peter Lang)

Trouillot, Michel-Rolph. 1995. *Silencing the Past: Power and the Production of History.* Boston: Beacon Press.

Twine, France Winddance. 1998. *Racism in a Racial Democracy: The Maintenance of White Supremacy in Brazil.* New Brunswick, NJ: Rutgers University Press.

Tyler, Kenneth M., A. Wade Boykin, and Tia R. Walton. 2006. "Cultural Considerations in Teachers' Perceptions of Student Classroom Behavior and Achievement." *Teaching and Teacher Education 22*: 998–1005.

Tyson, Karolyn. 2002. "Weighing In: Elementary-Age Students and the Debate on Attitudes Toward School Among Black Students." *Social Forces 80*: 1157–89.

Tyson, Timothy. 1999. *Radio Free Dixie: Robert F. Williams and the Roots of Black Power.* Chapel Hill: University of North Carolina Press.

UCLA/IDEA (Institute for Democracy, Education, & Access). 2004. "Funding Essentials for California Schools." Los Angeles: IDEA. Retrieved January 15, 2009 (http://just schools.gseis.ucla.edu/crisis/funding/index.html).

U.S. Census. 2001. *Statistical Abstracts of the United States 2001.* Washington, DC: Government Printing Office. Retrieved June 18, 2004 (http//www.census.gov/ prod/2002pubs/02statab/educ.pdf).

U.S. Department of Health and Human Services. 2004. *Temporary Assistance for Needy Families (TANF): Sixth Annual Report to Congress.* November. Washington, DC: U.S. Department of Health and Human Services, Administration for Children and Families, Office of Family Assistance.

Valencia, Reynaldo, Sonia R. García, Henry Flore, and José Roberto Juárez Jr. 2004. *Mexican Americans and the Law.* Tucson: University of Arizona Press.

Vargas, J.H.C. 2003. "The Inner City and the Favela: Transnational Black Politics." *Race and Class 44*(4): 19–40.

———. 2006. "When a Favela Dared to Become a Gated Condominium: The Politics of Race and Urban Space in Rio de Janeiro." *Latin American Perspectives 33*(4): 49–81.

Verspereny, C. 1982. "Desegregation Case Defense Outlined." *St. Louis Post-Dispatch,* July 18. (quoted in: Amy Stuart Wells and Robert L. Crain. 1997. *Stepping over the Color Line: African American Students in White Suburban Schools New Haven and London.* New Haven, CT: Yale University Press)

Von Eschen, Penny. 1997. *Race Against Empire: Black Americans and Anticolonialism, 1937–1957.* Ithaca, NY: Cornell University Press.

Wacquant, Loïc. 1987. "Symbolic Violence and the Making of the French Agriculturalist: An Enquiry into Pierre Bourdieu's Sociology." *Australian and New Zealand Journal of Sociology 23*(1): 65–88.

———. 2001. "The Penalisation of Poverty and the Rise of Neo-Liberalism." *European Journal on Criminal Policy and Research 9*(4): 401–11.

————. 2002. "From Slavery to Mass Incarceration: Rethinking the 'Race Question' in the US." *New Left Review 13*: 41–60.

Wade, Peter. 1993. *Blackness and Race Mixture: The Dynamics of Racial Identity in Colombia.* Baltimore: Johns Hopkins University Press.

Walcott, Rinaldo. 2005. "Outside in Black Studies: Reading from a Queer Place in the Diaspora." Pp. 90–105 in *Black Queer Studies: A Critical Anthology,* ed. E. P. Johnson and M. G. Henderson. Durham, NC: Duke University Press.

Walker, Erica N. 2007. "Why Aren't More Minorities Taking Advanced Math?" *Educational Leadership 65*(3). Retrieved January 15, 2009 (http://www.ascd.org/publications/educational_leadership/nov07/vol65/num03/Why_Aren't_More_Minorities_Taking_Advanced_Math?.aspx).

Walker, Samuel. 1998. *Sense and Nonsense About Crime.* Belmont, CA: Wadsworth.

Wallimann, Isidor, and Michael Dobkowski, eds. 1987. *Genocide and the Modern Age: Etiology and Case Studies of Mass Death.* New York: Greenwood.

Walsh, Jim. 1997. "Attorney General's Office Probes Roundup of Illegals." *Arizona Republic,* August 9, p. B1.

Walters, Pamela Barnhouse. 2001. "Educational Access and the State: Historical Continuities and Discontinuities in Racial Inequality in American Education." *Sociology of Education 74*(Extra Issue): 35–49.

Webb, Garry. 1999. *Dark Alliance: The CIA, the Contras, and the Crack Cocaine Explosion.* New York: Seven Stories Press.

Weber, Devra. 1994. *Dark Sweat, White Gold: California Farm Workers, Cotton and the New Deal.* Berkeley: University of California Press.

Weber, Max. 1946. *From Max Weber: Essays in Sociology* (trans. H. H. Gerth and C. Wright Mills). New York: Oxford University Press.

Weinberg, M. 1977. *A Chance to Learn: The History of Race and Education in the United States.* New York: Cambridge University Press.

Weiner, Mark S. 2001. "Teutonic Constitutionalism: The Role of Ethno-Juridical Discourse in the Spanish American War." Pp. 48–81 in *Foreign in a Domestic Sense: Puerto Rico, American Expansion, and the Constitution,* ed. Christina Duffy Burnett and Burke Marshall. Durham, NC: Duke University Press.

Wells, Amy Stuart, and Robert L. Crain. 1997. *Stepping Over the Color Line: African American Students in White Suburban Schools.* New Haven, CT: Yale University Press.

Wells, Amy Stuart, Jennifer Jellison Holme, Anita Tijerina Revilla, and Awo Korantemaa Atanda. 2009. *Both Sides Now: The Story of School Desegregation's Graduates.* Berkeley: University of California Press.

Werbner, Pnina. 2005. "Islamophobia: Incitement to Religious Hatred—Legislating for a New Fear?" *Anthropology Today 21*(1): 5–9.

Werneck, Jurema. 2007. "Of Ialodês and Feminists: Reflections on Black Women's Political Action in Latin America and the Caribbean." *Cultural Dynamics 19*(1): 99–114.

Western, Bruce. 2006. *Punishment and Inequality in America.* New York: Russell Sage Foundation.

Westra, Karen L., and John Routely. 2000. "Arizona Cash Assistance Exit Study: First Quarter 1998 Cohort." Report. Arizona Department of Economic Security, Phoenix.

Wheelock, Anne. 1992. *Crossing the Tracks: How "Untracking" Can Save America's Schools.* New York: New Press.

White, Janelle. 2004. "Our Silence Will Not Protect Us: Black Women Confronting Sexual and Domestic Violence." University of Michigan, Ann Arbor.

Wilderson, Frank B., III. 2005. "Gramsci's Black Marx: Whither the Slave in Civil Society?" *We Write* 2(1): 1–17.

Wilkins, David E. 1997. *American Indian Sovereignty and the U.S. Supreme Court: The Masking of Justice.* Austin: University of Texas Press.

Williams, Reed. 2004. "Police to Restrict DNA Testing." *Daily Progress* [Charlottesville, VA], April 16. Retrieved March 26, 2009 (http://george.loper.org/archives/2004/Apr/937.html).

Williams, William Appleman. 1980. *Empire as a Way of Life.* New York: Oxford University Press.

Willing, Richard. 2003. "La. Case Triggers Battle over DNA." *USA Today,* June 6. Retrieved March 26, 2009 (http://www.usatoday.com/tech/2003-05-28-dna-dragnet_x.htm).

Wilson, Carter A. 1986. "Exploding the Myths of a Slandered Policy." *Black Scholar* 17(3): 19–24.

Wilson, James G. 2002. *The Imperial Republic: A Structural History of American Constitutionalism from the Colonial Era to the Beginning of the Twentieth Century.* Burlington, VT: Ashgate.

Winant, Howard. 2001. *The World Is a Ghetto: Race and Democracy Since World War II.* New York: Basic Books.

———. 2004. *The New Politics of Race: Globalism, Difference, Justice.* Minneapolis: University of Minnesota Press.

Wise, Tim. 2001. "School Shootings and White Denial." *Multicultural Perspectives* 3(4): 3–4.

Wolfe, Patrick. 2006. "Settler Colonialism and the Elimination of the Native." *Journal of Genocide Research* 8(4): 387–409.

Woodson, Carter G. 1998 [1933]. *The Miseducation of the Negro.* Trenton, NJ: Africa World Press.

Wu, Chi-Fang, Maria Cancian, Daniel R. Meyer, and Geoffrey Wallace. 2006. "How Do Welfare Sanctions Work?" *Social Work Research* 30 (1): 33–51.

Yang, Caroline H. 2009. "Reconstruction's Labor: Racialized Workers in the Narratives of U.S. Culture and History, 1870–1930." Unpublished book manuscript.

Yee, James, and Aimee Molloy. 2005. *For God and Country: Faith and Patriotism Under Fire* (1st ed.). New York: Public Affairs.

Yelvington, Kevin A. 2001. "The Anthropology of Afro-Latin America and the Caribbean: Diasporic Dimensions." *Annual Review of Anthropology 30*: 227–60.

Zamora, Emilio. 1993. *The World of the Mexican Worker in Texas*. College Station: Texas A & M University Press.

Zulaika, Joseba, and William A. Douglass. 1996. *Terror and Taboo: The Follies, Fables, and Faces of Terrorism*. New York: Routledge.

CONTRIBUTORS

Eduardo Bonilla-Silva is professor of sociology at Duke University. He has published four books to date: *White Supremacy and Racism in the Post-Civil Rights Era* (Rienner, 2001); *Racism Without Racists* (Rowman & Littlefied, 2006); *White Out* (with Woody Doane) (Routledge, 2003); and *White Logic, White Methods: Racism and Methodology* (with Tukufu Zuberi) (Rowman & Littlefield, 2008). He is working on a book entitled *The Invisible Weight of Whiteness: The Racial Grammar of Everyday Life in America*. Bonilla-Silva is the 2008 recipient of the Lewis A. Coser Award for theoretical agenda-setting in sociology.

Richard Fording is professor of political science at the University of Kentucky. He is also associate director of the University of Kentucky Center for Poverty Research. His published research has appeared in the *American Political Science Review*, the *American Journal of Political Science*, the *Journal of Politics*, and other journals. He is coeditor of *Race and the Politics of Welfare Reform* (Michigan, 2003). The research analyzed in this chapter comes from a larger research project (see http://www.uky .edu/~rford/fla_project.htm), the results from which will be reported in a book tentatively entitled *Disciplining the Poor: Neoliberal Paternalism and the Persistent Power of Race*.

Joy James is professor of humanities and college professor in political science at Williams College. She is also a senior research fellow at the John Warfield Center for African and African American Studies at the University of Texas, Austin.

Moon-Kie Jung teaches sociology and Asian American studies at the University of Illinois, Urbana-Champaign.

Amanda E. Lewis is associate professor in the Department of Sociology at Emory University. Her research focuses on how race shapes educational opportunities from kindergarten through graduate school, and on how ideas about race get negotiated in everyday life. She is the author of several books, including the award-winning *Race in the Schoolyard: Negotiating the Color-Line in Classrooms and Communities* (Rutgers, 2003). Lewis is currently at work on a book (with John Diamond) entitled *Despite the Best Intentions: Why Racial Inequality Persists in Good Schools* (Oxford, forthcoming). She lectures and consults regularly on issues of educational equity and contemporary forms of racism.

George Lipsitz is professor of black studies and sociology at the University of California, Santa Barbara. He is the author of ten books, including *The Possessive Investment in Whiteness*. Lipsitz edits the Critical American Studies series for the University of Minnesota Press and is coeditor of the American Crossroads series at the University of California Press. He chairs the board of directors of the African American Policy Forum and is a member of the board of directors of the National Fair Housing Alliance.

Michelle Manno is a graduate student in the Department of Sociology at Emory University. She received her master's in sociology from the University of Illinois, Chicago, in 2008. Her research focuses on race, class, gender, sexuality, and sports. She is currently studying how female athletes negotiate conflicts between their athletic and gender identities and how those conflicts and the strategies women use for addressing them vary by race.

Sarah Mayorga is a doctoral candidate in the Department of Sociology at Duke University. Her dissertation research focuses on multigroup segregation in Durham, North Carolina. She is specifically interested in the effects of Latina/o migration on neighborhoods in this historically black and white city. Mayorga has also conducted research on contemporary racial humor, analyzing the inclusion of color-blind racism frames in television programs such as *Chappelle's Show* and *Mind of Mencia*.

Charles W. Mills is John Evans Professor of Moral and Intellectual Philosophy at Northwestern University. He works in the general area of oppositional political theory, with a special focus on race. He is the author of over sixty journal articles and book chapters, and five books: *The Racial Contract* (Cornell, 1997); *Blackness Visible: Essays on Philosophy and Race* (Cornell, 1998); *From Class to Race: Essays in White Marxism and Black Radicalism* (Rowman & Littlefield, 2003); *Contract and Domination* (with Carole Pateman) (Polity, 2007); and *Radical Theory, Caribbean Reality: Race, Class and Social Domination* (University of the West Indies Press, 2010).

Junaid Rana is associate professor of Asian American studies, with appointments in anthropology, at the Center for South Asian and Middle Eastern Studies and the Unit for Criticism and Interpretive Theory at the University of Illinois, Urbana-Champaign. His publications have appeared in *Cultural Dynamics*, *Souls*, and an edited anthology entitled *Pakistani Diasporas* (Oxford, 2009). He is the author of *Terrifying Muslims: Race and Labor in the South Asian Diaspora* (Duke, 2011).

Dylan Rodríguez is professor and chair of Ethnic Studies at the University of California, Riverside. As an activist and scholar, he engages with different political sites and historical moments of struggle against global racism, white supremacy, and other forms of institutionalized dehumanization. He is a founding member of Critical Resistance: Beyond the Prison Industrial Complex, a national movement-building collective that seeks to fulfill the social and historical vision of abolition. He is the author of two books, *Forced Passages: Imprisoned Radical Intellectuals and the U.S. Prison Regime* (Minnesota, 2006) and *Suspended Apocalypse: White Supremacy, Genocide, and the Filipino Condition* (Minnesota, 2010). His essays have appeared in a wide variety of scholarly journals and other print and online venues.

Mary Romero teaches at Arizona State University. She is the author of *Maid in the U.S.A.* (Routledge, 1992; 10th anniv. ed. 2002), and her recent coedited books include *Blackwell Companion to Social Inequalities* (Blackwell, 2005); *Latino/a Popular Culture* (NYU, 2002); *Women's Untold Stories: Breaking Silence, Talking Back, Voicing Complexity* (Routledge, 1999); and *Challenging Fronteras: Structuring Latino and Latina Lives in the U.S.* (Routledge, 1997). Her most recent articles are published in the *Indiana Law Journal*, *Aztlán*, the *International Journal of Sociology of the Family*, *Critical Sociology*, the *Contemporary Justice Review*, the *Law and Society Review*, the *British Journal of Industrial Relations*, the *Villanova Law Review*, and the *Cleveland State Law Review*. Her research also includes writings on social inequalities and justice, which incorporate the intersectionality of race, class, gender, and citizenship and link the parallels between racism against citizens and racism against noncitizens.

Sanford Schram teaches social theory and policy at the Graduate School of Social Work and Social Research, Bryn Mawr College. He has published articles in the *American Sociological Review*, the *American Political Science Review*, the *American Journal of Political Science*, and numerous other journals. His most recent book is *Welfare Discipline: Discourse, Governance, and Globalization* (Temple, 2006).

Andrea Smith is associate professor of media and cultural studies at the University of California, Riverside. She is the author of *Native Americans and the Christian Right: The Gendered Politics of Unlikely Alliances* (Duke, 2008).

Joe Soss is the Cowles Chair for the Study of Public Service at the University of Minnesota, where he holds faculty positions in the Hubert H. Humphrey Institute of Public Affairs, Department of Political Science, and Department of Sociology. His scholarship explores the politics of poverty and inequality, focusing particularly on the political sources and consequence of public policies that target socially marginalized groups.

João H. Costa Vargas teaches Black Diaspora studies at the University of Texas, Austin.

INDEX

abolitionist movement, 42

Adarand Constructors, Inc. v. Pena (1995), 126

advanced placement courses, 94

affirmative action, 44, 89, 93, 249, 266, 285n7

African Americans. *See* Blacks

Afro-Brazilians, 248–51, 263–65, 285n8

Afroreggae, 263

aggravated felonies, broadening definition of, 210

agribusiness, 209

Ahmad, Eqbal, 282n4

AIDS/HIV, 261, 264

Ainsworth-Darnell, James W., 96

Alito, Samuel, 110

Allen, Walter R., 85

Allen v. Wright (1984), 125–26

Amar, Paul, 265

American Civil Liberties Union, 118

American Dilemma, An (Myrdal), 35–36

American Indians. *See* Native Americans (Indians)

Americanization, 63

American Samoa, 18

Amirault, Gerald, 175–76

Anderson, Benedict, 2

Anderson, Carol, 285n13

Anderson, Warwick, 62

Anglo-Saxon civilization, 16, 41, 64–65

Ansalone, George, 104

anticolonialism, 36, 41, 42, 68

antidiscrimination efforts, seen as civil rights violations, 121

Apple, Michael, 108

Arab Americans, 213, 220, 221, 239

Armour v. Nix (1979), 118–19

Ashgar, Muhammad, 216–17, 218–20

Asians: capitalist exploitation of immigrants, 237; denial rates for mortgages, 84; internment of Japanese Americans, 191, 212; in sanitized histories of the United States, 34, 35; "yellow" peril, 212. *See also* Chinese; Philippines

Atwater, Lee, 164, 165

Ayala, Laura, 82

Bailey, Alison, 240

banking, racial discrimination in, 84, 278n15

Barry, Elizabeth, 166

Barry, Robert, 165–66

Bell, Derrick, 122

Bell, Griffin, 118

Beveridge, Albert, 62–63, 64–65

Billowitz, Lisa, 162

Birmingham Center for Contemporary Cultural Studies, 282n2

Black Diaspora: Black and Africa distinguished, 245–46; in Brazil, 248–53; as genocide, 243–70; the imperative revolt in, 245, 266; in Los Angeles, 251–53; supranational alliances in, 256, 269–70. *See also* Afro-Brazilians; Blacks

Black Panthers, 248, 286n19

Black Skin, White Masks (Fanon), 39, 78